Fodor's 91
Los Angeles

Fodor's Travel Publications
New York and London

Fodor's Los Angeles

Editor: Jillian Magalaner
Contributors: Bob Blake, Bruce David Colen, Pamela Faust, Marie Felde, Mary Jane Horton, Jane E. Lasky, Ellen Melinkoff, Linda K. Schmidt, Peter Segal, Deborah Smith, Aaron Sugarman
Art Director: Fabrizio La Rocca
Cartographer: David Lindroth
Illustrator: Karl Tanner
Cover Photograph: Mark Stephenson/Masterfile

Design: Vignelli Associates

Special Sales

Fodor's Travel Publications are available at special discounts for bulk purchases (100 copies or more) for sales promotions or premiums. Special editions, including personalized covers, excerpts of existing guides, and corporate imprints, can be created in large quantities for special needs. For more information write to Special Marketing, Fodor's Travel Publications, 201 East 50th St., New York, NY 10022. Inquiries from the United Kingdom should be sent to Fodor's Travel Publications, 20 Vauxhall Bridge Rd., London, England SW1V 2SA.

Contents

Foreword

While every care has been taken to ensure the accuracy of the information in this guide, the passage of time will always bring change, and consequently, the publisher cannot accept responsibility for errors that may occur.

All prices and opening times quoted here are based on information supplied to us at press time. Hours and admission fees may change, however, and the prudent traveler will avoid inconvenience by calling ahead.

Fodor's wants to hear about your travel experiences, both pleasant and unpleasant. When a hotel or restaurant fails to live up to its billing, let us know and we will investigate the complaint and revise our entries where the facts warrant it.

Send your letters to the editors of Fodor's Travel Publications, 201 E. 50th Street, New York, NY 10022.

Highlights'91 and Fodor's Choice

Highlights '91

Long known for its sights—palm trees, Johnny Carson, the Pacific—Los Angeles is increasingly recognizable by certain sounds: the roar of bulldozers, the pounding of steel girders, and all the other auditory trademarks of rampant real estate development. Much of the hammering and concrete-pouring comes courtesy of the travel industry, with a slew of new hotels and tourist attractions in the works.

The long-awaited redevelopment of **Hollywood** is probably causing the most noise. Despite the protests of some community groups, several buildings are on their way down and many more on their way up. The area surrounding Mann's Chinese Theater on Hollywood Boulevard will resemble a war zone, as the **Hollywood Promenade** rises phoenixlike from the rubble in 1993. The Promenade will house a 350-room hotel, 275,000 square feet of upscale shops and restaurants, a 19-story office tower, a state-of-the-art theater complex dubbed the American Cinematheque, and a film and broadcast museum known as the Hollywood Exposition.

Santa Monica is in the midst of a hotel boom. The beachfront, 195-room **Park Hyatt Santa Monica** at Pico Boulevard and the 253-room **Guest Quarters Suite Hotel,** on 4th Street near the Civic Auditorium opened in 1990, as did the stunning **Ritz Carlton** in Marina del Rey. The 148-room **Santa Monica Beach Hotel** on Pacific Coast Highway is set to open in 1992.

Always-competitive **West L.A.** has, not one, but two major art institutions under construction. The dueling museums are the **Armand Hammer Museum of Art and Cultural Center,** the future Westwood home of Hammer's $250-million collection, opening in 1991; and the **J. Paul Getty Center,** which will occupy a 110-acre hilltop site with views of the Pacific and the Los Angeles basin, scheduled to take its bow sometime in the mid-1990s.

Downtown L.A. is not quiet either. Construction should soon be under way on the **Walt Disney Concert Hall,** the future home of the Los Angeles Philharmonic. The hall is being designed by local hero Gehry, although word is the structure will be simpler and somewhat more conservative than typical Gehry creations.

The wave of redevelopment has even hit downtown **Huntington Beach** in Orange County. Best known as a surfing center, this classic Southern California beach town is adding a multiplex movie theater, restaurant, and retail center at the intersection of the Pacific Coast Highway and Main

Street. Scheduled to open in the summer of 1990, the complex will be known as **Pier Colony.** Across the street from the project, the **Huntington Beach pier** is in the midst of a total overhaul and will be closed for the year. A second phase of redevelopment will include two or three upscale waterside restaurants.

We reported here last year that the venerable Ambassador Hotel was in danger of being closed, after 68 years of trustworthy service. Not surprisingly, the Ambassador, L.A.'s premier hotel, the place where Rudolph Valentino, Douglas Fairbanks, and Greta Garbo played—and where Sen. Robert F. Kennedy was gunned down—has since closed its doors. The hotel was bought by Donald Trump—who intended to refurbish it—but with the Trumps' fortunes in a state of flux, the Ambassador's future remains uncertain.

No less capricious than the world of high finance, the elements of nature caused some chaos in the Los Angeles area in 1990. Santa Barbara experienced its worst fires in 30 years; nearly 500 homes were lost and 49,000 acres were burned, prompting President Bush to declare it a disaster area.

Fans of the **Farmers Market** will appreciate the massive redevelopment of this L.A. landmark, to be completed sometime in the mid-1990s. A movie theater, restaurants, and a 600-room hotel will be added to the market, which will also be enhanced by landscaping, fountains, plazas, and walkways, making this a much more attractive place in which to spend some time.

Fodor's Choice

No two people will agree on what makes a perfect vacation, but it's fun and helpful to know what others think. We hope you'll have a chance to experience some of Fodor's Choices yourself while visiting Los Angeles. For detailed information about each entry, refer to the appropriate chapters within this guidebook.

Postcard Sights

Griffith Park Observatory

Capitol Records Building

Malibu Beach seen from the Getty Museum

The Blue Whale, a.k.a. The Pacific Design Center

Melrose Avenue

Museums

Gene Autry Western Heritage Museum

J. Paul Getty Museum

Museum of Contemporary Art

Natural History Museum of Los Angeles

Norton Simon Museum

Parks and Gardens

Descanso Gardens

Eaton Canyon Park and Nature Center

Huntington Library and Botanical Garden

Will Rodgers State Park

William S. Hart County Park

Hotels

Bel Air Hotel *(Very Expensive)*

Century Plaza Hotel *(Very Expensive)*

The Regent Beverly Wilshire *(Very Expensive)*

The Ritz-Carlton, Marina del Rey *(Very Expensive)*

The Saint James's Club/Los Angeles *(Very Expensive)*

Restaurants

Bistro Garden *(Expensive)*

Chaya Brasserie *(Expensive)*

Spago *(Moderate–Expensive)*

L.A. Nicola *(Moderate)*

Tommy Tang's *(Moderate)*

Canter's *(Inexpensive–Moderate)*

Johnny Rockets *(Inexpensive)*

Special Moments

Christmas Boat Parade, Marina del Rey

Entering the Santa Monica Kite Festival

A walk in the Hollywood Hills, with view of Los Angeles and the ocean

Watching the filming of a live TV show

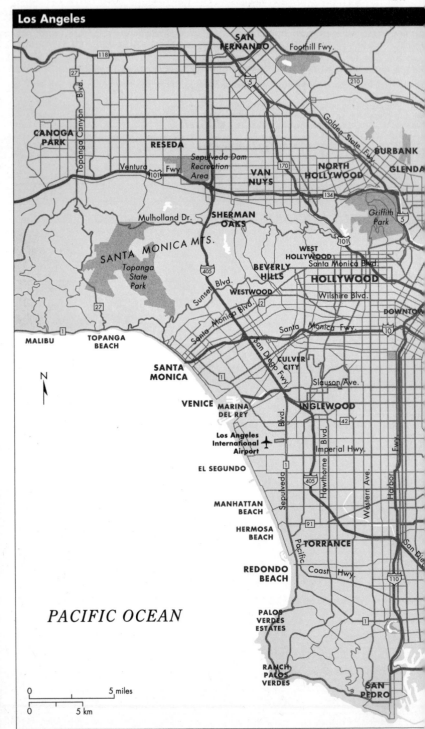

Los Angeles

SAN FERNANDO
Foothill Fwy.

CANOGA PARK

RESEDA

Topanga Canyon Blvd.

Golden State Fwy.

BURBANK

GLENDA

Ventura Fwy.

Sepulveda Dam Recreation Area

VAN NUYS

NORTH HOLLYWOOD

Mulholland Dr.

SHERMAN OAKS

Griffith Park

SANTA MONICA MTS.

Topanga State Park

WEST HOLLYWOOD

Santa Monica Blvd.

HOLLYWOOD

BEVERLY HILLS

Sunset Blvd.

WESTWOOD

Wilshire Blvd.

DOWNTON

MALIBU

TOPANGA BEACH

Santa Monica Blvd.

Santa Monica Fwy.

San Diego Fwy.

SANTA MONICA

CULVER CITY

Slauson Ave.

VENICE

MARINA DEL REY

INGLEWOOD

Los Angeles International Airport

Imperial Hwy.

EL SEGUNDO

MANHATTAN BEACH

HERMOSA BEACH

Sepulveda

Hawthorne Blvd.

Western Ave.

Harbor Fwy.

TORRANCE

San Diego

REDONDO BEACH

Coast Hwy.

Pacific

PACIFIC OCEAN

PALOS VERDES ESTATES

RANCH PALOS VERDES

SAN PEDRO

N

0   5 miles
0   5 km

Southern California

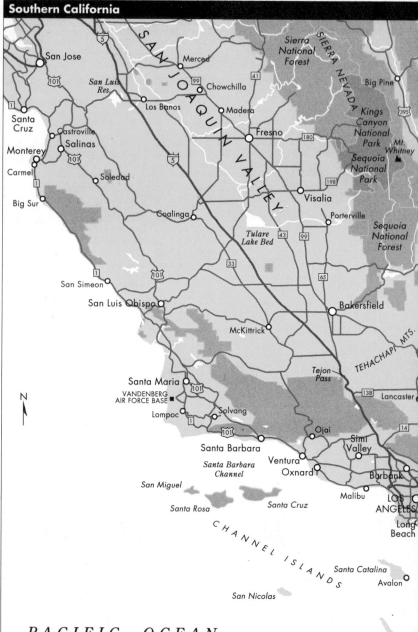

San Jose

San Luis Res.

SAN JOAQUIN VALLEY

Merced

Chowchilla

Madera

Sierra National Forest

SIERRA NEVADA

Big Pine

Santa Cruz

Castroville

Salinas

Monterey

Carmel

Soledad

Big Sur

Los Banos

Fresno

Kings Canyon National Park

Mt. Whitney

Sequoia National Park

Visalia

Porterville

Sequoia National Forest

Coalinga

Tulare Lake Bed

San Simeon

San Luis Obispo

McKittrick

Bakersfield

TEHACHAPI MTS.

Tejon Pass

Santa Maria

VANDENBERG AIR FORCE BASE

Lompoc

Solvang

Lancaster

Santa Barbara

Ojai

Simi Valley

Ventura

Oxnard

Burbank

Malibu

LOS ANGELES

Long Beach

Santa Barbara Channel

San Miguel

Santa Rosa

Santa Cruz

CHANNEL ISLANDS

Santa Catalina

Avalon

San Nicolas

N

PACIFIC OCEAN

San Clemente

0   50 miles

0   75 km

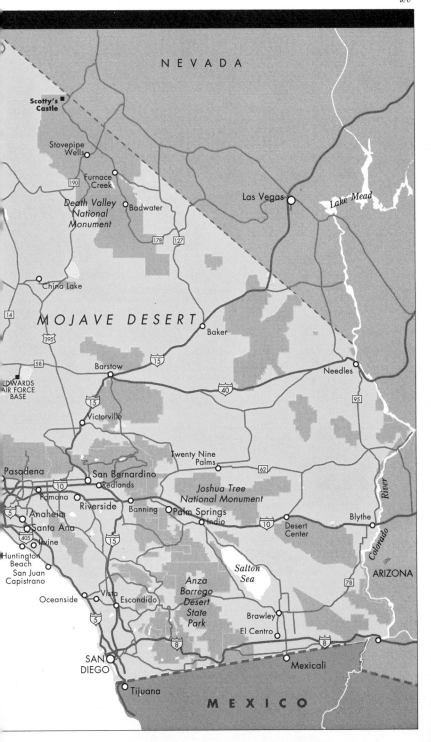

World Time Zones

MONDAY
SUNDAY

International Date Line

+12 | +13 | -9

-4

-3

3

7

-10

4

-7

5 -8 8 9

14 15

13

6 16

17

10

11

18

-11

-10

2

12

19 22

+11

-5

+12

20

-4 -3

1

23

-3

21 24

+11 | +12 - | -11 | -10 | -9 | -8 | -7 | -6 | -5 | -4 | -3 | -2

Numbers below vertical bands relate each zone to Greenwich Mean Time (0 hrs.).
Local times frequently differ from these general indications,
as indicated by light-face numbers on map.

Algiers, **29**	Berlin, **34**	Delhi, **48**	Istanbul, **40**
Anchorage, **3**	Bogotá, **19**	Denver, **8**	Jerusalem, **42**
Athens, **41**	Budapest, **37**	Djakarta, **53**	Johannesburg, **44**
Auckland, **1**	Buenos Aires, **24**	Dublin, **26**	Lima, **20**
Baghdad, **46**	Caracas, **22**	Edmonton, **7**	Lisbon, **28**
Bangkok, **50**	Chicago, **9**	Hong Kong, **56**	London (Greenwich), **27**
Beijing, **54**	Copenhagen, **33**	Honolulu, **2**	Los Angeles, **6**
	Dallas, **10**		Madrid, **38**
			Manila, **57**

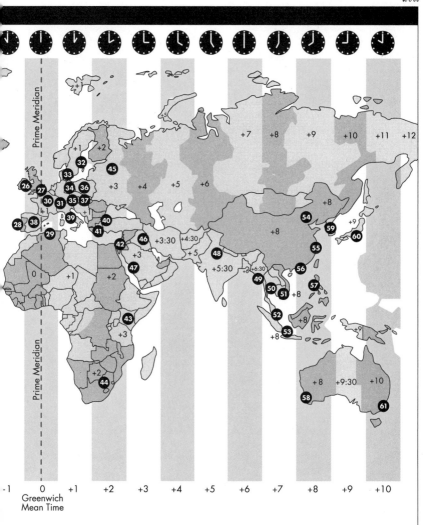

Introduction

by Jane E. Lasky

A syndicated newspaper columnist and author of several travel books, Jane Lasky also publishes articles in many national magazines, such as Vogue, Connoisseur, Travel & Leisure, *and* Esquire.

You're preparing for your trip to Los Angeles. You're psyching up with Beach Boys cassettes on your car radio or perhaps some Hollywood epics on the VCR. You've pulled out your tropical Hawaiian shirts and tennis shorts. You've studied the Mexican menu at Taco Bell. Maybe you're even doing a crash regimen at your local tanning salon and aerobics studio so you won't *look* like a tourist when you hit the coast.

Well, relax. *Everybody's* a tourist in LaLa Land. Even the stars are star-struck (as evidenced by the celebrities watching the other celebrities at Spago). Los Angeles is a city of ephemerals, of transience, and above all, of illusion. Nothing there is quite real, and that's the reality of it all. That air of anything-can-happen—and it often does—is what keeps thousands moving to this promised land each year and millions more vacationing in it. Not just from the East or Midwest, mind you, but from the Far East, Down Under, Europe, and South America. It's this influx of cultures that's been the lifeblood of Los Angeles since its Hispanic beginning.

We cannot predict what *your* Los Angeles will be like. You can laze on a beach or soak up some of the world's greatest art collections. You can tour the movie studios and stars' homes or take the kids to Disneyland, Magic Mountain, or the *Queen Mary/Spruce Goose*. You can shop luxurious Beverly Hills' Rodeo Drive or browse for hipper novelties on boutique-lined Melrose Avenue. The possibilities are endless—rent a boat to Catalina Island, watch the floats in Pasadena's Rose Parade, or dine on tacos, sushi, goat cheese pizza, or just plain hamburgers, hot dogs, and chili.

No matter how fast-forward Los Angeles seems to spin, the heart of the city—or at least its stomach—is still deep in the 1950s. Sure, the lighter, nouvelle-inspired California cuisine has made a big splash (no one here is ridiculed as a "health-food nut" for preferring a healthier diet), but nothing is more Californian than Johnny Rockets (a chrome-and-fluorescent burger paradise on Melrose with '57 Chevies galore) or Pink's (a greasy spoon of a chili-dog dive on La Brea popular with late-night carousers).

None of this was imagined when Spanish settlers founded their Pueblo de la Reina de Los Angeles in 1781. In fact, no one predicted a golden future for desert-dry Southern California until well after San Francisco and Northern California had gotten a good head start with their own gold rush. The dusty outpost of Los Angeles eventually had oil and oranges, but the golden key to its success came on the silver screen: the movies. If the early pioneers of Hollywood—

religiously conservative fruit farmers—had gotten their way, their town's name would never have become synonymous with cinema and entertainment.

The same sunshine that draws today's visitors and new residents drew Cecil B. De Mille and Jesse Lasky in 1911 while searching for a new place to make movies outside of New York City. Lesser filmmakers had been shooting reels for the nickelodeons of the day in Hollywood, but De Mille and Lasky made the first feature-length movie, far from New York's unpredictable weather. It took another fifteen years to break through the sound barrier in cinema, but the silent-film era made Hollywood's name synonymous with fantasy, glamour, and, as the first citizens would snicker in disgust, with sin.

Outrageous partying, extravagant homes, eccentric clothing, and money, money, money have been symbols of life in Los Angeles ever since. Even the more conservative oil, aerospace, computer, banking, and import/export industries on the booming Pacific Rim have enjoyed the prosperity that leads inevitably to fun living. But even without piles of money, many people have found a kindred spirit in Los Angeles for their colorful lifestyles, be they spiritually, socially, or sexually unusual. Tolerance reigns; live and let live—which explains why you, too, will fit in.

When you arrive in Los Angeles, turn your car radio to 94.7 FM. Ten years ago, we would have been guiding you to the Beach Boys (and they're still as great as ever in a convertible on a hot day), but "ninety-four-seven, the Way-ee-yave," as this station's identifiers croon it, plays New Age, mellow modern, and a synthesizer blend of soft jazz, gentle rock, and cosmic chords not easily found anywhere else on your dial. This is Muzak for tomorrow's world—the sixties cycled into the eighties; the tempo of Tinseltown, laid back and far out.

If cosmic music sounds corny to you, you will find excellent classical, contemporary, blues, soul, and rock stations here—and, believe us, with "drive time" what it is in Los Angeles, you will have plenty of time to find them. Disc jockey Rick Dees, the wacky composer of the eminently forgettable "Disco Duck," is a local institution (some say he should be *in* one), as is Gary Owens, formerly of television's "Laugh In." Game-show host Wink Martindale has a radio show here, and sex counselor Dr. Toni Grant hosts her syndicated talk show in Los Angeles.

No matter what you turn on and what turns you on while you drive the infamous freeways, these asphalt ribbons are your passage to the far-flung pleasures of Los Angeles. Getting there *can* be half the fun, outside of rush-crush hours (7–9 AM and 3–7 PM), but when the freeway bogs down with bumper-to-bumper Japanese imports, minipickups, and sleek Mercedes, tip your hat or raise your fist to Detroit.

It was the U.S. automakers and oil companies that, earlier this century, lobbied against an urban mass transit system in Southern California in order to sell more cars and gasoline. Free-spirited Californians drove blithely on, indulging their independence until one day, sometime in the late 1950s, the smog got thick enough to kill. Mandatory emission controls have helped clear up that problem. Nevertheless, check the papers daily to ascertain the air quality. Because the 700 miles of freeways are so full, a metro subway system is finally being dug, offering a possible solution to the smog problem someday. Perhaps not too little, but already too late: The first phase of the system won't be ready until sometime during the 1990s.

No city embraces the romance of the automobile as does Los Angeles. Cars themselves announce the wealth, politics, and taste of their drivers. Vanity license plates, a California innovation, condense the meaning of one's life into seven letters (MUZKBIZ). Sun roofs, ski racks, and cardboard windshield visors sell better here than anywhere else. You are what you drive—a thought worth remembering when you rent a car. Yes, Lamborghinis are available, even by the hour.

The distance between places in Los Angeles explains the ethnic enclaves that do not merge, regardless of the melting-pot appearance of the city. It would be misleading of us to gloss over the tensions between racial groups learning to share Los Angeles. More notable for visitors, however, is the rich cultural and culinary diversity this mix of peoples creates.

There's something about a shiny, better world that beckons so many diverse people to Los Angeles. "Have a nice day" may be a cliché by now, but the people here mean it. For some, a better world is self-enhancing —the building of the body beautiful, a personal fortune, or the hottest hot-rod. Others try to better their world through the arts, politics, or spiritual exploration. For some it is enough just to surf and sun. Southern California is, as historian Carey McWilliams calls it, "an island on the land." His book of the same name offers enriching insight into the mind-set of Los Angeles. Set off from the rest of the continent by mountains and desert, and from the rest of the world by an ocean, this incredible corner of creation has evolved its own identity that conjures envy, fascination, ridicule, and scorn—often all at once.

Those from purportedly more sophisticated cities note what Los Angeles lacks. Others from more provincial towns raise an eyebrow at what it has. Yet 12.5 million people visit the city annually, and 75% of them come back for more. Indeed, you cannot do Los Angeles in a day or a week or even two. This second largest city in America holds too many choices between its canyons and its coast to be exhausted in one trip; you will be exhausted first.

Angelenos have long felt forced to defend what they have and what they don't. Since the 1984 Olympics, though, a new pride has emerged. The sun and fun of Southern California warmed the world that summer, and the cultural sideshows of bright local artists and international performers put Los Angeles on the map. Ask anyone here about the quality of life in Los Angeles. Even the homeless, of which there are admittedly too many, come here to escape the less hospitable climate of Chicago or Colorado. It's not perfect, but as Randy Newman sings in what has become the city's unofficial anthem, "I Love L.A." We hope you do, too.

1 Essential Information

Before You Go

Visitor Information

The Los Angeles Visitors and Convention Bureau (LAVCB, 695 S. Figueroa St., Los Angeles 90017, tel. 213/689–8822) will provide you with extensive free information about the region. Los Angeles maintains a 24-hour toll-free line for information about community services (tel. 800/242–4612). A quarterly calendar of entertainment and special events in the Los Angeles area may be obtained by sending a self-addressed, stamped business-size envelope to "Datelines" (c/o LAVCB, Box 71608, Los Angeles 90071).

In addition, many of the communities in the Los Angeles area maintain visitors centers and chambers of commerce, all of them eager to give you information about their towns. A sampling:

Beverly Hills Visitors Bureau (239 S. Beverly Dr., Beverly Hills 90212, tel. 213/271–08174 or 800/345–02210).
Catalina Island Chamber of Commerce and Visitors Bureau (1 Green Pleasure Pier, Box 217, Avalon 90704, tel. 213/510–2266). Hotel reservations and transportation information are available by phone.
Glendale Chamber of Commerce (200 S. Louise St., Box 112, Glendale 91209, tel. 818/240–7870).
Hollywood Chamber of Commerce (6255 Sunset Blvd., Suite 911, Hollywood 90028, tel. 213/469–8311).
Long Beach Area Convention and Visitors Council (1 World Trade Center, Suite 300, Long Beach 90830, tel. 213/436–3645).
Oxnard Convention and Visitors Bureau (400 Esplanade Dr., Suite 100, Oxnard 93030, tel. 805/485–8833).
Palm Springs Convention and Visitors Bureau (Airport Park Plaza, #315, 2255 N. El Cielo, Palm Springs 92262, tel. 619/327–8411).
Pasadena Convention and Visitors Bureau (171 S. Los Robles Ave., Pasadena 91101, tel. 818/795–9311).
Santa Barbara Conference and Visitors Bureau (222 E. Anapamu St., Suite 24, Santa Barbara 93101, tel. 805/966–9222).

More information about the Los Angeles area is contained in a handsome and detailed 208-page book, *Discover the Californias*, available free of charge through the California Office of Tourism (tel. 800/862–2543). In addition, the California Office of Tourism (1121 L St., Suite 103, Sacramento 95814, tel. 916/322–1397) can answer many questions about travel in the state.

Tour Groups

Joining a tour group has some advantages: Someone else worries about travel arrangements, accommodations, and baggage transfer; you are likely to save money on airfare, hotels, and ground transportation; and you will probably cover a lot of territory. The major disadvantages are that you'll have to adjust to someone else's time schedule and pacing, and you won't be as free for independent explorations.

When considering a tour, be sure to find out (1) exactly what expenses are included, particularly tips, taxes, side trips, meals, and entertainment; (2) the ratings of all hotels on the itinerary and the facilities they offer; (3) the additional cost of single, rather than double, accommodations if you are traveling alone; and (4) the number of travelers in your group. Note whether the tour operator reserves the right to change hotels, routes, or even prices after you've booked, and check out the operator's policy regarding cancellations, complaints, and trip-interruption insurance. Many tour operators request that packages be booked through a travel agent; there is generally no additional charge for doing so.

General-Interest Tours A sampling of options is listed here; for additional possibilities, check with your travel agent or the Los Angeles Visitors and Convention Bureau (6th and S. Flower Sts., Los Angeles 90071, tel. 213/689–8822).

American Express Vacations (Box 5014, Atlanta, GA 30302, tel. 800/241–1700 or 800/282–0800 in GA).
California Parlor Car Tours (Hollywood Roosevelt Hotel, 7000 Hollywood Blvd., Hollywood 90028, tel. 800/227–4250).
Domenico Tours (751 Broadway, Bayonne, NJ 07002, tel. 800/554–8687).
Flair Tours Inc. (6922 Hollywood Blvd., Suite 421, Hollywood 90028, tel. 800/433–5247).
Globus-Gateway Cosmos Tours (150 S. Los Robles Ave., Suite 860, Pasadena 91101, tel. 800/556–5454).
Gray Line Tours (6541 Hollywood Blvd., Suite 200, Hollywood 90028, tel. 213/856–5900 or 800/538–5050).
Maupintour (Box 807, Lawrence, KS 66044, tel. 800/255–4266).

Special-Interest Tours The Rose Bowl Parade and football game, Pasadena's New Year's extravaganza, is the focal point for a tour offered by **Cartan Tours** (2809 Butterfield Rd., Oakbrook, IL 60521, tel. 800/422–7826 or 708/571–1400).

San Antonio Winery (737 Lamar St., Los Angeles, tel. 213/223–1401) allows self-guided tours during the week from 10 AM to 2 PM, but offers guided tours on the weekends from noon to 4. Wine-tastings are included in the free tours. There's also a gift shop and a restaurant on the premises.

A tour through the villages of the Santa Ynez Valley in Santa Barbara County, visiting some of the excellent small family-owned wineries and tasting a selection of wines, is provided by **Dee's Deluxe Tours** (1324 State St., Suite C, Santa Barbara 93101, tel. 805/962–9621).

Sierra Club (730 Polk St., San Francisco, CA 94109, tel. 415/776–2211) offers naturalist-led tours of the remarkable desert regions surrounding Los Angeles.

The Wilderness Institute, Inc. (28118 Agoura Rd., Agoura Hills 91301, tel. 818/991–7327). Wilderness experts and naturalists take you to hidden waterfalls, Western movie towns, and scenic vistas in Santa Monica Mountains National Park.

Package Deals for Independent Travelers

There is a wide range of packages available for independent travelers. Most airlines have packages that include car rentals and lodging along with your flight. American Airlines' (tel.

800/433–7300) "Vacation Enchantment" package to the Los Angeles area includes admission to Disneyland. USAir's (tel. 800/223–2929) "Great Escapes Vacations" package to Southern California gives you a choice of attractions, and special fares for children. Many major airlines have sightseeing tours in and around Los Angeles.

Hotels often have packages for weekends, or for off-season. Package possibilities sometimes cluster around major tourist attractions; hotels and motels near Disneyland in Anaheim will offer lodging and admission tickets in a package.

Amtrak offers tours to major attractions in California. For a brochure and specific information, call 800/USA–RAIL, or write to Amtrak Public Affairs (1 California St., Suite 1250, San Francisco 94111).

Tips for British Travelers

Passports You will need a valid 10-year passport You do not need a visa if you are staying for less than 90 days, have a return ticket, and are flying with a participating airline. There are some exceptions to this, so check with your travel agent or with the United States Embassy (Visa and Immigration Department, 5 Upper Grosvenor St., London W1A 2JB, tel. 071/499–3443). Note that the U.S. Embassy no longer accepts applications for visas made in person.

No vaccinations are required for entry into the United States.

Customs If you are 21 or over, you can take into the United States: 200 cigarettes, 50 cigars or 2 kilos tobacco; 1 liter of alcohol; duty-free gifts to a value of $100. Be careful not to try to take in meat or meat products, seeds, plants, fruits, etc., and avoid illegal drugs like the plague.

Returning to Britain, you may bring home: (1) 200 cigarettes or cigarillos or 50 cigars or 250 grams of tobacco; (2) two liters of table wine and, in addition, (a) one liter of alcohol over 22% by volume (most spirits) or (b) two liters of alcohol under 22% by volume (fortified or sparkling wine); (3) 60 milliliters of perfume and 1/4 liter of toilet water; and (4) other goods up to a value of £32.

Insurance We recommend that you insure yourself to cover health and motoring mishaps with **Europ Assistance** (252 High St., Croydon CRO 1NF, tel. 081/680–1234). Their excellent service is all the more valuable when you consider the possible costs of health care in the United States. It is also wise to insure yourself against trip cancellations and loss of luggage. For free general advice on all aspects of holiday insurance, contact the **Association of British Insurers** (Aldermarry House, Queen St., London EC4N 1TT, tel. 071/248–4477).

Tour Operators The price battle that has raged over transatlantic fares has meant that most tour operators now offer excellent budget packages to the United States. Among the best are

Thomas Cook Ltd. (Box 36, Thorpe Wood, Peterborough, Cambridgeshire PE3 6SB, tel. 0733–330300).
Cosmosair plc (Tourama House, 17 Homesdale Rd., Bromley, Kent BR2 9LX, tel. 0614/805799).
Jetsave (Sussex House, London Rd., East Grinstead, Sussex RH19 1LD, tel. 0342–312033).

Kuoni Travel Ltd. (Kuoni House, Dorking, Surrey RH5 4AZ, tel. 0306/740500).
Premier Holidays (Premier Travel Center, Westbrook, Milton Rd., Cambridge CB4 1YQ, tel. 0223–355977).
Speedbird (Pacific House, Hazelwick Ave., Three Bridges, Crawley, West Sussex RH10 1NP, tel. 0293/572856).

Airfares We suggest that you explore the current scene for budget-flight possibilities, including **Continental** and **Virgin Atlantic Airways.** Some of these fares can be extremely difficult to come by, so be sure to book well in advance. Also, check on APEX and other money-saving fares, as, quite frankly, only business travelers who don't have to watch the price of their tickets fly full-price these days—and find themselves sitting right beside APEX passengers!

At press time, an APEX round-trip fare to San Francisco or Los Angeles cost from £476 up and to San Diego from £479. Another good source of low-cost flights is in the small ads of daily and Sunday newspapers.

When to Go

Almost any time of the year is the right time to go to Los Angeles; the climate is mild and pleasant year-round. But you will want to take into consideration your specific needs and inclinations. The famous Los Angeles smog can be at its worst in the summer, and can cause problems for those with respiratory ailments. It will be much too hot to enjoy Palm Springs in the summertime.

The rainy season usually runs from November through March, with the heaviest downpours usually coming in January. Summers are virtually rainless.

Climate Seasons in Los Angeles and in Southern California generally are not as defined as in most other temperate areas of the world. The Pacific Ocean is the primary moderating influence. In addition, mountains along the north and east sides of the Los Angeles coastal basin act as buffers against the extreme summer heat and winter cold of the desert and plateau regions.

However, mild sea breezes and winds from the interior can mix to produce a variety of weather conditions; an unusual aspect of the Los Angeles climate is the pronounced difference in temperature, humidity, cloudiness, fog, rain, and sunshine over short distances.

The following are average daily maximum and minimum temperatures for Los Angeles.

Jan.	64F	18C	May	69F	21C	Sept.	75F	24C
	44	7		53	12		60	16
Feb.	64F	18C	June	71F	22C	Oct.	73F	23C
	46	8		57	14		55	13
Mar.	66F	19C	July	75F	24C	Nov.	71F	22C
	48	9		60	16		48	9
Apr.	66F	19C	Aug.	75F	24C	Dec.	66F	19C
	51	11		62	17		46	8

Current weather information on over 750 cities around the world—450 of them in the United States—is only a phone call

away. Dialing WeatherTrak at 900/370–8728 will connect you
to a computer, with which you can communicate by touch tone
—at a cost of 75¢ for the first minute and 50¢ a minute there-
after. The number plays a taped message that tells you to dial a
three-digit access code for the destination you're interested in.
The code is either the area code (in the United States) or the
first three letters of the foreign city. For a list of all access
codes, send a stamped, self-addressed envelope to Cities, Box
7000, Dallas, TX 75209. For further information, phone 214/869
–3035 or 800/247– 3282.

Festivals and Seasonal Events

Some of the major festivities scheduled for the greater Los Angeles area this year are listed here, month by month. "Datelines," a quarterly calendar of events, is available free of
charge at the Los Angeles Visitors Information Center in
downtown Los Angeles, Arco Plaza, Level B, 6th and S. Flower
streets, or by mail; send a stamped, self-addressed business-
size envelope to "Datelines," c/o LAVCB, Box 71608, Los Angeles 90071.

January **Tournament of Roses Parade and Game,** Pasadena. The 101st
annual parade took place on New Year's Day, 1990, with lavish
floral floats, marching bands, and equestrian teams moving
down Colorado Boulevard in Pasadena, followed by the Rose
Bowl Game. You can take a close-up look at the floats for two
days after the parade. *391 S. Orange Grove Blvd., Pasadena
91105, tel. 818/449–4100.*
Los Angeles City Metropolitan Tennis Tournament. For three
consecutive weekends, the city's best battle it out on the courts
of Griffith Recreation Center and Arroyo Seco Park. *Tel. 818/
246–5614.*
Moosehead Sled Dog Classic, Palm Springs. Sled dog races
are held at the top of the Palm Springs Aerial Tramway on the
second and third weekends in January. *Palm Springs
Aerial Tramway, 1 Tramway Rd., Palm Springs 92262, tel.
619/325– 1449.*
Martin Luther King Parade, Long Beach. This event begins
with a parade down 7th and Alameda streets and ends with a
festival in Martin Luther King Park. Local community leaders
speak on civil rights, while ethnic foods and music make the celebration. It's usually held the Saturday preceding the third
Monday in January. *Councilman Clarence Smith, 333 W.
Ocean Ave., Los Angeles 90802, tel. 213/590–6816.*
Whale Watching, California coast. Hundreds of gray whales
migrate from January through April and may be observed
along the California coast from San Diego to the Oregon border. *California Office of Tourism, 1121 L St., Suite 103, Sacramento 95814, tel. 916/322–1397.*

February **Bob Hope Chrysler Classic,** Indian Wells, La Quinta, and Ber-
muda Dunes. This PGA golf tournament, a celebrity-packed
pro-am, has been held in the desert in late January for the past
30 years. *Box 865, Rancho Mirage 92270, tel. 619/341–2299 or
346–8184.*
Chinese New Year and Golden Dragon Parade, Los Angeles.
Floats, bands, and dragon dancers move through the streets of
Chinatown. *Chinese Chamber of Commerce, 978 N. Broadway,
Suite 206, Los Angeles 90012, tel. 213/617–0396.*
National Date Festival, Indio. One of the country's more unusu-

al expositions, this 10-day affair in mid-February includes an Arabian Nights pageant, a horse show, and camel and ostrich races. *46350 Arabia St., Indio 92201, tel. 619/342–8247 or 347–0676.*

March   **Vintage Chrysler Invitational,** Indian Wells. The legends of golf compete for a $350,000 purse at this early-March stop on the PGA Senior Tour. *Box 1816, Palm Desert 92261, tel. 619/568–3579.*

Santa Barbara International Film Festival, Santa Barbara. This early-March festival has it all: premieres of international and U.S. films, a tribute to a film actor, documentaries and archival films, workshops and seminars headed by film-industry professionals, and a gala opening premiere. *1216 State St., Suite 201, Santa Barbara 93101, tel. 805/963–0023.*

Los Angeles Marathon, Los Angeles. Early in March, you can take part in this 26.2-mile run through the downtown streets, or watch others going for the finish. *11110 W. Ohio Ave., Suite 100, Los Angeles, tel. 213/444–5544.*

Santa Barbara International Cymbidium Orchid Show, Santa Barbara. This is a horticultural spectacular staged the second weekend in March. It features displays and demonstrations. *Box 3006, Santa Barbara 93130, tel. 805/687–0766.*

Fiesta de Las Golondrinas, San Juan Capistrano. Each year, in mid-March, there's a celebration of the arrival of the swallows on their journey from Argentina. *Mission San Juan Capistrano, 31815 Camino Capistrano, Suite C, San Juan Capistrano 92675, tel. 714/493–1424.*

Riverside Baseball Invitational Tournament, Riverside. At month's end, this round-robin tournament involves collegiate teams from across the country. *University of California Riverside PE Dept., Riverside 92521, tel. 714/787–4292.*

The Santa Monica Pier Kite Festival, Santa Monica. On the fourth Sunday in March, weather permitting, the largest noncompetitive kite festival in the country sends up hundreds of commercial and homemade kites. The wide variety reflects the ethnic diversity of Southern California. *13755 Fiji Way, Marina Del Rey 90292, tel. 213/822–2561.*

Nabisco Dinah Shore Invitational, Rancho Mirage. At the end of March, the finest women golfers in the world compete for the richest purse on the LPGA circuit. *1 Racquet Club Dr., Rancho Mirage 92270, tel. 619/324–4546.*

April   **Long Beach Grand Prix,** Long Beach. There is world-class auto racing on a mid-April weekend, with five races, entertainment, and celebrities. *100 W. Broadway, Suite 670, Long Beach 90802, tel. 213/437–0341.*

The Ramona Pageant, Hemet. On three weekends, from mid-April till the end of the month, the poignant love story of Ramona is presented by a large cast on a mountainside outdoor stage. *Ramona Pageant Association, 27400 Ramona Bowl Rd., Hemet 92344, tel. 714/658–3111.*

Conejo Valley Days, Thousand Oaks. Held at the end of April, this festival features a chili cook-off, picnic, parade, rodeo, whisker contest, carnival rides and games. *Conejo Valley Chamber of Commerce, 625 W. Hillcrest Dr., Thousand Oaks 91360, tel. 805/499–1993.*

May   **Cinco de Mayo,** Los Angeles. One of Mexico's most important holidays is celebrated with a fiesta in early May at El Pueblo de

Los Angeles State Historic Park in downtown Los Angeles. *622 N. Main St., Los Angeles 90006, tel. 213/628–1274.*

Wine Expo, Redondo Beach. Southern California's largest outdoor wine tasting takes place early in the month of May. Along with the wine, there is entertainment, and tasting of food from local restaurants. *Redondo Beach Chamber of Commerce, 1215 N. Catalina Ave., Redondo Beach 90277, tel. 213/376–6912.*

Queen Mary Jazz Festival, Long Beach. In mid-May, top-name jazz artists perform in an open-air theater off the bow of the *Queen Mary. Wrather Port Properties, Box 8, Long Beach 90801, tel. 213/435–3511.*

June **Semana Nautica Summer Sports Festival,** Santa Barbara. This festival, held from the latter part of June through the 4th of July, is over 50 years old, and includes some three dozen ocean, beach, and land events, most of them open to amateurs. *Semana Nautica Association, 5101 University Dr., Santa Barbara 93111, tel. 805/964–9425.*

July **Fourth of July Celebration,** Pasadena. The famous Rose Bowl is the site for an old-fashioned circus and a fireworks show produced by Pyro Spectaculars, who were responsible for the fireworks at the 1984 Olympics and at the celebration for the restored Statue of Liberty in New York Harbor. *Rose Bowl, 1001 Rose Bowl Dr., Pasadena 91103, tel. 818/577–3106.*

Orange County Fair, Costa Mesa. During its 10-day run from early to mid-July, there is top-name entertainment, a rodeo, food, music, arts and crafts, and hundreds of exhibits. *88 Fair Dr., Costa Mesa 92626, tel. 714/751–3247.*

Santa Barbara National Horse and Flower Show, Santa Barbara. Horses and riders compete in one of the nation's top horse shows, and at the same time, at the same showgrounds, a flower show features gardens, landscapes, and arrangements. Mid-month. *Santa Barbara National Horse and Flower Show, 19th District Agricultural Association, Earl Warren Showgrounds, Box 3006, Santa Barbara 93130, tel. 805/687–0766.*

International Surf Festival, Hermosa Beach, Manhattan Beach, Redondo Beach, and Torrance. July winds up with a three-day multicity celebration that includes lifeguard competitions, volleyball and body surfing tournaments, sand castle sculptures, and sand runs. *International Surf Festival Committee, 2600 Strand, Manhattan Beach 90266, tel. 213/545–4502.*

August **Old Spanish Fiesta Days,** Santa Barbara. In the first week of August the community celebrates the city's Hispanic heritage with costumes, parades, *mercados* (marketplaces), and a rodeo. *Old Spanish Days in Santa Barbara, Inc., 1122 N. Milpas St., Santa Barbara 93103, tel. 805/962–8101.*

Nisei Week Japanese Festival, Los Angeles. The rich Japanese cultural heritage is celebrated mid-month with parades, street dancing, and a carnival in Little Tokyo. *244 S. San Pedro St., Suite 501, Los Angeles 90012, tel. 213/687–7193.*

September **Los Angeles County Fair,** Pomona. This is the largest county fair in the world. It runs for more than two weeks, from mid-September into the first days of October. Horse racing, entertainment, fine arts, home arts, horse shows, agricultural displays, wine judging, and flower and garden shows are among the attractions. *Los Angeles County Fair Association, Box 2250, Pomona 91769, tel. 714/623–3111.*

October **Southern California Grand Prix at Del Mar,** Del Mar. This event on a mid-October weekend includes vintage grand prix races, an auto exposition, and national sports car championships. *100 W. Broadway, Suite 670, Long Beach 90802, tel. 213/437-0341.*

November **The Skins Game,** La Quinta. In the latter part of the month, four of the PGA's top golfing pros compete in a high-stakes hole-by-hole challenge. *Landmark Special Events, 8140 Calle Tampico, La Quinta 92253, tel. 619/564-8100.*
Hollywood Christmas Parade, Hollywood. Right after Thanksgiving comes this celebrity-studded parade. *Hollywood Chamber of Commerce, 6255 Sunset Blvd., Suite 911, Hollywood 90028, tel. 213/469-2337.*

December **Christmas Boat Parade of Lights,** Newport Beach. For six nights before Christmas, 200 decorated boats parade through the harbor. *1470 Jamboree Rd., Newport Beach 92660, tel. 714/644-8211.*
Queen Mary **New Year's Eve Party,** Long Beach. Billed as "the biggest party on earth," there are actually seven simultaneous parties, with a midnight fireworks display to welcome the new year. *WCO Port Properties, Ltd., Box 8, Long Beach 90801, tel. 213/435-3511.*

What to Pack

Clothing   The greatest single rule to bear in mind in packing for a Southern California vacation is to prepare for changes in temperature. An hour's drive can take you up or down many degrees; in addition, the variation from daytime to nighttime in a single location is often marked. Take along a sweater and a jacket. Clothes that can be layered are your best insurance for coping with variations in temperatures. Include shorts and/or cool cottons. Always tuck in a bathing suit; even if you're not a beach lover, the majority of overnight lodgings have a pool, a spa, or a sauna, and you'll want the option of using these facilities.

While casual dressing is a hallmark of the California lifestyle, men will need a jacket and tie for many good restaurants in the evening, and women will be more comfortable in something dressier than the regulation sightseeing garb of cotton dresses, walking shorts, or jeans and T-shirts.

Even though we're advising that you bring a variety of clothes, it's also important to pack light. Porters and luggage trolleys are not always easy to find. Try not to take more luggage than you can handle.

Be sure you take proven comfortable walking shoes with you. Even if you're not much of a walker at home, you're bound to find many occasions on a Southern California vacation when you'll want to hoof it, and nothing curtails the pleasures of sightseeing like sore feet. And who wants to spend precious vacation hours in shoe stores, looking for a pair of comfortable shoes?

Miscellaneous   While it is true that you can buy film, sunburn cream, aspirin, and most other necessities almost anywhere in Southern California, it's a nuisance to be searching for staples, especially when time is limited. An extra pair of glasses, contact lenses, or prescription sunglasses is always a good idea; the loss of your only pair can put a real crimp in your vacation.

It should go without saying that it is important to pack any prescription medicines you use regularly, as well as any that can be important upon occasion, such as allergy medication.

Cash Machines

Virtually all United States banks belong to a network of automatic teller machines (ATMs) which gobble up bank cards and spit out cash 24 hours a day in cities throughout the country.

There are some eight major networks; the largest are Cirrus, owned by MasterCard, and Plus, affiliated with Visa. Some banks belong to more than one network. Each network has a toll-free number you can call to locate machines in a given city; the Cirrus number is 800/4–CIRRUS; the Plus number is 800/THE–PLUS.

Bank cards are not issued automatically; you have to ask for them. If your bank doesn't belong to at least one ATM network, you should consider moving your funds, since ATMs are becoming even more useful than check cashing. Cards issued by MasterCard and Visa may also be used in the ATMs, but the fees are usually higher than the fees on bank cards, and there is a daily interest charge on the "loan," even if monthly bills are paid on time. Check with your bank for fees and for the amount of cash you can withdraw on any given day.

Traveling with Film

If your camera is new, shoot and develop a few rolls of film before leaving home. Pack some lens tissue and an extra battery for your built-in light meter. Invest about $10 in a skylight filter and screw it onto the front of your lens. It will protect the lens and reduce haze.

Film doesn't survive hot weather. If you're driving in summer, don't store film in the glove compartment or on the shelf under the rear window. Put it behind the front seat on the floor, on the side opposite the exhaust pipe.

On a plane trip, never pack unprocessed film in check-in luggage; if your bags get X-rayed, say goodbye to your pictures. Always carry undeveloped film with you through airport security and ask to have it inspected by hand. (It helps to isolate your film in a plastic bag, ready for quick inspection.) Inspectors at American airports are required by law to honor requests for hand inspection.

The newer airport scanning machines—used in all U.S. airports—are safe for anything from five to 500 scans, depending on the speed of your film. The effects are cumulative; you can put the same roll of film through several scans without worry. After five scans, though, you're asking for trouble.

If your film gets fogged and you want an explanation, send it to the National Association of Photographic Manufacturers (550 Mamaroneck Ave., Harrison, NY 10528), which will try to determine what went wrong. The service is free.

Traveling with Children

Hotels
: Many hotels and motels let children stay free in the same room with their parents, with nominal charges for cribs and $5–$10 charges for extra beds. The **Anaheim Hilton** (777 Convention Way, Anaheim 92802, tel. 800/HILTONS) has a free Kids Klub for children aged 5–15, with several counselors and a Kids Klub Corner in its restaurant. **Disneyland Hotel** (1150 W. Cerritos Ave., Anaheim 92802, tel. 714/778–6600) has supervised activities for children, a Yukon Klem Klub for children 4–12, and other family amenities. **Sheraton Grande** in Los Angeles and **Sheraton Universal Hotel** on the lot of Universal Studios (333 Universal Terrace Parkway, Universal City 91608, tel. 800/325 –3535) have family-oriented packages; one includes complimentary baby-sitting. The **Westin Bonaventure** (404 S. Figueroa St., Los Angeles 90071, tel. 213/624–1000) allows children under 18 to stay free with their parents and offers a special two-room family weekend special.

Baby-sitting Services
: For baby-sitting services, first check with the hotel concierge. **Sitters Unlimited** has franchises in Los Angeles County, Huntington Beach, and Long Beach (tel. 213/595–8186), Orange County (tel. 714/951–4580), Anaheim/Orange County (tel. 714/ 458–6646), and Irvine, Tustin, and Santa Ana (tel. 714/458– 6646).

Publications
: *L.A. Parent* (Box 3204, Burbank 91504, tel. 818/846–0400) is a monthly newspaper filled with events listings and resources; it is available free at such places as libraries, supermarkets, museums, and toy stores. For a small fee, you can have an issue sent to you before your trip.

: *Places to Go with Children in Southern California,* by Stephanie Kegan, is published by Chronicle Books; $7.95. *Family Travel Times,* an 8- to 12-page newsletter, is published 10 times a year by TWYCH (Travel with Your Children, 80 Eighth Ave., New York, NY 10011, tel. 212/206–0688). Subscription includes access to back issues and twice-weekly opportunities to call in for specific advice. *Great Vacations with Your Kids: The Complete Guide to Family Vacations in the U.S.,* by Dorothy Ann Jordon and Marjorie Adoff Cohen (E. P. Dutton, $12.95), details everything from city vacations to child-care resources.

Home Exchange
: Exchanging homes is a surprisingly low-cost way to enjoy a vacation in another part of the country. **Vacation Exchange Club, Inc.** (12006 111th Ave., Unit 12, Youngstown, AZ 85363, tel. 602/972–2186) specializes in domestic home exchanges. The club publishes one directory in February and a supplement in April. Membership is $24.70 per year, for which you receive one listing. Loan-a-Home (2 Park Lane, Mount Vernon, NY 10552, tel. 914/664–7640) is popular with academics on sabbatical and businesspeople on temporary assignment. There's no annual membership fee or charge for listing your home; however, one directory and a supplement costs $30.

Getting There
: On domestic flights, children under 2 not occupying a seat travel free. Various discounts apply to children 2–12 years of age. Regulations about infant travel on airplanes are in the process of changing. Until they do, however, if you want to be sure your infant is secured in his or her own safety seat, you must buy a separate ticket and bring your own infant car seat. (Check with

the airline in advance; certain seats aren't allowed. Or write for the booklet *Child/Infant Safety Seats Acceptable for Use in Aircraft,* from the Federal Aviation Administration, APA–200, 800 Independence Ave., SW, Washington, DC 20591, tel. 202/267–3479.) Some airlines allow babies to travel in their own safety seats at no charge if a spare seat is available on the plane; otherwise, safety seats will be stored and the child will have to be held by a parent. If you opt to hold your baby on your lap, do so with the infant outside the seatbelt so he or she won't be crushed in case of a sudden stop.

Also inquire about special children's meals or snacks. See the February 1990 and 1992 issues of *Family Travel Times,* for "TWYCH's Airline Guide," which contains a rundown of the children's services offered by 46 airlines.

Hints for Disabled Travelers

California is a national leader in providing access for disabled people to the attractions and facilities of the state. Since 1982, the state building code has required that all construction for public use must include access for the disabled. State laws more than a decade old provide such privileges as special parking spaces, unlimited parking in time-limited spaces, and free parking in metered spaces. Initia from states other than California are honored.

The Information Center for Individuals with Disabilities (Fort Point Pl., 1st floor, 27–43 Wormwood St., Boston, MA 02210, tel. 617/727–5540 or 800/462–5015) offers useful problem-solving assistance, including lists of travel agents who specialize in tours for the disabled.

Moss Rehabilitation Hospital Travel Information Service (12th St. and Tabor Rd., Philadelphia, PA 19141, tel. 215/329–5715) for a small fee provides information on tourist sights, transportation, and accommodations in destinations around the world.

Mobility International (Box 3551, Eugene, OR 97403, tel. 503/343–1284) has information on accommodations, organized study, and so forth around the world.

The Society for the Advancement of Travel for the Handicapped (26 Court St., Brooklyn, NY 11242, tel. 718/858–5483) offers access information. The annual membership is $40 or $25 for senior travelers and students. Send a stamped, self-addressed envelope.

The Itinerary (Box 2012, Bayonne, NJ 07002, tel. 201/858–3400) is a bimonthly travel magazine for the disabled. Call for a subscription ($10 for 1 year); it's not available in stores.

Greyhound/Trailways (tel. 800/531–5332) will carry a disabled person and companion for the price of a single fare. **Amtrak** (tel. 800/USA–RAIL) requests 24-hour notice to provide redcap service, special seats, and a 25% discount. For a free copy of Amtrak's *Travel Planner,* which includes services for elderly and disabled travelers, write to Amtrak (National Railroad Passenger Corporation, 400 N. Capitol St. NW, Washington, DC 20001).

In Los Angeles **The Junior League of Los Angeles** (Farmers' Market, 3rd and Fairfax Sts., Los Angeles 90036, tel. 213/937–5566) distributes a guide for the disabled, "Round the Town with Ease." Charge is $2.

The **Los Angeles Visitor and Convention Bureau** publishes "The Los Angeles Visitors Guide" and "The Los Angeles Lodging Guide." Both use symbols to indicate attractions and accommodations with facilities for the disabled. For copies contact the bureau's Travel Development Department (515 S. Figueroa St., Los Angeles 90071, tel. 213/624–7300).

Hints for Older Travelers

Discounts are available for meals, lodging, entry to various attractions, car rentals, tickets for buses and trains, campsites, and so on. The age that qualifies you for these senior discounts varies considerably. AARP, the American Association of Retired Persons, will accept you for membership at age 50, and your membership card will qualify you for many discounts. The state of California will reduce the cost of your campsite, but you must be at least 62.

Our advice, if you are 50, is to ask about senior discounts, even if there is no posted notice. Ask at the time you are making reservations, buying tickets, or being seated in a restaurant. Carry proof of your age, such as a driver's license, and of course any membership cards in organizations that provide discounts for seniors. Many discounts are given solely on the basis of your age, without any sort of membership requirement. A 10% cut on a bus ticket or a 10% cut on a pizza may not seem like a major saving, but they add up, and you can cut the cost of your trip appreciably if you remember to take advantage of these options.

The **American Association of Retired Persons** (AARP, 1909 K St. NW, Washington, DC 20049, tel. 202/872–4700) has two programs for independent travelers: (1) the Purchase Privilege Program, which offers discounts on car rentals, sightseeing, hotels, motels, and resorts; and (2) the AARP Motoring Plan, which furnishes emergency aid (road service) and trip-routing information for an annual fee of $33.95 for a single person or married couple. **American Express Vacations** (Box 5014, Atlanta, GA 30302, tel. 800/241–1700 or, in Georgia, 800/637–6200) arranges tours for AARP members. Annual dues are $5 per person or per couple.

Elderhostel (80 Boylston St., Suite 400, Boston, MA 02116, tel. 617/426–7788) is an innovative program for people 60 or over (only one member of a traveling couple needs to be 60 to qualify). Participants live in dorms on some 1,100 campuses in the United States and around the world. Mornings are devoted to lectures and seminars, afternoons to sightseeing and field trips. The fee includes room, board, tuition, and round-trip transportation.

National Council of Senior Citizens (925 15th St. NW, Washington, DC 20005, tel. 202/347–8800) is a nonprofit advocacy group with some 5,000 local clubs across the country. Annual membership is $12 per person or per couple. Members receive a monthly newspaper with travel information and an ID card for reduced-rate hotels and car rentals.

Mature Outlook (6001 N. Clark St., Chicago, IL 60660, tel. 800/336–6330), a subsidiary of Sears Roebuck & Co., is a travel club for people over 50, offering discounts at Holiday Inns and a bi-monthly newsletter. Annual membership is $9.95 per person or couple. Instant membership is available at participating Holiday Inns.

The Senior Citizen's Guide to Budget Travel in the United States and Canada is available for $4.95, including postage, from Pilot Books (103 Cooper St., Babylon, NY 11702, tel. 516/422–2225).

The Discount Guide for Travelers Over 55, by Caroline and Walter Weintz, lists helpful addresses, package tours, reduced-rate car rentals, and the like, in the United States and abroad. To order, send $7.95 plus $1.50 shipping and handling to NAL/Cash Sales (Bergenfield Order Dept., 120 Woodbine St., Bergenfield, NJ 07621, tel. 800/526–0275). Include ISBN 0–525–48358–6.

Further Reading

Much has been written about the fascinating city of Los Angeles. *Los Angeles: The Enormous Village, 1781–1981,* by John D. Weaver, and *Los Angeles: Biography of a City,* by John and LaRee Caughey, will give you a fine background in how it came to be the city it is today. The unique social and cultural life of the whole Southern California area is explored in *Southern California: An Island on the Land* by Carey McWilliams.

One of the most outstanding features of Los Angeles is its architecture. *Los Angeles: The Architecture of Four Ecologies,* by Reyner Banham, relates the physical environment to the architecture. *Architecture in Los Angeles: A Compleat Guide,* by David Gebhard and Robert Winter, is exactly what the title promises, and very useful.

Many novels have been written with Los Angeles as the setting. One of the very best, Nathanael West's *Day of the Locust,* was first published in 1939, but still rings true. Budd Schulberg's *What Makes Sammy Run?,* Evelyn Waugh's *The Loved One,* and Joan Didion's *Play It As It Lays* are unforgettable. Other novels that give a sense of contemporary life in Los Angeles are *Sex and Rage* by Eve Babitz and *Less Than Zero* by Bret Easton Ellis. Raymond Chandler and Ross Macdonald have written many suspense novels with a Los Angeles background.

Arriving and Departing

Trains, planes, buses, and even luxury ocean liners all converge on the city with great frequency. But a car is virtually a necessity in Los Angeles, so if you drive here you can expect to save a good deal of time and money.

By Plane

The new, improved Los Angeles International Airport or LAX (tel. 213/646–5252) is the largest airport in the area. It was revamped for the 1984 Olympics as a two-level airport, with departures on the upper level and arrivals on the lower level. Over 85 major airlines are serviced by LAX, the third largest airport in the world in terms of passenger traffic.

One special attraction at LAX is Skytel (tel. 2/417–0200). Located next to the Air France ticket counter in the Tom Bradley International Terminal, this mini hotel provides travelers with a tiny cabin complete with phone, television, bathroom, and work space. The cabinettes are rented by the half hour, up to eight hours. Rates start at $12.95 for a half hour and go to $47 for the full eight hours.

Airlines Among the major carriers that serve LAX are Air Canada (tel. 800/422–6232), America West (tel. 800/228–7862), American (tel. 800/433–7300), Braniff (tel. 800/752–4556), British Airways (tel. 800/247–9297), Continental (tel. 800/525–0280), Delta (tel. 800/221–1212), Eastern (tel. 800/327–8376), Japan Airlines (tel. 800/525–3663), Northwest (tel. 800/225–2525), Pan Am (tel. 800/221–1111), Southwest (tel. 800/531–5601), TWA (tel. 800/221–2000), United (tel. 800/241–6522), and USAir (tel. 800/428–4322).

Smoking As of late February 1990, smoking is banned on all scheduled routes within the 48 contiguous states; within the states of Hawaii and Alaska; to and from the U.S. Virgin Islands and Puerto Rico; and on flights of under six hours to and from Hawaii and Alaska. The rule applies to the domestic legs of all foreign routes but does not affect international flights.

On a flight where smoking is permitted, you can request a nonsmoking seat during check-in or when you book your ticket. If the airline tells you there are no seats available in the nonsmoking section, insist on one: Department of Transportation regulations require U.S. carriers to find seats for all nonsmokers, provided they meet check-in time restrictions.

Luggage Regulations *Carry-on Luggage* New rules have been in effect since January 1, 1988, on United States airlines regarding carry-on luggage. The model for these new rules was agreed to by the airlines in December 1987 and then circulated by the Air Transport Association with the understanding that each airline would present its own version.

Under the model, passengers are limited to two carry-on bags. For a bag you wish to store under the seat, the maximum dimensions are 9″ x 14″ x 22″. For bags that can be hung in a closet or on a luggage rack, the maximum dimensions are 4″ x 23″ x 45″. For bags you wish to store in an overhead bin, the maximum dimensions are 10″ x 14″ x 36″. Your two carry-ons must each fit one of these sets of dimensions, and any item that exceeds the specified dimensions will generally be rejected as a carry-on and handled as checked baggage. Keep in mind that an airline can adapt these rules to circumstances, so on an especially crowded flight, don't be surprised if you are allowed only one carry-on bag.

In addition to the two carry-ons, the rules list eight items that may also be brought aboard: a handbag (pocketbook or purse), an overcoat or wrap, an umbrella, a camera, a reasonable amount of reading material, an infant bag, and crutches, a cane, braces, or other prosthetic devices on which the passenger is dependent. Infant/child safety seats can also be brought aboard if parents have purchased a ticket for the child or if there is space in the cabin.

Note that these regulations are for U.S. airlines only. Foreign airlines generally allow one piece of carry-on luggage in tourist class in addition to handbags and bags filled with duty-free goods. Passengers in first and business class are also allowed to carry on one garment bag. It is best to check with the airline ahead of time to find out their exact rules regarding carry-on luggage.

Checked Luggage U.S. airlines generally allow passengers to check in two suitcases whose total dimensions (length plus width plus height) do not exceed 62″ and whose weight per bag does not exceed 70 pounds.

Rules governing foreign airlines vary from airline to airline, so check with your travel agent or the airline itself before you go. All the airlines allow passengers to check in two bags. In general, expect the weight restriction on the two bags to be not more than 70 lbs. each, and the size restriction on each bag to be 62″ total dimensions.

Luggage Insurance Airlines are responsible for lost or damaged property only up to $1,250 per passenger on domestic flights, $9.07 per pound (or $20 per kilo) for checked baggage on international flights, and up to $400 per passenger for unchecked baggage on international flights. If you're carrying valuables, either take them with you on the airplane or purchase extra insurance for lost luggage. Some airlines will issue additional luggage insurance when you check in, but many do not. One that does is **American Airlines.** Its additional insurance is only for domestic flights or flights to Canada. The rate is $1 for every $100 valuation, with a maximum of $25,000 valuation per passenger; hand luggage is not included.

Two companies providing luggage insurance are **Tele-Trip** (tel. 800/228–9792), a subsidiary of Mutual of Omaha, and **The Travelers Insurance Co.** (tel. 203/277–0111 or 800/243–3174). Tele-Trip operates sales booths at airports and issues insurance through travel agents. Tele-Trip will insure checked luggage for up to 180 days and for $500–$3,000 valuation. For 1–3 days, the rate for a $500 valuation is $8.25; for 180 days, $100. The Travelers Insurance Co. will insure checked or hand luggage for $500–$2,000 valuation per person, also for a maximum of 180 days. The rate for 1–5 days for $500 valuation is $10; for 180 days, $85. For more information, write: The Travelers Insurance Co. (Ticket and Travel Dept., 1 Tower Sq., Hartford, CT 06183). Both companies offer the same rates on domestic and international flights. Check the travel pages of your Sunday newspaper for the names of other companies that insure luggage. Before you go, itemize the contents of each bag in case you need to file an insurance claim. Be certain to put your home address on each piece of luggage, including carry-on bags. If your luggage is stolen and later recovered, the airline must deliver the luggage to your home free of charge.

From the Airport to the Hotels A dizzying array of ground transportation is available from LAX to all parts of Los Angeles and its environs. A taxi ride to downtown Los Angeles can take 20 minutes—*if* there is no traffic. But in Los Angeles, that's a big if. Visitors should request the flat fee ($24 at press time) to downtown or choose from the several ground transportation companies that offer set rates.

SuperShuttle offers direct service between the airport and hotels. The trip to downtown hotels runs about $11. The seven-passenger vans operate 24 hours a day. In the airport, phone 213/417–8988 or use the SuperShuttle courtesy phone in the luggage area; the van should arrive within 15 minutes. To be picked up anywhere in the Los Angeles area, phone 213/338–1111. **L.A. Top Shuttle** (9100 S. Sepulveda Blvd., #128, tel. 213/670–6666) features door-to-door service and low rates ($10 per person from LAX to hotels in the Disneyland/Anaheim area).

The following limo companies charge a flat rate for airport service, ranging from $65 to $75: **Jackson Limousine** (tel. 213/734–9955), **West Coast Limousine** (tel. 213/756–5466), and **Dav-El Livery** (tel. 213/550–0070). Many of the cars have bars, stereos, televisions, and cellular phones.

Flyaway Service (tel. 818/994–5554) offers transportation between LAX and the eastern San Fernando Valley for around $5. For the western San Fernando Valley and Ventura area, contact **The Great American Stage Lines** (tel. 805/656–4190). **RTD** (tel. 213/626–4455) also offers limited airport service.

Other Airports The greater Los Angeles area is served by several other local airports. **Ontario Airport** (tel. 714/984–1207), located about 35 miles east of Los Angeles, serves the San Bernardino–Riverside area. Domestic flights are offered by Air LA, Alaska Airlines, American, America West, Continental, Delta, Northwest, PSA, SkyWest, Southwest, TWA, United, United Express, and USAir. Ground transportation possibilities include Super-shuttle as well as Inland Express (tel. 714/626–6599), Empire Airport Transportation (tel. 714/884–0744), and Southern California Coach (tel. 714/978–6415).

Burbank Airport (tel. 818/840–8847) serves the San Fernando Valley with commuter, and some longer, flights. Alaska Airlines, Alpha Air, USAir, American, America West, TWA, United, Delta, LA Helicopter, SkyWest, States West, and United Express are represented.

John Wayne Airport, in Orange County (tel. 714/755–6510), is served by Jet America, TWA, SkyWest, American, Northwest, Alaska, American West, Continental, Delta, United, USAir, and States West.

Car Rentals

In Los Angeles, it's not a question of whether wheels are a hindrance or a convenience: They're a necessity. If you're renting a car, compare prices, and be sure you understand all the provisions of an agreement before you sign it. Often you will have to pay extra for the privilege of picking up a car in one location and dropping it in another; know the difference in cost, and know how important it is to you. Differing requirements for filling gas tanks can change the cost of the rental; ask questions.

More than 35 major companies and dozens of local rental companies serve a steady demand for cars at Los Angeles International Airport and various city locations. Here are toll-free numbers for some of the largest car rental agencies serving Los Angeles: **Agency Rent-A-Car** (tel. 800/843–1143), **American International Rent-A-Car** (tel. 800/527–0202), **Avis** (tel. 800/331–1212), **Budget Car and Truck Rental** (tel. 800/527–0700), **Dollar Rent-a-Car** (tel. 800/421–6868), **Hertz** (tel. 800/654–3131), **National Car Rental** (tel. 800/328–4567), and **Thrifty Car Rental** (tel. 800/367–2277).

Major budget car rental agencies are **Alamo** (tel. 800/327–9633), **General** (tel. 800/327–7607), and **Rent-A-Wreck** (tel. 800/525–5309).

If expense is no object, **Luxury Line** (8747 Wilshire Blvd., Beverly Hills, tel. 213/657–2800; 300 S. La Cienega, tel. 213/659–5555) rents anything from Toyota Tercels to Rolls Royces, Jaguars, and Ferraris. Do you see yourself cruising L.A. in a pink 1957 Thunderbird? Contact **National Car Rental's California Classics** (L.A. International Airport, tel. 213/670–9950).

Because Los Angeles is such a car-rental hub, rates are highly competitive; a little research can often pay off in a special rate. The larger companies charge $35–$45 per day for a subcompact, with, typically, 75–100 miles free. That's not a lot of miles for sprawling Los Angeles, and it might make sense to find a weekly rate offering more free miles.

By Train

Los Angeles can be reached by Amtrak. The *Coast Starlight* is a superliner that travels along the spectacular California coast. It offers service from Seattle-Portland and Oakland–San Francisco down to Los Angeles. Amtrak's *San Joaquin* train travels a route through the Central Valley from Oakland to Bakersfield, where passengers transfer to an Amtrak bus that takes them to Los Angeles. The *Sunset Limited* goes to Los Angeles from New Orleans, the *Eagle* from San Antonio, and the *Southwest Chief* and the *Desert Wind* from Chicago.

Union Station in Los Angeles is one of the grande dames of railroad stations. The Spanish Mission–style station is a remnant of the glory days of the railroads. It is located at 825 North Alameda Street.

For Amtrak information call 800/USA–RAIL; ask about special excursion fares, family plans, and discounts for disabled travelers and senior citizens.

By Bus

The Los Angeles **Greyhound/Trailways** terminal (tel. 800/237–8211) is located at 208 East 6th Street, on the corner of Los Angeles Street.

Staying in Los Angeles

Important Addresses and Numbers

Tourist Information

Visitor Information Center. Arco Plaza, Level B, 6th and S. Flower streets, 90071, tel. 213/689–8822. Open Mon.–Sat. 8–5. **Los Angeles Visitor and Convention Bureau.** 515 S. Figueroa, 90071, tel. 213/624–7300.
Beverly Hills Visitors and Convention Bureau. 239 S. Beverly Dr., 90212, tel. 213/271–8174. Open weekdays 8:30–5.
Santa Monica Visitors Center. 1400 Ocean Ave. (in Palisades Park), tel. 213/393–7593. Open daily 10–4. Write to 2219 Main St., 90405.
Hollywood Visitors Center. 6541 Hollywood Blvd., 90028, tel. 2/461–42. Open Mon.–Sat. 9–5.

Pasadena Convention and Visitors Bureau. 171 S. Los Robles Ave., 91101, tel. 818/795–9311. Open weekdays 9–5, Sat. 10–4.

Emergencies Dial 911 for **police** and **ambulance** in an emergency.

Doctor **Los Angeles Medical Association Physicians Referral Service,** tel. 213/483–6122. Open weekdays 8:45–4:45. Most larger hospitals in Los Angeles have 24-hour emergency rooms. A few are: **St. John's Hospital and Health Center** (1328 22nd St., tel. 213/829–5511), **Cedar-Sinai Medical Center** (8700 Beverly Blvd., tel. 213/855–5000), **Hollywood Presbyterian Medical Center** (1300 N. Vermont Ave., tel. 213/413–3000).

24-Hour Pharmacies **Horton and Converse Pharmacy** (6625 Van Nuys Blvd., Van Nuys, tel. 818/782–6251).

Bellflower Pharmacy (9400 E. Rosecrans Ave., Bellflower, tel. 213/920–4213).

Horton and Converse (11600 Wilshire Blvd., tel. 213/478–0801, and 3875 Wilshire Blvd., tel. 213/382–2236). Open until 2 AM.

Surf and Weather Report: Tel. 213/451–8761.

Community Services: Tel. 800/242–4612 (24 hours).

Getting around Los Angeles

By Bus A bus ride on the **Southern California Rapid Transit District (RTD)** (tel. 213/626–4455) costs $1.10 and 25 cents for each transfer.

By Taxi You probably won't be able to hail a cab on the street in Los Angeles. Instead, you should phone one of the many taxi companies. The metered rate is $1.60 per mile. Two of the more reputable companies are **Independent Cab. Co.** (tel. 213/385–8294 or 385–TAXI) and **United Independent Taxi** (tel. 213/653–5050). United accepts MasterCard and Visa.

By Limousine Limousines come equipped with everything from a full bar and telephone to a hot tub and a double bed—depending on your needs. Reputable companies include **Dav-El Livery** (tel. 213/550–0070), **First Class** (tel. 213/476–1960), and **Le Monde Limousine** (tel. 213/271–9270 or 818/887–7878).

By Car It's almost a necessity to have a car in Los Angeles. Rental agencies are listed in Planning Your Trip. The accompanying map of the freeway system should help you. If you plan to drive extensively, consider buying a *Thomas Guide*, which contains detailed maps of the entire county. Despite what you've heard, traffic is not always a major problem outside of rush hours (7–9 AM and 3–7 PM).

To the Airport **Supershuttle** (tel. 213/338–1111) will pick you up at your hotel or elsewhere and take you to the Los Angeles airport. The cost varies; it's about $11 from downtown. **Funbus Airlink Airport Service** (tel. 800/962–1976 in CA or 800/962–1975 nationwide) provides regular service from hotels to LAX. From the Valley, try **Flyaway Service** (Van Nuys, tel. 818/994–5554) or the **Great American Stage** (Woodland Hills, Thousand Oaks, Oxnard, Van Nuys, tel. 805/656–4190).

If you're driving, leave time for heavy traffic; it really can't be predicted.

Los Angeles Freeways

Guided Tours

Orientation Tours Los Angeles is so spread out and has such a wealth of sightseeing possibilities that an orientation bus tour may prove useful. The cost is about $25.

Gray Line (1207 W. Third St., 90017, tel. 213/856–5900), one of the best-known tour companies in the country, picks passengers up from more than 140 hotels. There are more than 24 tours to Disneyland, Universal Studios, the *Queen Mary*, Catalina Island, and other attractions.

All tours are fully narrated by a driver-guide. Reservations must be made in advance. Many hotels can book them for you.

Blue Line Tours (5600 Venice Blvd., Los Angeles, tel. 213/287–1111) offers city tours through downtown's Olvera Street, around Beverly Hills's stars homes, and along the glitzy Sunset Strip. Another tour goes to Universal Studios for the day. All tours are guide-driven, with lively narration. Buses or small vans pick you up and drop you off at your hotel.

StarLine Sightseeing Tours (6845 Hollywood Blvd., Hollywood 90028, tel. 213/463–3131) has been showing people around Los Angeles since 1935, with an emphasis on the homes of the stars. Like Gray Line, StarLine uses large touring buses and picks up at most area hotels. There are tours to Knott's Berry Farm, Disneyland, and other "musts"; but the company gets much of its business from its four-hour Stars' Home Tour, which takes visitors to more than 60 estates in Beverly Hills, Holmby Hills, and Bel Air. The tour departs from StarLine's Hollywood terminal at Mann's Chinese Theater hourly in the winter and every half hour in the summer. Hotel pickup can be arranged.

A more personalized look at the city can be had by planning a tour with **Casablanca Tours** (Roosevelt Hotel, 7000 Hollywood Blvd., Cabana 4, Hollywood 90028, tel. 213/461–0156), which offers an insider's look at Hollywood and Beverly Hills. The four-hour tour, which can be taken in the morning or afternoon, starts in Hollywood or in centrally located hotels. Tours are in minibuses with a maximum of people, and prices are equivalent to the large bus tours—about $25. Guides are college students with a high-spirited view of the city. The tour takes in the usual tourist spots—Hollywood Bowl, Mann's Chinese Theater, the Walk of Fame, and homes of such stars as Jimmy Stewart and Neil Diamond. It also includes a visit to the posh shops along Rodeo Drive.

Catalina Safari (Box 1566, Two Harbors, Catalina Island, 90704, tel. 213/510–0303) offers daily guided tours and field trips in Catalina's interior, where wild buffalo roam. Tours are in 14-passenger vans; pickup is at Catalina's Airport in the Sky or in Avalon. In addition to the natural-history tour, the company also offers hiking trips and snorkeling safaris.

Catalina Adventure Tours (Box 1314, Avalon, 90704, tel. 213/510–2888) has day and night glass-bottom-boat tours, city garden tours, harbor tram tours, and scenic island tours in 20 passenger buses.

Special-Interest Tours So much of Los Angeles is known to the world through Hollywood, it is fitting that many of the special-interest tours feature Hollywood and its lore.

Grave Line Tours (Box 931694, Hollywood, CA 90093, tel. 213/ 876–0920) digs up the dirt on notorious suicides and visits the scenes of various murders, scandals, and other crimes via a luxuriously renovated hearse. A clever, definitely off-the-beaten-track tour in the true sensationalist spirit of Hollywood. Tours daily at noon for two hours; $30 per person reserved, $25 standby.

Hollywood Fantasy Tours (1651 N. Highland, Hollywood, tel. 213/469–8184) has one tour that takes you through Beverly Hills, down Rodeo Drive, around Bel Air, and up and down colorful Sunset Strip, then on to exclusive Holmby Hills, home of *Playboy* magazine's Hugh Hefner. If you're only interested in Hollywood, ask about a tour of that area, pointing out television and film studios as well as famous stores, such as Frederick's of Hollywood.

Visitors who want something dramatically different should check with Marlene Gordon of **The Next Stage** (Box 35269, Los Angeles 90035, tel. 213/939–2688). This innovative tour company takes from four to 46 people, on buses or vans, in search of ethnic L.A., Victorian L.A., Underground L.A. (in which all the places visited are underground), and so on. The Insomniac Tour visits the flower market and other places in the wee hours of the morning. Marlene Gordon, who is a member of the L.A. Conservancy and the California Historical Society, also plans some spectacular tours outside of Los Angeles. Among them are a bald eagle tour to Big Bear with a naturalist; a whale-watching and biplane adventure; and a glorious garlic train, which tours Monterey and Carmel, and takes in the Gilroy Garlic Fest.

LA Today Custom Tours also has a wide selection of offbeat tours, some of which tie in with seasonal and cultural events, such as theater, museum exhibits, and the Rose Bowl. Groups range from 8 to 50, and prices from $6 to $50. The least expensive is a walking tour of hotel lobbies in downtown Los Angeles. The two-hour tour costs $6. For further information contact Elinor Oswald (LA Today, 14964 Camarosa Dr., Pacific Palisades, 90272, tel. 213/454–5730).

Architecture in Los Angeles is rich and varied. Guided and self-guided tours of the many design landmarks are becoming increasingly popular. Buildings run the gamut from the Victorian Bradbury Building in the downtown core, to the many fine examples of Frank Lloyd Wright's works—the Ennis-Brown House, Hollyhock House, and Snowden House among them. On the last Sunday of April each year the Los Angeles County Museum of Art (tel. 213/857–6500) holds a fund-raising tour of a selection of special houses in the city.

Walking Tours Walking is something that Angelenos do not do much of; Los Angeles is not a city where people stroll, except in Westwood and Beverly Hills, and in the various parks throughout the city. But there is no better way to see things close up.

A very pleasant self-guided walking tour of **Palisades Park** is detailed in a brochure available at the park's Visitors Center (1430 Ocean Blvd.). Many television shows and movies have been filmed on this narrow strip of parkland on a bluff overlooking the Pacific. The 26-acre retreat is always bustling with walkers, skaters, Frisbee throwers, readers, and sunbathers.

The **Los Angeles Conservancy** (tel. 213/623–CITY) offers low-cost walking tours of the downtown area. Each Saturday one of six different tours is offered. All tours leave at 10 AM from the Olive Street entrance of the Biltmore Hotel. Reservations are necessary. The Pershing Square Tour includes visits to buildings that span four decades of Los Angeles history, with such stops as the Biltmore Hotel, the Edison Building, and the Subway Terminal Building. On the Palaces of Finance Tour the elegant architecture of the Wall Street of the West is explored. Included are the stained-glass dome of Banco Popular, the Art Deco lobby of the Design Center of Los Angeles, and the Palm Court of the Alexandria Hotel. The Broadway Theaters Tour takes in splendid movie palaces—the largest concentration of pre–World War II movie houses in America. The Mecca for Merchants Tour explores the city's first shopping district. The Art Deco Tour explores great examples of this modernistic style at such places as the Oviatt Building, the green Sun Realty Building, and the turquoise Eastern Columbia Building. The Terra Cotta Tour takes a look at clay architectural ornamentation at the Palace Theater, the Wurlitzer Building, and other downtown locales.

Personal Guides Perhaps the best way to see Los Angeles, or any city, is with a guide who knows the city well and can gear sightseeing to your interests. One such service, **Tour Elegante** (15446 Sherman Way, Van Nuys, tel. 818/786–8466), offers the perk of a personal guide without the usual expense (under $50 per person). Tours run from three to six hours.

Elegant Tours for the Discriminating (tel. 213/472–4090) is a personalized sightseeing and shopping service for the Beverly Hills area. Joan Mansfield offers her extensive knowledge of Rodeo Drive to one, two, or three people at a time. Lunch is included.

Judith Benjamin Personally Designed Sightseeing (2210 Wilshire Blvd., #754, Santa Monica 90403, tel. 213/826–8810) also matches your interests with sightseeing outings. Judith will design architectural tours, museum tours, shopping tours, visits to jazz nightclubs—anything you might want to see or do in the area.

L.A. Nighthawks (Box 10224, Beverly Hills 902, tel. 213/859–1171) will arrange your nightlife for you. For a rather hefty price, you'll get a limousine, a guide, a gourmet dinner, as well as immediate entry into L.A.'s hottest night spots. For a group of eight, prices come down considerably because vans or tour buses are used. Nighthawks proprietor Charles Andrews, a music writer and 20-year entertainment-business veteran, has been featured on "Eye on LA" and other television shows for this innovative approach to nighttime entertainment.

Credit Cards

The following credit card abbreviations are used in this guide: AE, American Express; CB, Carte Blanche; DC, Diners Club; MC, MasterCard; V, Visa.

2 Portrait of Los Angeles

*Los Angeles is widely recognized as the land of hype and image. It's known for a hedonistic lifestyle in the sun, for (what remains of) the Hollywood mystique, for unending housing developments, and—of course—for the freeways. The image-making started early (*Sunset, *"the magazine of Western Living," started as a promotional publication of the Southern Pacific Railroad) and hasn't stopped yet.*

Reyner Banham's chapter on L.A.'s freeways (from his book Los Angeles: The Architecture of Four Ecologies) *is deservedly famous. It takes an imaginative look at the image and the reality of some more up-to-date Southern California mythology.*

Autopia

by Reyner Banham

The first time I saw it happen nothing registered on my conscious mind, because it all seemed so natural—as the car in front turned down the off-ramp of the San Diego freeway, the girl beside the driver pulled down the sun-visor and used the mirror on the back of it to tidy her hair. Only when I had seen a couple more incidents of the kind did I catch their import: that coming off the freeway is coming in from outdoors. A domestic or sociable journey in Los Angeles does not end so much at the door of one's destination as at the off-ramp of the freeway, the mile or two of ground-level streets counts as no more than the front drive of the house.

In part, this is a comment on the sheer vastness of the movement pattern of Los Angeles, but more than that it is an acknowledgement that the freeway system in its totality is now a single comprehensible place, a coherent state of mind, a complete way of life, the fourth ecology of the Angeleno. Though the famous story in *Cry California* magazine about the family who actually lived in a mobile home on the freeways is now known to be a jesting fabrication, the idea was immediately convincing (several other magazines took it seriously and wanted to reprint it) because there was a great psychological truth spoken in the jest. The freeway is where the Angelenos live a large part of their lives.

Such daily sacrifices on the altar of transportation are the common lot of all metropolitan citizens of course. Some, with luck, will spend less time on the average at these devotions, and many will spend them under far more squalid conditions (on the Southern Region of British Railways, or in the New York subway, for instance) but only Los Angeles has made a mystique of such proportions out of its commuting technology that the whole world seems to know about it—tourist postcards from London do not show Piccadilly Circus underground station, but cards from Los Angeles frequently show local equivalents like the "stack" intersection in downtown; Paris is not famous as the home of the Metro in the way Los Angeles is famous as the home of the Freeway (which must be galling for both Detroit and New York which have better claims, historically). There seem to be two major reasons for their dominance in the city image of Los Angeles and both are aspects of their inescapability; firstly, that they are so vast that you cannot help seeing them, and secondly, that there appears no alternative means of movement and you cannot help using them. There are other and useful streets, and the major boulevards provide an excellent secondary network in many parts of the city, but psychologically, all are felt to be tributary to the freeways.

Furthermore, the actual experience of driving on the freeways prints itself deeply on the conscious mind and unthinking reflexes. As you acquire the special skills involved, the Los Angeles freeways become a special way of being alive, which can be duplicated, in part, on other systems (England would be a much safer place if those skills could be inculcated on our motorways) but not with this totality and extremity. If motorway driving anywhere calls for a high level of attentiveness, the extreme concentration required in Los Angeles seems to bring on a state of heightened awareness that some locals find mystical.

That concentration is required beyond doubt, for the freeways can kill—hardly a week passed but I found myself driving slowly under police control past the wreckage of at least one major crash. But on the other hand the freeways are visibly safe—I never saw any of these incidents, or even minor ones, actually happening, even in weeks where I found I had logged a thousand miles of rush-hour driving. So one learns to proceed with a strange and exhilarating mixture of long-range confidence and close-range wariness. And the freeway system can fail; traffic jams can pile up miles long in rush-hours or even on sunny Sunday afternoons, but these jams are rarely stationary for as long as European expectations would suggest. Really serious jams seem to be about as frequent as hold-ups on London suburban railways, and might—if bad—disrupt the working day of about the same number of citizens, but for most of the time traffic rolls comfortably and driving conditions are not unpleasant. As one habituated to the psychotic driving (as Gerald Priestland has called it) in English cities, and the squalor of the driving conditions, I cannot find it in me to complain about the freeways in Los Angeles; they work uncommonly well.

Angelenos, who have never known anything worse than their local system, find plenty to complain about, and their conversations are peppered with phrases like "being stuck in a jam in the October heat with the kids in the back puking with the smog." At first the visitor takes these remarks

seriously; they confirm his own most deeply ingrained prej-
udices about the city that has "sold its soul to the motor
car." Later, I came to realize that they were little more
than standard rhetorical tropes, like English complaints
about the weather, with as little foundation in the direct
personal experience of the speakers.

This is not to minimize the jams, or even the smog, but both
need to be seen in the context of comparisons with other
metropolitan areas. On what is regarded as a normally clear
day in London, one cannot see as far through the atmosphere as on some officially smoggy days I have experienced in Los Angeles. Furthermore, the photochemical
irritants in the smog (caused by the action of sunlight on ni-
trogen oxides) can be extremely unpleasant indeed in high
concentrations, but for the concentration to be high enough
to make the corners of my eyes itch painfully is rare in my
personal experience, and at no time does the smog contain
levels of soot, grit, and corroding sulphur compounds that
are still common in the atmospheres of older American and
European cities.

It is the psychological impact of smog that matters in Los
Angeles. The communal trauma of Black Wednesday (8
September 1943), when the first great smog zapped the city
in solid, has left permanent scars, because it broke the legend of the land of eternal sunshine. It was only a legend; the
area was never totally pure of atmosphere. The Spaniards
called it the Bay of Smokes and could identify it from the
ocean by the persistence of smoke from Indian camp-fires,
while plots of land in South Cucamonga were advertised in
the eighties as being free from "fog-laden sea-breezes."
But there is a profound psychological difference between
fogs caused by Nature's land-forms and light breezes and
God-given water, and air-pollution due to the works of man.
To make matters worse, analysis showed that a large part of
the smog (though not all, one must emphasize) is due to ef-
fluents from the automobile. Angelenos were shocked to
discover that it was their favorite toy that was fouling up
their greatest asset.

But, psychologically shocked or no, most Angeleno
freeway-pilots are neither retching with smog nor
stuck in a jam; their white-wall tires are singing over
the diamond-cut anti-skid grooves in the concrete road surface, the selector-levers of their automatic gearboxes are
firmly in *Drive*, and the radio is on. And more important
than any of this, they are acting out one of the most spectacular paradoxes in the great debate between private freedom and public discipline that pervades every affluent,
mechanized urban society.

The private car and the public freeway together provide an
ideal—not to say idealized—version of democratic urban
transportation: door-to-door movement on demand at high
average speeds over a very large area. The degree of free-

dom and convenience thus offered to all but a small (but now conspicuous) segment of the population is such that no Angeleno will be in a hurry to sacrifice it for the higher efficiency but drastically lowered convenience and freedom of choice of any high-density public rapid-transit system. Yet what seems to be hardly noticed or commented on is that the price of rapid door-to-door transport on demand is the almost total surrender of personal freedom for most of the journey.

The watchful tolerance and almost impeccable lane discipline of Angeleno drivers on the freeways is often noted, but not the fact that both are symptoms of something deeper—willing acquiescence in an incredibly demanding man/machine system. The fact that no single ordinance, specification or instruction manual describes the system in its totality does not make it any less complete or all-embracing—or any less demanding. It demands, first of all, an open but decisive attitude to the placing of the car on the road-surface, a constant stream of decisions that it would be fashionable to describe as "existential" or even "situational," but would be better to regard simply as a higher form of pragmatism. The highway is not divided by the kind of kindergarten rule of the road that obtains on British motorways, with their fast, slow, and overtaking lanes (where there are three lanes to use!). The three, four, or five lanes of an Angeleno freeway are virtually equal, the driver is required to select or change lanes according to his speed, surrounding circumstances and future intentions. If everybody does this with the approved mixture of enlightened self-interest and public spirit, it is possible to keep a very large flow of traffic moving quite surprisingly fast.

But at certain points, notably intersections, the lanes are not all equal—some may be pre-empted for a particular exit or change-over ramp as much as a mile before the actual junction. As far as possible the driver must get set up for these pre-empted lanes well in advance, to be sure he is in them in good time because the topology of the intersections is unforgiving. Of course there are occasional clods and strangers who do not sense the urgency of the obligation to set up the lane required good and early, but fortunately they are only occasional (you soon get the message!), otherwise the whole system would snarl up irretrievably. But if these preparations are only an unwritten moral obligation, your actual presence in the correct lane at the intersection is mandatory—the huge signs straddling the freeway to indicate the correct lanes must be obeyed because they are infallible.

At first, these signs can be the most psychologically unsettling of all aspects of the freeway—it seems incredibly bizarre when a sign directs one into the far left lane for an objective clearly visible on the right of the highway, but the sign must be believed. No human eye at windscreen level can unravel the complexities of even a relatively simple intersection (none of those in Los Angeles is a symmetrical cloverleaf) fast enough for a normal human brain moving forward at up to sixty m.p.h. to make the right decision in time, and there is no alternative to complete surrender of will to the instructions on the signs.

But no permanent system of fixed signs can give warning of transient situations requiring decisions, such as accidents, landslips or other blockages. It is in the nature of a freeway accident that it involves a large number of vehicles, and blocks the highway so completely that even emergency vehicles have difficulty in getting to the seat of the trouble, and remedial action such as warnings and diversions may have to be phased back miles before the accident, and are likely to affect traffic moving in the opposite direction as well. So, inevitably the driver has to rely on other sources of rapid information, and keeps his car radio turned on for warnings of delays and recommended diversions.

Now, the source of these radio messages is not a publicly-operated traffic-control radio-transmitter; they are a public service performed by the normal entertainment stations, who derive the information from the police, the Highway Patrol, and their own "Sigalert" helicopter patrols. Although these channels of information are not provided as a designed component of the freeway system, but arise as an accidental by-product of commercial competition, they are no less essential to the system's proper operation, especially at rush hours. Thus a variety of commanding authorities—moral, governmental, commercial, and mechanical (since most drivers have surrendered control of the transmission to an automatic gearbox)—direct the freeway driver through a situation so closely controlled that, as has been judiciously observed on a number of occasions, he will hardly notice any difference when the freeways are finally fitted with automatic control systems that will take charge of the car at the on-ramp and direct it at properly regulated speeds and correctly selected routes to a pre-programmed choice of off-ramp.

But it seems possible that, given a body of drivers already so well trained, disciplined, and conditioned, realistic cost-benefit analysis might show that the marginal gains in efficiency through automation might be offset by the psychological deprivations caused by destroying the residual illusions of free decision and driving skill surviving in the present situation. However inefficiently organized, the million or so human minds at large on the freeway system at any time comprise a far greater computing capacity than could be built into any machine currently conceivable—why not put that capacity to work by fostering the illusion that it is in charge of the situation?

If illusion plays as large a part in the working of the freeways as it does in other parts of the Angeleno ecology, it is not to be deprecated. The system works as well as it does because the Angelenos believe in it as much as they do; they may squeal when the illusion is temporarily shattered or frustrated; they may share the distrust of the Division of Highways that many liberal souls currently (and understandably) seem to feel; but on leaving the house they still turn the nose of the car toward the nearest freeway ramp because they still believe the freeways are the way to get there. They subscribe, if only covertly, to a deep-seated mystique of freeway driving, and I often suspect that the scarifying stories of the horrors of the freeways are deliberately put about to warn off strangers.

Partly this would be to keep inexperienced and therefore dangerous hayseeds off the highways, but it would also be to prevent the profanation of their most sacred ritual by the uninitiated. For the Freeway, quite as much as the Beach, is where the Angeleno is most himself, most integrally identified with his great city.

3 Exploring Los Angeles

by Ellen Melinkoff

The author of L.A. Picnics *and two other books, Ellen Melinkoff writes two weekly columns for the Los Angeles Times.*

In a city where the residents think nothing of a 40-mile commute to work, visitors have their work cut out for them. To see the sites—from the Huntington Library in San Marino to the *Queen Mary* in Long Beach—requires a decidedly organized itinerary. Be prepared to put miles on the car. It's best to view Los Angeles as a collection of destinations, each to be explored separately, and not to jump willy-nilly from place to place. In our guide, the major sightseeing areas of Los Angeles have been divided into eight major tours: Downtown; Hollywood; Wilshire Boulevard; the Westside; Santa Monica, Venice, Pacific Palisades, and Malibu; Palos Verdes, San Pedro, and Long Beach; Highland Park, Pasadena, and San Marino; and the San Fernando Valley.

Each takes visitors to the major sites, augmented with bits of history and comments on the area, and occasional Time Out suggestions for meals. These main attractions are listed and numbered on the accompanying maps.

After the eight exploring sections, the rest of Los Angeles's most noteworthy attractions have been organized into six miscellaneous sections. Other Places of Interest includes the sites that are located outside the map areas but are definitely worth visiting. Historic Buildings and Sites, Museums, Parks and Gardens, Los Angeles for Free, What to See and Do with Children, and Off the Beaten Track all contain both new sites not found elsewhere in the book and an alphabetical checklist of sites which are fully explained in the exploring sections. For example, the Huntington Museum is fully described in the Highland Park, Pasadena, and San Marino tour, and then cross-referenced in the Museums section, where every noteworthy museum in Los Angeles is listed.

Tour 1: Downtown Los Angeles

Numbers in the margin correspond with points of interest on the Tour 1: Downtown Los Angeles map.

All those jokes about Los Angeles being a city without a downtown are simply no longer true. They might have had some ring of truth to them a few decades ago when Angelenos ruthlessly turned their back on the city center and hightailed to the suburbs without a look back. There *had* been a downtown, once, when Los Angeles was very young, and now the city core is enjoying a resurgence of attention from urban planners, real estate developers, and intrepid downtown office workers who have discovered the advantages of living close to the office.

Downtown Los Angeles can be explored on foot (or better yet, on DASH—more about that in a minute). The natives might disagree, but these are the same natives who haven't been downtown since they took out a marriage license at city hall 30 years ago; don't follow their advice. During the day, downtown is relatively safe and quite interesting. A tour of downtown cuts through more than a century of history and colorful ethnic neighborhoods.

Getting around to the major sites in downtown Los Angeles is actually quite simple, thanks to DASH (Downtown Area Short Hop). This minibus service travels in a loop past most of the at-

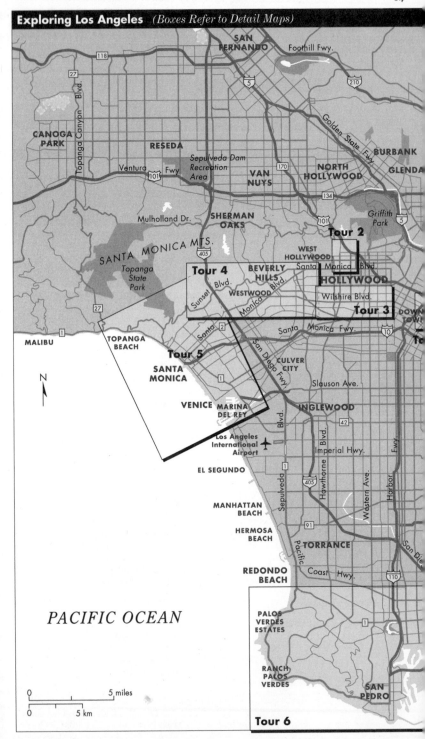

Exploring Los Angeles *(Boxes Refer to Detail Maps)*

SAN FERNANDO
Foothill Fwy.
118
5
210
Golden State Fwy.
CANOGA PARK
BURBANK
RESEDA
GLEND
Topanga Canyon Blvd.
Sepulveda Dam Recreation Area
170
NORTH HOLLYWOOD
Ventura 101 Fwy.
VAN NUYS
134
Mulholland Dr.
SHERMAN OAKS
Griffith Park
5
101
SANTA MONICA MTS.
405
WEST HOLLYWOOD
Tour 2
Topanga State Park
Tour 4
BEVERLY HILLS
Santa Monica Blvd.
HOLLYWOOD
27
Sunset Blvd.
WESTWOOD
Monica Blvd.
Wilshire Blvd.
Tour 3
DOWN TOW
Santa 2
Santa Monica Fwy.
10
MALIBU
1
TOPANGA BEACH
Tour 5
Santa
San Diego Fwy.
To
SANTA MONICA
1
CULVER CITY
Slauson Ave.
VENICE
MARINA DEL REY
INGLEWOOD
Los Angeles International Airport
Blvd.
42
Imperial Hwy.
Fwy.
EL SEGUNDO
Sepulveda
1
405
Hawthorne Blvd.
Western Ave.
Harbor
San Die
MANHATTAN BEACH
HERMOSA BEACH
91
TORRANCE
Pacific
San Die
REDONDO BEACH
Coast Hwy.
110
1

PACIFIC OCEAN

N

0   5 miles
0   5 km

PALOS VERDES ESTATES
1
RANCH PALOS VERDES
SAN PEDRO
Tour 6

tractions listed here. Every ride costs 25 cents so if you hop on and off to see attractions, it'll cost you every time. But the cost is worth it, since you can travel quickly and be assured of finding your way. Whether you begin your tour at ARCO, as suggested, or decide to start at Olvera Street in Chinatown, DASH will get you around. The bus stops every two blocks or so. DASH (tel. 800/874–8885) runs weekdays 6:30–6:30, Saturday 9–5.

Begin your walk in the Los Angeles of today. The new downtown is a collection of eastside streets, paralleling the Harbor Freeway. Your walk will take you from the most modern buildings back in time past Art Deco movie palaces to the very oldest adobe in the city.

ARCO Plaza is hidden directly under the twin ARCO towers. This subterranean shopping mall is jam-packed with office workers during the week, nearly deserted on weekends. The
❶ **Los Angeles Visitor and Convention Bureau** is housed on level B. It offers free information about attractions as well as advice on public transportation. *Fifth St. and Figueroa St., tel. 213/ 689–8822. Open weekdays 9–5.*

❷ Just north of ARCO, the **Westin Bonaventure Hotel** (404 S. Figueroa St., tel. 213/624–1000) is unique in the L.A. skyline: five shimmering cylinders in the sky, with not a 90 degree angle in sight. Designed by John Portman in 1974, it remains a science fiction fantasy. Nonguests can use only one elevator, which rises through the roof of the lobby to soar through the air outside to the revolving restaurant and bar on the 35th floor. Food is expensive here. A better bet is to come for a drink (still over-priced) and nurse it for an hour as Los Angeles makes a full circle around you.

In the 19th century, Bunker Hill was the site of many stately mansions. Thanks to bulldozers, there's not much of a hill left, but this downtown area is being redeveloped, and two major sites here showcase visual arts (painting, sculpture, and environmental work) and media and performing arts.

❸ The **Museum of Contemporary Art** houses a permanent collection of international scope, representing modern art from 1940 to the present. Included are works by Mark Rothko, Franz Kline, and Susan Rothenberg. The red sandstone building was designed by one of Japan's renowned architects, Arata Isozaki, and opened in late 1986. Pyramidal skylights add a striking geometry to the seven-level, 98,000 square foot building. Don't miss the gift shop or the lively Milanese-style cafe. *250 S. Grand Ave., tel. 213/626–6222. Admission: $4 adults, children under 12 free; free to all Thurs. and Fri. after 5 PM. Open Tues., Wed., Sat., and Sun. 11–6, Thurs. and Fri. 11–8.*

❹ Walk north to the **The Music Center,** which has become the cultural center for Los Angeles since it opened in 1969. For years, it was the site of the Academy Awards each March: the limousines arrived at the Hope Street drive-through and celebrities whisked (sometimes more than once) through the crowds to the Dorothy Chandler Pavilion, the largest and grandest of the three theaters. It was named after the widow of the publisher of the Los Angeles *Times*, who was instrumental in fundraising efforts to build the complex.

Tour 1: Downtown Los Angeles

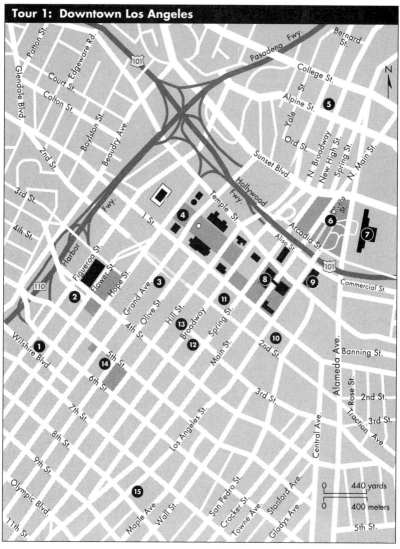

Biltmore Hotel, **14**

Bradbury Building, **12**

Chinatown, **5**

El Pueblo State
Historic Park, **6**

Garment District, **15**

Grand Central
Market, **13**

Little Tokyo, **10**

Los Angeles Children's
Museum, **9**

Los Angeles City
Hall, **8**

Los Angeles *Times*, **11**

Los Angeles Visitor
and Convention
Bureau, **1**

Museum of
Contemporary Art, **3**

The Music Center, **4**

Union Station, **7**

Westin Bonaventure
Hotel, **2**

The round, center building, the Mark Taper Forum, seats only 750 and seems almost cozy. Most of its offerings are of an experimental nature, many of them on a pre-Broadway run. The Ahmanson, at the north end, is the venue for many musical comedies. The plaza has a fountain and sculpture by Jacques Lipchitz. *First St. and Grand Ave., tel. 213/972–7211. Free 1-hr, 10-min tours are offered Tues.–Sat. 10–1:30. Call for reservations.*

⑤ L.A.'s **Chinatown** runs a pale second to San Francisco's Chinatown but it still offers visitors an authentic slice of life, beyond the tourist hokum. The neighborhood is bordered by Yale, Bernard, Alameda, and Ord, and the main street is North Broadway, where, every February, giant dragons snake down the center of the pavement during Chinese New Year celebrations. More than 15,000 Chinese and Southeast Asians (mostly Vietnamese) actually live in the Chinatown area, but many times that regularly frequent the markets (filled with exotic foods unfamiliar to most Western eyes) and restaurants (dim sum parlors are currently the most popular).

⑥ **El Pueblo State Historic Park** preserves the "birthplace" of Los Angeles (no one knows exactly where the original 1781 settlement was), the oldest downtown buildings, and some of the only remaining pre-1900 buildings in the city. The state park, comprising 44 acres and including the Plaza and Olvera Street, is bounded by Alameda, Arcadia, Spring, and Macy streets. *The Visitors Center is in Sepulveda House, 622 N. Main St., tel. 213/628–1274. Open weekdays 10–3, Sat. 10–4:30. Most shops and restaurants in the park are open daily 10–9.*

Olvera Street is the heart of the park and one of the most popular tourist sites in Los Angeles.

With its cobblestone walkways, pinatas, mariachis, and authentic Mexican food, Olvera Street should not be dismissed as a mere approximation of Old Mexico, a gringo version of the real thing. Mexican families come here in droves, especially on weekends and Mexican holidays—to them it feels like the old country.

Begin your walk of the area at the Plaza, between Main and Los Angeles streets, a wonderful Mexican-style park with shady trees, a central gazebo, and plenty of benches and walkways for strolling. On weekends there are often mariachis and folkloric dance groups here. You can have your photo taken in an oversize velvet sombrero, astride a stuffed donkey (a take-off of the zebra-striped donkeys that are a tradition on the streets of Tijuana).

Head north up Olvera Street proper. Mid-block is the Sepulveda House, which houses the Visitors Center and is now undergoing renovations. The Eastlake Victorian was built in 1887 as a hotel and boardinghouse. Pelanconi House, built in 1855, was the first brick building in Los Angeles and has been used by La Golondrina restaurant for more than 50 years. During the 1930s, famed Mexican muralist David Alfaro Siquieros was commissioned to paint a mural on the south wall of the Italian Hall building. The patrons were not prepared for the anti-imperialist mural depicting the oppressed workers of Latin America held in check by a menacing American eagle; it was immediately whitewashed into oblivion. It remains, under the paint, to this day, as preservationists from the Getty Conservation Trust work on ways of restoring the mural. (Ask to see copies of the mural at the visitors center.)

Walk down the east side of Olvera Street to mid-block, passing the only remaining sign of Zanja Ditch (mother ditch), which supplied water to the area in the earliest years. Avila Adobe (open weekdays 10–3), built in 1818, is generally considered the oldest building still standing in Los Angeles. This graceful, simple adobe is designed with the traditional interior courtyard. It is furnished in typical 1840s fashion.

On weekends, the restaurants are packed, and there is usually music in the plaza and along the street. Two Mexican holidays, Cinco de Mayo (May 5) and Independence Day (September 16), also draw huge crowds—and long lines for the restaurants. To see Olvera Street at its quietest and perhaps loveliest, visit on a late weekday afternoon. The long shadows heighten the romantic feeling of the street and there are only a few strollers and diners milling about.

South of the plaza is an ambitious area that has undergone recent renovation but remains largely underutilized. Except for docent-led tours, these magnificent old buildings remain closed, awaiting some commercial plan (à la Ghiradelli Square in San Francisco) that never seems to come to fruition. Buildings seen on tours include the Merced Theater, Masonic Temple, Pico House, and the Garnier Block—all ornate examples of the late 19th-century style. Under the Merced and Masonic Temple are the catacombs, secret passageways and old opium dens used by Chinese immigrants. Tours depart Tuesday–Saturday 10–1, on the hour. Meet at the Old Firehouse (south side of plaza), an 1884 building that contains early fire-fighting equipment and old photographs.

Time Out The Olvera Street dining ranges from fast-food stands to comfortable, sit-down restaurants. The most authentic food is at **La Luz del Dia,** at the southwest corner of the street. Here they serve traditional Mexican favorites like barbecued goat and pickled cactus as well as standbys like tacos and enchiladas. Best of all are the handmade tortillas. You haven't tasted real tortillas until you've tried handmade ones like these (the only ones on the street), which are patted out in a practiced rhythm by the women behind the counter. **La Golondrina** and **El Paseo** restaurants, across from each other in mid-block, have delightful patios and extensive menus.

---

❼ Union Station (800 N. Alameda St.), directly east of Olvera Street across Alameda, is one of those quintessentially Californian buildings that seemed to define Los Angeles to moviegoers all over the country in the 1940s. Built in 1939, its Spanish Mission style is a subtle combination of Streamline Moderne and Moorish. The majestic scale of the waiting room is definitely worth a walk over. Imagine it in its heydey, as Carole Lombard or Groucho Marx or Barbara Stanwyck might alight from a train and sashay through.

❽ Los Angeles City Hall is another often-photographed building. It's been used in "Dragnet," "Superman," and other television shows. Opened in 1928, the 27-story City Hall remained the only building to break the -story height limit (earthquakes, you know) until 1957. Although other buildings (e.g., the Bonaventure) may offer higher views, City Hall offers a 45-minute tour and ride to the top-floor observation deck. *200 N. Spring St., tel. 213/485–4423. Tours are by reservation only, weekday mornings at 10 and 11.*

❾ Los Angeles Children's Museum was the first of several strictly-for-kids museums now open in the city. All the exhibits here are hands-on, from Sticky City (where kids get to pillow fight with abandon in a huge pillow-filled room) to a TV studio (where they can put on their own news shows). *310 N. Main St., tel. 213/687–8800. Admission: $4. Open during school sessions Wed.–Thurs. 2–4 and weekends 10–5; during summer vacations, open weekdays 11:30–5, weekends 10–5.*

❿ Little Tokyo is the original ethnic neighborhood for Los Angeles's Japanese community. Most have deserted the downtown center for suburban areas like Gardena and West Los Angeles but Little Tokyo remains a cultural focal point. Nisei (the name for second-generation Japanese) Week is celebrated here every August with traditional drums, obon dancing, a carnival and huge parade. Bound by First, San Pedro, Third, and Los Angeles streets, Little Toyko has dozens of sushi bars, tempura restaurants, trinket shops, and even an eel-only restaurant. The Japanese American Cultural and Community Center presents events such as kabuki theater straight from Japan.

⓫ The **Los Angeles *Times*** complex is several buildings, supposedly harmoniously combining several eras and styles but ending up as pretty much of a hodge-podge. *Public, 1-hr tours weekdays 11:15 and 3. Enter at the 202 W. First St. entrance. Children must be at least 10 years old. Park at the lot at 213 S. Spring St. and it will be validated at end of tour. Reservations are required, tel. 213/237–5000.*

Broadway between First and Ninth is one of Los Angeles's busiest shopping streets. The shops and sidewalk vendors cater to the Hispanic population with bridal shops, immigration lawyers, and cheap stereos. First-floor rental space is said to be the most expensive in the city, even higher than in Beverly Hills. It can be an exhilarating slice-of-life walk, past the florid old movie theaters like the Mayan and the Million Dollar and the still-classy-no-matter-what Bradbury Building.

⓬ The five-story **Bradbury Building** (304 S. Broadway, tel. 213/489–1893) remains a marvelous specimen of architecture, serenely anchoring the southeast corner of Third and Broadway and keeping its nose above the hustle and bustle of the street like a real lady. Once the site of turn-of-the-century sweatshops, it now houses genteel law offices. The interior courtyard with its glass skylight and open balconies and elevator is picture perfect—and naturally another popular movie locale. The building is only open during the week, and its owners prefer that you not wander too far past the lobby.

⓭ Grand Central Market is the most bustling market in the city, and a testimony to the city's diversity. The block-through market of colorful and exotic produce, herbs, and meat draws a faithful clientele from the Hispanic community, senior citizens on a budget, and money-is-no-object Westside matrons seeking rare foodstuffs for their recipe adventures. Even if you don't plan to buy even one banana, Grand Central Market is a delightful place to browse. The butcher shops display lamb heads, bulls' testicles, pigs' tails. The produce stalls are piled high with the ripest reddest tomatoes. The herb stalls promise remedies for all your ills. Mixed among them are fast food stands (one Chinese but most Mexican). *317 S. Broadway. Open Mon.–Sat. 9–6, Sun. 10–4.*

⑭ The **Biltmore Hotel** (515 S. Olive St.) rivals Union Station for sheer majesty in the Spanish Revival tradition. The public areas have recently been restored; the magnificent, hand-painted wood beams brought back to their former glory.

⑮ **The Garment District** (700–800 blocks of Los Angeles St.) is an enclave of jobbers and wholesalers that sell off the leftovers from Los Angeles's considerable garment industry production. The Cooper Building (860 S. Los Angeles St.) is the heart of the district and houses several of what local bargain-hunters consider to be the best pickings.

Tour 2: Hollywood

Numbers in the margin correspond with points of interest on the Tour 2: Hollywood map.

"Hollywood": The name once defined movie stars, glamour, the Big Time. The big studios were here; starlets lived in sorority-like buildings in the center of town; the latest movies premiered at the Chinese and the Pantages.

Those days are gone. Paramount is the only major studio left; some celebrities may live in the Hollywood Hills, but certainly not in the "flats." Hollywood is no longer "Hollywood." These days it is, even to its supporters, a seedy town that could use a good dose of urban renewal (some projects are, in fact, finally underway). Why visit? Because the legends of the golden age of the movies are heavy in the air. Because this is where "they" were: Judy Garland lived here, so did Marilyn Monroe and Lana Turner. Because visitors are able to look past the junky shops and the lost souls who walk the streets to get a sense of yesterday. Even today, no visit to Los Angeles is truly complete without a walk down Hollywood Boulevard.

❶ Begin your tour of Hollywood simply by looking to the **Hollywood sign** in the Hollywood Hills that line the northern border of the town. Even on the smoggiest days, the sign is visible for miles. It is north of Beachwood Canyon, which is approximately one mile east of Hollywood and Vine. The sign was erected in 1923 as a promotional scheme for a real estate development called Hollywoodland. (The sign originally read "Hollywoodland"; "land" was taken down in 1949.) Standing high on Mount Lee, the 50-foot-high letters seem to be an ongoing lure for vandals and pranksters. There has been only one known suicide off the letters (in 1932), but every year there are several alterations (dopers turning it into "Hollyweed", right wingers into "Ollywood" during the Iran-Contra hearings).

❷ **Hollywood and Vine** was once considered the heart of Hollywood. The mere mention of the intersection inspired thoughts of starlets and movie moguls passing by, on foot and in jazzy convertibles. These days, Hollywood and Vine is far from the action. Pedestrian traffic is—well, pedestrian. No stars. No starlets. The big Broadway department store on the southwest corner is closed. The intersection is little more than a place for visitors to get their bearings.

Tour 2: Hollywood

Capitol Records
Building, **3**

Frederick's of
Hollywood, **7**

Hollywood Bowl, **10**

Hollywood High
School, **12**

Hollywood Memorial
Cemetery, **13**

Hollywood sign, **1**

Hollywood Studio
Museum, **11**

Hollywood and Vine, **2**

Hollywood Walk of
Fame, **6**

Hollywood Wax
Museum, **8**

Mann's Chinese
Theater, **9**

The Palace, **4**

The Pantages
Theater, **5**

❸ **Capitol Records Building.** When Capitol decided to build its headquarters building just north of Hollywood and Vine, at 1756 N. Vine Street, two big Capitol talents of the day (singer Nat King Cole and songwriter Johnny Mercer) suggested that it be done in the shape of a stack of records. It opened in 1956, the very picture of fifties chic. These days, it doesn't seem so odd.

❹ **The Palace,** just across the street at 1735 N. Vine Street, was opened in 1927 as the Hollywood Playhouse. It has played host to many shows over the years from Ken Murray's *Blackouts* to Ralph Edwards's *This Is Your Life.* It is now the site of popular rock concerts.

❺ **The Pantages Theater,** at 6233 Hollywood, just east of Vine, opened in 1930, the very height of movie-theater opulence. From 1949 to 1959, it was the site of the Academy Awards.

❻ **The Hollywood Walk of Fame** is at every turn as you make your way through downtown Hollywood on foot. The sidewalks of Hollywood feature dark gray terrazzo circles embedded by pink-colored stars, with the name of a Hollywood legend in brass in the center. The first eight stars were unveiled in 1960 at the northwest corner of Highland Avenue and Hollywood Boulevard. Some names have stood the test of time better than others: the eight were Olive Borden, Ronald Colman, Louise Fazenda, Preston Foster, Burt Lancaster, Edward Sedgwick, Ernest Torrence, and Joanne Woodward. In the more than 20 years since, 1,800 others have been added. Being walked on, day after day, may be a celebrity's dream but it does not come cheap. The personality in question (or, for instance, the record company) must pay for the honor: $3,500. Walk a few blocks and you'll quickly find that not all the names are familiar. Many are stars from the earliest days of Hollywood. To aid in the identification, celebrities are identified by one of five logos: a motion picture camera, a radio microphone, a television set, a record, or theatrical masks. Here's a guide to a few of the more famous stars on the Walk of Fame: Marlon Brando at 1765 Vine, Charlie Chaplin at 6751 Hollywood, W.C. Fields at 7004 Hollywood, Clark Gable at 1608 Vine, Marilyn Monroe at 6774 Hollywood, Rudolph Valentino at 6164 Hollywood, and John Wayne at 1541 Vine.

❼ **Frederick's of Hollywood** (6608 Hollywood Blvd., tel. 213/466–8506) is one of Hollywood's more infamous spots. Until 1989, a gaudy lavender building, Frederick's was finally restored to its original understated Art Deco look. Inside houses the famous name in trashy lingerie and is a very popular tourist spot, if only for a good giggle.

❽ **Hollywood Wax Museum.** It's not the same as seeing them in the flesh, but the museum can offer visitors sights that real life no longer can (Mary Pickford, Elvis Presley, and Clark Gable) and a few that even real life never did (Rambo and Conan). A short film on Academy Award winners is shown daily. *6767 Hollywood Blvd., tel. 213/462–8860. Admission: $7 adults, $6 senior citizens, $5 children. Open Sun.–Thurs. 10 AM–midnight, Fri. –Sat. 10 AM–2 AM.*

❾ It took the residents quite a few years to stop calling **Mann's Chinese Theater** (6925 Hollywood Blvd., tel. 213/464–8111) "Grauman's Chinese," but now the new owners seem to have a firm hold on the place in the public's eye. The theater opened in

1927 with the premiere of Cecil B. De Mille's *King of Kings*. The architecture is a fantasy of Chinese pagodas and temples as only Hollywood could turn out. Although you'll have to buy a movie ticket to appreciate both the interior trappings and the exterior excess, the famous courtyard is open for browsing. You'll see the famous cement hand- and footprints. The tradition is said to have begun at the premiere itself, when actress Norma Talmadge accidentally stepped in the wet cement. Now more than 160 celebrities have added their footprints, handprints, even a few oddball prints like Jimmy Durante's nose. Space has pretty much run out and, unlike the Walk of Fame on the sidewalks, these cement autographs are by invitation only.

10 Summer evening concerts at the **Hollywood Bowl** have been a tradition since 1922, although the shell has been replaced several times. The 17,000-plus seating capacity ranges from boxes (where local society matrons put on incredibly fancy alfresco preconcert meals for their friends) to cement bleachers in the rear. Some people prefer the back rows of the bleachers for their romantic appeal.

The official concert season begins in early July and runs through mid-September with performances on Tuesdays, Thursdays, and weekends. The program ranges from jazz to pop to classical. Evenings can be chilly (even on 90-degree days), so bring a sweater and wear comfortable shoes. A night at the Bowl involves considerable walking. *2301 N. Highland Ave., tel. 213/850-2000. Grounds open daily summer, 9-sunset. Call for program schedule.*

11 The **Hollywood Studio Museum** sits in the Hollywood Bowl parking lot, east of Highland Boulevard. The building, recently moved to this site, was once called the Lasky–De Mille Barn and it was where Cecil B. De Mille produced the first feature-length film, *The Squaw Man*. In 1927, the barn became Paramount Pictures, with the original company of Jesse Lasky, Cecil B. De Mille, and Samuel Goldwyn. The museum shows the origin of the motion picture industry. There's a re-creation of Cecil B. De Mille's office, with original artifacts and a screening room offering vintage film footage of Hollywood and its legends. A great gift shop sells quality vintage memorabilia like autographs, photographs, and books. *2100 N. Highland Ave., tel. 213/874-2276. Admission: $3.50 adults, $2.50 children. Open weekends 10-4.*

12 Such stars as Carol Burnett, Linda Evans, Rick Nelson, and Lana Turner have attended **Hollywood High School** (1521 N. Highland Ave.). Today, the student body is as diverse as Los Angeles itself with every ethnic group represented.

13 Many of Hollywood's stars, from the silent-screen era on, are buried in **Hollywood Memorial Cemetery,** a few blocks from Paramount Studios. Walk from the entrance to the lake area and you'll find the crypt of Cecil B. De Mille and the graves of Nelson Eddy and Douglas Fairbanks Sr. Inside the Cathedral Mausoleum is Rudolph Valentino's crypt (where fans, the press, and the famous Lady in Black turn up every August 23, the anniversary of his death). Other stars interred in this section are Peter Lorre and Eleanor Powell. In the Abbey of Palms Mausoleum, Norma Talmadge and Clifton Webb are buried. *6000 Santa Monica Blvd., tel. 213/469–1181. Open daily 8–5.*

Tour 3: Wilshire Boulevard

Numbers in the margin correspond with points of interest on the Tour 3: Wilshire Boulevard map.

Wilshire Boulevard begins in the heart of downtown Los Angeles and runs west, through Beverly Hills and Santa Monica, ending at the cliffs above the Pacific Ocean. In 16 miles it moves through poor immigrant neighborhoods and middle-class ones and on through a corridor of the highest priced high-rise condos in the city. Along the way (within a few blocks of each other) are many of Los Angeles's top architectural sites, museums, and shops.

This linear tour can be started at any point along the way but to really savor a true cross-section of the city, it takes a Bullocks-west-the-sea approach. It would be better to skip Koreatown and Larchmont and pare down the museum time than to do only one stretch. All these sites are on Wilshire or within a few blocks north or south.

"One" Wilshire is just another anonymous office building in downtown Los Angeles. Begin, instead, a few miles westward. As Wilshire Boulevard moves from its downtown genesis, it quickly passes through neighborhoods now populated by recent Central American immigrants. In the early years, however, this area was home to many of the city's wealthy citizens, as the faded Victorian houses on the side streets attest.

As the population crept westward, the distance to downtown shops began to seem insurmountable and the first suburban department branch store, **I. Magnin Wilshire** (3050 Wilshire Blvd., tel. 213/382–6161), was opened in 1929. It remains in excellent condition today and is still operating. To appreciate the real splendor of the store, enter from the rear door. The behind-the-store parking lot was quite an innovation in 1929 and the first accommodation a large Los Angeles store made to the automobile age. Look up at the ceiling of the porte cochere, where a mural depicts early 20th-century history. Inside, the store remains a well-preserved monument to the Art Deco age. The walls, the elevators, and the floors are the height of late 1920s style.

Koreatown begins almost at I. Magnin Wilshire's backdoor. Koreans are one of the latest and largest groups in our ethnically diverse city. Arriving from the old country with generally more money than most immigrant groups do, Koreans nevertheless face the trauma of adjusting to a new language, new alphabet, and new customs. Settling in the area south of Wilshire Boulevard, along Olympic Boulevard between Vermont and Western avenues, the Korean community has slowly grown into a full-fledged enclave with active community groups and newspapers. The area is teeming with Asian restaurants (not just Korean but also Japanese and Chinese, because Koreans are fond of those cuisines). Many of the signs in this area are in Korean only.

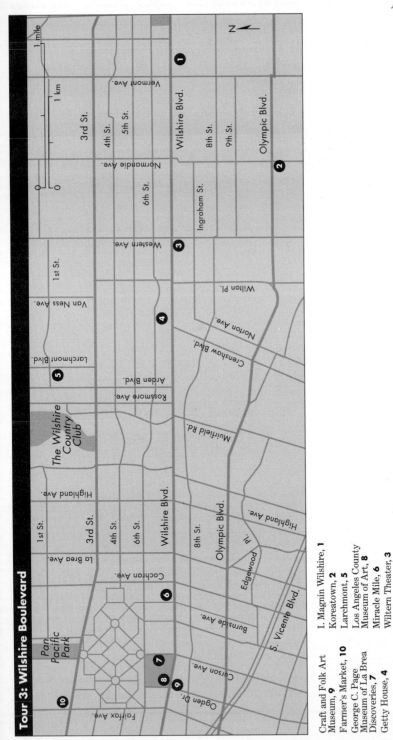

Tour 3: Wilshire Boulevard

Craft and Folk Art
Museum, **9**
Farmer's Market, **10**
George C. Page
Museum of La Brea
Discoveries, **7**
Getty House, **4**

I. Magnin Wilshire, **1**
Koreatown, **2**
Larchmont, **5**
Los Angeles County
Museum of Art, **8**
Miracle Mile, **6**
Wiltern Theater, **3**

At the southwest corner of Wilshire and Western Avenue sits
❸ **Wiltern Theater,** one of the city's best examples of Art
Moderne. The 1930s zigzag design has been recently restored
to its splendid turquoise hue. Inside, the theater is magnifi-
cently opulent, in the grand tradition.

Continuing west on Wilshire, the real estate values start to
make a sharp climb. The mayor of Los Angeles has his official
❹ residence in **Getty House** (605 S. Irving Blvd.), one block north
of Wilshire in the Hancock Park district. This is one of the city's
most genteel neighborhoods, remaining in vogue since its development in the 1920s. Many of L.A.'s old monied families live
here in English Tudor homes with East Coast landscaping
schemes that seem to defy the local climate and history. The
white-brick, half-timber Getty House was donated to the city
by the Getty family.

The genteel Hancock Park folks have their own little suburb-in-
❺ a-city shopping street: **Larchmont.** Named after the New York
suburb, Larchmont is a very un–Los Angeles shopping district. Larchmont Boulevard, between Third Street and Beverly Boulevard, is a bit of small-town America in the middle of the
city. The tree-lined street has 45 degree parking and a cozy,
everybody-knows-everybody feeling. Many celebrities live in
the area and can be seen darting in and out of the boutiques,
health food store, and old-time five-and-dime. There are also
several chic restaurants here including Chan Dara and De Milo.

Drop back down to Wilshire Boulevard again and continue
❻ westward. **Miracle Mile,** the strip of Wilshire Boulevard between La Brea and Fairfax avenues, was so dubbed in the 1930s
as a promotional gimmick to attract shoppers to the new stores.
The buildings went into a decline in the fifties and sixties but
the area is now enjoying a strong comeback. Exceptionally
strong Art Deco buildings like the Darkroom (5370 Wilshire)
and the El Rey Theater (5519 Wilshire) stand out as examples
of period design. In the Callender's Restaurant (corner of Wilshire and Curson), there are recent murals and old photographs that effectively depict life on the Miracle Mile during its
heyday.

Across Curson Avenue is Hancock Park, the park, not to be
confused with Hancock Park, the residential neighborhood.
The park is home to two of the city's best museums as well as
the city's only world-famous fossil source, the **La Brea Tar Pits.**
Despite the fact that "la brea" means tar in Spanish and to say
"La Brea Tar Pits" is redundant, the name remains firm in local
minds. These tar pits were known to the earliest inhabitants of
the area and were long used to seal leaky boats and roofs. In the
early 20th century, geologists discovered that the sticky goo
contained the largest collection of Pleistocene fossils ever
found at one location. More than 200 varieties of birds, mammals, plants, reptiles, and insects have been discovered here.
The statues of mammoths in the big pit near the corner of Wilshire and Curson depict how many of them were entombed:
Edging down to a pond of water to drink, animals were caught
in the tar and unable to extricate themselves, as other animals
looked on helplessly.

The pits were formed about 35,000 years ago when deposits of
oil rose to the Earth's surface, collected in shallow pools, and
coagulated into sticky asphalt. Over 100 tons of fossil bones

have been removed in the 70 years since excavations began here. There are several pits scattered around Hancock Park. They are a reminder of nature's superiority over man. Construction in the area has had to accommodate these oozing pits, and in nearby streets and along sidewalks, little bits of tar ooze up, unstoppable.

❼ Also in Hancock Park, the **George C. Page Museum of La Brea Discoveries** is a satellite of the Los Angeles County Museum of Natural History. The Page Museum is situated at the tar pits, a modern facility that is set, bunkerlike, half underground; a bas-relief around four sides depicts life in the Pleistocene era. The museum has over one million Ice Age fossils. Exhibits include reconstructed, life-size skeletons of mammals and birds whose fossils were recovered from the pits: saber-tooth cats, mammoths, wolves, sloths, eagles, and condors. Several large murals and colorful dioramas depict the history of the Pleistocene. The glass-enclosed Paleontological Laboratory permits observation of the ongoing cleaning, identification, and cataloguing of fossils excavated from the nearby asphalt deposits. *The La Brea Story* and *Dinosaurs, the Terrible Lizards* are short documentary films shown every 15–30 minutes as museum traffic requires. A hologram magically puts flesh on "La Brea Woman," and a tar contraption shows visitors just how hard it would be to free oneself from the sticky mess. An excellent gift shop offers nature-oriented books and trinkets. *5801 Wilshire Blvd., tel. 213/936–2230. Admission: $3 adults, 75¢ children; free the second Tues. of the month. Open Tues.–Sun. 10–5.*

❽ The **Los Angeles County Museum of Art,** also in Hancock Park and the largest museum complex in Los Angeles, has grown considerably in the past few years with generous donations from local patrons who are determined to put Los Angeles on the map, art-wise. The original buildings (Ahmanson Gallery, Frances and Armand Hammer Wing, and Leo S. Bing Center) have been joined by the Robert O. Anderson Building and the Pavilion for Japanese Art. The museum's new Wilshire Boulevard facade sports spiffy glass tile.

The Ahmanson Gallery, built around a graceful central atrium, houses a permanent collection of paintings, sculptures, graphic arts, costumes, textiles, and decorative arts from a wide range of cultures and periods, prehistoric to present. Included are works by Picasso, Rembrandt, Veronese, Durer, Hals, de la Tour, and Homer. One of the Western world's largest collections of Indian, Nepalese, and Tibetan art is housed here. Major changing exhibitions are presented in the Frances and Armand Hammer Wing.

The Robert O. Anderson Building was completed in fall 1986. This 115,000-square-foot gallery houses 20th-century art from the museum's permanent collection and traveling exhibits. The new Pavilion for Japanese Art houses the Sinen-Kan collection of over 300 Japanese scroll paintings and screens.

The Leo S. Bing Center contains the Art Rental Gallery, the Bing Theater, Art Research Library, and the indoor/outdoor cafeteria-style Plaza Cafe. The museum offers the community many cultural activities, including film series, concerts, lectures, tours of the collections, and student programs. The Art Research Library, with more than 75,000 volumes and an extensive collection of slides, is open for scholarly research. The Museum Shop features a selection of books, magazines, postcards, posters, antiquities, jewelry, and gifts.

The museum, as well as the adjoining Page Museum and Hancock Park itself, is brimming with visitors on warm weekend days. Although crowded, it can be the most exciting time to visit the area. Mimes and itinerant musicians ply their trades. Street vendors sell fast food treats and there are impromptu soccer games on the lawns. To really study the art though, a quieter weekday visit is recommended. *5905 Wilshire Blvd., tel. 213/857–6111. Open Tues.–Fri. 10–5, weekends 10–6. Admission: $5 adults, $3 children ($2 for special exhibits).*

9 The **Craft and Folk Art Museum,** across Wilshire, offers consistently fascinating exhibits of both contemporary crafts and folk crafts from around the world. The museum's collections include Japanese, Mexican, American, and East Indian folk art, textiles, and masks. Six to eight major exhibitions are planned each year. The museum's library and media resources center are open to the public. The museum shop carries displays of merchandise relating to each current exhibition as well as quality work by expert craftspeople, folk art from around the world, original postcards, and educational materials. *5814 Wilshire Blvd., tel. 213/937–5544. Admission free. Open Tues.–Sun. 10–5.*

Time Out Located on the mezzanine of the Craft and Folk Art Museum, overlooking the exhibitions, is the **Egg and the Eye,** which serves 40 exotic varieties of omelets as well as other dishes. *Tel. 213/933–5596. Reservations recommended. Open Tues.–Sun. 11–3.*

Continue west on Wilshire a few blocks to the corner of Fairfax Avenue. On the northeast corner is the May Co. department store, another 1930s landmark with a distinctive curved corner.

10 Head north on Fairfax a few blocks to the **Farmer's Market.** Thanks to tour bus operators and its own easygoing, all-year-outdoor setting, the Farmer's Market is a popular stop of L.A. city tours. When it first opened in 1934, the market sold farm-direct produce at bargain prices. These days, the produce is still tantalizing but definitely high priced. No longer farm-direct, the stands offer out-of-season peppers and tiny seedless champagne grapes from Chile at top prices. In addition to produce stands, there are dozens of cooked-food stalls offering Cajun gumbos, Mexican enchiladas, fish and chips, frozen yogurt, pizza, and hamburgers. *6333 W. Third St., tel. 213/933–9211. Open Mon.–Sat. 9–6:30, Sun. 10–5. Open later during summer.*

Time Out **Kokomo** is not only the best place to eat in the Farmer's Market, it's got some of the best new-wave diner food anywhere in L.A. Lively, entertaining service is almost always included in the reasonable prices. *Located on the Third St. side of the market, tel. 213/933–0773. Reservations. No credit cards. Open Mon.–Sat. to 7 and Sun. to 6 during summers.*

North of the market, Fairfax becomes the center of Los Angeles's Jewish life. The shops and stands from Beverly Boulevard north are enlivened with friendly conversations between shop-keepers and regular customers. Canter's Restaurant, Deli, and Bakery (419 N. Fairfax, tel. 213/651–2030) is the traditional hangout.

Tour 4: The Westside

Numbers in the margin correspond with points of interest on the Tour 4: Westside map.

The Westside of Los Angeles, which to residents means from La Brea Avenue westward to the ocean, is where the rents are the most expensive, the real estate values sky high, the restaurants (and the restaurateurs) the most famous, the shops the most chic. It's the good life Southern California style and to really savor the Southland, spend a few leisurely days or half days exploring the area. Short on traditional tourist attractions like amusement parks, historic sites, and museums, it more than makes up for those gaps with great shopping districts, exciting walking streets, outdoor cafes, and lively nightlife.

The Westside can be best enjoyed in at least three separate outings, allowing plenty of time for browsing and dining. Attractions #1 through #4 are in the West Hollywood area; #5 through #8 in Beverly Hills; and #9 through #11 in Westwood. But the Westside is small enough that you could pick four or five of these sites to visit in a day, depending on your interests.

West Hollywood is a glitzy section of Los Angeles. Once an almost forgotten parcel of county land surrounded by L.A. city and Beverly Hills, it became an official city in 1984. The West Hollywood attitude—trendy, stylish, plenty of disposable income—spills over beyond the official city borders.

❶ **Melrose Avenue,** which isn't exactly in West Hollywood, nevertheless remains firmly fixed in residents' minds as *very* West Hollywood. If you're entertained by punks and other people in spiked hairdos, just about the most outlandish ensembles imaginable, Melrose is the place for you. Would-be rock stars and weekend punkers hang out and provide a wonderful show for the ordinary folks. The busiest stretch of Melrose is between Fairfax and La Brea avenues. Here you'll find one-of-a-kind boutiques and small, chic restaurants for more than a dozen blocks. Park on a side street (the parking regulations around here are vigorously enforced: a rich vein for the city's coffers) and begin walking. The quintessential Melrose shops are Soap Plant and Wacko, on the same block near Martel Avenue. Gaudy both inside and out and offering the most bizarre trinkets and books, these shops are just plain fun. Other busy shops: War Babies (clothes from the armies of the world) and Rene's (offbeat records and a local skateboarders' hangout as well).

Time Out Melrose has no shortage of great eateries. Part of any visit here is trying to pick one from the dozens of choices: Thai, Mexican, sausages, yogurt, Italian, and more. The ultimate Melrose "joint" is **Johnny Rocket's** (7507 Melrose Ave., tel. 213/651–3361), a very hip fifties-style diner near the corner of Gardner Street. It's just stools at a counter, the best of old-time rock and roll on tape, and great hamburgers, shakes, and fries—

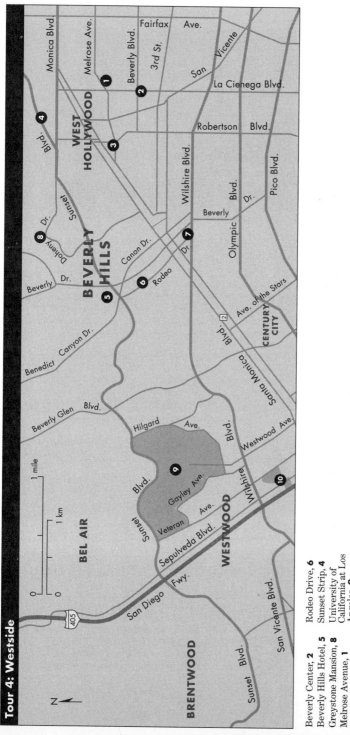

Tour 4: Westside

Beverly Center, **2**
Beverly Hills Hotel, **5**
Greystone Mansion, **8**
Melrose Avenue, **1**
The Pacific Design
Center, **3**
Regent Beverly
Wilshire Hotel, **7**

Rodeo Drive, **6**
Sunset Strip, **4**
University of
California at Los
Angeles, **9**
Westwood Memorial
Park, **10**

and almost always crowded, with people lined up behind the stools to slip in the moment they are vacated. Off-hours are best.

② Beverly Center (8500 Beverly Blvd. at La Cienega, Los Angeles, tel. 213/854–0070) is that hulking monolith dominating the corner of La Cienega and Beverly Boulevard. Designed as an all-in-one stop for shopping, dining, and movies, it has been a boon to Westsiders—except those who suffer the congestion by living too close. Parking is on the second through fifth floors, shops on the sixth and seventh, and movies and restaurants on the eighth. The first floor features Irvine Ranch Market, a state-of-the-art gourmet grocery that is a booby trap for impulse buyers who love to try new foods. At the northwest corner, the Hard Rock Cafe (look for the vintage green Cadillac imbedded in the roof) always has a line of hungry customers (salivating for both burgers and a chance to see celebrities that often come here). Upstairs in the center proper are two major department stores, dozens of upscale clothing boutiques, 14 movie theaters, and a wide variety of restaurants (Mandarin Cove, Siam Orchid, Tea Room St., Petersburg plus cookie shops, pizza parlors, and hamburger stands).

③ West Hollywood is the center of Los Angeles's thriving interior decorating business. **The Pacific Design Center** (8687 Melrose Ave., West Hollywood, tel. 213/657–0800) has been dubbed the "Blue Whale" by residents. The all-blue-glass building designed by Cesar Pelli in 1975 houses to-the-trade-only showrooms filled with the most tempting furnishings, wallpapers, and accessories. Last year, the center added a second building by Pelli, this one clad in green glass. Most of the showrooms discourage casual browsers but the building is open and anyone can stroll the halls and rubberneck in the windows.

The same rules apply for "Robertson Boulevard," the name given to the outside-PDC showrooms that surround the Blue Whale. They are not confined to Robertson Boulevard but are well represented on Beverly Boulevard and Melrose Avenue. This section is exceptionally walkable, and residents often walk their dogs here in the evening (even driving them to the area to do their walking) so they can browse the well-lit windows. A few of the showrooms will accommodate an occasional retail buyer so if you see something to die for, it's worth a timid inquiry inside.

④ Sunset Strip was famous in the fifties, as in "77 Sunset Strip," but it was popular even in the 1930s when nightclubs like Ciro's and Mocambo were in their heyday. This windy, hilly stretch is a visual delight, enjoyed both by car (a convertible would be divine) or on foot. Drive it once to enjoy the hustle-bustle, the vanity boards (huge billboards touting new movies, new records, new stars), the dazzling shops. Then pick a section and explore a few blocks on foot. The Sunset Plaza section is especially nice, with very expensive shops and a few outdoor cafes (Tutto Italia, Chin Chin) that are packed for lunch and on warm evenings. At Horn Street, Tower Records (a behemoth of a record store with two satellite shops across the street), Book Soup (finally, a literary bookstore in L.A.!), and Spago (tucked a half block up the hill on Horn) make a nice browse, especially in the evening.

The glitz of the Strip ends as suddenly as it begins at Doheny Drive, where Sunset Boulevard enters the world-famous and glamorous city of Beverly Hills. Suddenly the sidewalk street life gives way to expansive, perfectly manicured lawns and palatial homes, all representative of what the name Beverly Hills has come to mean.

❺ West of the Strip a mile or so is the **Beverly Hills Hotel** (9641 Sunset Blvd., Beverly Hills, tel. 213/276–2251). Dubbed the "Pink Palace," its quiet Spanish Colonial Revival architecture and soft pastel exterior belie the excitement inside, where Hollywood moguls make deals over margaritas in the Polo Lounge and where many stars keep permanent bungalows as second homes.

It is on this stretch of Sunset, especially during the daytime, that you'll see hawkers peddling maps of stars' homes. Are the maps reliable? Well, that's a matter of debate. Stars do move around, so it's difficult to keep any map up to date. But the fun of looking at some of these magnificent homes, irrespective of whether they're owned by a star of the moment, makes many people buy such maps and embark on tours.

Beverly Hills was incorporated as a city early in the century and has been thriving ever since. As a vibrant, exciting city within the larger city, it has retained its reputation for wealth and luxury, an assessment with which you will agree as you drive along one of its main thoroughfares, Santa Monica Boulevard (which is actually two parallel streets at this point: "Big Santa Monica" is the northern street; "Little Santa Monica," the southern one).

Within a few square blocks in the center of the city are some of the most exotic, not to mention high-priced, stores in Southern California. Here one can find such items as $200 pairs of socks wrapped in gold leaf and stores that take customers only by appointment. A fun way to spend an afternoon is to stroll famed
❻ **Rodeo Drive** between Santa Monica and Wilshire boulevards. Some of the Rodeo (pronounced ro-DAY-o) shops may be familiar to you since they supply clothing for major network television shows and their names often appear among the credits. Others such as Gucci have a worldwide reputation. Fortunately, browsing is free (and fun), no matter how expensive the store is. Several nearby restaurants have outside patios where you can sit and sip a drink while watching the fashionable shoppers stroll by.

❼ The **Regent Beverly Wilshire Hotel** (9500 Wilshire Blvd., tel. 213/275–4282) anchors the south end of Rodeo, at Wilshire. Opened in 1928, and vigorously expanded and renovated since, the hotel is often home to visiting royalty and celebrities, who arrive amid much fanfare at the porte cochere in the rear of the old structure. The lobby is quite small for a hotel of this size and there is little opportunity to meander; you might stop for a drink or meal in one of the hotel's restaurants.

❽ The **Greystone Mansion** was built by oilman Edward Doheny in 1923. This Tudor-style mansion, now owned by the city of Beverly Hills, sits on 16 landscaped acres and has been used in such films as *The Witches of Eastwick* and *All of Me*. The gardens are open for self-guided tours and peeking in the windows (only) is permitted. *905 Loma Vista Dr., Beverly Hills, tel. 213/550–4796. Admission free. Open daily 10–5.*

One of Beverly Hills' mansions opens its grounds to visitors. The **Virginia Robinson Gardens** are 6.2 terraced acres on the former estate of the heir to the Robinson Department Store chain. A guide will take you on an hour tour of the gardens and the exquisite exteriors of the main house, guest house, servants' quarters, swimming pool, and tennis court. A highlight of the tour is the collection of rare and exotic palms. Since the gardens' administration is trying to keep a low profile to avoid congestion in the cul-de-sac where the gardens are situated, visitors must call for reservations and be told the address and directions. *Tel. 213/276-5367. Admission: $3. Tours Tues.– Thurs. 10 AM and 1 PM and Fri. 10 AM.*

Westward from Beverly Hills, Sunset continues to wind past palatial estates and passes by the **University of California at Los Angeles.** Nestled in the Westwood section of the city and bound by LeConte, Sunset, and Hilgard, the parklike UCLA campus is an inviting place for visitors to stroll. The most spectacular buildings are the original ones, Royce Hall and the library, both in Romanesque style. In the heart of the north campus is the Franklin Murphy Sculpture Garden with works by Henry Moore and Lachaise dotting the landscaping. For a gardening buff, UCLA is a treasure of unusual and well-labeled plants. The Mildred Mathias Botanic Garden is located in the southeast section of campus and is accessible from Tiverton Avenue. Maps and information are available at drive-by kiosks at major entrances, even on weekends. Free 90-minute, guided walking tours of the campus are offered on weekdays. The campus has several indoor and outdoor cafes plus bookstores that sell the very popular UCLA Bruins paraphernalia. *Tours (tel. 213/825–4574) weekdays at 10:30 AM and 1:30 PM. Meet at 10945 LeConte St., room 1417, on the south edge of the campus, facing Westwood.*

The **Hannah Carter Japanese Garden,** located in Bel Air just north of the campus, is owned by UCLA and may be visited by making phone reservations two weeks in advance (tel. 213/825–4574).

Directly south of the campus is Westwood, once a quiet college town and now one of the busiest places in the city on weekend evenings—so busy that during the summer, many streets are closed to car traffic and visitors must park at the Federal Building (Wilshire and Veteran) and shuttle over. However you arrive, Westwood remains a delightful village filled with clever boutiques, trendy restaurants, movie theaters, and colorful street life.

The village proper is delineated on the south by Wilshire Boulevard, which is now a corridor of cheek-by-jowl office buildings whose varying architectural styles can be jarring, to say the least. Tucked behind one of these behemoths is **Westwood Memorial Park** (1218 Glendon Ave.). In this very unlikely place for a cemetery is one of the most famous graves in the city. Marilyn Monroe is buried in a simply marked wall crypt. For 25 years after her death, her former husband Joe DiMaggio had six red roses placed on her crypt three times a week. Also buried here is Natalie Wood.

Tour 5: Santa Monica, Venice, Pacific Palisades, and Malibu

Numbers in the margin correspond with points of interest on the Tour 5: Santa Monica and Venice map.

The towns that hug the coastline of Santa Monica Bay reflect the wide diversity of Los Angeles, from the rich-as-can-be Malibu to the cheek-by-jowl Yuppie/seedy mix of Venice. Life is lived outdoors here and the emphasis is on being out in the sunshine, always within sight of the Pacific. Visitors might savor the area in two sections: Santa Monica to Venice in one day and Pacific Palisades to Malibu in another.

From Santa Monica to Venice

Santa Monica is a sensible place. It's a tidy little city, two miles square, whose ethnic population is largely British (there's an English music hall and several pubs here), attracted perhaps by the cool and foggy climate. The sense of order is reflected in the economic/geographic stratification: The most northern section has broad streets lined with superb, older homes. Driving south, real estate prices drop $50,000 or so every block or two. The middle class lives in the middle and the working class, to the south, along the Venice border.

❶ Begin exploring at **Santa Monica Pier,** located at the foot of Colorado Avenue and easily accessible for beach-goers as well as drive-around visitors. Cafes, gift shops, a psychic advisor, bumper cars, and arcades line the truncated pier, which was severely damaged in a storm a few years ago. The 46-horse carousel, built in 1922, has seen action in many movie and television shows, most notably the Paul Newman/Robert Redford film *The Sting. Tel. 213/394–7554. Rides: 50¢ adults, 25¢ children. Carousel open in summer, Tues.–Sun. 10–9; in winter, weekends 10–5.*

❷ **Palisades Park** is a ribbon of green that runs along the top of the cliffs from Colorado Avenue to just north of San Vicente Boulevard. The flat walkways are usually filled with casual strollers as well as joggers who like to work out with a spectacular view of the Pacific as company. It is especially enjoyable at sunset.

The Visitor Information Center is located in the park, at Santa Monica Boulevard. It offers bus schedules, directions, and information on Santa Monica–area attractions. *Tel. 213/393–7593. Open daily 10–4.*

❸ Santa Monica has grown into a major center for the L.A. art community, and the brand-new **Santa Monica Museum of Art** promises to boost that reputation. Designed by local architect Frank Gehry, the museum presents the works of performance and video artists and exhibits works of lesser-known painters and sculptors. *2437 Main St., Santa Monica, tel. 213/399–0433. Open Wed. and Thurs. 11–8, Fri.–Sun. 11–6. Admission: $3 adults, $1 artists, students, and senior citizens.*

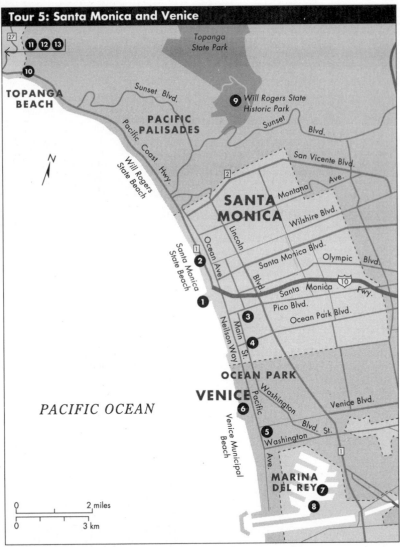

Tour 5: Santa Monica and Venice

Topanga State Park

PACIFIC OCEAN

Will Rogers State Historic Park 9

Sunset Blvd.

PACIFIC PALISADES

Pacific Coast Hwy.

Will Rogers State Beach

TOPANGA BEACH

11 12 13

10

27

San Vicente Blvd.

SANTA MONICA

Montana Ave.

Wilshire Blvd.

Lincoln Blvd.

Ocean Ave.

Santa Monica State Beach

Santa Monica Blvd.

Olympic Blvd.

Santa Monica Fwy.

Pico Blvd.

Ocean Park Blvd.

Main St.

Neilson Way

OCEAN PARK

VENICE

Pacific

Washington

Venice Blvd.

Venice Municipal Beach

Washington Blvd. St.

Ave.

MARINA DEL REY 7

8

1

2

3

4

5

6

0 ——— 2 miles

0 ——— 3 km

❹ The **Santa Monica Heritage Museum**, housed in an 1894-vintage, late-Victorian home once owned by the founder of the city, was moved to its present site on trendy Main Street in the mid-1980s. Three rooms have been fully restored: the dining room in the style of 1890 to 1910; the living room, 1910–1920; and the kitchen, 1920–1930. The second-floor galleries feature photography and historical exhibits as well as shows by contemporary Santa Monica artists. *2612 Main St., Santa Monica, tel. 213/392–8537. Open Thurs.–Sat. 11–4, Sun. noon–4.*

The museum faces a companion home, another Victorian delight moved to the site that is now the Chronicle restaurant. These two dowagers anchor the northwest corner of the funky Main Street area of Santa Monica. Several blocks of old brick buildings here have undergone a recent rejuvenation (and considerable rent increases) and now house galleries, bars, cafes, omelet parlors, and boutiques. With its close proximity to the beach, parking can be tight on summer weekend days. Best bets are the city pay lots behind the Main Street shops, between Main and Neilsen Way.

Venice was a turn-of-the-century fantasy that never quite came true. Abbot Kinney, a wealthy Los Angeles businessman, envisioned his little piece of real estate, which then seemed so far from downtown, as a romantic replica of Venice, Italy. He developed an incredible 16 miles of canals, floated gondolas on them, and built scaled-down versions of the Saint Marks Palace and other Venice landmarks. The name remains but the connection with the Old World Venice is flimsy. Kinney's project was bothered by ongoing engineering problems and disasters and
❺ soon went into disrepair. Three small **canals** and bridges remain and can be viewed from the southeast corner of Pacific Avenue and Venice Boulevard. Gone are the amusement park, swank seaside hotels, and the gondoliers.

What's left is a colorful mishmash of street life: the liveliest waterfront walkway in Los Angeles, known as both Ocean Front
❻ Walk and the **Venice Boardwalk.** It begins at Washington Street and runs north. Save this visit for a weekend. There is plenty of action year-round: bikini-clad roller skaters gather a crowd around them as they put on impromptu demonstrations, vying for attention with the unusual breeds of dogs that locals love to prance along the walkway. A local body-building club works out on the adjacent beach, and strollers find it impossible not to stop to ogle at the pecs as these strong men lift weights.

At the south end of the boardwalk, along Washington Street, near the Venice Pier, roller skates and bicycles (some with baby seats) are available for rent.

Time Out The boardwalk is lined with fast food stands and food can then be brought a few feet away to be enjoyed as a beachy picnic. But for a somewhat more relaxing meal, stand in line for a table at **Sidewalk Cafe** (1401 Ocean Front Walk, tel. 213/399–5547). Wait for a patio table, where you can watch the wildly dressed free spirits parade by. Despite their flamboyant attire, they seem like Sunday wild ones, and it's amusing to imagine them in their sedate Monday-go-to-work suits.

Venice locals are a grudgingly thrown together mix of aging hippies, Yuppies with the disposable income to spend on inflated rents, senior citizens who have lived here for decades, and the homeless.

Just south of Venice is a quick shift of the time frame. Forget Italy of the Renaissance, or even the turn of the century. Marina del Rey is a modern and more successful, if less romantic, dream than Venice. It is the largest man-made boat harbor in the world, with a commercial area catering to the whims of boatowners and boat groupies.

❼ Burton Chase Park, For boatless visitors, the best place to savor the marina is from **Burton Chase Park,** at the end of Mindinao Way. Situated at the tip of a jetty and surrounded on three sides by water and moored boats, this small, six-acre patch of green offers a cool and breezy place to watch boats move in and out of the channel, and it's great for picnicking.

❽ Fisherman's Village is a collection of cute Cape Cod clapboards housing shops and restaurants. It's not much of a draw unless you include a meal or a snack or take one of the 45-minute marina cruises offered by Hornblower Dining Outs that depart from the village dock. *13755 Fiji Way, tel. 213/301–6000. Tickets: $5 adults, $3.50 senior citizens, $4 children. Open in summer, daily 11 AM–4 PM; in winter, weekends 11–4. Cruises leave every hour, Mon.–Fri. 12–3, weekends 11–5.*

A Tour of Pacific Palisades and Malibu

The drive on Pacific Coast Highway north of Santa Monica toward Malibu is one of the most pleasant in Southern California, day or evening. The narrow-but-expensive beachfront houses were home to movie stars in the 1930s.

❾ Spend a few hours at **Will Rogers State Historic Park** in Pacific Palisades and you will understand quite easily why all of America fell in love with this cowboy/humorist in the 1920s and 1930s. The two-story ranch house on Rogers's 187-acre estate is a folksy blend of Navajo rugs and Mission-style furniture. Rogers's only extravagance was raising the roof several feet (he waited till his wife was in Europe to do it) to accommodate his penchant for practicing his lasso technique indoors. The nearby museum features Rogers memorabilia. The short films showing his roping technique will leave even sophisticated city slickers breathless, and hearing his homey words of wisdom is a real mood elevator.

Rogers was quite a polo fan, and in the 1930s, his front-yard polo field attracted friends like Douglas Fairbanks for weekend games. The tradition continues with free games scheduled most summer weekends. The park's broad lawns are excellent for picnicking. For postprandial exercise, there's hiking on miles of eucalyptus-lined trails. Those that make it to the top will be rewarded with a panoramic view of the mountains and ocean. Neighborhood riders house their horses at the stable up the hill and are usually agreeable to some friendly chatter (no rental horses, alas). *14253 Sunset Blvd., Pacific Palisades, tel. 213/454–8212. Call for polo schedule.*

❿ The **J. Paul Getty Museum** contains one of the country's finest collections of Greek and Roman antiquities (also a few items of uncertain provenance). The building is a re-creation of a 1st-century Roman villa. The main level houses sculpture, mosaics, and vases. Of particular interest are the 4th-century Attic stelai (funerary monuments) and Greek and Roman portraits. The newly expanded decorative arts collection on the upper level features furniture, carpets, tapestries, clocks, chandeliers, and small decorative items made for the French, German, and Italian nobility, with a wealth of royal French treasures (Louis XIV to Napoleon). Richly colored brocaded walls set off the paintings and furniture to great advantage.

All major schools of Western art from the late 13th century to the late 19th century are represented in the painting collection, which emphasizes Renaissance and Baroque art and includes work by Rembrandt, Rubens, de la Tour, Van Dyck, Gainsborough, and Boucher. Newly added are Old Master drawings, and medieval and Renaissance illuminated manuscripts.

The museum itself has an interesting history. Getty began collecting art in the 1930s, concentrating on the three distinct areas that are represented in the museum today: Greek and Roman antiquities, Baroque and Renaissance paintings, and 18th-century decorative arts. In 1946 he purchased a large Spanish-style home on 65 acres of land in a canyon just north of Santa Monica to house the collection. By the late 1960s, the museum could no longer accommodate the rapidly expanding collection and Getty decided to build an entirely new museum, which was completed in 1974. Getty's estimated $1.3 billion bequest upon his death in 1976 has appreciated to $2.1 billion with the 1984 takeover of Getty Oil by Texaco.

The museum building is a re-creation of the Villa dei Papiri, a luxurious 1st-century Roman villa that stood on the slopes of Mount Vesuvius overlooking the Bay of Naples. Located just south of the ancient city of Herculaneum, the villa is thought to have once belonged to Lucius Calpurnius Piso, the father-in-law of Julius Caesar. The two-level, 38-gallery building and its extensive gardens (which includes trees, flowers, shrubs, and herbs that might have grown 2,000 years ago at the villa) provide an appropriate and harmonious setting for Getty's Greek and Roman antiquities. The climate here is similar to that of southern Italy.

The bookstore carries art books, reproductions, calendars, and a variety of scholarly and general-interest publications. A self-service lunch is available in the indoor/outdoor Garden Tea Room. There are no tours but docents give 15-minute orientation talks. Summer evening concerts (reservations are required) are given on an irregular basis with the lower galleries open at intermission. Parking reservations are necessary and there is no way to visit the museum without using the parking lot unless you are dropped off or take a tour bus. They should be made one week in advance by telephoning or writing to the museum's Reservations Office. *17985 Pacific Coast Hwy., Malibu, tel. 213/458-2003. Admission free. Open Tues.–Sun. 10–5.*

⓫ **Adamson House** is the former home of the Rindge family, which owned much of the Malibu Rancho in the early part of the 20th century. Malibu was quite isolated then, with all visitors and supplies arriving by boat at the nearby Malibu Pier (and it can still be isolated these days by rock slides that close the highway). The Moorish-Spanish home, built in 1928, has been recently opened to the public and may be the only chance most visitors get to be inside a grand Malibu home. The Rindges led an enviable Malibu lifestyle, decades before it was trendy. The house is right on the beach (high chain-link fences keep out curious beach-goers). The family owned the famous Malibu Tile Company and their home is predictably encrusted with some of the most magnificent tilework in rich blues, greens, yellows, and oranges. Even an outside dog shower, near the servants' door, is a tiled delight. Docent-led tours help visitors to envision family life here as well as to learn about the history of Malibu and its real estate (you can't have one without the other). *23200 Pacific Coast Hwy., Malibu, tel. 213/456-8432. Admission free. Open Wed.-Sat. 10-1:30.*

⓬ Adjacent to Adamson House is **Malibu Lagoon State Park** (23200 Pacific Coast Hwy., Malibu), a haven for native and migratory birds. Visitors must stay on the boardwalks so that the egrets, blue herons, avocets, and gulls can enjoy the marshy area. The signs that give opening and closing hours refer only to the parking lot; the lagoon itself is open 24 hours and is particularly enjoyable in the early morning and at sunset. Luckily, streetside parking is available then (but not midday).

⓭ **Pepperdine University** (24255 Pacific Coast Hwy., Malibu) looks exactly like a California school should. Designed by William Pereira, this picture-perfect campus is set on a bluff above the Pacific. The school's fine athletic facilities have been used for those televised "Battle of the Network Stars" workouts.

Tour 6: Palos Verdes, San Pedro, and Long Beach

Numbers in the margin correspond with points of interest on the Tour 6: Palos Verdes, San Pedro, and Long Beach map.

Few local residents take advantage of Long Beach's attractions. If they should take a day to see the *Queen Mary* when their in-laws are here from Michigan, they are astounded to discover Long Beach's impressive skyline. How could this big city, the fifth largest in the state, be right here and they never really knew about it? Allow a generous half day or more to explore the *Queen Mary* complex. Plump up the itinerary with a glorious drive through Palos Verdes and a few short stops at local historic sites and parks.

Palos Verdes Peninsula is a hilly haven of horse lovers and other gentrified folks, many of them executive transplants from east of the Mississippi. The real estate in these small peninsula towns, ranging from expensive to very expensive, are zoned for stables and you'll often see riders along the streets (they have the right of way).

The drive on Pacific Coast Highway around the water's edge takes you soaring high above the cliffs. An aerial shot of this area was used in the original opening on television's "Knots Landing." Marineland once stood on these cliffs but it was recently closed and demolished.

❶ **Wayfarers Chapel** (5755 Palos Verdes Dr. S, Rancho Palos Verdes, tel. 213/377-1650) was designed by architect Frank Lloyd Wright in 1949. He planned his modern glass church to blend in with an encircling redwood forest. The redwoods are gone (they couldn't stand the rigors of urban encroachment),

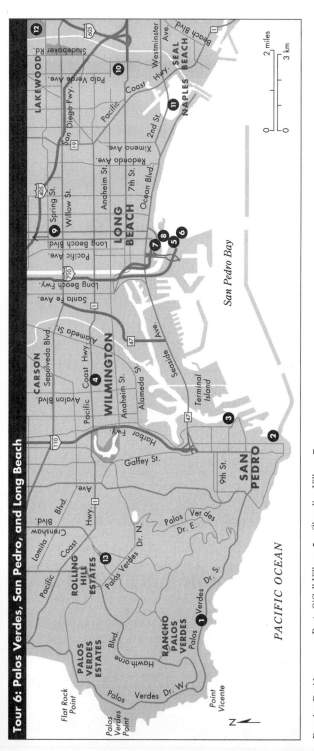

Tour 6: Palos Verdes, San Pedro, and Long Beach

PACIFIC OCEAN

San Pedro Bay

Banning Residence Museum and Park, **4**
Cabrillo Marine Museum, **2**
El Dorado Regional Park, **12**
Naples, **11**

Ports O'Call Village, **3**
Queen Mary, **5**
Rancho Los Alamitos, **10**
Rancho Los Cerritos, **9**
Shoreline Aquatic Park, **8**

Shoreline Village, **7**
South Coast Botanic Garden, **13**
Spruce Goose, **6**
Wayfarers Chapel, **1**

but another forest has taken their place and the breathtaking combination of ocean, trees, and structure remains. This "natural church" is a popular wedding site.

San Pedro shares the peninsula with the Palos Verdes towns, but little else. Here, the cliffs give way to a hospitable harbor. The 1950s-vintage executive homes give way to tidy 1920s-era white clapboards, and horses give way to boats. San Pedro (the locals ignore the correct Spanish pronunciation—it's "San Pee-dro" to them) is an old seafaring community with a strong Mediterranean and Eastern European flavor. There are enticing Greek and Yugoslavian markets and restaurants throughout the town.

➋ **Cabrillo Marine Museum** is a gem of a small museum dedicated to marine life that flourishes off the Southern California coast. Recently moved from a nearby boathouse to a modern Frank O. Gehry–designed building right on the beach, the museum is popular with school groups because its exhibits are especially instructive as well as fun. The 35 saltwater aquaria include a shark tank and a see-through tidal tank gives visitors a chance to see the long view of a wave. On the back patio, docents supervise as visitors reach into a shallow tank to touch starfish and sea anemones. *3720 Stephen White Dr., San Pedro, tel. 213/548–7546. Parking $4. Admission free. Open Tues.–Fri. noon–5, weekends 10–5.*

If you're lucky enough to visit at low tide, take time to explore the tide pool on nearby Cabrillo Beach (museum staff can direct you).

➌ **Ports O' Call Village** is a commercial rendition of a New England shipping village, an older version of Fisherman's Village in Marina del Rey, with shops, restaurants, and fast food windows. *Berth 77, San Pedro, tel. 213/831–0996. Fare: $7 adults, $3 children. 1-hr cruises depart from the village dock. Call for schedule.*

➍ **Banning Residence Museum and Park,** in Wilmington, is a pleasant, low-keyed stop before the razzle-dazzle of the *Queen Mary.* In order to preserve transportation and shipping interests for the city of Los Angeles, Wilmington was annexed in the late 19th century. A narrow strip of land, mostly less than a half mile wide, follows the Harbor Freeway from downtown south to the port.

General Phineas Banning was an early entrepreneur in Los Angeles, and is credited with developing the harbor into a viable economic entity and naming the area Wilmington (he was from Delaware). Part of the estate has been preserved in a 20-acre park that offers excellent picnicking possibilities. A 100-year-old wisteria, near the arbor, blooms in the spring. *401 E. M St., Wilmington, tel. 213/548–7777. Admission: $2. The interior of the house can only be seen on docent-led tours, Tues.–Thurs., Sat., and Sun. 12:30–3:30 on the half hour.*

Long Beach began as a seaside resort in the 19th century and during the early part of the 20th century was a popular destination for Midwesterners and Dust Bowlers in search of a better life. They built street after street of modest wood homes.

➎ The first glimpse of the *Queen Mary,* the largest passenger ship ever built, as she sits so smugly in Long Beach Harbor is disarming. What seemed like sure folly when Long Beach officials bought her in 1964 has turned out to be an attention-getting and money-making bonanza that has put the city on the proverbial map. She stands permanently moored at Pier J.

The 50,000-ton *Queen Mary* was launched in 1934, a floating treasure of Art Deco splendor. It took a crew of 1,100 to minister to the needs of 1,900 demanding passengers. This most luxurious of luxury liners is completely intact, from the extensive wood paneling to the gleaming nickel- and silver-plated handrails and the hand-cut glass. Tours through the ship are available; guests are invited to browse the 12 decks and witness close-up the bridge, staterooms, officers' quarters, and engine rooms. There are several restaurants on board, and visitors may even spend the night in the first-class cabins, now the Queen Mary Hotel. *Pier J, Long Beach, tel. 213/435–3511. Admission: $17.50 adults, $9.50 children for an all-day combination ticket to both the* Queen Mary *and the* Spruce Goose. *Guided 90-min tours are $5 and leave every half hour beginning at 10:30 AM. Open July 4–Labor Day, daily 9–9; rest of year, daily 10–6.*

❻ Just a short walk away from this most amazing ship is a most amazing plane, the ***Spruce Goose,*** housed in a 12-story aluminum dome. The *Spruce Goose* was Howard Hughes's folly. It is the largest wooden aircraft ever built, with a 320-foot wingspan. Designed by Hughes in 1942, it made its first and only flight on November 2, 1947. Multimedia displays surround the plane explaining its history. Howard Hughes memorabilia is also on view. New under the *Spruce Goose* dome is *Time Voyager,* "a multi-sensory entertainment journey," with a narration aimed at children, in which passengers board a 100-seat flight module to experience time periods past and present. Free with admission. *See Queen Mary for times and prices.*

❼ **Shoreline Village** is the most successful of the pseudo–New England harbors here. Its setting, between the Long Beach skyline and the *Queen Mary,* is reason enough to stroll here, day and evening (when visitors can enjoy the lights of the ship twinkling in the distance). In addition to gift shops and restaurants there's a 1906 carousel with bobbing giraffes, camels, and horses. *Corner of Shoreline Dr. and Pine Ave., tel. 213/590–8427. Rides: 75¢. The carousel is open daily 10–10 in summer, 10–9 the rest of the year.*

❽ **Shoreline Aquatic Park** (205 Marina Dr.) is literally set in the middle of Long Beach Harbor (another inspired landfill project) and is a much-sought-after resting place for RVers. Kiteflyers also love it, because the winds are wonderful here. Casual passersby can enjoy a short walk, where the modern skyline, the quaint Shoreline Village, the *Queen Mary,* and the ocean all vie for attention like four clamoring kids. One at a time, please! The park's lagoon is off-limits for swimming but aquacycles and kayaks can be rented during the summer months. Contact **Long Beach Water Sports** (730 E. 4th St., Long Beach, 90802, tel. 213/432–0187) for information on sea kayaking lessons, rentals, and outings.

❾ **Rancho Los Cerritos** is a charming Monterey-style adobe built by the Don Juan Temple family in 1844. Monterey-style homes can be easily recognized by two features: They are always two-storied and have a narrow balcony across the front. Imagine Zorro here, that swashbuckling hero of the rancho era, jumping from the balcony to rescue Don Juan Temple's lovely daughter. The 10 rooms have been furnished in the style of the period and are open for viewing. Don't expect a Southwest fantasy with primitive Mexican furniture and cactus in the garden. The Temple family shared the prevalent taste of the period. They might live in Southern California, but the East Coast and Europe still set the style, emphasizing fancy, dark woods and frou-frou Victorian bric-a-brac. The gardens here were designed in the 1930s by well-known landscape architect Ralph Cornell and have been recently restored. *4600 Virginia Rd., Long Beach, tel. 213/424–9423. Open Wed.–Sun. 1–5. Self-guided tours on weekdays. Free 50-min guided tours on weekends hourly 1–4.*

⑩ **Rancho Los Alamitos** is said to be the oldest one-story domestic building still standing in the county. It was built in 1806 when the Spanish flag still flew over California. There's a blacksmith shop in the barn. *6400 E. Bixby Hill Rd., Long Beach, tel. 213/431–3541. Open Wed.–Sun. 1–5. Hour-long, free tours leave every half hour.*

⑪ The **Naples** section of Long Beach is known for its pleasant and well-maintained canals. Canals in Naples, you ask? You're right, this is a bit of a misnomer. But better misnamed and successful in Naples than aptly named and a big bust in Venice, a few miles north. Naples is actually three small islands in man-made Alamitos Bay. It is best savored on foot. Park near Bay-shore Drive and Second Street, and walk across the bridge where you can begin meandering the quaint streets with very Italian names. This well-restored neighborhood boasts eclectic architecture—vintage Victorians, Craftsman bungalows, and Mission Revivals. You may spy a real gondola or two on the canals. You can hire them for a ride but not on the spur of the moment. Gondola Getaway offers one-hour rides, usually touted for romantic couples, although the gondolas can accommodate up to four people. *5437 E. Ocean Blvd., Naples, tel. 213/433–9595. Rides: $45 a couple, $10 for each additional person. Reservations essential, at least 1 to 2 wks in advance.*

⑫ **El Dorado Regional Park** (7550 E. Spring St., Long Beach) played host to the 1984 Olympic Games archery competition and remains popular with local archery enthusiasts. Most visitors, however, come to this huge, 800-acre park for the broad, shady lawns and walking trails and the lakes. Several small lakes are picturesquely set among cottonwoods and pine trees. This is wonderful picnicking country. Fishing is permitted in all the lakes (stocked with catfish, carp, and trout) but the northernmost one is favored by local anglers. Pedal boats are available by the hour (one hour of pedaling is more than enough). The Nature Center is a bird and native plant sanctuary.

⑬ **South Coast Botanic Gardens** began life ignominiously—as a garbage dump–cum–landfill. It's hard to believe that as recently as 1960, truckloads of waste (3.5 million tons) were being deposited. With the intensive ministerings of the experts from the L.A. County Arboreta department, the dump soon boasted lush gardens with plants from every continent except Antarctica. The gardens are undergoing an ambitious five-year reorganization at the end of which all the plants will be organized into color groups. Self-guided walking tours take visitors past flower and herb gardens, rare cacti, and a lake with ducks. Picnicking is limited to a lawn area outside the gates. *26300 Crenshaw Blvd., Rancho Palos Verdes, tel. 213/377–0468. Open daily 9– 4:30. Admission: $3 adults, $1.50 children.*

Tour 7: Highland Park, Pasadena, and San Marino

Numbers in the margin correspond with points of interest on the Tour 7: Highland Park, Pasadena, San Marino map.

The suburbs north of downtown Los Angeles have much of the richest architectural heritage in Southern California as well as several fine museums. The Highland Park area can be explored in a leisurely afternoon. Pasadena could take a full day, more if you want to savor the museums' collections.

A Tour of Highland Park

To take advantage of the afternoon-only hours of several sites here, and to enjoy a relaxed Old California patio lunch or dinner, this tour is best scheduled in the afternoon.

Once past Chinatown, the Pasadena Freeway (110) follows the curves of the arroyo (creek bed) that leads north from downtown. It was the main road north during the early days of Los Angeles where horses-and-buggies made their way through the chaparral-covered countryside to the small town of Pasadena. In 1942, the road became the Arroyo Seco Parkway, the first freeway in Los Angeles, later renamed the Pasadena Freeway. It remains a pleasant drive in nonrush hour traffic, with the freeway lined with old sycamores and winding up the arroyo like a New York parkway.

Highland Park, midway between downtown Los Angeles and Pasadena, was a genteel suburb in the late 1800s, where the Anglo population tried to keep an Eastern feeling alive in their architecture despite the decidedly Southwest landscape. The streets on both sides of the freeway are filled with faded beauties, classic old clapboards that have gone into decline in the past half century.

❶ **Heritage Square** is the ambitious attempt by the Los Angeles Cultural Heritage Board to preserve some of the city's architectural gems of the 1865–1914 period from the wrecking ball. During the past 20 years four residences, a depot, a church, and a carriage barn have been moved to this small park from all over the city. The most breathtaking building here is Hale House, built in 1885. The almost-garish colors of both the interior and exterior are not the whim of some aging hippie painter, but rather a faithful re-creation of the palette that was actually in fashion in the late 1800s. The whitewashing we associate with these old Victorians was a later vogue. The Palms Depot, built in 1886, was moved to the site from the Westside of L.A. The night the building was moved, down city streets and up freeways, is documented in photomurals on the depot's walls. *3800 Homer St., Highland Park, off Ave. 43 exit, tel. 818/449–0193. Admission: $4.50 adults, $3 children 12–17. Open weekends noon–4. Tours begin at 12:15, 1:15, 2:15, 3:15 on Sun. only.*

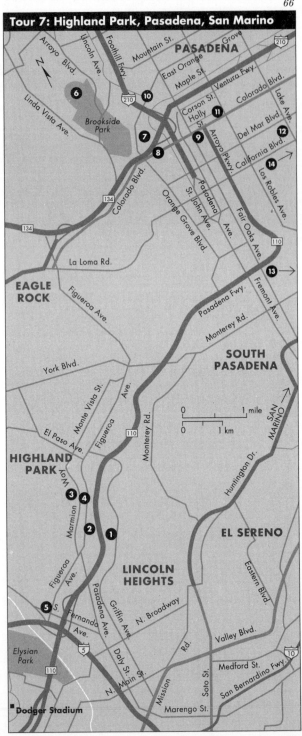

② El Alisal was the home of eccentric Easterner-turned-Westerner-with-a-vengeance Charles Lummis. This Harvard graduate was captivated by Indian culture (he founded the Southwest Museum), often living the lifestyle of the natives, much to the shock of the staid Angelenos of the time. His home, built from 1898 to 1910, is constructed of boulders from the arroyo itself, a romantic notion until recent earthquakes have made the safety of such homes questionable. The Art Nouveau fireplace was designed by Gutzon Borglum, the sculptor of Mount Rushmore. *200 E. Ave. 43, Highland Park, tel. 213/222–0546. Admission free. Open Thurs.–Sun. 1–4.*

③ The Southwest Museum is the huge Mission Revival building that stands half way up Mount Washington and can be seen from the freeway. It contains an extensive collection of Native American art and artifacts, with special emphasis on the people of the Plains, Northwest Coast, Southwest U.S., and Northern Mexico. The basket collection is outstanding. *234 Museum Dr., Highland Park, off the Ave. 43 exit, tel. 213/221–2163. Admission: $3 adults, children free. Open Tues.–Sun. 11–5.*

④ Casa de Adobe is a satellite of the Southwest Museum and located directly below it at the bottom of the hill. What appears to be the well-preserved, authentically furnished hacienda of an Old California don is actually a 1917 re-creation of a 19th-century rancho. The central courtyard plan is typical. *4605 Figueroa St., Highland Park, tel. 213/221–2163. Admission free. Open Tues.–Sun. 11–5.*

Time Out **Lawry's California Center** is a more recent attempt to capture
⑤ the romance of Old Mexico—Zorro and Ramona all rolled up in one—but this one leaves no doubt that it is a recent construction. It is *Sunset* magazine come to life, with bougainvillea-covered patios and flowers in pots at every turn, winter and summer. A spice blending company, Lawry's offers free tours of its plant on weekdays, but the best reason to come here is to enjoy a patio meal. Lunches, both cafeteria-style and full service, are served year-round 11–3. Fiesta dinners are served (May–Oct.) nightly under the stars to the accompaniment of strolling mariachis. Wine and gourmet shops stay open late for after-dinner browsing. *570 W. Ave. 26, Los Angeles, tel. 213/225–2491. Open daily.*

Pasadena and San Marino

Although now absorbed into the general Los Angeles sprawl, Pasadena was once a distinctly defined, and refined, city. Its varied architecture, augmented by lush landscaping, is the most spectacular in Southern California. With only a few hours to spend, visitors should consider driving past the Gamble House, through Old Town, and then on to the grand old neighborhood of the Huntington Library, spending most of their time there.

⑥ The Rose Bowl (991 Rosemont Ave., Pasadena) is set at the bottom of a wide area of the arroyo in an older wealthy neighborhood that must endure the periodic onslaught of thousands of cars and party-minded football fans. The stadium is closed except for games and special events such as the monthly

Rose Bowl Swap Meet. Held the second Sunday of the month, it is considered the granddaddy of West Coast swap meets.

❼ Gamble House, built by Charles and Henry Greene in 1908, is the most spectacular example of Craftsman-style bungalow architecture. The term bungalow can be misleading since the Gamble House is a huge two-story home. To wealthy Easterners such as the Gambles, who commissioned the Greenes to build them a vacation home, this type of home seemed informal compared to their accustomed mansions. What makes visitors swoon here is the incredible amount of hand craftsmanship: the hand-shaped teak interiors, the Greene-designed furniture, the Louis Tiffany glass door. The dark exterior has broad eaves, with many sleeping porches on the second floor. *4 Westmoreland Pl., Pasadena, tel. 818/793–3334. Open Thurs.– Sun. noon–3. Admission: $4 adults, children free. Tours are given Tues. and Thurs. approximately every hour, Sun. noon– 12:45.*

❽ The Norton Simon Museum will be familiar to television viewers of the Rose Parade. The TV cameras position themselves to take full advantage of the sleek, modern building as a background for the passing floats. Like the more famous Getty Museum, the Norton Simon is a tribute to the art acumen of an extremely wealthy businessman. In 1974, Simon reorganized the failing Pasadena Museum of Modern Art and assembled one of the world's finest collections, richest in its Rembrandts, Goyas, Degas, and Picassos—and dotted with Rodin sculptures throughout.

Rembrandt's development can be traced in three oils—"The Bearded Man in the Wide Brimmed Hat," "Self Portrait," and "Titus." The most dramatic Goyas are two oils—"St. Jerome" and the portrait of "Dona Francisca Vicenta Chollet y Caballero." Down the walnut and steel staircase is the Degas gallery, enriched in 1984 with "Waiting," a delicate study of two ballerinas, acquired jointly with the Getty Museum. Picasso's renowned "Woman with Book" highlights a comprehensive collection of his paintings, drawings, and sculptures.

The museum's collections of Impressionist (van Gogh, Matisse, Cézanne, Monet, Renoir, et al.) and Cubist (Braque, Gris) work is extensive. Older works range from Southeast Asian artworks from 100 B.C., bronze, stone and ivory sculptures from India, Cambodia, Thailand, and Nepal.

The museum's wealth of Early Renaissance, Baroque, and Rococo artworks could fill an art history book. Church works by Raphael, Guariento, de Paolo, Filippino Lippi, and Lucas Cranach give way to robust Rubens maidens and Dutch landscapes, still lifes, and portraits by Frans Hals, Jacob van Ruisdael, and Jan Steen. And a magical Tiepolo ceiling highlights the Rococo period. The most recent addition to the collection are seven 19th-century Russian paintings.

The bookstore has posters, prints, and postcards. There are no dining facilities. *411 W. Colorado Blvd., Pasadena, tel. 818/ 449–6840. Admission: $4 adults, $2 students and senior citizens. Open Thurs.–Sun. noon–6.*

❾ Half a mile east of the museum, **Old Town Pasadena** is an ambitious, ongoing restoration. Having fallen into seedy decay in the past 50 years, the area is being revitalized as a blend of restored brick buildings with a Yuppie overlay. Rejuvenated buildings include bistros, elegant restaurants, and boutiques. On Raymond Street, the Hotel Green, now the Castle Apartments, dominates the area. Once a posh resort hotel, the Green is now a faded Moorish fantasy of domes, turrets, and balconies reminiscent of the Alhambra but with, true to its name, a greenish tint. Holly Street, between Fair Oaks and Arroyo, is home to several shops offering an excellent selection of vintage 50s objects, jewelry, and clothes. This area is best explored on foot. Old Town is bisected by Colorado Boulevard, where on New Year's Day throngs of people line the street for the Rose Parade.

Time Out If browsing the Holly Street shops leaves you both nostalgic and hungry, walk down Fair Oaks Avenue to the **Rose City Diner.** Classic diner fare, from chicken-fried steak and eggs to macaroni and cheese, is served in an *American Graffiti* setting. Bebop singers roam the joint from 11 AM to 3 PM every Sunday for added '50s flavor. *45 S. Fair Oaks Ave., tel. 818/793–8282. Open daily 6:30 AM–2 AM.*

---

10 The **Pasadena Historical Society** is housed in Fenyes Mansion. The 1905 mansion still holds the original furniture and paintings on the main and second floors; in the basement, the focus is on the history of the city. There are also four acres of well-landscaped gardens. *170 N. Orange Grove Blvd., Pasadena, tel. 818/795–3002. Historical Society Museum, 470 W. Walnut St., tel. 818/577–1660. Admission: $3 adults, children free. Open Tues., Thurs., and Sun. 1–4.*

11 The **Pacific Asia Museum** is the gaudiest Chinese-style building in Los Angeles outside of Chinatown. Designed in the style of a Northern Chinese imperial palace with a central courtyard, it is devoted entirely to the arts and crafts of Asia and the Pacific Islands. Most of the objects are on loan from private collections and other museums, and there are usually changing special exhibits that focus on the objects of one country. A bookstore and the Collectors Gallery shop sell fine art items from members' collections. The extensive research library can be used by appointment only. *46 N. Los Robles Dr., Pasadena, tel. 818/449–2742. Admission: $3 adults, children free. Open Wed.–Sun. noon–5.*

12 **Kidspace** is a children's museum housed in the gymnasium of an elementary school. Here kids can talk to a robot, direct a television or radio station, dress up in the real (and very heavy) uniforms of a firefighter, an astronaut, a football player, and more. A special "Human Habitrail" challenges children by changing architectural environments and "Illusions" teases one's ability to perceive what is real and what is illusion. *390 S. El Molino Ave., Pasadena, tel. 818/449–9144. Admission: $3. Open during the school year, weekends noon–4, Wed. 2–5; longer hours during summer and other school vacation periods.*

13 The **Huntington Hotel and Cottages** (1401 S. Oak Knoll Ave., Pasadena, tel. 818/792–0266) is situated in Pasadena's most genteel neighborhood of Oak Knoll, close to San Marino. Although all the original buildings were closed in 1986 because of an inability to conform to earthquake regulations, this hotel, built in 1906, is still worth a visit, if only for its 23 acres of beautifully landscaped grounds, where visitors may walk (in selected areas). Features include the Japanese Garden and the Picture Bridge. You can still make reservations here, but only for the 106 newer rooms.

⑭ The **Huntington Library, Art Gallery, and Botanical Gardens** is the area's most important site. If there's only time for a quick drive through the area and one stop, this should be it. Railroad tycoon Henry E. Huntington built his hilltop home in the early 1900s. It has established a reputation as one of the most extraordinary cultural complexes in the world, annually receiving more than a half million visitors. The library contains six million items, including such treasures as a Gutenberg Bible, the earliest known edition of Chaucer's *Canterbury Tales*, George Washington's genealogy in his own handwriting, and first editions by Ben Franklin and Shakespeare. In the library's hallway are five tall hexagonal towers displaying important books and manuscripts.

The art gallery, devoted to British art from the 18th and 19th centuries, contains the original "Blue Boy" by Gainsborough, "Pinkie," a companion piece by Lawrence, and the monumental "Sarah Siddons as the Tragic Muse" by Reynolds.

The Huntington's awesome 130-acre garden, formerly the grounds of the estate, now includes a 12-acre Desert Garden featuring the largest group of mature cacti and other succulents in the world, all arranged by continent. The Japanese Garden offers traditional Japanese plants, stone ornaments, a moon bridge, a Japanese house, a bonsai court, and a Zen rock garden. Besides these gardens, there are collections of azaleas and 1,500 varieties of camellias, the world's largest public collection. The 1,000-variety rose garden displays its collection historically so that the development leading to today's roses can be observed. There are also herb, palm, and jungle gardens plus a Shakespeare garden, where plants mentioned in Shakespeare's plays are grown.

Because of the Huntington's vastness, a variety of orientation options is available for visitors. They include: a 12-minute slide show introducing the Huntington; an hour-and-a-quarter guided tour of the gardens; a 45-minute audio tape about the art gallery (which can be rented for a nominal fee); a 15-minute introductory talk about the library; and inexpensive, self-guided tour leaflets.

In 1980, the first major facility constructed on the Huntington grounds in more than 60 years opened. The $5 million Huntington Pavilion offers visitors unmatched views of the surrounding mountains and valleys and houses a bookstore, displays, and information kiosks as well. Both the east and west wings of the pavilion display paintings on public exhibition for the first time. The Ralph M. Parsons Botanical Center at the pavilion includes a botanical library, a herbarium, and a laboratory for research on plants. No picnicking or pets. A refreshment room is open to the public. *Oxford Rd., San Marino, tel. 818/405–2275. Open Tues.–Sun. 1–4:30. Reservations required Sun. (tel. 818/449–3901). Donation requested.*

The San Fernando Valley

The San Fernando Valley lies northwest of downtown Los Angeles, past Hollywood and accessible through the Cahuenga Pass (where the Hollywood Freeway now runs). Although there are other valleys in the Los Angeles area, this is the one that people refer to simply as "the Valley." Sometimes there is a note of derision in their tone, since the Valley is still struggling with its stepchild status. City people still see it as a mere collection of bedroom communities, too bovine to merit serious thought. But the Valley has come a long way since the early 20th century when it was mainly orange groves and small ranches.

The Valley is now home to over one million people (it even has its own monthly magazine). For many, this area is idyllic: Neat bungalows and ranch-style homes are situated on tidy parcels of land; shopping centers are never too far away. It boasts fine restaurants and even several major movie and television studios.

We are grouping the major attractions of the Valley into one Exploring section to give readers a sense of the place. Because the Valley is such a vast area, however, focus on one or two attractions and make them the destination for a half- or full-day trip. Try to avoid the rush hour traffic jams on the San Diego and Hollywood freeways. They can be brutal.

If you drive into the area on the Hollywood Freeway, through the Cahuenga Pass, you'll come first to one of the most recently developed areas of the Valley: Universal City. It is a one-industry town and that industry is Universal Studios. Its history goes back decades as a major film and television studio but in the past few years it has also become a major tourist attraction. Today this hilly area boasts the Universal Studios Tour, the Universal Amphitheater, a major movie complex, hotels, and restaurants.

Universal Studios is the best place in Los Angeles to see behind the scenes of the movie industry. The five- to seven-hour Universal tour is an enlightening and amusing (if a bit sensational) day at the world's largest television and movie studio, complete with live shows based on "Miami Vice," *Conan the Barbarian*, and "Star Trek." The complex stretches across more than 400 acres, many of which are traversed during the course of the tour by trams featuring witty running commentary provided by enthusiastic guides. Visitors experience the parting of the Red Sea, an avalanche, and a flood, and have the opportunity to meet a 30-foot-tall version of the legendary King Kong, as well as Kit, the talking car from the NBC television series "Knightrider." They live through an encounter with a runaway train and an attack by the ravenous killer shark of *Jaws* fame and endure a confrontation by aliens armed with death rays— all without ever leaving the safety of the tram. And now, thanks to the magic of Hollywood, visitors can experience the perils of The Big One—an all-too-real simulation of an 8.3 earthquake, complete with collapsing earth, deafening train wrecks, floods, and other life-threatening amusements. There are a New England village, an aged European town, and the same New York street that Kojak and Columbo once walked. Visitors relax in the snack bar and picnic area, before going on to the Entertainment Center, the longest and last stop of the day, where they stroll around to enjoy various shows. In one theater animals beguile you with their tricks. In another you can pose for a photo session with the Incredible Hulk. Visit Castle Dracula and confront a variety of terrifying monsters. At the Screen Test Theater, visitors may find themselves being filmed as extras in films already released and recut to include them. *100 Universal Pl., Universal City, tel. 818/508-9600. Box office open daily 9:30-3:30. Admission: $21 adults, $15.50 senior citizens and children 3-11.*

Warner Brothers and Columbia Studios share the lot of **Burbank Studios,** where a two-hour guided walking tour is available. Because the tours involve a lot of walking, dress comfortably and casually. This tour is somewhat technical, centered more on the actual workings of filmmaking than the one at Universal. It varies from day to day to take advantage of goings-on on the lot. Most tours see the backlot sets, prop construction department, and sound complex. *400 Warner Blvd., Burbank, tel. 818/954-1008. Tours given weekdays at 10 and 2. Admission: $22. No children under 10 permitted. Reservations essential, 1 wk in advance.*

NBC Television Studios are also in Burbank as any regular viewer of the Johnny Carson show can't help knowing. Ninety-minute guided tours of the largest color television facilities in the United States explain communication satellites and videotape processes. Studio 1, where "The Tonight Show" is taped, is also part of the tour, as are the huge prop warehouse and makeup and wardrobe departments. There are lucky groups that have a chance to see NBC stars like Carson arrive for their shows. The morning tours are recommended since there is more activity then. Tickets are also available for tapings of NBC shows. *3000 W. Alameda Ave., Burbank, tel. 818/840-3537. Admission: $6.75 adults, 50¢ children. Tours weekdays 8:30-4, Sat. 10-3, and Sun. 10-2.*

San Fernando, in the northeast corner of the valley that bears its name, is one of the few separate cities in the Valley (and the only one in the Valley proper since Burbank and Glendale are really at the junction of the San Fernando and San Gabriel valleys). It has only one attraction of any remote interest to visitors, the mission, but that one offers such a spectacularly vivid glimpse of early California life that it is definitely worth the trip.

Mission San Fernando Rey de España was one of a chain of 21 missions established by 1823, which extend from San Diego to Sonoma. Approximately a day's travel apart in those days (30 miles), the missions dotted the coastal route known as The Camino Real. Today U.S. 101 parallels the historic Mission Trail, one of the state's most popular tourways.

San Fernando Mission was established in 1797 and named in honor of Ferdinand III of Spain. Fifty-six Indians joined the mission to make it a self-supportive community. Soon wheat, corn, beans, and olives were grown and harvested there. In addition workshops produced metalwork, leather goods, cloth, soap, and candles. Herds of cattle, sheep, and hogs also began to prosper. By 1833, after Mexico extended its rule over California, a civil administrator was appointed for the mission and the priests were restricted to religious duties. The Indians began leaving and what had been flourishing one year before became unproductive. Thirteen years later the mission, along with its properties (the entire San Fernando Valley), was sold for $14,000. During the next 40 years, the mission buildings were neglected; settlers stripped roof tiles, and the adobe walls were ravaged by the weather.

Finally in 1923 a restoration program was initiated that resulted in a recovery of the rustic elegance and the feeling of history within the mission walls. Today, as you walk through the mission's arched corridors, you may experience déjà vu and you probably have, vicariously, through an episode of "Gunsmoke," "Dragnet," or dozens of movies. The church's interior is decorated with Indian designs and artifacts of Spanish craftsmanship depicting the mission's 18th-century culture. There is a small museum and gift shop. *15151 San Fernando Mission Rd., San Fernando, tel. 818/361–0186. Admission: $2 adults, $1 children. Open daily 9–4:15.*

The main attraction at **Los Encinos State Historic Park** is the early California dwelling, which was built in 1849 by Don Vicente de la Osa and is furnished with historically accurate furniture, household goods and tools, and a two-story French-style home, dated 1870. The grounds are quite serene, especially on weekdays, with a duck pond and plenty of shade trees. *16756 Moorpark St., Encino, tel. 818/706–1310. Tours available Wed.–Sun.*

Calabasas, in the southwest corner of the Valley, was once a stagecoach stop on the way from Ventura to Los Angeles. The name means "pumpkins" in Spanish. The little town has retained some of the flavor of its early days. The **Leonis Adobe** is one of the most charming adobes in the county, due in part to its fairly rural setting and barnyard animals, especially the Spanish red hens. With a little concentration, visitors can imagine life in the early years. The house was originally built as a one-story adobe, but in 1844 Miguel Leonis decided to remodel rather than move and added a second story with a balcony. Voila! A Monterey-style home. The furnishings are authentic to the period. Highly recommended for history buffs who can appreciate a small but very moving slice of the old days. *23537 Calabasas Rd., Calabasas, tel. 818/712–0734. Open Wed.– Sun. 1–4.*

Time Out   **The Sagebrush Cantina** (23527 Calabasas Rd., Calabasas, tel. 818/888–6062), just next door to the Leonis Adobe, is a casual, outdoorsy place. It's perfect for families. The food is a mix of hamburgers, pasta, and trendy salads. There's a large bar for the singles set and outdoor tables for leisurely meals. It's busy —and best—on weekends.

Los Angeles for Free

In Los Angeles, every day is a free event in terms of nature; the sun, sand, and ocean alone can fill a vacation. But there are plenty of other free activities, events, and cultural attractions to keep even those with limited budgets busy.

Cabrillo Marine Museum. *See* Palos Verdes, San Pedro, and Long Beach above.

California Museum of Science and Industry. *See* Museums above.

Carroll Avenue. *See* Historic Buildings and Sites above.

Christmas Boat Parades. During December, many local marinas celebrate Christmas in a special way. Boat owners decorate their boats with strings of lights and holiday displays and then cruise in a line for dockside visitors to see. Call for specific dates (Marina del Rey, tel. 2/822–0119; Port of Los Angeles, tel. 2/519–3508).

El Alisal. *See* Highland Park, Pasadena, and San Marino above.

El Pueblo State Historic Park. Olvera Street is a year-round freebie for strolling and soaking up Mexican ambience. The tours are also free. Best yet is to enjoy Olvera Street during one of the seasonal events. The Blessing of the Animals, at 2 P.M. on the Saturday before Easter, is Olvera Street at its best. On a warm, springtime day, merchants and their families dress in traditional Mexican folkloric costumes. Residents bring their pets (not just dogs and cats but horses, pigs, cows, birds, hamsters, and more) all freshly groomed and sporting bows and ribbons to be blessed by a local priest. Everyone lines up to make a "paseo" around the plaza for a sprinkling of holy water. It's wonderfully colorful and perfect for photos. Las Posadas takes place every night from Dec. 16 to 24. This is a tradition commemorating Mary and Joseph's search for shelter on Christmas Eve. The parade of merchants and visitors up and down the cobblestoned street is led by children dressed up as angels. They sing a haunting song and the evening ends with a pinata breaking in the plaza. This is a low-keyed, raggle-taggle procession (at the far end of the spectrum from Disney on Parade) but quite special in its authenticity. *See* Downtown Los Angeles above.

Forest Lawn Memorial Park. *See* Other Places of Interest above.

Hebrew Union College Skirball Museum. *See* Museums above.

Hollywood. Most of the Hollywood attractions are free walk-by and walk-through activities.

Huntington Library, Art Gallery, and Botanical Gardens. *See* Highland Park, Pasadena, and San Marino above.

J. Paul Getty Museum. *See* Santa Monica, Venice, Pacific Palisades, and Malibu above.

La Brea Tar Pits. *See* Wilshire Boulevard above.

Laurel and Hardy's Piano Stairway. *See* Off the Beaten Track below.

Leonis Adobe. *See* The San Fernando Valley above.

Mulholland Drive. *See* Other Places of Interest above.

Pig Murals. *See* Off the Beaten Track below.

Polo Games at Will Rogers State Historic Park. *See* Santa Monica, Venice, Pacific Palisades, and Malibu above.

Rancho Los Alamitos. *See* Palos Verdes, San Pedro, and Long Beach above.

Rancho Los Cerritos. *See* Palos Verdes, San Pedro, and Long Beach above.

Rose Parade. Seen from the streets (rather than the bleachers), the Rose Parade is as free as it is on television. Arrive before dawn and dress warmly. Thousands of residents prefer to watch on television and then go out to East Pasadena a day or two later to view the floats, which are parked there for a few days for observation. *Corner of Sierra Madre Blvd. and Washington St., Pasadena. Call for viewing hours, tel. 818/449-7673.*

Santa Anita Racetrack Workouts. *See* What to See and Do with Children below.

Santa Monica Mountains Nature Walks. The rangers and docents of the many parks in the Santa Monica Mountains offer an ambitious schedule of walks for all interests, ages, and levels of exertion. These include wildflower walks, moonlight hikes, tidepool explorations, and much more. Several outings are held every day. For updated information, call the National Park Service (tel. 818/597-9192).

Travel Town. *See* What to See and Do with Children below.

UCLA. *See* The Westside above.

Watts Towers. *See* Other Places of Interest above.

Westwood Memorial Park. *See* The Westside above.

What to See and Do with Children

The kids of Los Angeles have plenty going for them: their own museums, our museums, a world-class zoo, children's theater every weekend, nature walks, pony rides, art classes, and much more.

In addition to the attractions listed here, check the Parks and Gardens section above for more places to take children. Also, the Los Angeles *Times* provides ideas for the upcoming week in two regular columns: "54 Hours," which runs on Thursdays in the View section, and "Family Spots," which runs on Saturdays in View. *L.A. Parent*, a monthly tabloid devoted to family life, has a monthly calendar.

California Museum of Science and Industry. *See* Museums above.

Children's Museum at La Habra. Housed in a 1923-vintage Union Pacific railroad depot, with old railroad cars resting nearby, this museum combines permanent and special exhibitions all designed to stimulate young minds—the painless way. In Grandma's Attic, kids can try on old clothes and parade in front of a mirror. There's a real beehive (behind glass) and dozens of stuffed animals. A recent special exhibit focused on the world of handicapped children and allowed visitors to try out crutches and wheelchairs and learn a bit of sign language. *301 S. Euclid St., La Habra, tel. 714/526-2227. Admission: $2 adults, $1.50 children. Open Mon.-Sat. 10-4.*

Junior Arts Center. In this age of plenty of high-priced thrills for kids but few moderately priced ones, the Junior Arts Center is a beacon in Los Angeles. It offers low-priced arts-and-crafts classes year-round. Every Sunday, the center's patio is set up with worktables and art supplies for a two-hour free workshop where parents and kids work together on special projects supervised by local artists. There are also gallery exhibits with strong kid appeal. *Barnsdall Park, 4800 Hollywood Blvd., Hollywood, tel. 213/485-4474. Open Tues.-Sat. 10-5, Sun. noon-5.*

Kidspace. *See* Highland Park, Pasadena, and San Marino above.

La Brea Tar Pits and George C. Page Museum of La Brea Discoveries. *See* Wilshire Boulevard above.

Lomita Railroad Museum. Don't be surprised if you think you've gotten lost in this typical suburban neighborhood before you find the museum. Look closely, and you'll discover a replica of a turn-of-the-century Massachusetts train station. Beyond the gate, discover one of the largest collections of railroad memorabilia in the West. Climb aboard a real steam engine and take a look at the immaculate interior of the car itself. *2137 250th St., Lomita, tel. 213/326-6255. Admission: 50¢. Open Wed.-Sun. 10-5.*

Long Beach Children's Museum. Recently moved to expanded quarters in a Long Beach mall, the museum features the regulation-issue children's-museum exhibits such as The Art Cafe and Granny's Attic. All exhibits welcome curious minds and eager hands. *445 Long Beach Blvd. at Long Beach Plaza, Long Beach, tel. 213/495-1163. Admission: $2.95. Open Thurs.-Sun. noon-4.*

Los Angeles Children's Museum. *See* Downtown Los Angeles above.

Los Angeles Zoo. The zoo, one of the major zoos in the United States, is noted for its breeding of endangered species. Koala bears and white tigers are the latest additions. The 113-acre compound holds more than 2,000 mammals, birds, amphibians, and reptiles. Animals are grouped according to the geographical areas where they are naturally found—Africa, Australia, Eurasia, North America, and South America. A tram is available for stops at all areas. Seeing the zoo calls for a lot of walking, seemingly all uphill, so strollers or backpacks are recommended for families with young children. The zoo is beautifully landscaped and areas for picnicking are available. Not-to-be-missed features at the zoo include Adventure Island, a new children's zoo offering interactive exhibits and featuring animals of the American Southwest; a walk-through bird exhibit with more than 50 different species from all over the world; and a koala area, where the furry creatures live amid eucalyptus trees in an environment resembling their native Australia. *Junction of the Ventura and Golden State freeways, Griffith Park, tel. 213/666-4090. Admission: $5.50 adults, $2.25 children. Open daily 10-5.*

Magic Mountain. The only real amusement park actually in Los Angeles County, there are 260 acres of rides, shows, and entertainments. The roster of major rides is headlined by Viper, the world's largest looping roller coaster. The first drop is 18 stories high, and three vertical loops turn you upside down seven times. There's also the Roaring Rapids, a simulated white-water wilderness adventure complete with whirlpools, waves, and real rapids; the Colossus, the largest dual-track wood roller coaster ever built, offering two "drops" in excess of 100 feet and experiencing speeds up to 62 miles per hour; and the Revolution, a steelcoaster with a 360 degree, 90-foot vertical loop. On the Z-Force ride, passengers ride upside down, and recent addition Ninja is a suspended roller coaster. Children's World is a minipark with scaled-down rides, such as the Red Baron's Airplane and the Little Sailor Ride. Other attractions at the park include a puppet theater, celebrity musical revues, Dixieland jazz, rock concerts, and the Aqua Theater high-diving shows. Spillikin's Handcrafters Junction is a 4-acre compound in which craftsmen exhibit skills and wares from blacksmithing to glassblowing. *26101 Magic Mountain Pkwy., off I–5, Valencia, tel. 818/992–0884. Admission: $22 adults, $11 senior citizens, $11 children 4 ft tall and under. Open daily May 19–Labor Day 10–10 (later on weekends); rest of the year, open weekends and holidays.*

Merry-Go-Round in Griffith Park. Just up the road from the real pony rides, this 1926-vintage carousel offers safe and melodic rides for families. The broad lawn nearby was the scene of some of the most colorful love-ins of the 1960s.

Merry-Go-Round at Santa Monica Pier. *See* Santa Monica, Venice, Pacific Palisades, and Malibu above.

"Mothers' Beach" (Admiralty Way and Via Marina, Marina del Rey). The real name is Marina Beach, but its nickname is popular with local families. Nestled in between the sleek sloops and singles condos and bars, this tiny crescent of man-made beach offers a wonderfully protected environment for families with very young children.

Nature Walks for Children. Walks in the Santa Monica Mountains for preschoolers and their parents are offered by two local groups: the William O. Douglas Outdoor Classroom (WODOC) at Franklin Canyon Ranch (tel. 213/858–3834) and Nursery Nature Walks at the Pacific Palisades YMCA (tel. 213/454–5591). Both groups schedule several walks every week where specially trained docents help the littlest hikers to learn about the plants and animals in the parks by smelling sage and searching for footprints. All walks require advanced reservations.

Natural History Museum Of Los Angeles County. *See* Museums above.

Pierce College Farm Tour (6201 Winnetka Ave., Woodland Hills, tel. 818/719–6425). The agriculture students at this junior college offer regular tours of their working farm. Kids can see all the usual farm animals—goats, cows, chickens—in a surprisingly bucolic setting considering the surrounding city.

Pony Rides. Most kids in Los Angeles (and their parents before them) had their first pony ride at the track in Griffith Park. Two-year-olds are routinely strapped on and paraded around on the slowest of old nags, and these days, the event is dutifully recorded on video camera. The ponies come in three versions: slow, medium, and fast. The slow ones are the best, for all ages. The faster ones are jarring, and the kids seem disappointed. To round out an eventful morning (the lines are long in late afternoon), there are stagecoach rides and a miniature train ride that makes a figure eight near the pony rides. *Crystal Springs*

Dr., Griffith Park, tel. 213/664–3266. Use entrance near Golden State Freeway (I–5) and Los Feliz Blvd. Pony rides $1 for two rounds; stagecoach rides $1; miniature train rides $1.50 adults, $1.25 children. Open in summer, weekdays 10–5:30, weekends 10–6:30; rest of year, open Tues.–Fri. 10–4:30, weekends 10–5.

Queen Mary and Spruce Goose. *See* Palos Verdes, San Pedro, and Long Beach above.

Raging Waters. Los Angeles's major water park is situated in Bonelli Regional Park, using 44 acres for swimming pools, lagoons, water slides, and other water-related activities. There are slides for all ages and levels of daring. For nonwater-types there are sunny "beaches" and special pools for the tiniest visitors. Bring your own towels. Picnicking spots available as well as fast food stands. *111 Raging Waters Dr., San Dimas, tel. 714/592–6453. Admission: $14.95 adults, $8.50 children 42–48 inches tall. Open late May–mid-Oct., weekdays 10–9, weekends 9 AM–10 PM.*

Santa Anita Racetrack Workouts. During the racing season (December 26–late April), the public is welcome to come out early in the morning to watch the workouts from the grandstands. There is an announcer who'll keep you advised of the horses' names and times. Breakfast is available in the restaurant. *Santa Anita Park, 285 W. Huntington Dr., Arcadia, tel. 818/574–7223. Enter Gate 8 off Baldwin Ave. or Gate 3 off Huntington Dr. Open 7:30 AM–9:30 AM.*

Travel Town. Fifteen vintage railroad cars are resting here, all welcoming the onslaught of climbing and screaming children, who love to run from car to car, jump in the cab, run through the cars, and jump off the high steps. The collection includes a narrow-gauge sugar train from Hawaii, a steam engine, and an old L.A. trolley. Travel Town goes beyond just trains with a collection of old planes such as World War II bombers. There's also an old fire engine, milk wagon, buggies, and classic cars. A miniature train takes visitors on a ride around the area. *5200 Zoo Dr., Griffith Park, tel. 213/662–5874. Admission free. Open weekdays 10–4, weekends 10–6.*

Universal Studios. *See* The San Fernando Valley above.

Van Nuys Airport Tour. Free, 1½-hour tours of this small, small-aircraft center are offered in buses. It's mostly a drive-by, but kids do have the chance to climb in a huge California Air National Guard cargo carrier. Reservations are required. *8030 Balboa Blvd., Van Nuys, tel. 818/785–8838. Tours weekends and some Sat., 9:30 and 11. Reservations required.*

Wonderworld Puppet Theater. Local puppeteer Ric Morton presents Saturday-morning puppet shows for an audience of short attention spans and curious young minds. After the adventure-filled performance, the curtains come down and kids can come up to the stage and see how it was all done. Call for schedule. *Torrance Community Theater, 1522 Cravens Ave., Torrance, tel. 213/532–1741. Admission: $4.*

Off the Beaten Track

The Flower Market. Just east of the downtown high rises, in the 700 block of Wall Street, is a block-long series of stores and stalls that open up in the middle of the night to sell wholesale flowers and house plants to the city's florists, who rush them to their shops to sell that day. Many of the stalls stay open until late morning to sell leftovers to the general public at the same bargain prices. And what glorious leftovers they are: Hawaiian ginger, Dutch tulips, Chilean freesia. The public is welcome after 9 AM and the stock is quickly depleted by 11 AM. Even if you don't buy, it's a heady experience to be surrounded by so much fragile beauty.

Laurel and Hardy's Piano Stairway. One of the most famous scenes in the history of movies is one in *The Music Box* where Laurel and Hardy try to get a piano up an outdoor stairway. This Sisyphean tale was filmed in 1932 at 923-927 Vendome Street (where the stairway remains today much as it was then), in the Silverlake section of Los Angeles, a few miles northeast of downtown.

Orcutt Ranch Horticultural Center (23600 Roscoe Blvd., Canoga Park, tel. 818/883–6641). Once owned by William Orcutt, a well-known geologist who was one of the excavators of the La Brea Tar Pits, this ranch is a surprisingly lush and varied garden in the west San Fernando Valley. Orcutt is filled with interesting little areas to explore such as the rose garden, herb garden, and stream banked with shady trees and ferns (a wonderful picnic site). On the last Sunday of the month, the house, where the Orcutts lived, is open to the public. Two weekends a year (late June or early July) the extensive orange and grapefruit groves are open for public picking. It's a chance to enjoy the Valley as it was in the years when groves like these covered the landscape for miles. You'll need an A-frame ladder or a special pole for dislodging the fruit up high. Bring along grocery sacks.

Pig Murals (3049 E. Vernon Ave., Vernon). Vernon Avenue is the heart of Los Angeles's meat-packing industry and to be stuck in traffic on Vernon Avenue on a hot summer afternoon is an odorific experience not soon forgotten. Nevertheless, for aficionados of offbeat sites and/or street murals, the Pig Murals on the outside walls of the Farmer John Company are great fun. Probably the first public murals in Los Angeles, they were painted originally by Leslie Grimes who was killed in a fall from the scaffolding while painting. They depict bucolic scenes of farms and contented pigs, rather an odd juxtaposition to what goes on inside the packing plant.

Sightseeing Checklists

Historical Buildings and Sites

When Los Angeles celebrated its bicentennial in 1981, it came as something of a shock to many Americans. Until then most people had assumed that Los Angeles came into being in the 1920s or thereabouts. The city's historical heritage has not always been carefully preserved. In fact, city officials and developers have been quite cavalier about saving many of the best examples of the city's architectural past. However, active restoration projects are taking place all the time and there is a great deal to be seen that predates the arrival of moving pictures.

Adamson House. *See* Santa Monica, Venice, Pacific Palisades, and Malibu above.

Banning Residence Museum. *See* Palos Verdes, San Pedro, and Long Beach above.

Bradbury Building. *See* Downtown Los Angeles above.

Carroll Avenue (1300 block Carroll Ave., Angelino Heights, tel. 213/250–5976). Angelino Heights is one of the oldest neighborhoods in Los Angeles, developed when the upper middle class of the 1880s sought out homes in this hilly section just northwest of downtown. Although the entire area has many fine examples of Victorian architecture, the 1300 block of Carroll Avenue has the highest concentration of Victorian homes in the city and has been designated a historical monument. Living on Carroll Avenue carries a certain implied mandate these days. Most of the homes have been renovated with a careful eye for historical accuracy. The Carroll Avenue Foundation sponsors several events during the year which include hour tours to the best restored homes. The Sessions House, at 1330 Carroll, is one of the finest.

De Mille Barn. *See* Hollywood Studio Museum in Hollywood above.

El Alisal. *See* Highland Park, Pasadena, and San Marino above.

El Pueblo State Historic Park. *See* Downtown Los Angeles above.

Gamble House. *See* Highland Park, Pasadena, and San Marino above.

Heritage Square. *See* Highland Park, Pasadena, and San Marino above.

Hollyhock House. *See* Other Places of Interest above.

Leonis Adobe. *See* The San Fernando Valley above.

I. Magnin Wilshire. *See* Wilshire Boulevard above.

Mission San Gabriel Archangel. Over 200 years ago Father Junipero Serra dedicated this mission to the great archangel and messenger from God, Saint Gabriel. As the founders approached the mission site, they were confronted with savage Indians. In the heat of battle, one of the padres produced the canvas painting "Our Lady of Sorrows," which so impressed the Indians that they laid down their bows and arrows. The miracle produced another painting, which is on display at the mission today. Within the next 50 years, the San Gabriel Archangel became the wealthiest of all California missions.

In 1833 the Mexican government passed the "Decree of Desecularization," and following their confiscation of the mission, it began to decline, as did Mission San Fernando Rey. In 1855 the United States government returned the mission to the church. Unfortunately by this time the Franciscans had departed. Not much happened until 1908, when the Claretian Fathers took charge. In the following years, much care and respect was poured into the mission.

Today Mission San Gabriel Archangel's adobe walls preserve an era of history unchanged by the outside world. The magnificent cemetery tells the history of the mission through the people that lived, died, and were buried there. Over 6,000 Indians stricken by horrible cholera and smallpox epidemics in 1825 are buried in the cemetery.

The magnificent church and museum housing relics reflecting the history of the padres and early visitors to San Gabriel have been closed for repairs since the October 1988 earthquake. The gardens, cemetery, and gift shop are still open. *537 W. Mission Dr., San Gabriel, tel. 818/282–5191. Open daily 9:30–4:15.*

Mission San Fernando Rey de Espana. *See* The San Fernando Valley above.

Rancho Los Alamitos. *See* Palos Verdes, San Pedro, and Long Beach above.

Rancho Los Cerritos. *See* Palos Verdes, San Pedro, and Long Beach above.

Santa Monica Heritage Museum. *See* Santa Monica, Venice, Pacific Palisades, and Malibu above.

Watts Towers. *See* Other Places of Interest above.

Will Rogers State Historic Park. *See* Santa Monica, Venice, Pacific Palisades, and Malibu above.

William S. Hart County Park. *See* Parks and Gardens below.

Wiltern Theater. *See* Wilshire Boulevard above.

Museums

Banning Residence Museum. *See* Palos Verdes, San Pedro, and Long Beach above.

Cabrillo Marine Museum. *See* Palos Verdes, San Pedro, and Long Beach above.

California Museum of Science and Industry. This museum was vastly expanded for the 1984 Olympics. The Aerospace Complex features a DC3, DC8, rockets, and satellites plus an IMAX motion picture theater. The Taper Hall of Economics and Finance has 62 3-D exhibits, most of them computer interactive for visitors. And a new miniature winery complements McDonald's Computer Chef exhibit of behind-the-scenes fast food cooking (McDonald's is also open for business and quite a lure for kids). The redesigned Hall of Health reveals the inner workings of the body and has a new Health for Life Arcade. There are exhibits on fiber optics, robotics, high technology, and also the ever-popular hatchery where 150 baby chicks hatch daily for all to see. This museum is especially intriguing to children, with many exhibits kids can operate by punching buttons, twisting knobs, or turning levers. *700 State Dr., Exposition Park, tel. 213/744–7400. Admission free. Open daily 10–5.*

Children's Museum at La Habra. *See* What to See and Do with Children below.

Craft and Folk Art Museum. *See* Wilshire Boulevard above.

George C. Page Museum of La Brea Discoveries. *See* Wilshire Boulevard above.

Hebrew Union College Skirball Museum. The collection comprises Judaic art, Palestinian archeology, and anthropological material from the Negev Desert. Also in the collection are rare manuscripts, historical coins and medals, ceremonial art, ancient Israeli artifacts, and an extensive display of painting, graphics, and sculptures. The museum offers a unique opportunity to explore Judaism and its history and culture through esthetic and material treasures of the Jewish people. The museum itself is of architectural note because of its series of arches representative of the Ten Commandments. *3077 University at 32nd and Hoover Sts., Los Angeles, tel. 213/749-3424. Admission free. Open Tues.-Fri. 11-4, Sun. 10-5. Public tours on Sun. at 1.*

Hollywood Studio Museum (De Mille Barn). *See* Hollywood above.

Huntington Library, Art Gallery, and Botanical Gardens. *See* Highland Park, Pasadena, and San Marino above.

J. Paul Getty Museum. *See* Santa Monica, Venice, Pacific Palisades, and Malibu above.

Lomita Railroad Museum. *See* What to See and Do with Children below.

Long Beach Children's Museum. *See* What to See and Do with Children below.

Los Angeles Children's Museum. *See* Downtown Los Angeles above.

Los Angeles County Museum of Art. *See* Wilshire Boulevard above.

Museum of Contemporary Art. *See* Downtown Los Angeles above.

Natural History Museum of Los Angeles County. The fourth largest natural history museum in the United States covers a span of history ranging from the prehistoric to the present. So many aspects of natural history are presented here that all couldn't possibly be absorbed in one visit. Opened in 1913, the 400,000-square-foot museum contains more than 35 halls and galleries displaying permanent as well as special, temporary exhibits. The main building is an attraction in itself: Spanish Renaissance in structure, the museum contains travertine columns, walls, and domes; an inlaid marble floor heightens the overall effect of magnificence. The museum is rich in its collection of prehistoric fossils, both reptile and mammal. It also houses an extensive bird and marine life exhibit, as well as a vast display of insect life. A brilliant display of stones can be seen in the museum's Hall of Gems and Minerals. In addition, the museum features an elaborate taxidermy exhibit of North American and African mammals in their natural habitats. The settings are excellent replicas of the real thing. Exhibits typifying various cultural groups include pre-Columbian artifacts and a display of crafts from the South Pacific. The Hall of American History presents everything from the paraphernalia of prominent historical figures to old American cars. The museum's new Ralph M. Parsons Discovery Center is a barn-size room that is a cross between a natural history museum and a children's museum with many hands-on, science-oriented exhibits. The museum has three excellent gift shops: an ethnic arts shop, an extensive bookstore, and the Dinosaur Shop, where kids will find coloring books, crafts, books, tapes, stuffed animals, and much more—many with a dinosaur motif. *900 Exposition Blvd., Exposition Park, tel. 213/744–3466 or 213/744–6292. Admission: $3 adults, $1.50 senior citizens and students, 75¢ children; free the first Tues. of every month. Open Tues.–Sun. 10–5.*

Norton Simon Museum. *See* Highland Park, Pasadena, and San Marino above.

Pacific Asia Museum. *See* Highland Park, Pasadena, and San Marino above.

Santa Monica Heritage Museum. *See* Santa Monica, Venice, Pacific Palisades, and Malibu above.

Southwest Museum. *See* Highland Park, Pasadena, and San Marino above.

Parks and Gardens

The extensive Los Angeles park system provides a welcome oasis after the myriad concrete freeways and urban sprawl. They range from small, grassy knolls for picnicking and relaxing to huge wilderness areas offering a wide spectrum of recreational facilities, including tennis courts, golf courses, and lakes.

The **Los Angeles Department of Parks and Recreation** (tel. 213/485–5555) provides helpful information on locating and identifying park facilities. Parks and Rec also sponsors various activities such as marathon races, inter-park sports contests, poetry readings, art shows, and chess tournaments.

Banning Park. *See* Palos Verdes, San Pedro, and Long Beach above.

Burton Chase Park. *See* Santa Monica, Venice, Pacific Palisades, and Malibu above.

Descanso Gardens. Once part of the vast Spanish Rancho San Rafael that covered more than 30,000 acres, Descanso Gardens now encompasses 165 acres of native chaparral-covered slopes. A forest of California live oak trees furnishes a dramatic backdrop for thousands of camellias, azaleas, and a 4-acre rose garden. Descanso's Tea House features pools, waterfalls, a Zen garden, and a gift shop as well as a relaxing spot to stop for refreshments. Flower shows (including chrysanthemum, daffodil, camellia, and bonsai demonstrations) are held at various times of the year. Guided tours are available; trams traverse the grounds. *1418 Descanso Dr., La Canada, tel. 818/790–5571. Admission: $3 adults, $1.50 senior citizens and students, 75¢ children; free the third Tues. of every month. Open daily 9–4:30.*

Douglas Park (1155 Chelsea Ave., Wilshire Blvd. near 25th St., Santa Monica). This postage-stamp-size park (four acres) is jam-packed every weekend with Westside families. It offers pleasant spots for blanket picnics close to the playgrounds so parents can monitor their children and read the Sunday *Times* at the same time. The playground area seldom has an empty swing. A former wading pool is now a dry track for tiny kids and their three-wheelers. Well-kept and frequented by friendly people, this park deserves its favorable word-of-mouth among locals.

Eaton Canyon Park and Nature Center (1750 N. Altadena Dr., Pasadena). This park celebrates native plants and animals in a big but low-keyed way. It may look a bit dry and scrubby, compared to parks planted with lush East Coast trees and bushes, but this is the real thing and for those who take the time to study the variety of plants and how they have learned to adapt to the meager rainfall, it is well worth a trip. The Nature Center helps to orient visitors before they start down the trails. From September to June (the best times to visit), docents offer easy, guided walks. They leave the flagpole beginning at 9 AM.

Echo Park (1632 Bellevue Ave., Echo Park). Perhaps the most evocative park in Los Angeles, Echo Park manages to rise above the seedy, urban patina it can't escape. If you're a half-full kind of person, you'll find plenty to rave about here. There's a feeling of romance, of a bygone era, of history, stories untold. Set in one of the older, tougher neighborhoods in the city, Echo Park is mostly lake with a little edging all around. The lake itself is famous for its lotus pads, and visitors can rent boats and paddle right up to them. There are a few palm-filled islands near the north end, tropical-feeling and very inviting. Echo Park is at its best in the late afternoon, when the area takes on a warm glow as the sun sets. Weekdays are quiet; weekends, filled with families.

El Dorado Park. *See* Palos Verdes, San Pedro, and Long Beach above.

Elysian Park (929 Academy Rd., Los Angeles, tel. 213/225–2044). This 575-acre park is on hilly acreage overlooking downtown Los Angeles. Despite its size, Elysian Park should be classified as an "urban" park, as it offers refuge to downtowners who live in cramped apartments. It can be a lively excursion for those who like seeing families enjoying some fresh air on weekends, and these crowded family areas are the safest parts of the park (despite the presence of the L.A. Police Academy in the park, solo wanderings should be taken with caution). Much of the park is still wilderness and there is a 10-acre rare tree grove completely labeled for convenient identification. The recreation center has volleyball and basketball courts. Plentiful play areas for children, nature trails for hiking, plus nine picnic spots with tables round out the park's offerings. Perched on the southeast corner, high above the smog, is Dodger Stadium, home of the Los Angeles Dodgers professional baseball team.

Franklin Canyon Ranch (1736 N. Lake Dr., north of Beverly Hills, tel. 2/858–3834). Westside nature-buff do-gooders have embraced this park with a vengeance, turning this relatively close-in park into a busy-all-the-time spot for special-interest hikes and other outdoor events. The big draw is the nature walks for preschoolers and their parents but the schedule is also filled with aerobic walks and moonlit hikes (to the top of the ridge for a breathtaking view of the city). There is a nice broad lawn for games and good picnicking.

Griffith Park (entrances at north end of Vermont Ave., Los Feliz district, tel. 213/665–5188). Donated to the city in 1896 by mining tycoon Griffith J. Griffith, this is the largest city park in the United States. It contains 4,000 acres. There are seemingly endless picnic areas, as well as hiking and horseback riding trails. Travel Town, with its miniature railroad, is a favorite with kids. Pony rides and stagecoach rides are also available. The park is home to two 18-hole golf courses (Harding and Wilson) and one nine-hole executive course (Roosevelt), a pro shop, a driving range, and tennis courts. A swimming pool and soccer fields are nearby. The world-famous Los Angeles Zoo (*see* What to See and Do with Children, above) is on the park's north side. The Griffith Park Observatory and Planetarium is located on the park's south side, high atop the Hollywood Hills (*see* Other Places of Interest, below). Near the Western Avenue entrance is Fern Dell, a half mile of shade that includes paths winding their way amid waterfalls, pools, and thousands of ferns.

MacArthur Park (2230 W. Sixth St., Los Angeles). During the 1920s and 1930s, MacArthur Park was a popular hangout for the elite, a favorite spot for a leisurely stroll, boating, or an afternoon concert. How times have changed! The surrounding neighborhood is no longer a fledgling suburb of the Anglo well-to-do but a rundown section of town that is teeming with Mexican and Central American immigrants and more than its share of winos. The park has suffered, but it remains well-used by the local population. For people who enjoy street life and consider themselves urban explorers, MacArthur Park still has something to offer. Dress to blend in (no Yuppie duds here) and relax. It's best to visit on weekends when the crowds provide some safety as well as a wonderfully rich panoply of human life. The grassy areas surrounding the lake are the most picturesque. The rental pedal-boats allow visitors to observe the human condition from a safe distance.

Malibu Creek State Park (¼ mi south of intersection of Las Virgenes Rd. and Mulholland Hwy., Malibu). Nestled deep in the Santa Monica Mountains, this park crystallizes what the mountains are all about: an incredibly varied chaparral landscape and a get-away-from-it-all feeling. Century Lake, a small, man-made lake a mile from the road, is an excellent picnic site.

Malibu Lagoon State Park. *See* Santa Monica, Venice, Pacific Palisades, and Malibu above.

Peter Strauss Ranch (30,000 Mulholland Hwy., Agoura, tel. 818/620–3508). A perfectly lovely setting, this park is named for its former owner, actor Peter Strauss, who lived in the splendidly cozy stone house, now park headquarters. What makes this park such a pleasant spot to visit is the sense of being at someone's country home, not a public park. It's like joining in a big family reunion. The broad front lawn beckons Frisbees and kites. The hiking trails are easy enough for the whole family. Throughout the year there is an ambitious schedule of weekend entertainments, from folk dance ensembles to puppet shows.

Placerita Canyon Nature Center (19152 Placerita Canyon Rd., Newhall, tel. 805/259–7721). This 350-acre park is perfect for hiking with 8 miles of trails through both flat and hilly terrain

along a streambed and through oak trees. Warm days, winter
and spring, are the best times to visit, because there is a chance
of water (and tadpoles) in the stream then. The deeply shaded
picnic area is highly recommended and is an excellent meeting
place for picnics. Because the park is a wildlife refuge, picnicking is limited to the designated area. The half-mile ecology trail
focuses on the flora and fauna of the area. Gold was first discovered in California in 1842, in this park (not in the Mother Lode
as most assume) at a site designated by the Oak of the Golden
Dream. The Nature Center features dioramas, indigenous animals, and a small museum.

Roxbury Park (471 S. Roxbury Dr., at Olympic Blvd., Beverly
Hills, just east of Century City, tel. 213/550–4761). This centrally located park is under the Beverly Hills Parks and Recreation Department's jurisdiction and attracts a good crowd every
weekend. Young families hover around the playground and picnic tables (fully booked in advance for preschoolers' birthday
parties), couples toss blankets on the flat lawns to catch some
sun, and senior citizens head for the lawn bowling area. The
park also offers a softball diamond and tennis courts. It has recently undergone a major facelift (typical Beverly Hills!).

Shoreline Aquatic Park. *See* Palos Verdes, San Pedro, and Long
Beach above.

Vasquez Rocks (10700 E. Escondido Rd., Aqua Dulce, off Antelope Valley Frwy.). Here is one of Los Angeles County's best
photo opportunities. Sure, it's a two-hour drive from downtown but that doesn't stop the dozens of film, television, and ad-
agency crews who truck out here each year to use the rocks as
the archetypal Western backdrop. These 45-degree angled
rocks (our fault line in action) will seem very familiar. Bad guys
jumped off them to hoodwink the good guys; Chevys and Fords
have been paraded in front of them. The stark rock landscape is
best visited during the cool months since there is very little
shade here. The park is named for early California bandit
Tiburcio Vasquez, who used the rocks as his between-robberies
hideout.

William S. Hart County Park. Cowboy star William S. Hart
took his movie money and bought a large tract of land in the
Santa Clarita Valley, which, in those days, was far in the country. Hart has long since died, civilization (in the guise of housing tracts and shopping malls) has surrounded the area, but 253
acres remain a bucolic and very Western preserve. The park
has nice flat lawns for picnics and games. Up the hill, Hart's
home has been kept just as it was when he lived here in the
1920s. Docents lead tours through the exquisite Spanish Revival–style rooms, filled with priceless Russells and
Remingtons, Navajo rugs, and cowboy relics. *24151 Newhall
Ave., Newhall, tel. 805/259–0855. House open Wed.– Fri. 10–
12:30 and weekends 11–3:30 with tours every half hour.*

Will Rogers State Historic Park. *See* Santa Monica, Venice, Pacific Palisades, and Malibu above.

Other Places of Interest

Scattered across Los Angeles County are attractions that don't
fit neatly into any organized drive or walk. Some are major
sites such as Dodger Stadium. Others are quirky places, such

as the Pig Murals in Vernon. If Los Angeles is anything, it's a something-for-everybody city.

Dodger Stadium. The stadium has been home of the Los Angeles Dodgers since 1961, when Chavez Ravine was chosen as the site of the newly-arrived-from-Brooklyn team's home base. The stadium seats 56,000 and parking is fairly easy. *1000 Elysian Park Ave., tel. 213/224-1400, accessible from the Pasadena Freeway just north of downtown Los Angeles. No tours, open only during games.*

El Mercado. Olvera Street may draw both Mexican and gringo customers, but El Mercado in East Los Angeles, the heart of the Mexican barrio, is the real thing. This huge, three-story marketplace is as close as a north-of-the-border market gets to places like Libertadad in Guadalajara. There are trinkets (piñatas and soft-clay pottery) to buy here, but the real draw is the authentic foods and mariachi music. The mid-level food shops offer hot tortillas, Mexican herbs, sauces, and cheeses. Upstairs is where the action is, especially on weekends when several local mariachi bands stake out corners of the floor and entertain—all at the same time. You'll either love it or hate it. The food on the top floor is only so-so, but the feeling of Old Mexico is palpable. *3425 First St., East Los Angeles, tel. 213/ 268-3451. Open daily 9-9, later on weekends.*

Exposition Park (Figueroa St. at Exposition Blvd., Los Angeles). This beautiful park was the site of the 1932 Olympics and the impressive architecture still stands. Adjoining the University of Southern California, Exposition Park is the location of two major museums: the California Museum of Science and Industry and the Natural History Museum (*see* Museums, above). Also included in the 114-acre park is the Los Angeles Swimming Stadium (home of Los Angeles aquatic competitions), which is open to the public in summer, and the Memorial Coliseum, the site of college football games. There are plenty of picnic areas on the grounds as well as a sunken rose garden.

Forest Lawn Memorial Park. This 300-acre formally landscaped area features a major collection of marble statuary and art treasures, including a replica of Leonardo da Vinci's "The Last Supper" done entirely in stained glass. In the Hall of the Crucifixion–Resurrection is one of the world's largest oil paintings incorporating a religious theme, "The Crucifixion" by artist Jan Styka. The picturesque grounds are perfect for a leisurely walk. Forest Lawn was the model for the setting of Evelyn Waugh's novel *The Loved One.* Many celebrities are buried here, some more flamboyantly than others. Silent-screen cowboy star Tom Mix is said to be buried in his good-guy clothes: white coat, white pants, and a belt buckle with his name spelled out in diamonds. Markers for Walt Disney and Errol Flynn are near the Freedom Mausoleum. Inside the mausoleum are the wall crypts of Nat King Cole, Clara Bow, Gracie Allen, and Alan Ladd. Clark Gable, Carole Lombard, Theda Bara, and Jean Harlow are among the luminaries buried in the Great Mausoleum. *1712 S. Glendale Ave., Glendale, tel. 213/ 254-3131. Open daily 8-5.*

Forest Lawn Memorial Park–Hollywood Hills. Just west of Griffith Park on the north slope of the Hollywood Hills, this 340-acre sister park to Forest Lawn Glendale is dedicated to the ideal of American liberty. Featured are bronze and marble statuary, including Thomas Ball's 60-foot Washington Memorial and a replica of the Liberty Bell. There are also reproductions of Boston's Old North Church and Longfellow's Church of the Hills. The film *The Many Voices of Freedom* is shown daily and Revolutionary War documents are on permanent display. Among the famous people buried here are Buster Keaton, Stan Laurel, Liberace, Charles Laughton, and Freddie Prinze. *6300 Forest Lawn Dr., Hollywood, tel. 213/254-7251. Open daily 8-5.*

Gene Autry Western Heritage Museum. The American West, both the movie and real-life versions, is celebrated via memorabilia, artifacts, and art in a structure that draws on Spanish mission and early Western architecture. The collection includes Teddy Roosevelt's Colt revolver, Buffalo Bill Cody's saddle, and Annie Oakley's gold-plated Smith and Wesson guns, alongside video screens showing clips from old Westerns. *4700 Zoo Dr., Los Angeles, tel. 213/667-2000. Admission $4.75 adults, $3.50 senior citizens, $2 children 2-12. Open Tues.-Sun. 10-5.*

Griffith Park Observatory and Planetarium. Located on the south side of Mount Hollywood in the heart of Griffith Park, the planetarium offers dazzling daily shows that duplicate the starry sky. A guide narrates the show and points out constellations. One of the largest telescopes in the world is open to the public for free viewing every clear night. Exhibits display models of the planets with photographs from satellites and spacecraft. A Laserium show is featured nightly, and other special astronomy shows are offered frequently. The Observatory sits high above Los Angeles and from the outside decks and walkways offers a spectacular view of the city, very popular on warm evenings. *Griffith Park, tel. 213/664-1191. Enter at the Los Feliz Blvd. and Vermont Ave. entrance. Hall of Science and telescope are free. Planetarium shows: $3 adults, $1.50 children. Laserium show: $6 adults, $5 children. Call for schedule. Open Tues.-Fri. 2-10, weekends 12:30-10.*

Hollyhock House. Frank Lloyd Wright designed a number of homes in the Los Angeles area. Hollyhock House was his first, built in 1921 and commissioned by heiress Aline Barnsdall. It was done in the pre-Columbian style Wright was fond of at that time. As a unifying theme, he used a stylized hollyhock flower, which appears in a broad band around the exterior of the house and even on the dining room chairs. Now owned by the city, as is Barnsdall Park, where it is located, Hollyhock House has been restored and furnished with original furniture designed by Wright and reproductions. His furniture may not be the comfiest in the world, but it sure looks perfect in his homes. *4800 Hollywood Blvd., Hollywood, tel. 213/662-7272. Admission: $1.50 adults, children free. Tours conducted Tues.-Thurs. at 10, 11, noon, and 1; Sat. and the 1st, 2nd, and 3rd Sun. of the month at noon, 1, 2, and 3.*

Mulholland Drive. One of the most famous streets in Los Angeles, Mulholland makes its very windy way from the Hollywood Hills across the spine of the Santa Monica Mountains west almost to the Pacific Ocean. Driving its length is slow, but the reward is sensational views of the city, the San Fernando Valley, and the expensive homes along the way. For a quick shot, take Benedict Canyon north from Sunset Boulevard, just west of the

Beverly Hills Hotel, all the way to the top and turn right at the crest, which is Mulholland. There's a turnout within a few feet of the intersection, and at night, the view of the valley side is incredible.

University of Southern California (USC). Called simply "SC" by the locals, this school is the oldest major private university on the West Coast. The pleasant campus is home to close to 30,000 students and has 191 buildings. The campus is often used as a backdrop for television shows and movies. Two of the more notable buildings are the Romanesque Doheny Memorial Library and Widney Hall, the oldest building on campus, a two-story clapboard dated 1880. The Mudd Memorial Hall of Philosophy contains a collection of rare books from the 13th through 15th centuries. *Bounded by Figueroa, Jefferson, Exposition, and Vermont, and adjacent to Exposition Park, tel. 213/743–2983. Free 1-hr campus tours, weekdays 10–2. Reservations required.*

Watts Towers (1765 E. 107th St.). This is the folk-art legacy of an Italian immigrant tile-setter, Simon Rodia, and one of the great folk structures in the world. From 1920 until 1945, without helpers, this eccentric and driven man erected three cement towers, using pipes, bed frames, and anything else he could find, and embellished them with bits of colored glass, broken pottery, sea shells, and assorted discards. The tallest tower is 107 feet. Plans are under way to stabilize and protect this unique monument, often compared to the 20th-century architectural wonders created by Barcelona's Antonio Gaudi. Well worth a pilgrimage for art and architecture buffs (or anyone else, for that matter).

4 Shopping

by Jane E. Lasky   Most Los Angeles shops are open from 10 to 6 although many remain open until 9 or later, particularly at the shopping centers, on Melrose Avenue, and in Westwood Village during the summer. Melrose shops, on the whole, don't get moving until 11 AM but are often open on Sundays, too. At most stores around town, credit cards are almost universally accepted and traveler's checks are also often allowed with proper identification. If you're looking for sales, check the Los Angeles *Times*.

Shopping Districts

When asked where they want to shop, visitors to Los Angeles inevitably answer, "Rodeo Drive." This famous thoroughfare is not only high-high-end—and therefore, somewhat limited—it is also only one of many shopping streets Los Angeles has to offer. Visitors should also consider other shopping districts within this huge metropolitan area. Remember that distances between each can be vast, so don't choose too many different stops in one day. If you do, you'll spend more time driving than shopping.

Downtown   Although downtown Los Angeles has many enclaves to explore, we suggest that the bargain hunter head straight for the **Cooper Building** (860 S. Los Angeles St., tel. 213/622–1139). Eight floors of small clothing and shoe shops (mostly for women) offer some of the most fantastic discounts in the city. Grab a free map in the lobby, and seek out as many of the 82 shops as you can handle. Nearby are myriad discount outlets selling everything from shoes to suits to linens.

Near the Hilton Hotel, **Seventh Street Marketplace** (tel. 213/955–7150) was erected in 1986 and is worth a visit. It's an indoor/outdoor multilevel shopping center with an extensive courtyard that boasts many busy cafes and lively music. The stores surrounding this courtyard include **G.B. Harb** (tel. 213/629–5051), a fine menswear shop, and **Bullocks** (tel. 213/624–9494), a small version of the big department store geared to the businessperson.

Melrose Avenue   West Hollywood, especially Melrose Avenue, is where young shoppers should try their luck, as should those who appreciate vintage styles in clothing and furnishings. The 1½ miles of intriguing, one-of-a-kind shops and bistros stretch from La Brea to a few blocks west of Crescent Heights; it is definitely one of Los Angeles's hottest shopping areas. A sampling of the stores that operate there:

Art Deco L.A. Antiques (7300 Melrose Ave., tel. 213/936–9860) is full of lacquered furniture, porcelain radios, neon clocks, and jukeboxes.
Betsey Johnson (7311 Melrose Ave., tel. 213/931–4490) offers the designer's vivid, hip women's fashions. Watch for twice-yearly sales.
Cottura (7215 Melrose Ave., tel. 213/933–1928) offers Italian ceramics.
Ecru (7428 Melrose Ave., tel. 213/653–8761) displays elemental men's and women's shoes and finely designed clothing, including couture lines by Ana Salazar, John Galliano, and Uomo, in a worthy architectural space.
Emphasis (7361 Melrose Ave., tel. 213/653–7174) offers a pristine collection of fashion-foward clothes for women, including hats, belts, accessories, and a selection of unique lingerie.

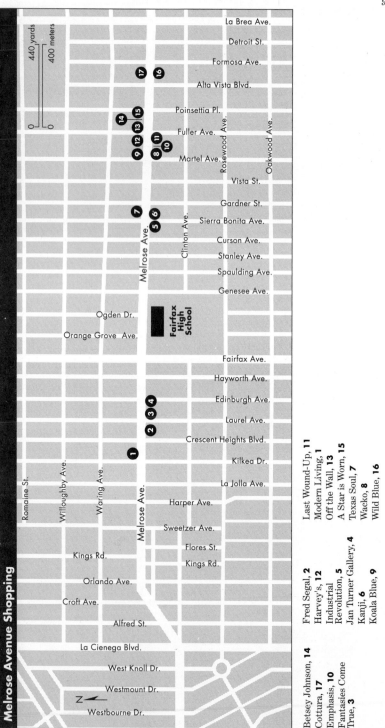

Melrose Avenue Shopping

La Brea Ave.
Detroit St.
Formosa Ave.
Alta Vista Blvd.
Poinsettia Pl.
Fuller Ave.
Martel Ave.
Rosewood Ave.
Oakwood Ave.
Vista St.
Gardner St.
Sierra Bonita Ave.
Clinton Ave.
Curson Ave.
Stanley Ave.
Spaulding Ave.
Genesee Ave.

Melrose Ave.

Ogden Dr.
Orange Grove Ave.

Fairfax High School

Fairfax Ave.
Hayworth Ave.
Edinburgh Ave.
Laurel Ave.
Crescent Heights Blvd.
Kilkea Dr.
La Jolla Ave.
Harper Ave.
Sweetzer Ave.
Flores St.
Kings Rd.

Romaine St.
Willoughby Ave.
Waring Ave.

Melrose Ave.

Kings Rd.
Orlando Ave.
Croft Ave.
Alfred St.
La Cienega Blvd.
West Knoll Dr.
Westmount Dr.
Westbourne Dr.

N

440 yards
400 meters

Betsey Johnson, **14**
Cottura, **17**
Emphasis, **10**
Fantasies Come
True, **3**

Fred Segal, **2**
Harvey's, **12**
Industrial
Revolution, **5**
Jan Turner Gallery, **4**
Kanji, **6**
Koala Blue, **9**

Last Wound-Up, **11**
Modern Living, **1**
Off the Wall, **13**
A Star is Worm, **15**
Texas Soul, **7**
Wacko, **8**
Wild Blue, **16**

Fantasies Come True (8012 Melrose Ave., tel. 213/655–2636) greets you with "When You Wish Upon A Star" playing from a tape deck. The store, needless to say, is packed with Walt Disney memorabilia.

Fred Segal (8118 Melrose Ave., tel. 213/651–1935) has a collection of shops providing stylish clothing for men and women. Among the designers and manufacturers they carry: Nancy Heller, New Man, Ralph Lauren, Calvin Klein. Children's clothing, accessories, and shoes—an impressive array—are also stocked at the Melrose store.

Harvey's (7367 Melrose Ave., tel. 213/852–1271) has everything from Victorian through 1950s-era designer pieces but specializes in the latter. Rattan is in one room, Art Deco furniture in the other.

Industrial Revolution (7560 Melrose Ave., tel. 213/651–2893) has high-tech furniture and furnishings.

Kanji (7547 Melrose Ave., tel. 213/655–7244) carries an alluring mixture of conservative fashions and clothing with flair. You'll find European-style dresses, pants, and suits.

Koala Blue (7366 Melrose Ave., tel. 213/655–3596) is Australian singer Olivia Newton-John's shop, filled with goodies from her homeland.

The Last Wound-Up (7374 Melrose Ave., tel. 213/653–6703) has an impressive collection of wind-up toys and music boxes.

Modern Living (8125 Melrose Ave., tel. 213/655–3898) is a gallery of 20th-century design, representing renowned international furniture designers, including Phillippe Starck, Ettore Sottsass, and Massino Isosaghini.

Off The Wall (7325 Melrose Ave., tel. 213/930–1185) specializes in "antiques and weird stuff."

A Star Is Worn (7303 Melrose Ave., tel. 213/939–4922) sells secondhand clothing once worn by celebrities.

Texas Soul (7515 Melrose Ave., tel. 213/658–5571) is the place for western wear.

Wacko (7416 Melrose Ave., tel. 213/651–3811) is a wild space crammed with all manner of blow-up toys, cards, and other semiuseless items that make good Los Angeles keepsakes.

Wild Blue (7220 Melrose Ave., tel. 213/939–8434) is a fine shop/gallery specializing in functional and wearable art.

Larchmont One of L.A.'s most picturesque streets is Larchmont Boulevard, adjacent to the expensive residential neighborhood of Hancock Park. New stores that have made Larchmont Village worth a detour include **Hollyhock** (214 N. Larchmont Blvd., tel. 213/931–3400), for exceptional new and antique furnishings; and **Robert Grounds** (121 N. Larchmont Blvd., tel. 213/464–8304), for distinctive gifts and antiques. Farther up the boulevard are: **Lavender & Lace** (656 N. Larchmont Blvd., tel. 213/856–4846), specializing in antique textiles, linens, and English pine furniture and **The Hat Gallery** (just around the corner, at 5632 Melrose Ave., tel. 213/463–3163), offering the exceptional creations of owner Elizabeth Marcel.

Westwood Westwood Village, near the UCLA campus, is a young and lively area for shopping. The atmosphere is invigorating, especially during summer evenings when there's a movie line around every corner, all kinds of people strolling the streets (an unusual phenomenon in L.A. where few of us ever walk anywhere), and cars cruising along to take in the scene. Among the shops worth scouting out in this part of the city:

Aah's (1087 Broxton, tel. 213/824–1688) is good for stationery and fun gift items.

Chanin's (1030 Westwood Blvd., tel. 213/208–4500), with the best in casual wear, undoubtedly reflects the UCLA influence in the youthful and fun fashions sold here.

Copelands Sports (1001 Westwood Blvd., tel. 213/208–6444) offers cornucopia of sportswear, beachwear, shoes, and shorts, along with a variety of skiing, camping, and other outdoor equipment.

Jazz'd (1069 Broxton, tel. 213/208–7950) sports work-out attire.

Morgan and Company (1131 Glendon, tel. 213/208–3377) is recommended for California jewelry.

Shanes Jewelers (1015 Broxton, tel. 213/208–8404) is a youth-oriented jewelry store specializing in earrings, engagement rings, chains, and watches. There is a good repair department.

The Wilger Company (10924 Weyburn, tel. 213/208–4321) offers fine men's clothing.

Z Gallery (1138 Westwood Blvd., tel. 213/824–2383) sells high-tech furniture and furnishings, including contemporary posters and lithographs.

The Beverly Center and Environs Mall shopping is so important in Los Angeles that it is actually a sociological phenomenon. The **Beverly Center** (tel. 213/854–0070), bound by Beverly Boulevard, La Cienega Boulevard, San Vicente Boulevard, and Third Street, covers more than seven acres and contains some 200 stores. Since its opening in spring 1982, the mall has continually catered to an upscale market. Many French designers—Daniel Hechter, Rodier, and others—have opened retail outlets here, as have unusual American shops. Examples are **By Design** and **Conran's,** for home furnishings and furniture; **By Oliver,** for fashionable women's clothes; **Alexio,** for fashionable men's clothes; and two stores called **Traffic** for contemporary clothing for both genders.

The shopping center is anchored by the Broadway department store on one end, and Bullocks on the other. Inside, there are also some interesting restaurants (like the Kisho-an, a Japanese restaurant known for its fine sushi, and The Hard Rock Cafe, known for its bargain cuisine and fascinating decor, including a 1959 Caddy that dives into the roof of the building above the restaurant) and one of Los Angeles's finest cineplexes with 14 individual movie theaters.

It's worthwhile to venture outside the confines of the Beverly Center to discover some very interesting shops. For instance:

Esprit (841 Santa Monica Blvd., tel. 213/659–9797) is a high-styled shop that was once a roller disco. Customers at this sporting clothing outlet use grocery carts to push purchases through the store.

Freehand (8413 W. Third St., tel. 213/655–2607) is a gallery shop featuring contemporary American crafts, clothing, and jewelry, mostly by California artists.

Maxfield (8825 Melrose Ave., tel. 213/274–8800) is among the most elite clothing stores in L.A. Designers carried here include Azzedine Alaia, Comme des Garçons, Maud Frizon, Issey Miyake, Giorgio Armani, Byblos, Missoni. The store also houses Yohiji Yamamoto's only L.A. boutique. Maxfield is the supplier of choice for sundry celebrities as well as the wardrobe people responsible for dressing the more fashionable shows on television.

The **Pacific Design Center** (corner of Melrose Ave. and San Vicente Blvd., tel. 213/657–0800) is where leading interior designers find the best in home furnishings and accessories for clients who aim to impress. Set in two startlingly big colored-glass buildings—known to locals as the Blue Whale and the Green Giant—the PDC's exclusive showrooms sell only to the trade. If you would like to do more than look here, contact LA Design Concepts, an interior-design shopping service (8811 Alden Dr., tel. 213/276–2109). A design professional will guide you through the PDC for $15 an hour, offer advice, and order items for you at less than half the standard industry markup of 33%.

Trashy Lingerie (402 N. La Cienega, tel. 213/652–4543) is just what the name suggests. This is a place for the daring; models try on the sexy garments to help customers decide what to buy.

Century City **Century City Shopping Center & Marketplace** (tel. 213/277–3898) is set among gleaming steel office buildings. Here, in the center of a thriving business atmosphere, is a city kind of mall—open-air. Besides the Broadway and Bullocks, both department stores, you'll find **Sasha of London** for trendy shoes and bags; **Ann Taylor** for stylish but not outlandish clothing and Joan & David shoes; and **The Pottery Barn** for contemporary furnishings at comfortable prices. **Heaven** is a whimsical boutique with fun and funky T-shirts, ashtrays, and other weird things. **Go Sport** is a gigantic European sporting goods store. **Brentano's** is one of the city's largest bookstores. You'll find California wines, a great gift to take home, at **Gelson's,** a gourmet food market.

Besides dozens of stores, there are five restaurants on the premises—which, incidentally, used to be Twentieth Century Fox Film Studios' backlot. Among them are Langan's Brasserie, the offspring of a famous London dining spot, and Stage Deli, the kind of New York–style deli that previously was hard to find in L.A. Also at Century City is the AMC Century 14 Theater Complex, which opened in 1987.

West Los Angeles The **Westside Pavilion** (tel. 213/474–6255) is a pastel-colored postmodern mall on Pico and Overland boulevards. The two levels of shops and restaurants run the gamut from high-fashion boutiques for men and women to a store devoted solely to travelers' needs, large and small. Among them are **Muppet and Stuff,** filled with novelties commemorating the television show; **The May Company** and **Nordstrom,** two full-scale department stores; **Mr Gs for Kids,** a good place for children's gifts; **The Cashmere People,** filled with fine woolens; and **Victoria's Secret,** a lingerie boutique.

Santa Monica Another worthwhile and multifaceted area, farther west and next to the ocean, offers both malls and street shopping.

Santa Monica Place Mall (315 Broadway, tel. 213/394–5451) is a three-story enclosed mall that's nothing special. Some of the stores inside are **Splash Wear,** selling super bathing suits; **Karl Logan,** for special men's and women's classic clothes; **Devon Becke,** for upscale fashions; **Aprons,** for soaps and scents; and **Wherehouse Records,** for the latest tunes.

Next door, **Santa Monica Promenade** (tel. 213/393–8355) is an open-air arena of shops with pedestrian walkways and a landscaped island. A light, airy atrium views all three floors of the mall at once, and from particular points you can see the Pacific in the background. Robinson's and The Broadway are department stores in this complex.

Montana Avenue is a stretch of a dozen blocks that has evolved into an L.A. version of New York City's Columbus Avenue. Boutique after boutique of quality goods can be found along Montana from Seventh to Seventeenth streets. Among them:

A.B.S. Clothing (1533 Montana Ave., tel. 213/393–8770) sells contemporary sportswear designed in Los Angeles.
Brenda Himmel (1126 Montana, tel. 213/395–2437) offers fine stationery and gifts.
Jona (1325 Montana, tel. 213/458–0071) is a personalized women's clothing store for those who like help in choosing a wardrobe.
Lisa Norman Lingerie (1134 Montana, tel. 213/451–2026) sells high-quality lingerie from Europe and the United States—slips, camisoles, robes, silk stockings, and at-home clothes.
Seventh Heaven (710 Montana, tel. 213/451–0077) is a gourmet deli for California products.
Weathervane II (1209 Montana, tel. 213/393–5344) is one of the street's larger shops, with a friendly staff which makes browsing among the classic and offbeat fashions more fun.

The stretch of **Main Street** leading from Santa Monica to Venice (Pico Blvd. to Rose Ave.) makes for a pleasant walk, with a collection of quite good restaurants, unusual shops and galleries, and an ever-present ocean breeze.

San Fernando and San Gabriel Valleys The San Fernando Valley is a great place to shop, but it is important to get your bearings and directions straight before you set out, as this is a sprawling area. "The Valley" refers to the San Fernando Valley, which is north of Los Angeles, but there's a lot more "out there." East of Los Angeles is the San Gabriel Valley and nearby are Pasadena, Glendale, and dozens of other communities.

This is mall country; among the many are **Sherman Oaks Galleria** (tel. 818/783–2547), **Woodland Hills Promenade** (tel. 818/884–7090), **Glendale Galleria** (tel. 818/246–2401), and **Town and Country Shopping Center** and **Plaza de Oro** in Encino (tel. 818/788–6100).

Aside from shopping centers, this area includes hundreds of places to shop. Some stand out, particularly in the Valley, along sections of Ventura Boulevard, which runs through Universal City, Sherman Oaks, Topanga, and Calabasas. Among the top shops:

Dazzles (13805 Ventura Blvd., Sherman Oaks, tel. 818/990–5488) is an Art Deco store dominated by a pristine jewelry collection and some furniture and furnishings, like frames and ashtrays that look like airplanes.
Jona (12532 Ventura Blvd., Sherman Oaks, tel. 818/762–5662) is a wardrobe/consultation service and store rolled into one. The store's buyer has impeccable taste in his choice of women's clothing.
Sharper Image (14559 Ventura Blvd., Sherman Oaks, tel. 818/907–1557) has unique high-tech gift items.
The Shoe & Clothing Connections (17404 Ventura Blvd., Encino, tel. 818/784–2810), a two-level shop packed with the

latest women's fashions and shoes, some with the store's own label, offers lots of interesting leather outfits.

Beverly Hills We've saved the most famous section of town for last. **Rodeo Drive** is often compared to famous streets such as Fifth Avenue in New York and the Via Condotti in Rome. Along the several blocks between Wilshire and Santa Monica boulevards, you'll find an abundance of big-name retailers—but don't shop Beverly Hills without shopping the streets that surround illustrious Rodeo Drive. There are plenty of treasures to be purchased on those other thoroughfares as well.

Some of the many shops, boutiques, and department stores in Beverly Hills:

Fashions and Home Decor **Polo/Ralph Lauren** (444 N. Rodeo Dr., tel. 213/281–7200), an instant smash hit when it opened last year, serves up a complete presentation of Lauren's all-encompassing lifestyle philosophy. The men's area, reminiscent of a posh British men's club, offers roughwear and activewear. Some 200 antiques are used as a backdrop for the women's area. Upstairs resides the most extensive selection of Lauren's home-furnishing designs in the world.

Women's Fashions **Alan Austin and Company** (9533 Brighton Way, tel. 213/275–1162) has traditional clothing in a wide selection of fabrics and colors. The store manufactures its own designs, so clothing can be made to order.

Ann Taylor (357 N. Camden Dr., tel. 213/858–7840) is the flagship shop of this chain of women's clothing stores, offering the epitome of the young executive look, and a good selection of casual clothing and Joan & David shoes as well.

Celine (460 N. Rodeo Dr., tel. 213/273–1243) is for luggage, shoes, and accessories as well as traditionally tailored clothing made of fine fabrics. Expect Old World craftsmanship and classic designs.

Fred Hayman (273 N. Rodeo Dr., tel. 213/271–3000). At this illustrious store, one does not merely shop for glitzy American and European clothing, accessories, and footwear; one also refreshes oneself at the stunning Oak Bar that separates the women's from the men's clothes.

Jaeger International Shop (19699 Wilshire Blvd., tel. 213/276–1062) is one of Britain's best-known clothiers, with a complete line of cashmere and woolen separates available in traditionally designed fashions.

Theodore (453 N. Rodeo Dr., tel. 213/276–9691) offers trendy items in fabulous fabrics for men and women from Kenzo, Sonia Rykiel, and Claude Montana. Everything is done with a real eye for color.

Torie Steele boutiques (414 N. Rodeo Dr., tel. 213/271–5150) is a collection of six designers, including Valentino, Fendi, Maud Frizon, Luciano Soprani, and Krizia. Artisans were flown in from Europe to paint the stone-textured trompe l'oeil facade.

Men's Fashions **Alfred Dunhill of London** (201 N. Rodeo Dr., tel. 213/274–5351) is an elegant shop selling British-made suits, shirts, sweaters, and slacks. Pipes, tobacco, and cigars, however, are this store's claim to fame.

Battaglia (306 N. Rodeo Dr., tel. 213/276–7184) features accessories, shoes, and men's apparel—the richest Italian fashions in luxurious silks, woolens, cottons, and cashmeres.

Bernini (362 N. Rodeo Dr., tel. 213/278–6287) specializes in

Beverly Hills Shopping

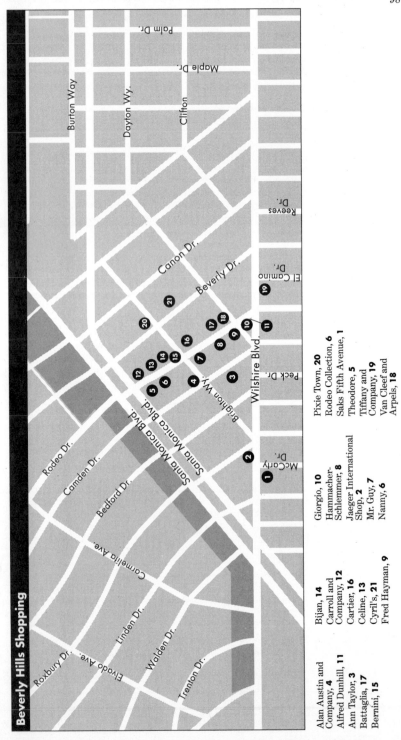

Alan Austin and
Company, **4**
Alfred Dunhill, **11**
Ann Taylor, **3**
Battaglia, **17**
Bernini, **15**

Bijan, **14**
Carroll and
Company, **12**
Cartier, **16**
Celine, **13**
Cyril's, **21**
Fred Hayman, **9**

Giorgio, **10**
Hammacher-
Schlemmer, **8**
Jaeger International
Shop, **2**
Mr. Guy, **7**
Nanny, **6**

Pixie Town, **20**
Rodeo Collection, **6**
Saks Fifth Avenue, **1**
Theodore, **5**
Tiffany and
Company, **19**
Van Cleef and
Arpels, **18**

contemporary Italian designer fashions. Look for fine leather accessories from Zilli.

Bijan (420 N. Rodeo Dr., tel. 213/273–6544) is a store where you shop by appointment only. Bijan claims that many Arabian sheiks and other royalty shop here, along with some of the wealthiest men in the United States. Many designs are created especially by the owner.

Carroll and Co. (466 N. Rodeo Dr., tel. 213/273–9060) is a conservative man's shop that's been in business for nearly a decade. It's known for quality, service, and its professional and celebrity clientele.

Cyril's (370 N. Beverly Dr., tel. 213/278–1330) features fine clothing in the latest European styles and carries labels like Valentino, Cerruti, and Michel Axel.

Mr. Guy (301 N. Canon Dr., tel. 213/275–4143) offers all the needs of the well-dressed man under one roof.

Children's Fashions **Nanny** (421 N. Rodeo Dr., tel. 213/276–6422) sells beautiful one-of-a-kind children's clothing and shoes imported from France, Greece, and Italy for infants up to size 14. It's good for nursery furnishings, shower gifts, and toys to take home to the little ones.

Pixie Town (400 N. Beverly Dr., tel. 213/272–6415) has everything from baby clothes and accessories to impeccably designed clothing for boys and girls.

Jewelry **Cartier** (370 N. Rodeo Dr., tel. 213/275–4272) offers all manner of gifts and jewelry bearing the double-C logo.

Tiffany and Company (9502 Wilshire Blvd., tel. 213/273–8880), in the Beverly Wilshire Hotel, needs no introduction. This store is a bit smaller than one might expect but every jewelry and gift purchase will still be packaged in the famous blue Tiffany box.

Van Cleef and Arpels (300 N. Rodeo Dr., tel. 213/276–1161) sells expensive baubles and fine jewelry.

Gifts **Hammacher-Schlemmer** (309 N. Rodeo Dr., tel. 213/859–7255) is a fabulous place to unearth those hard-to-find presents for adults who never grew up. For $25,000, the store will even sell you a submarine.

Even Beverly Hills has a shopping center, though owners wouldn't dare call their collection of stores and cafes a mall. It's the **Rodeo Collection** (tel. 213/276–9600) located between Brighton Way and Santa Monica Boulevard, and it's the epitome of opulence and high fashion. Many famous European designers who have never had freestanding stores on the West Coast have opened their doors in this piazzalike area of marble and brass. Among them: Cerruti, a designer known in Europe for his own fabrics; Louis Vuitton, known throughout the world for fine luggage; Nina Ricci, with everything from accessories to evening gowns in a dramatic setting complete with crystal chandelier; Gianni Versace, trendsetting Italian designer represented here by one of his largest U.S. clothing collections; Fendi, for leather goods; and Pratesi, selling fine bed linens where a single sheet can be priced as high as $900.

Department Stores

The Broadway (The Beverly Center, 8500 Beverly Blvd., tel. 213/854–7200). This complete department store offers merchandise in the moderate price range, from cosmetics, to housewares, to linens, to clothing for men and women. There are stores throughout Los Angeles.

Buffums (Glendale at 145 S. Central Ave. in the Glendale Galleria, tel. 818/240–8600). These are conservative and not very impressive department stores carrying moderately priced goods of all descriptions.

Bullocks (3050 Wilshire Blvd., tel. 213/382–6161). More upscale than the Broadway, Bullocks carries an extensive collection of clothing for men and women as well as housewares and cosmetics. Stores are throughout Southern California, with the flagship store at the Beverly Center (8500 Beverly Blvd., tel. 213/854–6655).

I. Magnin (Wilshire District, 3050 Wilshire Blvd., tel. 213/382–6161). This large store with many designer labels for men and women and a good handbag and luggage department has stores throughout Southern California. The flagship store (I. Magnin Wilshire) is an Art Deco landmark.

The May Company (Downtown at 6067 Wilshire Blvd., tel. 213/938–4211). Modestly priced clothing and furniture without glitz or glitter are offered in these stores throughout Southern California.

Nordstrom (Westside Pavilion at 500 N. Pico Blvd., in West Los Angeles, tel. 213/470–6155). This Seattle-based department store infiltrated Southern California within the past decade and has brought with it a wide selection of clothing for men and women as well as a reputation for fine customer service, a huge shoe department, and the entertainment of popular music played on the store's grand piano.

Robinson's (9900 Wilshire Blvd., Beverly Hills, tel. 213/275–5464). This high-end department store has many women's selections, a few men's selections, a good housewares department, and stores throughout Southern California.

Saks Fifth Avenue (9600 Wilshire Blvd., Beverly Hills, tel. 213/275–4211). The Los Angeles version of this New York store isn't as impressive as the one you'll find next to St. Patrick's in Manhattan. Still, the buyers have good taste.

Specialty Shops

Antiques La Cienaga Boulevard, between Santa Monica Boulevard and Beverly Boulevard, is lined with antiques dealers selling everything from Chinese to French to Viennese collectibles.

Nearby lies L.A.'s poshest antiquarian niche: Melrose Place. **Rose Tarlow Antiques** (8454 Melrose Pl., 213/653–2122), **Licorne** (8432 Melrose Pl., tel. 213/852–4765), and **Le Lion et La Licorne** (8445 Melrose Ave., tel. 213/653–7470), operated by French emigres, sell fine 17th-century furnishings. **Panache** (8445 Melrose Ave., tel. 213/653–9436) provides an eclectic assortment of furniture and objects at the most reasonable prices in the area.

For more intrepid hunters, Western Avenue (between First and Second streets) offers some valuable finds in some very low-key shops, including: **French Kings Antiques** (135 S. Western Ave., tel. 213/383–4430) with furniture, bronzes, and clocks; **Used Stuff** (151 S. Western Ave., tel. 213/487–5336), for

English imported furniture; and **Antiques Etcetera** (153 S. Western Ave., tel. 213/487–5226), which resembles a jumble of estate and garage sales.

At **The Antique Guild** (8800 Venice Blvd., Los Angeles, tel. 213/838–3131), you'll find treasures from all over the world and a gigantic inventory in a warehouse-size space.

Books **Artworks** (170 S. La Brea, West Hollywood, tel. 213/934–2205). All manner of art and photography books are stocked in this tiny space that shares a building with several art galleries and a terrific little cafe.

The Bodhi Tree (8585 Melrose, West Hollywood, tel. 213/659–1733). If the metaphysical is of interest, this is the place to learn about it.

Book Soup (8818 Sunset, West Hollywood, tel. 213/659–3110). This Sunset Strip shop stocks a wide variety of volumes, with particularly strong photography, film, new fiction, and international magazines sections.

Children's Clothing **Splash** (12109 Ventura Blvd., Studio City, tel. 818/762–6123). Shop here if you like to dress your child (newborn to toddler) in the latest fashions.

Gifts and Crafts **Del Mano Gallery** (11981 San Vicente Blvd., Brentwood, tel. 213/476–8508). For a decade, owners Jan Peters and Ray Leier have been handling the work of contemporary artists. Del Mano stocks everything from hand-crafted handbags to glass and ceramic treasures.

Tesoro (319 S. Robertson, tel. 213/273–9890) is a large boutique that stocks everything from trendy Swid-Powell dishware to Southwestern blankets, ceramics, and art furniture. The wide-ranging work by area artists is well worth browsing.

Wilder Place (7975 ½ Melrose Ave., tel. 213/655–9072) is a cozy shop offering a carefully edited selection of handcrafted ceramics, pottery, cutlery, and small furniture.

Leather **North Beach Leather** (8500 Sunset, West Hollywood, tel. 213/652–3224). Here is a great selection of clothing made of leather and suede, for both men and women.

Musical Recordings **Aron's Record** (7725 Melrose, Los Angeles, tel. 213/653–8170). You'll find an extensive selection of old records, perhaps the largest on the West Coast, and low prices on new albums.

CD Bonzai (8250 W. 3rd St., Los Angeles, tel. 213/653–0800). This is an all-CD shop that's tiny but full of finds.

Second-hand Clothing **American Rag** (150 S. La Brea Ave., tel. 213/935–3154) offers inexpensive, downtown-chic clothes for men and women. Much of the stock is "previously owned," though some items are on the racks for the first time.

Charlie's (115 N. LaBrea, tel. 213/931–2486). This West Hollywood shop sells a cornucopia of '50s and '60s clothes, with a few choice furnishings as well. This place has vintage evening gowns in impeccable condition.

Toys **Imaginarium** (Century City Shopping Center, 10250 Santa Monica Blvd., tel. 213/785–0227). Children are encouraged to play in this store, known for toys that are both nonviolent and educational.

5 Sports and Fitness

Participant Sports

If you're looking for a good work-out, you've come to the right city. Los Angeles is one of the major sports capitals in the United States. Whether your game is basketball, golf, Laser Tag, or bowling, L.A. is a dream town for athletes. Not only does the near-perfect climate allow sports enthusiasts to play outdoors almost year-round, but during some seasons it's not impossible to be surfing in the morning and snow skiing in the afternoon . . . all in the same city!

While there are almost as many sports in Los Angeles as there are people, the following list is a compilation of the more popular activities. For any additional information on facilities closer to where you're staying or on other sports not listed, two agencies will gladly assist you: **City of Los Angeles Department of Recreation and Parks** (200 N. Main St., 13th fl., City Hall East, L.A. 90012, tel. 213/485–5515); **Los Angeles County Parks and Recreation Department** (433 S. Vermont Ave., L.A. 90020, tel. 213/738–2961).

Bicycling and Roller Skating

In the last few years, Los Angeles has made a concerted effort to upgrade existing bike paths, and to designate new lanes along many major boulevards for cyclists' use. Perhaps the most famous bike path in the city, and definitely the most beautiful, can be found on the beach. The path starts at Temescal Canyon, and works its way down to Redondo Beach. San Vicente Boulevard in Santa Monica has a nice wide lane next to the sidewalk for cyclists. The path continues for about a five-mile stretch. Balboa Park in the San Fernando Valley is another haven for two-wheelers. For more information about other bike trails in the city, contact the **L.A. Bicycle Club Association** (tel. 213/806–4646).

All of the cycling areas mentioned above are also excellent for roller skating, even though cyclists still have the right of way. Venice Beach is the skating capital of the city.

If you're looking to get off the streets, there are a number of skating rinks in L.A. **Moonlight Skating Rink** (5110 San Fernando Rd., Glendale, tel. 818/241–3630) and **Skateland** (18140 Parthenia St., Northridge, tel. 818/885–1491) are two of the more popular rinks in the city.

Bowling

Bowling is seeing a resurgence in popularity. While there are a number of bowling alleys all over the city, a few are attracting the attention of the renaissance bowler. **Sports Center Bowl** (12655 Ventura Blvd. in the Valley, tel. 818/769–7600) has a special "Moonlight Madness" party every Friday night, midnight–3 AM. Nothing is "spared," as the lights are turned down and the stereo volume is turned up, making this a dangerously fun rock-and-roll blowout! For a different taste, **Little Tokyo Bowl** (333 S. Alameda Ave., in Little Tokyo, tel. 213/626–7376) is perhaps the most modern facility in the city. But what spices this place up is the sushi bar! For bowling alleys in your area, check the phone book.

Fishing

The best lakes for **freshwater fishing** in the L.A. area are Big Bear and Arrowhead. Rainbow trout, bass, and catfish are the typical catch, and the scenery in the mountains is anything but ordinary. Juniper Point on the north shore of Big Bear Lake is a favorite trout hangout. For fishing information in the area, call 714/866-5796.

If the fish stories are becoming more abundant than the fish on your plate, a sure catch can be found at **Trout Dale** (in Agoura, 3 mi south of the Ventura Frwy. on Kanan Rd., tel. 818/889-9993). Three picturesque ponds are set up for picnicking or "force" fishing. A $2 entry fee includes your license and pole, but there's an extra charge for each trout you push up onto the banks. Open Wed.–Sun. 10–5. **L.A. Harbor Sportfishing** (tel. 213/547-9916) offers whale-watching off Berth 79 at the San Pedro Harbor, as well as just plain fishing.

Saltwater fishing in L.A. offers the gamesman a number of different ways to enjoy the fresh catch of the Pacific. Shore fishing is excellent on many of the beaches (*see* Beaches, below). Pier fishing is another popular method of hooking your dinner. The Malibu, Santa Monica, and Redondo Beach piers each offer nearby bait-and-tackle shops, and you can generally pull in a healthy catch. If you want to break away from the piers, however, the **Malibu Pier Sport Fishing Company** (2300 Pacific Coast Hwy., tel. 213/456-8030) and the **Redondo Sport Fishing Company** (233 N. Harbor Dr., tel. 213/372-2111) have half-day and full-day charters. Half-day charters, 8 AM–1 PM, run about $16 per person, while a full day goes for about $45. You can rent a pole for $5.50. Sea bass, halibut, bonita, yellowtail, and barracuda are the usual catch.

For something with a little more bite, there are a number of fishing charters out of Marina Del Rey, like **The Widow Maker** (tel. 213/306-9793), that will take you hunting for thresher shark. Threshers are common in the Santa Monica Bay, and are equally as challenging and almost as big as marlin. Rates range from $360 to $480.

The most popular and most unique form of fishing in the L.A. area involves no hooks, bait, or poles. The great **grunion runs**, which take place March–August, are a spectacular natural phenomenon in which hundreds of thousands of small, silver fish wash up on Southern California beaches to spawn and lay their eggs in the sand. The Cabrillo Museum in San Pedro (tel. 213/548-7562) has entertaining and educational programs about grunion during most of the runs. In certain seasons, touching the grunion is prohibited, so it's advisable to check with the Fish and Game Department (tel. 213/590-5132) before going to see them wash ashore.

Golf

The L.A. Open and the famous Pebble Beach Tournament to the north have made California a popular state on the PGA tour. In addition, there are a number of public courses that will satisfy the most discerning amateur tastes. The Department of Parks and Recreation lists seven public 18-hole courses in Los Angeles. **Rancho Park Golf Course** (10460 W. Pico Blvd., tel.

213/838–7373) is one of the most heavily played links in the entire country. Rancho is a beautifully designed course with enough towering pines to make those who slice or hook want to forget they ever learned how to play golf. There's a two-story driving range, a nine-hole pitch'n'put (tel. 213/838–7561), a snack bar, and a pro shop where you can rent clubs.

Several good public courses are located in the San Fernando Valley. The **Balboa and Encino Golf Courses** are located right next to each other at 16821 Burbank Boulevard in Encino, tel. 818/995–1170. The **Woodley Golf Course** (6331 Woodley Ave. in Van Nuys, tel. 818/780–6886) is a carpenter's dream . . . flat as a board, and with no trees! During the summer months, the temperature in the Valley can get high enough to fry an egg on your putter, so be sure to bring lots of sunscreen and plenty of water. Down the road in Pacoima, you'll find little escape from the heat in the summer, but the **Hansen Dam Public Golf Course** (10400 Glen Oaks Blvd., tel. 818/899–2200) has a dining area that serves plenty of cold drinks, as well as a driving range where you can warm up. It's the only place in Pacoima where you can drink and "drive" without touching your car keys.

Perhaps the most concentrated area of golf courses in the city can be found in **Griffith Park.** Here you'll find two splendid 18-hole courses along with a challenging nine-hole course. **Harding Golf Course** and **Wilson Golf Course** (both on Crystal Springs Dr., tel. 213/663–2555) are located about a mile and a half inside the Griffith Park entrance at Riverside and Los Feliz. Peaceful bridle paths surround the outer fairways, as the San Gabriel Mountains make up the rest of the gallery in a scenic background. The nine-hole **Roosevelt Course** (tel. 213/665–2011) can be found by entering Griffith Park at the Hillhurst Street entrance.

Yet another course in the Griffith Park vicinity (where there usually is no wait) is the nine-hole **Los Feliz Pitch'n'Put** (3207 Los Feliz Blvd., tel. 213/663–7758). Other pitch'n'put courses in Los Angeles include **Holmby Hills** (601 Club View Dr., West L.A., tel. 213/276–1604) and **Penmar** (1233 Rose Ave., Venice, tel. 213/396–6228).

Miniature Golf For the super-amateur linkster, or just for the heck of it, you might want to jot down a few of the more spectacular miniature golf facilities in the L.A. area. **Malibu Castle Park** (4989 Sepulveda Blvd., Sepulveda, tel. 818/990–8100) is the San Fernando Valley's Cadillac of "mini" courses. **Topanga Golf** (6262 Topanga Canyon Blvd., Woodland Hills, tel. 818/999–0666) is yet another favorite place to putter around.

Health Clubs

Many movies, TV shows, and songs have depicted the L.A. body as some kind of mythological creature possessing the secret of the three *T*s: tanning, toning, and tightening! Well, those chiseled muscles don't just grow on you when you get off the plane at LAX . . . it involves hard work!

There are dozens of health-club chains in the city that offer monthly and yearly memberships. **Nautilus Plus** and **Holiday Spa Health Clubs** are the most popular chains. The Holiday Club located south of Hollywood Boulevard (1607 Gower St., tel. 213/461–0227) is the flagship operation. This place has everything, including racquetball courts, indoor running tracks, pools, men's and women's weight and aerobics rooms, and a juice bar. **Sports Club L.A.** (1835 Sepulveda Blvd., West L.A., tel. 213/473–1447) is a hot spot, attracting such diverse celebrities as James Woods, Magic Johnson, and Princess Stephanie of Monaco. Not only does the gym have valet parking, it also contains the newest technology in fitness equipment. This is the place to go if you're looking to get fit or just looking.

Probably the most famous body-pumping facility of this nature in the city is **Gold's Gym** (360 Hampton Dr., Venice, tel. 213/392–6004). This is where all the "incredible hulks" pump themselves into modern art. For $8 a day or $25 a week, several tons of weights and Nautilus machines can be at your disposal. **World's Gym** (in the Valley, 23210 Ventura Blvd., tel. 818/999–6753, and another at 812 Main St., Venice, tel. 213/399–9888) is another famous iron person's club.

Hotel Health Facilities A few hotels in the city also have health spas, and some are open to the public. The Century Plaza Hotel (in Beverly Hills, tel. 213/277–2000) also has weights, aerobics, and saunas. The spa is open to hotel guests only, at $15 per session. And if you're in town briefly on a lay over, the Marriott hotel at LAX (tel. 213/641–5700) has Universal weights, life cycles, a sauna, and an Olympic-size pool—all free to guests. *See* Lodging for other details on these hotels.

Hiking

What makes Los Angeles the hiker's paradise is a multitude of different land- and seascapes to explore. **Arrowhead, Big Bear,** many parts of the **Angeles National Forest,** and the **Angeles Crest** area have spectacular mountain hiking trails. Much of the terrain here is rugged, and if you're not familiar with these regions, it's advisable to contact the National Forest Service (tel. 818/790–1151) for information before you go.

Closer to the city, **Will Rogers State Park** off of Sunset Boulevard near Pacific Palisades, has a splendid nature trail that climbs from the polo fields up to the mountaintop where you can get a spectacular view of the ocean. Other parks in the L.A. area that also have hiking trails include **Brookside Park, Elysian Park,** and **Griffith Park.** For more information on the parks, *see* Parks and Gardens in Exploring Los Angeles.

In the Malibu area, **Leo Carillo Beach** and the top of **Corral Canyon** offer incredible rock formations and caves to be explored on foot. In the hills east of **Paradise Cove,** a horse trail winds back into the canyons along a stream for several miles, eventually winding up at a beautiful waterfall. *See* Beaches below.

For further information on these or any other hiking locations in Los Angeles, contact the **Sierra Club** (3550 W. 6th St., Suite 321, tel. 213/387–4287).

Horseback Riding

Although horseback riding in Los Angeles is extremely popular, stables that rent horses are becoming an endangered species. Of the survivors, **Bar "S" Stables** (1850 Riverside Dr., in Glendale, tel. 818/242–8443) will rent you a horse for $13 an hour. Riders who come here can take advantage of over 50 miles of beautiful trails in the Griffith Park area. **Sunset River Trails** (on Rush St., at the end of Peck Rd., in El Monte, tel. 818/444–2128) offers riders the nearby banks of the San Gabriel River to explore. **Los Angeles Equestrian Center** (480 Riverside Dr., Burbank, tel. 818/840–8401) rents pleasure horses—both English and Western—for riding along bridle paths throughout the Griffith Park hills. Horses cost $13 per hour. **Sunset Stables** (at the end of Beachwood Dr. in Hollywood, tel. 213/469–5450) offers a $25 "dinner cruise." Riders take a trail over the hill into Burbank at sunset where they park their horses and have a feast at a Mexican restaurant.

Jogging

Most true joggers don't care where they run, but if you've got the time to drive to a choice location to commence your leg-pumping exercises, here are a few suggestions: First of all, just about every local high school and college in the city has a track. Most are public and welcome runners, and the private schools usually don't give a hoot who jogs on their tracks between 5 AM and 8 AM. A popular scenic course for students and downtown workers can be found at Exposition Park. Circling the Coliseum and Sports Arena is a jogging/workout trail with pull-up bars, and other simple equipment spread out every several hundred yards. San Vicente Boulevard in Santa Monica has a wide grassy median that splits the street for several picturesque miles. Griffith Park offers several thousand acres of grassy hills for a course with more challenging terrain. Of course, the premium spot in Los Angeles for any kind of exercise can be found along any of the beaches.

Laser Tag

For an electrifying new sport, you might want to try the most technologically advanced game to hit this town since Pac Man! It's called Laser Tag. You've seen it in the toy stores, and now you can play it in a number of modern sport complexes popping up in the southland. The laser guns shoot a harmless light which, when it hits an opponent's laser detector, scores points for your team. Many companies have formed laser leagues, making this the new "corporate softball." **Photon** (9380 Warner Ave., Fountain Valley, tel. 714/968–2508) will supply you with your gun, helmet, and laser detector for $3.50 per game.

Racquetball and Handball

As with tennis, there are dozens of high schools and colleges all over town that have three-walled courts open to the public. The only catch is you have to wait until the weekend or until school's out.

For more serious players—or just for rainy days—there are several new indoor racquetball facilities throughout the city: **The Racquet Center,** located in the San Fernando Valley (10933 Ventura Blvd., tel. 818/760–2303) offers court time for $8–$12, depending on when you play. There's another Racquet Center in South Pasadena at 920 Lohman Lane (tel. 213/258–4178). The **John Wooden Center** on the UCLA campus has several spectacular glass-enclosed courts. These facilities are open to the public if you are sponsored by a student. Court time goes for $4 per hour. **YMCAs** throughout the city also have courts available based on hourly rates.

Tennis

And on the eighth day, God created the tennis court! At least, it seems that way when you drive around most L.A. neighborhoods. If you want to play tennis, you'll have no problem finding a court in this town—although you might have to wait a while when you get there. Many public parks have courts that require an hourly fee. **Lincoln Park** (Lincoln and Wilshire Blvd., Santa Monica), **Griffith Park** (Riverside and Los Feliz), and **Barrington Park** (Barrington just south of Sunset in L.A.), all have well-maintained courts with lights.

For less of a wait, and no fee at all, there are a number of local high schools and colleges that leave their court gates unlocked on the weekends. There are several nice courts on the campus of **USC** (off the Vermont St. entrance), a few on the campus of **Paul Revere Junior High School** (in Brentwood at Sunset and Mandeville Canyon Rd.), and a few more at **Palisades High School** (in Pacific Palisades on Temescal Canyon Rd.)—and that's only the tip of this iceberg!

For a full rundown of all the public tennis courts in Los Angeles, contact the L.A. Department of Recreation and Parks (tel. 213/485–5515) or the **Southern California Tennis Association** Los Angeles Tennis Center, UCLA Campus, (Box 240015, Los Angeles 90024, tel. 213/208–3838).

Hotels with Tennis Courts If you're just in town for a few days and you don't have time to drive around looking for a court, you may very well be staying at a hotel that has facilities. The Century Plaza in Beverly Hills (tel. 213/277–2000) has eight rooftop courts overlooking the city; the Sheraton Town House (2961 Wilshire Blvd., tel. 213/382–7171) has four courts; and downtown, the L.A. Bonaventure (tel. 213/624–1000) has eight courts for their guests. *See* Lodging for other details on these hotels.

Water Sports

When the surf's up in L.A., the Pacific coast becomes an amusement park for water sports. But the ocean isn't the only place where Southern Californians can get wet. Los Angeles is a mecca for aqua-sports enthusiasts, offering everything from crystal mountain-lake fishing to jet skiing in the Pacific.

Boating **Sailing** is still one of the most popular activities in Southern California, and you don't have to own a boat to be the captain of your own ship. **Rent-A-Sail** (13560 Mindanao Way, Marina Del Rey, tel. 213/822–1868) will rent you everything from canoes to power boats or 14–25-foot sailboats for anywhere from $14 to $34 per hour. No boating licenses are required, but if you've got your eye on one of the larger vessels, you must have prior sailing experience.

If you'd rather leave the driving to someone else, there are a number of spectacular sailing yachts that can be chartered for dinner cruises or weekend trips. **Charter Concepts** (4051 Glencoe, #7, tel. 213/823–2676) has a remarkable fleet of yachts ranging in size from 40 to 140 feet.

If you don't care what the boat looks like, and you just want to go for a ride, **Catalina Cruises** (in San Pedro, tel. 213/514–3838) will take you round-trip to the "island of romance" for about $25 per person, on L.A.'s version of the New York ferry boats (without the cars, garbage, or exhaust). Catalina Cruises also runs an extremely popular whale-watching excursion from December through the first week in April.

Paddleboats in **MacArthur Park** near downtown offer a less salty and more sedentary form of water navigation. For information about rentals, you can call the boathouse (tel. 213/387–6427).

Big Bear and **Lake Arrowhead** open up a whole different world of freshwater adventure for aqua athletes. Canoes, motor boats, and waterskiing equipment can be rented from a number of outfits in both towns. Big Bear even offers parasailing for those who'd rather be above it all. For information about both of these lakes and nearby rental facilities, contact the Big Bear Chamber of Commerce (tel. 714/866–4607).

Jet Skiing This is another booming sport in the southland. You'll find as many jet skiers on the lakes at Big Bear and Arrowhead as you will in Marina Del Rey. Jet skis are expensive to rent. Two of the more popular places that carry them are **Del Rey Jet Ski,** in Marina Del Rey (tel. 213/821–4507), and in the summer, a parking lot concession across the street from **Zuma Jay's** (22775 Pacific Coast Hwy., Malibu, tel. 213/456–8044), which rents machines for about $45 an hour.

Scuba Diving and Snorkeling Diving and snorkeling off Leo Carillo Beach, Catalina, and the Channel Islands is considered some of the best on the Pacific coast. Dive shops like **New England Divers** (4148 Viking Way, Long Beach, tel. 213/421–8939) and **Dive & Surf** (504 N. Broadway, Redondo Beach, tel. 213/372–8423) will provide you with everything you need for your voyage to the bottom of the sea. Snorkeling equipment runs $15–$20 per day, while full scuba gear for certified divers runs $35–$55 per day. Diving charters to Catalina and the Channel Islands as well as certification training can be arranged through these outfits.

Surfing The signature water sport in L.A. has got to be surfing . . . and rightfully so! Southern California beaches offer a wide variety of surfing venues, along with a number of places to rent boards. For a complete listing of the best surfing areas, *see* Beaches below.

Swimming Pools For a slightly slower pace, there are a number of conventional public swimming pools in the L.A. area. Right next to the L.A. Coliseum is perhaps the most famous of all the public pools still functioning. The **Exposition Park** pool was originally built and used for the 1932 summer Olympic Games. The huge grandstands still make this an ominous place for an afternoon dip. Another popular pool is **The Keyhole,** located in Glendale next to the Civic Auditorium on N. Glendale Avenue. This is a much more woodsy setting than the old Olympic pool, and there is a public park right next door. The **Griffith Park** pool at the intersection of Los Feliz and Riverside Drive is another favorite L.A. splash, as is the **Magnolia Park** public pool off the Hollywood Freeway at Magnolia Avenue in the San Fernando Valley.

Water Parks If playing Jacques Cousteau is a bit too sophisticated for your tastes, there's a new water-sport craze in the southland that's much simpler and yet equally as challenging. **Raging Waters** off I–210 in San Dimas (tel. 714/592–6453) is the aquatic version of Disneyland. Mammoth water slides, water swings, and inner-tube rapids designed to bump you, spin you, and throw you have made this "the" place to be on a hot day. Palm Springs has a water park similar to this called **Oasis** (tel. 619/325–7873).

Windsurfing "Hanging" ten has traditionally involved a surfer, a few toes, and a board; a recent addition to this classic sport is the sail. In fact, on a brisk day, you'll see as many windsurfers out on the waves as conventional surfers. Good windsurfing can be found all along the coast, and there are a number of places to rent equipment for certified windsurfers. **Wind Surfing West** (4047 Lincoln Blvd., Marina Del Rey, tel. 213/821–5501) will rent you a rig for $10 an hour, and $35 a day. For novices, a six-hour lesson with an instructor will run you about $75. Further north, contact **Natural Progression** (22935 Pacific Coast Hwy., Malibu, tel. 213/456–6302).

Winter Sports

Winter in Los Angeles means mild temperatures, and usually sunny skies. But there are parts of the city that offer some of the best snow skiing in the state! And whether or not you enjoy swooshing down the slopes or simply strolling through a peaceful winter wonderland, there are many snowy regions within minutes from downtown.

Cross-country Skiing If you're into cross-country skiing, **Idyllwild,** located above Palm Springs, offers excellent trails during most of the heavy-snow seasons. For information, call the Idyllwild Chamber of Commerce (tel. 714/659–3259).

Ice Skating Rinks are located all over the city. In the Valley, there's **Ice Capades Chalet Ice Arena** (6100 Laurel Canyon Blvd., North Hollywood, tel. 818/985–5555) and the **Pickwick Ice Arena** (1001 Riverside Dr., Burbank, tel. 818/846–0032). In Pasadena, try the **Ice Skating Center** (300 E. Green St., tel. 818/578–0800) and in Rolling Hills, try the **Ice Capades Chalet Ice Arena** (550 Deep Canyon Dr., tel. 213/541–6630).

Skiing Just north of Pasadena, in the San Gabriel Mountains, there are two ski areas perfect for day trips. **Mt. Waterman** (tel. 818/440–1041) and **Kratka Ridge** (tel. 818/449–1749) have a couple of lifts, and a range of slopes to satisfy both beginning and advanced skiers. Further east is **Mt. Baldy** (tel. 714/981–3344), located off I–10 at the top of Mountain Avenue. This is another good ski area for day trips.

Ski resorts with accommodations can be found within 90 minutes from Los Angeles proper. **Big Bear** is one of the most popular ski retreats on the West Coast. A full range of accommodations, several new ski lifts, night skiing, and the largest snow-making operation in California make this a great weekend getaway spot. For information about Big Bear ski conditions, hotels, and special events, contact the Tourist and Visitor's Bureau (tel. 714/866–4601) or the Chamber of Commerce (tel. 714/866–5652).

Other ski areas located in the general vicinity of Big Bear include **Snow Forest** (tel. 714/866–8891), **Goldmine** (tel. 714/585–2517), **Snow Valley** (tel. 714/867–5151), **Mountain High** (tel. 714/874–7050), and **Snow Summit** (tel. 714/866–4621). All of these areas also have snow-making capabilities, and many of them have lights for night skiing. Contact the phone numbers listed for directions, and for information about ski conditions.

Sledding   If you're just looking for an afternoon of local sledding and tobogganing, **Fraser Park,** located at the top of the Grapevine off I–5, has plenty of open hillsides.

Spectator Sports

If you enjoy watching professional sports, you'll never hunger for action in this town. Los Angeles is the home of some of the greatest franchises in pro basketball, football, and baseball. And while most cities would be content to simply have one team in each of those categories, L.A. fans can root for two.

Baseball

The **Dodgers** will try to muster up the old glory of "Dodger Blue," in another eventful season at the ever-popular Dodger Stadium. For ticket information, call 213/224–1400. Down the freeway a bit in Anaheim, the **California Angels** continue their race for the pennant in the American League West. For Angel ticket information, contact Angel Stadium: tel. 213/625–1123.

Basketball

While the great American pastime may be baseball, in the town where the perennial world champion **Los Angeles Lakers** display what they call "showtime," basketball is king. The Lakers' home court is the Fabulous Forum in Inglewood. Ticket information: tel. 213/419–3182. L.A.'s "other" team, the **Clippers,** make their home at the L.A. Sports Arena downtown next to the Coliseum. Ticket information: tel. 213/748–6131.

Boxing and Wrestling

Championship competitions take place in both of these sports year-round at the **Great Western Forum** (3900 W. Manchester, Inglewood, tel. 213/673–1773).

College Basketball

USC plays at the L.A. Sports Arena, while the Bruins' home court is the famous Pauley Pavilion on the UCLA campus; these two schools mix it up in Pac 10 competition each season. Another local team to watch for is the Lions of Loyola Marymount University.

College Football

The University of Southern California (USC) Trojans' home turf is the Coliseum, and the University of California at Los Angeles (UCLA) Bruins pack 'em in at the Rose Bowl in Pasadena. Each season, the two rivals face off against one another in one of college football's oldest and most exciting rivalries. For USC tickets, tel. 213/743–2311; for UCLA tickets, tel. 213/825–4321.

Football

With a 50% chance that owner Al Davis will move his team to Oakland, you may have only until 1992 to catch the **Los Angeles Raiders** at the L.A. Coliseum (3911 S. Figueroa, downtown, tel. 213/747–7111). The **Los Angeles Rams** will continue their struggle to get back to the Super Bowl this year. The team plays out of Anaheim Stadium. Ticket information: tel. 213/625–1123.

Golf

The hot ticket each Feburary in this town is the **Los Angeles Open** (tel. 213/482–1311). The tournament attracts the best golfers in the world, and is played in Pacific Palisades at the Riviera Country Club.

Hockey

The **L.A. Kings** put their show on ice at the Forum, November–April. Ticket information: tel. 213/419–3182.

Horse Racing

Santa Anita Race Track (Huntington Dr. and Colorado Pl., Arcadia, tel. 818/574–7223) is still the dominant site for exciting Thoroughbred racing. From Pincay to Shoemaker, you can always expect the best racing in the world at this beautiful facility.

Several grand-prix jumping competitions and western riding championships are held throughout the year at the **Los Angeles Equestrian Center** in Burbank (tel. 818/840–9063).

Hollywood Park is another favorite racing venue. The new Cary Grant Pavilion was recently completed, bringing back a style that has been lacking from this once-great park for some time. The track is next to the Forum in Inglewood, off of Century Boulevard, tel. 213/419–1500. Open late April–mid-July.

For harness racing, **Los Alamitos** has both day and night racing. Track information: tel. 213/431–1361.

Polo

Will Rogers State Park offers lovely picnic grounds where you can feast while enjoying an afternoon chukker of polo. Polo season information: tel. 213/454–8212. If it doesn't rain during the week, games are played Saturdays at 2 and Sundays at 10.

Tennis

The Volvo/Los Angeles Pro Tournament is held in September at UCLA. The competition usually attracts some of the top-seeded players on the pro tennis circuit.

Beaches

The beach scene is very much a part of the Southern California lifestyle. There is no public attraction more popular in L.A. than the white, sandy playgrounds of the deep blue Pacific.

From the L.A. Civic Center, the easiest way to hit the coast is by taking the Santa Monica Freeway (I–10) due west. Once you reach the end of the freeway, I–10 turns into the famous Highway 1, better known in Southern California as the Pacific Coast Highway (PCH), and continues up to Oregon. Other basic routes from the downtown area include Pico, Olympic, Santa Monica, or Wilshire boulevards, which all run east–west through the city. Sunset Boulevard offers a less direct but more scenic drive to the beaches, starting near Dodger Stadium, passing through Hollywood, Beverly Hills, and Pacific Palisades, and eventually reaching the Pacific Ocean one mile south of Malibu. The RTD bus lines, L.A.'s main form of public transportation until the new Metro Rail is completed, runs every 20 minutes to and from the beaches along each of these boulevards.

Los Angeles County beaches (and the state beaches operated by the county) have lifeguards. Public parking (for a fee) is available at most. The following beaches are listed in north–south order. Some are excellent for swimming, some for surfing (check with lifeguards for current conditions for either activity), others better for exploring.

Leo Carillo State Beach. This beach along a rough and mountainous coastline is most fun at low tide, when a spectacular array of tide pools blossom for all to see. Rock formations on the beach create some great secret coves for picnickers looking for solitude. There are hiking trails, sea caves, and tunnels, and whales, dolphins, sea lions, and otters are often seen swimming in the offshore kelp beds. The waters here are rocky and best for experienced surfers and scuba divers; fishing is good. Picturesque campgrounds are set back from the beach. *36000 block of PCH, Malibu, tel. 818/706–1310. Facilities: parking, lifeguard, rest rooms, showers, fire pits.*

Zuma Beach County Park. This is Malibu's largest and sandiest beach, and a favorite spot for surfing. It's also a haven for high school students who've discovered NautilusPlus. *30050 PCH, Malibu, tel. 213/457–9891. Facilities: parking, lifeguard, rest rooms, showers, food, playground, volleyball.*

Westward Beach/Point Dume State Beach. Another favorite spot for surfing, this half-mile-long sandy beach has tide pools and sandstone cliffs. *South end of Westward Beach Rd., Malibu, tel. 213/457–9891. Facilities: parking, lifeguard, rest rooms, food.*

Paradise Cove. With its pier and equipment rentals, this sandy beach is a mecca for sport-fishing boats. Though swimming is allowed, there are lifeguards during the summer only. *28128 PCH, Malibu, tel. 213/457–2511. Facilities: parking, rest rooms, food.*

Surfrider Beach/Malibu Lagoon State Beach. The steady 3-to-5-foot waves make this beach, just north of Malibu Pier, a great long-board surfing beach. The International Surfing Contest is

Los Angeles Area Beaches

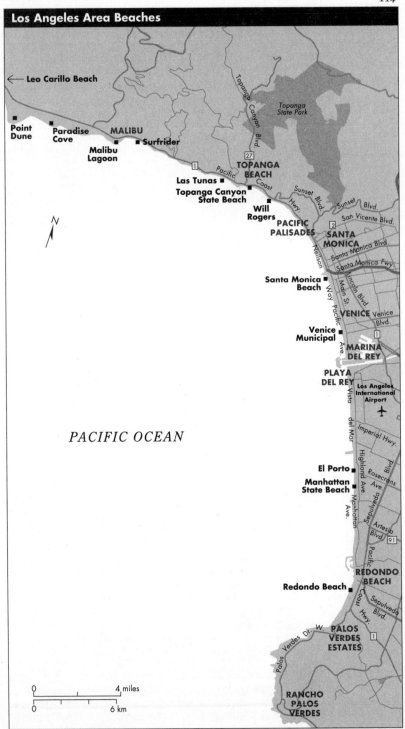

← Leo Carillo Beach

Point Dune

Paradise Cove

MALIBU

Malibu Lagoon

Surfrider

Topanga Canyon Blvd.

Topanga State Park

27

TOPANGA BEACH

Las Tunas

Topanga Canyon State Beach

Will Rogers

Pacific Coast Hwy.

Sunset Blvd.

Sunset Blvd.

San Vicente Blvd.

2

PACIFIC PALISADES

SANTA MONICA

Santa Monica Blvd.

Santa Monica Fwy.

Neilson Way

Lincoln Blvd.

Santa Monica Beach

Main St.

VENICE

Venice Blvd.

1

Venice Municipal

Pacific Ave.

MARINA DEL REY

PLAYA DEL REY

Los Angeles International Airport

Vista del Mar

Imperial Hwy.

PACIFIC OCEAN

El Porto

Manhattan State Beach

Highland Ave.

Manhattan Ave.

Rosecrans Ave.

Aviation Blvd.

Artesia Blvd.

91

Pacific

REDONDO BEACH

Redondo Beach

Coast Hwy.

Sepulveda Blvd.

Palos Verdes Dr. W.

PALOS VERDES ESTATES

1

RANCHO PALOS VERDES

0   4 miles

0   6 km

held here in September. Water runoff from Malibu Canyon forms a natural lagoon, a sanctuary for many birds. Take a romantic sunset stroll along the nature trails. *23200 block of PCH, Malibu, tel. 818/706–1310. Facilities: parking, lifeguard, rest rooms, picnicking, visitor center.*

Las Tunas State Beach. Las Tunas is small (1,300 feet long, covering a total of only two acres), narrow, and sandy, with some rocky areas, set beneath a bluff. Surf fishing is the biggest attraction here. There is no lifeguard, and swimming is not encouraged because of steel groins set offshore to prevent erosion. *19400 block of PCH, Malibu, tel. 213/457–9891. Facilities: parking, rest rooms.*

Topanga Canyon State Beach. The rocky beach stretches from the mouth of the canyon, which is great for surfing, down to Coastline Drive. Catamarans dance in these waves and skid onto the sands of this popular beach, where dolphins sometimes come close enough to shore to startle sunbathers. *18500 block of PCH, Malibu, tel. 213/394–3266. Facilities: parking, lifeguard, rest rooms, food.*

Will Rogers State Beach. This wide, sandy beach is several miles long, with an even surf. Parking is limited at the Castle Rock section, but there is plenty of beach, volleyball, and bodysurfing parallel to the pedestrian bridge. *15100 PCH, Pacific Palisades, tel. 213/394–3266. Facilities: parking, lifeguard, rest rooms.*

Santa Monica Beach. This is one of L.A.'s most popular beaches. In addition to a pier and a promenade, a man-made breakwater just offshore has caused the sand to collect and form the widest stretch of beach on the entire Pacific coast. Wider beaches mean more bodies! If you're up for some sightseeing on land, this is one of the more popular gathering places for L.A.'s young, toned, and bronzed. All in all, the 2-mile-wide beach is well equipped with bike paths, facilities for the disabled, playgrounds, and volleyball. *West of PCH, Santa Monica, tel. 213/394–3266. Facilities: parking, lifeguard, rest rooms, showers.*

Venice Municipal Beach. While the surf and sands of Venice are fine, the main attraction here is the boardwalk. Venice combines the pure beef of some of L.A.'s most serious bodybuilders with the productions of lively crafts merchants and street musicians. There are roller skaters and break dancers to entertain you and cafes to feed you. You can rent bikes at Venice Pier Bike Shop (21 Washington St.) and skates at Roller Skates of America (64 Windward Ave.) or Skatey's (102 Washington St.). *1531 Ocean Front Walk, Venice, tel. 213/394–3266. Facilities: parking, rest rooms, showers, food, picnicking.*

Playa Del Rey. South of Marina Del Rey lies a beach not quite as famous as its neighbors, but known to its nearby residents as one of the more underrated beaches in Southern California. Its sprawling white sands stretch from the southern tip of Marina Del Rey almost two miles down to Dockweiler Beach. The majority of the crowds that frequent these sands are young.

One of the more attractive features of this beach is an area called Del Rey Lagoon. Located right in the heart of Playa Del Rey, this grassy oasis surrounds a lovely pond inhabited by dozens of ducks, and it offers picnickers barbecue pits and tables to help stave off starvation on afternoon outings. *6660 Esplanade, Playa Del Rey. Facilities: Parking, lifeguard, rest rooms, food.*

Dockweiler State Beach. There are consistent waves for surfing at this beach, and it is not crowded, due to an unsightly power plant with towering smokestacks parked right on the beach. While the plant presents no danger to swimmers in the area, its mere presence, combined with the jumbo jets taking off overhead from L.A.'s International Airport, makes this beach a better place to work out than to lay out. There is firewood for sale for barbecues on the beach; beach fires are legal in this area as long as they are contained within the special pits that are already set up along the beach. *Harbor Channel to Vista Del Mar and Grand Ave., Playa Del Rey, tel. 213/322–5008. Facilities: parking, lifeguard, rest rooms, showers.*

Manhattan State Beach. Here are 44 acres of sandy beach for swimming, diving, surfing, and fishing. Polliwog Park is a charming, grassy landscape a few yards back from the beach. Ducks waddle around a small pond, picnickers enjoy a full range of facilities including grills and rest rooms, and there is even a series of rock and jazz concerts held here in the summer. *West of Strand, Manhattan Beach, tel. 213/372–2166. Facilities: parking, lifeguard, rest rooms, showers, food.*

Redondo State Beach. The beach is wide, sandy, and usually packed in summer; parking is limited. The Redondo Pier marks the starting point of the beach area, which continues south for more than 2 miles along a heavily developed shoreline community. Storms have damaged some of the restaurants and shops along the pier, but plenty of others are still functioning. Excursion boats, boat launching ramps, and fishing are other attractions. *Foot of Torrance Blvd., Redondo Beach, tel. 213/372–2166. Facilities: parking, lifeguard, rest rooms, showers, food.*

6   Dining

by Bruce David
Colen

*For the past 15
years, Bruce
David Colen has
been the
restaurant and
food critic for* Los
Angeles Magazine.
*He has also
written on food
and travel for*
Town & Country,
Architectural
Digest, Bon
Appetit,
Connoisseur,
Signature, *and*
Endless Vacations.

This past decade has seen Los Angeles emerge as a top gastronomic capital of the world. It has been an amazing and delicious transformation. Where once the city was only known for its chopped Cobb salad, Green Goddess dressing, drive-in hamburger stands, and outdoor barbecues, today it is home to some of the best French and Italian restaurants in the United States, plus so many places featuring international cuisines that listing them all would sound like a roll call at the United Nations. Actually, there are so many new, *good* dining establishments opening every week that, currently, there are more chairs, banquettes, and booths than there are bodies to fill them. Net result? The fierce competition among upscale restaurateurs has made L.A. one of the least expensive big cities—both here and abroad—in which to eat well.

The natives tend to dine early, between 7:30 and 9 PM, a hangover from when this was a "studio" town, and film-making started at 6 AM. Advance reservations are essential at the "starred" restaurants, and at almost all restaurants on weekend evenings.

Highly recommended restaurants are indicated by a star ★.

Category	Cost*
Very Expensive	over $70
Expensive	$40–$70
Moderate	$20–$40
Inexpensive	under $20

*per person, without tax (6.5%), service, or drinks

American

Beverly Hills
★ **The Grill.** The closest Los Angeles comes in looks and atmosphere to one of San Francisco's venerable bar and grills, with their dark wood paneling and brass trim. The food is basic American, cleanly and simply prepared, and includes fine steaks and chops, grilled fresh salmon, corned beef hash, braised beef ribs, and a creamy version of the Cobb salad. *9560 Dayton Way, tel. 213/276–0615. Reservations required. Dress: casual. AE, DC, MC, V. Valet parking eve. Closed Sun. Moderate.*

Ed Debevic's. This is a good place to take the kids and yourself, if you are yearning for the nostalgia of youth. Old Coca-Cola signs, a blaring juke box, gum-chewing waitresses in bobby sox, and meat loaf and mashed potatoes will take you back to the diners of the fifties. *134 N. La Cienega, tel. 213/ 659–1952. No weekend reservations; weekday reservations advised. Dress: casual. No credit cards. Valet parking. Inexpensive.*

RJ'S the Rib Joint. There is a large barrel of free peanuts at the door, sawdust on the floor, and atmosphere to match. The outstanding salad bar has dozens of fresh choices and return privileges, and there are big portions of everything—from ribs, chili, and barbecued chicken, to mile-high layer cakes—at very reasonable prices. *252 N. Beverly Dr., tel. 213/274–RIBS. Reservations advised. Dress: casual. AE, DC, MC, V. Valet parking eve. Inexpensive.*

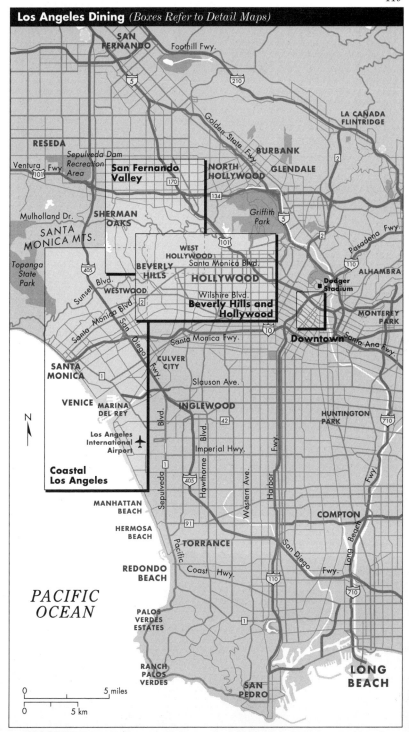

Los Angeles Dining (Boxes Refer to Detail Maps)

Downtown Los Angeles Dining

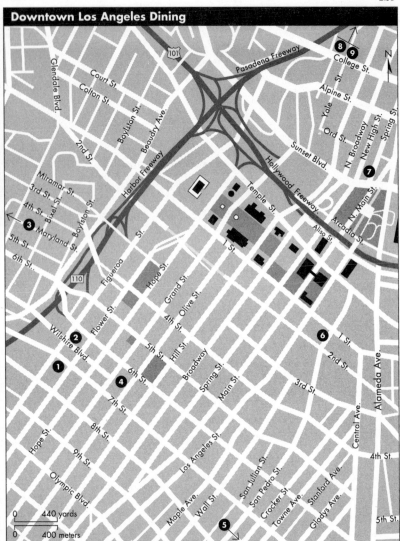

The Chronicle, **9**
Engine Co. #28, **2**
Lawry's California
Center, **8**
Mon Kee Seafood
Restaurant, **7**

Pacific Dining Car, **3**
Restaurant
Horikawa, **6**
Rex Il Ristorante, **4**
Seventh Street
Bistro, **1**
Vickman's, **5**

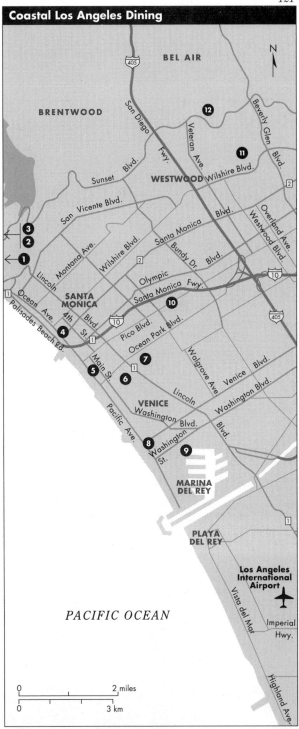

Beaurivage, **1**
The Bel-Air Hotel, **12**
Chinois on Main, **7**
Dynasty Room, **11**
Edie's Diner, **9**
Fennel, **4**
Gilliland's, **5**
Gladstone's 4 Fish, **3**
La Scala-Malibu, **2**
Orleans, **6**
Valentino, **10**
West Beach Cafe, **8**

Coastal Los Angeles Dining

Beverly Hills and Hollywood Dining

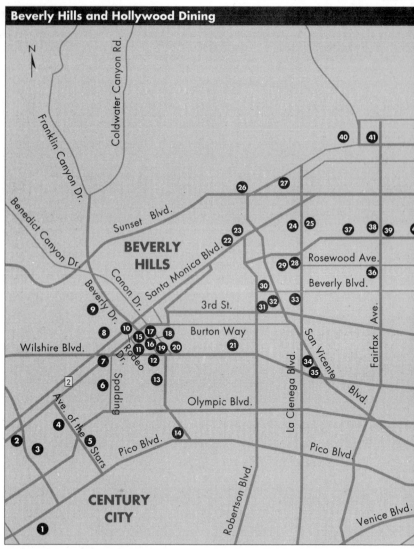

Antonio's Restaurant, **45**
The Bistro, **19**
The Bistro Garden, **20**
Border Grille, **39**
California Pizza Kitchen, **13**
Canter's, **36**
Carnegie Deli, **17**
Cha Cha Cha, **55**
Champagne, **2**
Chan Dara, **51**
Chopstix, **44**

Chasen's, **30**
Citrus, **50**
Columbia Bar and Grill, **49**
Dan Tana's, **8**
The Dining Room, **12**
Ed Debevic's, **34**
El Cholo, **53**
El Coyote Spanish Cafe, **46**
The Garden Pavilion, **3**
Greenblatt's, **41**
The Grill, **11**

Hard Rock Cafe, **33**
Harry's Bar & American Grill, **5**
Jimmy's, **6**
Johnny Rockets, **42**
Kate Mantilini, **21**
L.A. Nicola, **56**
La Chaumiere, **4**
La Masia, **22**
La Toque, **40**
Le Chardonnay, **37**
Le Dome, **27**
L'Ermitage, **25**

Lew Mitchell's Orient Express, **47**
Locanda Veneta, **31**
L'Orangerie, **24**
Lucy's El Adobe, **52**
The Mandarin, **15**
Mandarin Wilshire, **35**
Morton's, **29**
Nate 'n Al's, **18**
The Palm, **23**
Pane Caldo, **32**
Pastel, **10**
Pierre's Los Feliz Inn, **58**

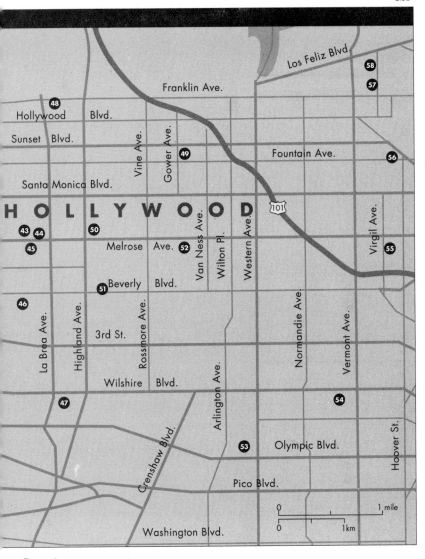

Prego, **9**
Primi, **1**
RJ's the Rib Joint, **16**
Restaurant Katsu, **57**
The Ritz Cafe, **14**
Spago, **26**
Tommy Tang's, **43**
Trader Vic's, **7**
Trumps, **28**
Tuttobene, **38**
The Windsor, **54**
Yamashiro, **48**

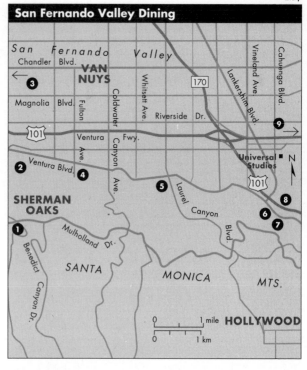

Downtown **Pacific Dining Car.** This is one of L.A.'s oldest restaurants, located in a 1920s railroad car that has been expanded over the years. Best known for well-aged steaks, rack of lamb, and an extensive California wine list at fair prices, it's a favorite haunt of politicians and lawyers around City Hall, and of sports fans after the Dodger games. *1310 W. Sixth St., tel. 213/483–6000. Reservations advised. Dress: casual. MC, V. Valet parking. Moderate–Expensive.*

Engine Co. #28. The ground floor of this National Historic Site was recently refurbished and refitted; now it's a very polished, "uptown" downtown bar and grill. It has been crowded from day one. Reason? All-American food carefully prepared and served with obvious pride. Don't miss the corn chowder, "Firehouse" chili, grilled pork chop, smoked rare tenderloin, and grilled ahi tuna. And there's a great lemon meringue pie. *Corner of Figueroa St. and Wilshire Blvd., tel. 213/624–6966. Reservations required. Dress: Jacket and tie suggested for lunch; casual for dinner. AE, MC, V. Valet parking. Closed weekend lunches. Moderate.*

Lawry's California Center. What out-of-towners envision when they think of dining under the stars in the Big Orange: a terraced courtyard lush with flowers, ferns, and palm trees. There is a strolling mariachi band and, on weekends, a jazz group. The food is not special, but the entrées—charbroiled New York steak, swordfish, grilled salmon, and hickory-smoked chicken—come with the works: a garden salad, freshly baked herb bread, corn on the cob, steamed vegetables, and a tortilla casserole. *570 West Ave. 26, tel. 213/225–2491. Reserva-*

tions advised for dinner. Dress: casual. AE, MC, V. Parking lot. Closed Sun. lunch. Garden dining May–mid-Nov. Inexpensive–Moderate.

Vickman's. Located next to the L.A. Produce Market, this bustling cafeteria opens at 3 AM to accommodate fleets of truck drivers, restaurant and hotel buyers, stall owners, curious nightpeople, and customers at the nearby flower mart. The dishes are simple, hearty, and bountiful: ham and eggs, grits, stuffed pork chops, giant sandwiches, and a famous fresh strawberry pie. It's a fun place to go if you can't sleep. *1228 E. Eighth St., tel. 213/ 622–3852. No reservations. Dress: casual. No credit cards. Closed 3 PM–3 AM. Inexpensive.*

Eastside
(Downtown Los Angeles Dining map)
The Chronicle. You will think you are in San Francisco's Sam's or the Tadish Grill, both very good places to be. The Chronicle's steaks, chops, prime rib, oysters and other shellfish are excellent, and it has one of the best California wine lists south of the Napa Valley. *897 Granite Dr., tel. 818/792–1179. Reservations advised. Jacket and tie required. AE, MC, V. Valet parking. Moderate.*

Hollywood
Columbia Bar & Grill. Located front and center in the heart of Tinsel Town, this comfortably contemporary restaurant, with Jasper Johns and Hockneys on the walls, is the daytime mecca for people from the surrounding television and film studios. The food is definitely above par. Don't pass up the crab cakes; Caesar salad; or the fish, fowl, and meats grilled over a variety of flavor-filled woods. *1448 N. Gower St., tel. 213/461–8800. Reservations required. Dress: casual. AE, DC, MC, V. Closed Sun. Valet parking. Moderate–Expensive.*

L.A. Nicola. Owner/chef Larry Nicola spent his early years in his family's produce market. His appreciation for fresh vegetables, greens, and meats is evident in all his offerings, as is his penchant for off-beat American cooking, utilizing the bounty from California's farms and waters. Nicola raises the lowly hamburger to a place of eminence. And don't miss the grilled shark, veal chop with capers, or the appetizer of fried artichoke hearts. Perhaps the nicest thing about this California-style bistro, with its white walls and huge pails of fresh flowers, is its hideaway atmosphere. It is a place with style but no pretensions. *4326 Sunset Blvd., tel. 213/660–7217. Reservations advised. Dress: casual. AE, DC, MC, V. Valet parking. Closed Sun. Moderate.*

San Fernando Valley
Paty's. Located near NBC, Warner Brothers, and the Disney Studio, Paty's is a good place to stargaze without having to mortgage your home for the meal. This is an all-American-style upgraded coffee shop with a comfortable, eclectic decor. Breakfasts are charming; the omelets are plump, and the biscuits are homemade and served with high-quality jam. Lunches and dinners include Swiss steak and a hearty beef stew that is served in a hollowed-out loaf of home-baked bread. Roast turkey is served with dressing and a moist, sweet loaf of home-baked nut or raisin bread. All desserts are worth saving room for: New Orleans bread pudding with a hot brandy sauce is popular, and the Danishes are gigantic. *10001 Riverside Dr., Toluca Lake, tel. 818/760–9164. No reservations. Dress: casual. No credit cards. Inexpensive.*

West Hollywood   **Chasen's.** It may no longer be Hollywood's "in" spot, but the clublike rooms are full of nostalgia and have a quaintly formal charm. The dishes that Alfred Hitchcock, Gary Cooper, and Henry Fonda loved—and George Burns still does—are as good as ever: hobo steak, double-rib lamb chops, boiled beef with matzo dumplings, and the late Dave Chasen's famous chili. For the finales, try the sensational banana shortcake or frozen eclair. This is a place for special celebrations. *9039 Beverly Blvd., tel. 213/271–2168. Weekend reservations advised. Jacket and tie required. No credit cards. Valet parking. Closed Mon. and lunch. Expensive.*

The Palm. If you don't mind the roar of the jocks, or having the New York–style waiters rush you through your Bronx cheesecake, this is where you'll find the biggest and best steamed Maine lobster, good steaks and chops, great french-fried onion rings, and paper-thin potato slices. If you have the roast beef hash for lunch, you'll have to skip dinner. A three-deep bar adds to the noise. *9001 Santa Monica Blvd., tel. 213/550–8811. Reservations advised. Dress: casual. AE, DC, MC, V. Valet parking. Closed weekend lunches. Expensive.*

Morton's. When the brother-and-sister owners of this trendy restaurant decided to open an upscale clubhouse for the music and entertainment industry, it was only natural that choice steaks should be the cornerstone of the menu—their father owns several steak houses in Chicago. Good broiled fish and chicken have since been added to the fare. Don't be intimidated by the celebrity-fawning waiters, all hoping for an acting job. *8800 Melrose Ave., tel. 213/276–5205. Reservations required. Jacket required. AE, MC, V. Valet parking. Closed Sun. Moderate.*

The Hard Rock Cafe. Big burgers, rich milkshakes, banana splits, BLTs and other pre-yuppie food delights, along with loud music, have made this '50s-era barn of a cafe the favorite of local teenagers. There is a large and busy bar for curious adults, many of whom are parents watching the kids. The place drew national attention—and spawned other Hard Rocks—for its fish-tail Cadillac jutting out of the roof, Fonzie's leather jacket on the wall, and Elvis's motorcycle. *8600 Beverly Blvd., tel. 213/276–7605. No reservations. Dress: casual. AE, DC, MC, V. Valet parking. Inexpensive.*

Westside   **West Beach Cafe.** It seems that owner Bruce Madder can do no
(Coastal   wrong. Ten years ago, he opened this upscale restaurant within
Los Angeles   a frisbee toss of all the voyeur action on the Venice Beach
Dining map)   strand. Next came **Rebecca's,** just across the street, where
★   Mexican food is treated as semi-*haute cuisine* and idolized by the yuppie set. Then last year came the instant winner **DC-3,** a 21st-century architectural extravaganza at the Santa Monica Airport. Best at the West Beach are: Caesar salad, filet Mignon taco, braised lamb shank, ravioli with port and raddichio, fisherman's soup and what many consider the best hamburger and fries in all of Los Angeles. There's also a fabulous selection of French wines and after-dinner liqueurs. *60 N. Venice Blvd., tel. 213/823–5396. Reservations advised. Dress: casual. AE, DC, MC, V. Valet parking. Moderate–Expensive.*

Gilliland's. While Gerri was teaching cooking in her native Ireland, she took a vacation in southern California—and never went back. She created this charming restaurant, which offers the best of both culinary worlds, and showcases her fascination with Mediterranean dishes. The soda bread, Irish stew, and corned beef and cabbage are wonderful; and marvelous is the only word for her bitter lemon tart. Be sure to try the pasta dishes with California sauces or Provençal herbs. The place is warm and friendly, just like its owner. *2424 Main St., Santa Monica, tel. 213/392–3901. Reservations advised. Dress: casual. AE, MC, V. Moderate.*

Gladstone's 4 Fish. This is undoubtedly the most popular restaurant along the entire California coast, serving well over a million beachgoers a year. Perhaps the food is not the greatest in the world, but familiar seashore fare is prepared adequately and in large portions, and the prices are certainly right. Best bets: crab chowder, steamed clams, three-egg omelets, hamburgers, barbecue ribs, and chili. And then there's the wonderful view, especially from the beach-side terrace—ideal for whale-, porpoise-, and people-watching. *17300 Pacific Coast Hwy. (corner of Sunset Blvd.), Pacific Palisades, tel. 213/GL4 –FISH. Dress: casual. Reservations advised. AE, DC, MC, V. Valet parking. Moderate.*

Cajun

Westside **Orleans.** Jambalaya and gumbo dishes are hot—in more ways
(Coastal than one—at this spacious eatery, where the cuisine was cre-
Los Angeles ated with the help of New Orleans chef Paul Prudhomme. The
Dining map) blackened redfish is probably the best catch on the menu. *11705 National Blvd., W. Los Angeles, tel. 213/479–4187. Reservations advised. Dress: casual. AE, DC, MC, V. Moderate.*

California

Beverly Hills **The Dining Room.** Located in the remodeled Regent Beverly
★ Wilshire, this elegant, European-looking salon is the best thing to happen to L.A. hotel dining in decades. Wonderful California cuisine, plus splendid service at surprisingly non-posh prices. Adjoining is an equally attractive, sophisticated cocktail lounge, with romantic lighting and a show-tune pianist. *9500 Wilshire Blvd., tel. 213/275–5200. Reservations advised. Jacket and tie required. AE, DC, MC, V. Valet parking. Moderate–Expensive.*

California Pizza Kitchen. This is the place to go if you hanker for a good pizza at a fair price but don't feel like the usual pizza-parlor surroundings. There's an immaculate, pleasingly modern dining room, plus counter service by the open kitchen, and a wide, rather esoteric choice of pizza toppings. The pastas are equally interesting and carefully prepared. The few sidewalk tables are in great demand. *207 S. Beverly Dr., tel. 213/272–7878. No reservations. Dress: casual. AE, MC, V. Inexpensive–Moderate.*

Century City **The Bistro Garden.** The flower-banked outdoor dining terrace
(Beverly Hills makes this the quintessential Southern California luncheon ex-
and Hollywood perience. It's chic and lively without being pretentious or "Hol-
Dining map) lywood." There's excellent smoked salmon, fresh cracked crab, steak tartare, calf's liver with bacon, and a unique apple pancake. *176 N. Canon Dr., tel. 213/550–3900. Reservations required. Jacket and tie required at dinner. AE, DC, MC, V. Valet parking. Closed Sun. Moderate–Expensive.*

West Hollywood **Citrus.** Tired of being known only as one of the country's great-
★ est pastry chefs, Michel Richard opened this contemporary restaurant to display the breadth of his talent. He creates superb

dishes by blending French and American cuisines. You can't miss with the delectable tuna burger, the thinnest angel-hair pasta, or the deep-fried potatoes, sauteed foie gras, rare duck, or sweetbread salads. Best get your doctor's permission before even looking at Richard's irresistible desserts. *6703 Melrose Ave., tel. 213/857–0034. Reservations advised. Jacket required. AE, MC, V. Valet parking. Closed Sun. Moderate–Expensive.*

★ **Spago.** This is the restaurant that propelled owner/chef Wolfgang Puck into the national and international culinary spotlights. He deserves every one of his accolades for raising California cuisine to an imaginative and joyous gastronomic level, using only the finest West Coast produce. The proof is in the tasting: grilled baby Sonoma lamb, pizza with Santa Barbara shrimp, thumbnail-size Washington oysters topped with golden caviar, grilled free-range chickens, and, from the North Pacific, baby salmon. As for Puck's incredible desserts, he's on Weight Watchers' Most Wanted List. This is the place to see *People* magazine live, but you'll have to put up with the noise in exchange. Be safe: Make reservations at least two weeks in advance. *1114 Horn Ave., tel. 213/652–4025. Reservations required. Jacket required. AE, DC, MC, V. Valet parking. Closed lunch. Moderate–Expensive.*

Trumps. A smartly designed contemporary adobe building, with striking abstract art on the pure-white walls. But the best artist in the house is chef/co-owner Michael Roberts, an imaginative young American who takes special pleasure in combining off-beat flavors that result in a delectable whole: brie-and-apple bisque, salmon tartare with tomatillo, corn pancakes with mussels, duck breast and pickled pumpkin, and gingersnap cheesecake. This is the perfect cure for jaded appetites, and a popular rendezvous for L.A.'s tastemakers. It serves the best afternoon tea in town. *8764 Melrose Ave., tel. 213/855–1480. Reservations advised. Jacket required. AE, DC, MC, V. Closed weekend lunches. Moderate–Expensive.*

Westside
(Coastal Los Angeles Dining map)
★
The Bel-Air Hotel. Even if the food were terrible, one would not care, since the romantic, country-garden setting is so satisfying. But the California-Continental cooking is first-rate, be it breakfast, lunch, or dinner. A meal at the Bel-Air is a not-to-be-missed experience. *701 Stone Canyon Rd., Bel Air, tel. 213/472–1211. Reservations advised. Jacket and tie required. AE, DC, MC, V. Valet parking. Expensive.*

Caribbean

Hollywood
Cha Cha Cha. When the Cajun food craze cooled off among L.A. foodies, Caribbean cooking became the trend, and this small shack of a place became the hottest spot in town. There's cornmeal chicken, spicey swordfish, fried banana chips, and assorted flans. This is a hangout for celebrities gone slumming. *656 N. Virgil Ave., tel. 213/664–7723. Reservations required, but expect to wait. Dress: casual. AE, DC, MC, V. Valet parking. Moderate.*

Chinese

Beverly Hills
★
The Mandarin. Who said you only find great Chinese food in hole-in-the-wall places with oilcloth tabletops? Here is a good-looking restaurant with the best crystal and linens, serving an

equally splendid mixture of Szechuan and Chinese country-cooking dishes. Minced squab in lettuce-leaf tacos, Peking duck, a superb beggars chicken, scallion pancakes, and any of the noodle dishes are recommended. *430 N. Camden Dr., tel. 213/272-0267. Reservations required. Jacket required. AE, DC, MC, V. Valet parking. Closed weekend lunches. Moderate.*

Downtown **Mon Kee Seafood Restaurant.** The name says it all—except how good the cooking is and how morning-fresh the fish are. The delicious garlic crab is addictive; the steamed catfish is a masterpiece of gentle flavors. In fact, almost everything on the menu is excellent. This is a crowded, messy place; be prepared to wait for a table. *679 N. Spring St., tel. 213/628-6717. No reservations. Dress: casual. MC, V. Pay parking lot. Inexpensive–Moderate.*

Mid-Wilshire **Mandarin Wilshire.** Roger Lee, formerly chef at the Mandarin
(Beverly Hills in Beverly Hills (*see* above), and his wife opened this unpreten-
and Hollywood tious, cheerful cafe, in a mini-shopping center on the outskirts
Dining map) of Beverly Hills. The menu lists nearly 150 dishes, a repertoire that only a master such as Lee could handle in so modest a setting. Expect large portions, reasonable prices, and a helpful staff. *8300 Wilshire Blvd., tel. 213/658-6928. Reservations required. Dress: casual. AE, DC, MC, V. Free parking. Closed Sun. lunch. Inexpensive.*

San Fernando **Fung Lum.** Located in the Universal Studios complex, this or-
Valley nate Chinese restaurant cost millions to build. It's a replica of a Chinese palace, and the interior design includes hand-carved, -painted, and -embroidered panels; rosewood and teak furniture; and breathtaking hand-woven carpeting. The menu is long and primarily Cantonese. It's best to come here in a large group so you can taste a multitude of courses. The minced squab in lettuce leaves is wonderful; the service is not. *100 Universal City Plaza, Universal City, tel. 818/763-7888. No reservations. Dress: casual. AE, DC, MC, V. Moderate.*

West Hollywood **Chopstix.** Never underestimate the ability of Californians to adopt, and adapt, an ethnic-food vogue. In this case it is dim sum, subtly doctored for non-oriental tastes. The result is nouvelle Chinese junk-food served in a mod setting, at high-stool tables or at a dinerlike counter. The dishes are appetizing, but don't expect a native Chinese to agree. *729 Melrose Ave., tel. 213/935-2944. No reservations. Dress: casual. AE, DC, MC, V. Inexpensive.*

Continental

Beverly Hills **The Bistro.** The kitchen is not quite as good as Jimmy's (*see* below), but nobody has ever questioned that this replica of a Parisian boîte is one of the most stylish dining rooms west of Europe. The original owner, director Billy Wilder, was responsible for the interior design: mirrored walls, etched-glass partitions, giant bouquets of fresh flowers, and soft lighting. The food is more American bistro than French. There is a delicious, juicy chopped steak, good veal medallions, Eastern lobster on tagliatelli and, most likely, the greatest chocolate souffle you've ever tasted. *246 North Canon Dr., tel. 213/273-5633. Reservations required. Jacket and tie required. AE, DC, MC, V. Valet parking. Closed Sat. lunch and Sun. Moderate–Expensive.*

Century City
(Beverly Hills and Hollywood Dining map)

Jimmy's. When the Beverly Hills C.E.O.s are not entertaining, they head here or to the Bistro (*see* above). Owner Jimmy Murphy provides the warmth in this expensive, decorator-elegant restaurant. The best dishes on the broad menu include smoked Scottish salmon, prawns with herbs and garlic, saddle of lamb, Chateaubriand, and pheasant breast with wild blueberry sauce. There's steak tartare at lunch. *201 Moreno Dr., tel. 213/ 879–2394. Reservations required. Jacket and tie required. AE, DC, MC, V. Valet parking. Expensive.*

Mid-Wilshire
(Beverly Hills and Hollywood Dining map)

The Windsor. This is what an upscale L.A. restaurant was like 40 years ago: a dark, quiet retreat with red-leather booths and banquettes, where captains prepare dishes table-side. Talk about the old days, the menu even has Baked Alaska and Crepes Suzette. Stick with the steak and chop entrées and the Caesar salad. *3198 West 7th St., tel. 213/382–1261. Reservations required. Jacket and tie required. AE, DC, MC, V. Valet parking. Moderate.*

San Fernando Valley

Victoria Station. Located atop the Universal Studios hill, this restaurant has been built to resemble (sort of) a British railway station. The service is cheerful and efficient. Recommended are the quality top sirloin and good teriyaki steak; gooey, cheesy baked potato skins provide a perfect appetizer. The ribs here are a bit greasy, but they have a nice smoky flavor. There's a great children's menu charging reasonable prices. Dinners come with soup of the day or a pleasant salad bar and whole-grain bread. No matter what age you are, don't leave without trying the peanut-butter pie: It's a nutty peanut-butter filling frozen into a graham-cracker crust with whipped cream on top and chocolate hot fudge sauce on the side. You'll find good value here. Check the phone book for other locations. *3850 Lankershim Blvd., Universal City, tel. 818/760–0714. Reservations accepted. Dress: casual. AE, DC, MC, V. Moderate–Expensive.*

Europa. The menu here roams the world: great goulash, terrific teriyaki—even matzoball soup. The dining room is tiny and casual; reservations are a must, as this is a community favorite. *14929 Magnolia Blvd., Sherman Oaks, tel. 818/501–9175. Reservations advised. Dress: casual. MC, V. Closed Sun. and lunch. Inexpensive–Moderate.*

L'Express. This is a cheerful brasserie where people from Hollywood's soundstages meet, mingle, and relax. Contemporary art and lots of neon add color to this already lively dining spot. It's a great place for late-night snacks, croque monsieur, pizzas of all types, and delicious desserts. There is a full bar (and quite a bar scene). *14190 Ventura Blvd., Sherman Oaks, tel. 818/990–8683; 3573 Cahuenga Blvd., Universal City, tel. 818/876–3778; and 11620 Wilshire Blvd., Brentwood, tel. 213/ 477–3463. No reservations. Dress: casual. AE, MC, V. Inexpensive–Moderate.*

Westwood
(Coastal Los Angeles Dining map)

Dynasty Room. This peaceful, elegant room in the Westwood Marquis Hotel has a European flair and tables set far enough apart for privacy. Besides well-handled Continental fare, there is a *cuisine minceur* menu for calorie counters. There's an expecially lavish, excellent Sunday brunch. *930 Hilgard Ave., tel. 213/208–8765. Reservations required. Jacket and tie required. AE, DC, MC, V. Valet parking. Closed lunch. Moderate.*

Deli

Beverly Hills **Carnegie Deli.** Marvin Davis, the oil millionaire, got tired of jetting cheesecake, pastrami, and lox back from the parent Carnegie in New York City, so he financed a Beverly Hills taste-alike to challenge Nate 'n Al's preeminence. His big guns are corned beef and pastrami sandwiches that are 4 1/2 inches high, cheese blintzes under a snowcap of sour cream, and wonderfully creamy cole slaw. *300 N. Beverly Dr., tel. 213/275–3354. No reservations. Dress: casual. AE, DC, MC, V. Inexpensive.*
Nate 'n Al's. A famous gathering place for Hollywood comedians, gag writers, and their agents. Nate 'n Al's serves first-rate matzo-ball soup, lox and scrambled eggs, cheese blintzes, potato pancakes, and the best deli sandwiches west of Manhattan. *414 N. Beverly Dr., tel. 213/274–0101. No reservations. Dress: casual. CB, DC. Free parking. Inexpensive.*

San Fernando Valley **Art's Delicatessen.** One of the best Jewish-style delicatessens in the city serves breakfast, lunch, and dinner daily. The sandwiches are mammoth and are made from some of the best corned beef, pastrami, and other cold cuts around. Matzo-ball soup and sweet-and-sour cabbage soup are specialties, and there is good chopped chicken liver. *12224 Ventura Blvd., Studio City, tel. 818/769–9808. No reservations. Dress: casual. No credit cards. Inexpensive–Moderate.*

West Hollywood **Greenblatt's.** Who ever heard of a deli famous for its extensive wine list? This one also serves wood-smoked ribs, rotisserie chicken, and 20 different salads, along with the usual sandwiches. *8017 Sunset Blvd., tel. 213/656–0606. No reservations. Dress: casual. MC, V. Parking lot. Inexpensive.*

French

Beverly Hills **Pastel.** The most successful business in the ultrachic Rodeo Drive collection of high-fashion boutiques is proof that the natives are hungry for dining bargains. Pastel's prix-fixe dinners, which include a half bottle of wine are bargains indeed, at $28.50. For starters, there is duck pâté and a giant basket of crudités; next comes charbroiled prime rib, a perfect roasted chicken, or fresh grilled fish. And there is a choice of seven lovely desserts. *421 Rodeo Dr., tel. 213/274–9775. Reservations advised. Jacket required. AE, DC, MC, V. Parking. Closed Sun. Moderate.*

Century City **(Beverly Hills and Hollywood Dining map)** ★ **Champagne.** Patrick Healy, another young American who trained under some of the best chefs in France, has opened this attractive restaurant, where cuisine, not people-watching, keeps patrons returning week after week. They have their choice of contemporary or traditional French dishes and spa cuisine selections. Two specialties include a three-layered eggplant and crayfish cake, plus a real farmhouse cassoulet. The desserts are light and lovely. *10506 Santa Monica Blvd., tel. 213/470–8446. Reservations required. Jacket and tie required. AE, DC, MC, V. Valet parking. Closed for lunch and Mon. Moderate.*

Downtown ★ **Seventh Street Bistro.** Set in a landmark Art Deco office building, this ground-floor restaurant is full of light and beautifully designed. It has all the sophistication and panache of a townhouse in Paris or Manhattan. The *nouvelle* Franco-Californian cuisine is splendid. The menu changes monthly but the enthusiasm of the bistro's loyal customers is a constant. *811 W. Seventh St., tel. 213/627–1242. Reservations advised. Jacket and tie required. Valet parking eve. Closed Sat. lunch and Sun. Moderate–Expensive.*

West Hollywood
★ **L'Ermitage.** Although they are served in a sedate, French country-house setting, there's nothing imitative about chef Michel Blanchet's three-star classic French-California dishes. Specialties include escargot pancake, smoked salmon ravioli with leeks and caviar, sea bass in a pastry crust, sweetbread stew, salmon tartare, and fabulous desserts. *730 N. La Cienega Blvd., tel. 213/652–5840. Reservations required. Jacket and tie required. AE, DC, MC, V. Valet parking. Closed lunch and Sun. Very Expensive.*

★ **L'Orangerie.** For sheer elegance and classic good taste, it would be hard to find a lovelier restaurant in this country. And the cuisine, albeit *nouvelle*-light, is as French as the l'orangerie at Versailles. Specialties include coddled eggs served in the shell and topped with caviar, squab with *foie gras, pot au feu,* rack of lamb for two, and an unbeatable apple tart served with a jug of double cream. *903 N. La Cienega Blvd., tel. 213/652–9770. Reservations required. Jacket and tie required. AE, DC, MC, V. Valet parking. Closed lunch. Expensive.*

La Toque. Amidst the hurly-burly of Sunset Strip is this small, unassuming, one-story building. Step through the door, and you'll imagine you've entered a French country inn. The charming hideaway is the province of Ken Frank, one of the nation's best American, French-cooking chefs. Each day some new delight graces the menu: raviolis stuffed with foie gras and pheasant, fettucine with egg and black truffle, venison seared with armagnac, or grilled duck breast in a calvados sauce. Be sure to order the roasted, shredded potato pancake with golden caviar and crème fraîche. *8171 Sunset Blvd., tel. 213/656–7515. Reservations required. Jacket required. AE, DC, MC, V. Valet parking. Closed Sat. lunch, Sun. Moderate–Expensive.*

Le Chardonnay. The interiors are Art Deco in this unabashed copy of a famous Left Bank bistro, circa 1920. Despite the high noise level, it's a most romantic rendezvous, with comfortable, cozy booths. Specialties include warm sweetbread salad, goat cheese ravioli, roast venison, grilled fish, Peking duck with a ginger and honey sauce, and lots of lush desserts. *8284 Melrose Ave., tel. 213/655–8880. Reservations required. Jacket required. AE, MC, V. Valet parking. Closed Sat. lunch, Sun. Moderate.*

Le Dome. For some reason, local food critics have never given this brasserie the attention it deserves. Perhaps they are intimidated by the hordes of show- and music-biz celebrities that keep the place humming. By and large the food is wonderful, honest, down-to-earth French: cockles in white wine and shallots, veal ragout, marvelous veal sausage with red cabbage, and a genuine, stick-to-the-ribs cassoulet. *8720 Sunset Blvd., tel. 213/659–6919. Reservations required. Dress: casual. AE, DC, MC, V. Valet parking. Closed Sun. Moderate.*

Westside
(Coastal Los Angeles Dining map)
★ **Fennel.** Ocean Avenue has often been compared to a sea bluff boulevard on the French Riviera; and Fennel is the closest you can come to the latest true Parisian cooking in California. It is very, very trendy with L.A.'s francophiles. Call in advance to find out which of three French chefs is in residence. *1535 Ocean*

Ave., tel. 213/394–2079. Reservations required. Jacket required. AE, DC, MC, V. Valet parking. Closed weekend lunches in winter. Expensive.

★ **Chinois on Main.** The second of the Wolfgang Puck pack of restaurants, this one is designed in tongue-in-cheek kitsch by his wife, Barbara Lazaroff. Both the look of the place and Puck's merging of Chinese and French cuisines for contemporary tastes are great good fun. A few of the least resistable dishes on an irresistable menu include Mongolian lamb with eggplant, poach-curried oysters, whole catfish garnished with ginger and green onions, and rare duck with a wonderous plum sauce. The best desserts are three differently flavored *cremes brulees.* This is one of L.A.'s most crowded spots—and among the noisiest. Bring earplugs. *2709 Main St., Santa Monica, tel. 213/392–9025. Reservations required for dinner. Dress: casual. AE, DC, MC, V. Valet parking, evenings. Closed Sat.– Tues. lunch. Moderate–Expensive.*

Beaurivage. A charming, romantic restaurant designed in the fashion of an auberge on the Cote D'Azur, this is the best of the Malibu dining places with a view of the beach and ocean. The menu compliments the Provençal atmosphere: roast duckling Mirabelle, pasta with shellfish, mussel soup, filet mignon with a three-mustard sauce and, in season, wild game specials. It's a satisfying getaway. *26025 Pacific Coast Highway, tel. 213/456–5733. Reservations required. Dress: casual. Parking lot. Open Mon.–Sat. 5–11, Sun. 11–4 and 5– 11. Moderate.*

Greek

San Fernando Valley **Great Greek.** This joint is jumping with Greek music and Old World dancing where everyone joins in. The food is a delight: loukaniki, Greek sausages; butter-fried calamari; and two kinds of shish kebab. *13362 Ventura Blvd., Sherman Oaks, tel. 818/905–5250. Reservations advised. Dress: casual. AE, DC, MC, V. Valet parking. Moderate.*

Health Food

San Fernando Valley **The Good Earth.** Eating healthfully doesn't have to mean eating a diet of alfalfa sprouts and wheat germ. The menus of this health-oriented chain feature whole-grain breads, desserts baked with honey, and entrées heavy on fruit and vegetables rather than on meat. Even the decor, with earth-tone walls and furnishings and macrame-and wicker baskets on the walls, is earthy. Breakfast items include turkey sausages, 10-grain sourdough pancakes, and a choice of omelets. Vegetarian burgers, curried chicken, and Zhivago's beef Stroganoff are superior lunch and dinner specialties. *17212 Ventura Blvd., Encino, tel. 818/986–9990; 1002 Westwood Blvd., Westwood, tel. 213/208 –8215; and 23397 Mulholland Dr., Woodland Hills, tel. 818/ 888–6300. Reservations accepted. Dress: casual. MC, V. Inexpensive–Moderate.*

Italian

Beverly Hills **Primi.** Valentino's younger, less expensive brother, with a menu that features a wide variety of appetizer-size portions of Northern Italian treats, including pasta and salad selections.

This is a cheerful, contemporary setting, with a pleasant outside terrace. *10543 W. Pico Blvd., tel. 213/475–9235. Reservations advised. Jacket and tie required. AE, DC, MC, V. Valet parking. Closed Sun. Moderate.*

Prego. This is a super bargain in the highest of high-rent districts. The baby lamb chops, large broiled veal chop, and Florentine rib steak are among the best, dollar for dollar, in town. The baked in-house bread sticks are great. *362 N. Camden Dr., tel. 213/277–7346. Reservations advised. Dress: casual. AE, DC, MC, V. Valet parking at night. Closed Sun. lunch. Inexpensive–Moderate.*

Century City
(Beverly Hills and Hollywood Dining map)

Harry's Bar & American Grill. A more private, posh, uptown version of Prego, run by the same management. The decor and selection of dishes are acknowledged copies of Harry's Bar in Florence. But you'll find that for first-rate food—paper-thin carpaccio, excellent pastas, grilled fish and steaks, along with a fine hamburger—the check will be lower than in Italy. This is the best place to dine before or after seeing a movie in the area. *2020 Ave. of the Stars, tel. 213/277–2333. Reservations advised. Jacket required. AE, DC, MC, V. Valet parking. Closed Sun. lunch. Moderate.*

Downtown
★

Rex Il Ristorante. Owner Mauro Vincenti probably knows more about Italian cuisine than any other restaurateur in this country. The Rex is the ideal showcase for his talents: Two ground floors of a historic Art Deco building were remodeled to resemble the main dining salon of the circa-1930 Italian luxury liner Rex. The cuisine is equally special, the lightest of *cucina nuevo*. Be prepared for small and costly portions. *617 S. Olive St., tel. 213/627–2300. Reservations required. Jacket and tie required. AE, DC, MC, V. Valet parking. Closed Mon. and Sat. lunch and Sun. Very Expensive.*

San Fernando Valley

Adriano's Ristorante. A five-minute drive north of Sunset Boulevard through one of L.A.'s loveliest residential canyons, brings you to this countrified retreat, near the top of the Santa Moncia Mountains. There's nothing backwoods about the food, though. Specialties include lobster with linguini, a t-bone veal chop, polenta risotto, roasted quail, and a delicious cheese souffle. *2930 Beverly Glen Circle, tel. 213/475–9807. Reservations required. Jacket required. AE, DC, MC, V. Free parking. Closed weekend lunches and Mon. Moderate–Expensive.*

West Hollywood
★

Locanda Veneta. The food may be more finely wrought at one or two other spots, but the combination of a splendid Venetian chef, Antonio Tomassi, and a simpatico co-owner, Jean Louis De Mori, have recreated the atmospheric equivalent of a genuine Italian trattoria, *at reasonable* prices. Specialties include fried white-bait, risotto with porcini mushrooms, veal chop, ricotta and potato dumplings, linguini with clams, lobster ravioli with saffron sauce, and pear tart. *8638 W. Third St., tel. 213/274–1893. Reservations required. Jacket required. AE, DC, MC, V. Valet parking. Closed Sat. lunch and Sun. Moderate.*

Tuttobene. If Silvio de Mori, Jean Louis's older brother, served nothing more than peanut-butter sandwiches, his place would be doing SRO business. But this best-loved restaurateur, a genuinely gracious, caring host, happens to provide some of the most delectable trattoria dishes west of Tuscany. There are different, freshly baked breads every day, superb down-to-earth pastas and gnocci, luscious rissotto with wild mushrooms, picked-that-morning arugula salad—all at very fair prices. *945 N. Fairfax Ave., tel. 213/655–7051. Reservations required. Dress: casual. AE, MC, V. Valet parking. Moderate.*

Westside **Valentino.** Rated among the best Italian restaurants in the na-
(Coastal tion, Valentino is generally considered to have the best wine
Los Angeles list outside Italy. Owner Piero Selvaggio is the man who intro-
Dining map) duced Los Angeles to the best and lightest of modern-day Ital-
★ ian cuisine, and the natives have loved him ever since. There's
superb prosciutto, bresola, fried calamari, lobster cannelloni,
fresh broiled porcini mushrooms, and osso buco. *3115 Pico
Blvd., Santa Monica, tel. 213/829–4313. Reservations required.
Jacket required. AE, DC, MC, V. Valet parking. Closed Sat.–
Thur. lunch and Sun. Expensive.*

La Scala Malibu. Malibu's most celebrity-crowded hangout has
moved to brand-new, cheerful quarters, and, in the process,
the Northern Italian food has greatly improved, and the prices
have come down a notch. You can't quite see the ocean, but,
"There's Cher over there talking to Olivia Newton-John and
Jack Lemmon, next to the table with Larry Hagman and Walter Mathau." *3874 Cross Creek Rd., tel. 213/456–1979. Reservations advised. Dress: casual. AE, MC, V. No lunch
weekends. Moderate.*

Japanese

Downtown **Restaurant Horikawa.** A department store of Japanese cuisines
including sushi, teppan steak tables, tempura, sashimi, shabu-
shabu, teriyaki, and a $50-per-person *kaiseki* dinner. All are
good or excellent, but the sushi bar is the best. The decor is traditional Japanese, with private sit-on-the-floor dining rooms
for 2 to 24. *111 S. San Pedro St., tel. 213/680–9355. Reservations advised. Jacket and tie required. AE, DC, MC, V. Valet
parking. Closed weekend lunches. Moderate–Expensive.*

Los Feliz **Restaurant Katsu.** A stark, simple, perfectly designed sushi
(Beverly Hills bar with a small table area, serving the most exquisite and deli-
and Hollywood cious delicacies in all of Southern California. This is a treat for
Dining map) eye and palate. *1972 N. Hillhurst Ave., tel. 213/665–1891. No
★ lunch reservations, dinner reservations advised. Dress: casual. AE, MC, V. Valet parking. Closed Sat. lunch. Moderate.*

Mexican

Hollywood **El Cholo.** This progenitor of the present-day, upscale Southland chain, has been packing them in since the '20s. It serves
good bathtub-size Margaritas, a zesty assortment of tacos,
make-your-own tortillas, and, from June to September, green-
corn tamales. It's friendly and fun, with large portions at peso
prices. *1121 S. Western Ave., tel. 213/734–2773. Reservations
advised. Dress: casual. AE, MC, V. Parking lot. Inexpensive.*

West Hollywood **Border Grill.** This is a very trendy, very loud storefront place,
owned by two women chefs with the most eclectic tastes in
town. The menu ranges from crab tacos to vinegared-and-
peppered grilled turkey to pickled pork sirloin. It's worth
dropping by, if you don't mind the noise while you're there.
*7407 ½ Melrose Ave., tel. 213/658–7495. Reservations advised.
Dress: casual. AE, MC, V. Moderate.*

Antonio's Restaurant. Don't let the strolling mariachis keep
you from listening to the daily specials, the true Mexico City
dishes that put this unpretentious favorite several cuts above

the ubiquitous taco-enchilada cantinas. The *chayote* (squash) stuffed with ground beef; ricotta in a spicy tomato sauce; pork ribs in a sauce of pickled chipotle peppers; veal shank with garlic, cummin, and red pepper; and chicken stuffed with apples, bananas and raisins are definitely worth trying. Have the flan for dessert. *7472 Melrose Ave., tel. 213/655-0480. Dinner reservations advised. Dress: casual. AE, MC, V. Valet parking. Inexpensive–Moderate.*

Polynesian

Beverly Hills **Trader Vic's.** Sure, it's corny, but this is the most restrained and elegant of the late Victor Bergeron's South Sea extravaganzas. Besides, who says corn can't be fun—and tasty, too. The crab Rangoon, grilled cheese wafers, skewered shrimp, grilled pork ribs, and the steaks, chops, and peanut-butter–coated lamb cooked in the huge clay ovens, are just fine. As for the array of exotic rum drinks, watch your sips. *9876 Wilshire Blvd., tel. 213/274-7777. Reservations required. Jacket and tie required. AE, DC, MC, V. Valet parking. Closed lunch. Moderate–Expensive.*

Thai

Hollywood **Chan Dara.** Here you'll find excellent Thai food in a bright and shiny Swiss chalet! Try any of the noodle dishes, especially those with crab and shrimp. There is noise here, but it's bearable. *310 N. Larchmont Blvd. tel. 213/467-1052. Reservations advised for parties of more than 4. Dress: casual. AE, MC, V. Inexpensive.*

West Hollywood **Tommy Tang's.** A very "in" grazing ground for yuppies and celebs alike. So much people-watching goes on, nobody seems to notice the small portions on their plates. The kitchen features crisp duck marinated in ginger and plum sauce, blackened sea scallops, and a spinach salad tossed with marinated beef. There is also a sushi bar. *7473 Melrose Ave., tel. 213/651-1810. Reservations advised. Dress: casual. AE, DC, MC, V. Valet parking. Closed for lunch. Moderate.*

7 Lodging

by Jane E. Lasky

You can find almost any kind of accommodation in Los Angeles, from a simple motel room that allows you to park right in front of your room to a posh hotel like the Beverly Hills, where an attendant will park your car and whisk you off to a spacious room or to your own bungalow.

Because L.A. is so spread out—it's actually a series of suburbs connected by freeways—it's a good idea to select a hotel room not only for its ambience, amenities, and price but also for a location that is convenient to where you plan to spend most of your time.

West Hollywood and Beverly Hills are at the heart of the city, equidistant from the beaches and downtown. These are also the primary shopping districts of Los Angeles, with Rodeo Drive the central axis of Beverly Hills, and Melrose Avenue the playground for trendier purchases.
the Pacific, so if it's the beach that lures you to L.A., book a room on the Westside.

Downtown is attractive if you are interested in Los Angeles's cultural offerings since this is where the Music Center and the Museum of Contemporary Art are located. It is also the heartland for Los Angeles's conventions.

The more recently developed Century City, located between Westwood and Beverly Hills, and built around the back lot of Twentieth Century Fox, offers top-notch hotels, a terrific mall, movie and legitimate theaters—and quick access to Rodeo Drive shopping. It's also an important Los Angeles business center.

Hollywood itself, unfortunately, has lost much of its legendary glamour, even though it does take center stage in the geographic scheme of Los Angeles, so don't book a room in this part of town thinking you'll be in the lap of luxury. Parts of Hollywood, in fact, are downright seedy.

The San Fernando Valley is a good place to stay if you're looking for a suburban setting and quarters close to the movie and television studios on that side of the hill.

It's best to plan ahead and reserve a room; many hotels offer special prices for weekend visits and offer tickets to amusement parks or plays. A travel agent can help in making your arrangements.

Hotels are listed in categories, determined first by location: Downtown, Mid-Wilshire, Hollywood/West Hollywood, Beverly Hills/Bel Air, West Los Angeles, Santa Monica, Marina del Rey, South Bay Beach Cities, the Airport, and the San Fernando Valley. They are further divided, under location, into categories determined (roughly) by the price of a room for two people, on the European plan.

The most highly recommended accommodations are indicated by a star ★.

Category	Cost*
Very Expensive	over $155
Expensive	$110–$155

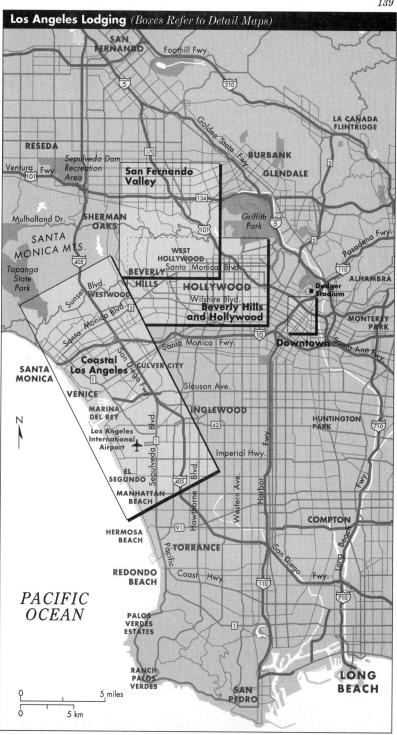

Los Angeles Lodging *(Boxes Refer to Detail Maps)*

SAN FERNANDO

Foothill Fwy.

210

LA CANADA
FLINTRIDGE

RESEDA

Golden State Fwy.

BURBANK

2

GLENDALE

Ventura Fwy

101

Sepulveda Dam
Recreation
Area

170

**San Fernando
Valley**

134

Griffith
Park

5

Pasadena Fwy.

Mulholland Dr.

SHERMAN
OAKS

SANTA
MONICA MTS.

101

WEST
HOLLYWOOD
Santa Monica Blvd.

ALHAMBRA

110

Topanga
State
Park

405

BEVERLY
HILLS

WESTWOOD

Sunset Blvd.

2

HOLLYWOOD

Wilshire Blvd.

**Beverly Hills
and Hollywood**

Dodger
Stadium

MONTEREY
PARK

Santa Monica Blvd.

San Diego Fwy.

Santa Monica Fwy.

10

Downtown

Santa Ana Fwy.

SANTA
MONICA

1

**Coastal
Los Angeles**

CULVER CITY

Slauson Ave.

VENICE

MARINA
DEL REY

Sepulveda Blvd.

1

INGLEWOOD

42

HUNTINGTON
PARK

710

Los Angeles
International
Airport

Hawthorne Blvd.

405

Imperial Hwy.

Western Ave.

Harbor Fwy.

EL
SEGUNDO

MANHATTAN
BEACH

HERMOSA
BEACH

91

TORRANCE

San Diego Fwy.

Long Beach Fwy.

COMPTON

710

N

REDONDO
BEACH

Pacific Coast Hwy.

110

*PACIFIC
OCEAN*

PALOS
VERDES
ESTATES

1

**LONG
BEACH**

RANCH
PALOS
VERDES

SAN
PEDRO

0   5 miles

0   5 km

Moderate	$70–$110
Inexpensive	under $70

*for a double room

Downtown

Very Expensive **The Biltmore Hotel.** Since its 1923 opening, the Biltmore has hosted such notables as Mary Pickford, J. Paul Getty, Eleanor Roosevelt, Princess Margaret, and several U.S. presidents. Now a historic landmark, it was renovated in 1986 for $35 million, with modern, updated guest rooms decorated in pastels. The lobby ceiling was painted by Italian artist Giovanni Smeraldi; imported Italian marble and plum-color velvet grace the Grand Avenue Bar, which features excellent jazz nightly. Bernard's is an acclaimed Continental restaurant. The private, swank health club has a Roman bath motif. Banquet and meeting rooms serve up to 1,200; the special club floor boasts a library, wide-screen TV, and pocket billiards room. *506 S. Grand Ave., 90013, tel. 213/624–1011, or 800/245–8673. 704 rooms. Facilities: restaurants, lounge, entertainment, health club (fee). AE, DC, MC, V.*

Checkers Hotel. With its excellent pedigree and smaller scale, the brand-new Checkers is a sophisticated, welcome addition to the downtown hotel scene. Set in one of downtown's few remaining historic buildings—opened as the Mayflower Hotel in 1927—Checkers boasts the same management as the acclaimed Campton Place in San Francisco (one of the nation's top hotels). Rooms are furnished with oversized beds, upholstered easy chairs, writing tables, and mini-bars. A library is available for small meetings or tea. *535 S. Grand Ave., 90071, tel. 213/624–0000 or 800/628–4900. 190 rooms. Facilities: restaurant, rooftop spa and lap pool, exercise studio. AE, DC, MC, V.*

Hyatt Regency, Los Angeles. The Hyatt is located in the heart of the "new" downtown financial district, minutes away from the Convention Center, Dodger Stadium, and the Music Center. Each room has a wall of windows with city views. The Regency Club has a private lounge. The hotel is part of the Broadway Plaza, comprising 35 shops. Nearby tennis and health club facilities are available at an extra cost. *711 S. Hope St., 90017, tel. 213/683–1234 or 800/233–1234. 500 rooms. Facilities: restaurant, coffee shop, lounge, entertainment. AE, DC, MC, V.*

Los Angeles Hilton Hotel. Located on L.A.'s most accessible street, the Hilton contains a fine Italian restaurant, Cardini, as well as a Japanese eatery. The rooms are conservatively decorated in beige and green. It's near Dodger Stadium, museums, Chinatown, and the Music Center. Parking is expensive. *930 Wilshire Blvd., 90017, tel. 213/629–4321. 901 rooms. Facilities: restaurants, lounge, 24-hr coffee shop, pool, large banquet and meeting facilities. AE, DC, MC, V.*

★ **Sheraton Grande Hotel.** Opened in 1983, this 14-story, 550-room mirrored hotel is near Dodger Stadium, the Music Center, and downtown's Bunker Hill District. Rooms have dark wood furniture, sofas, minibars; colors are aqua or copper; baths are marble. Butler service on each floor. Stay in the penthouse suite if you can afford it. Limousine service is available, and there are privileges at a local health club. *333 S. Figueroa*

141

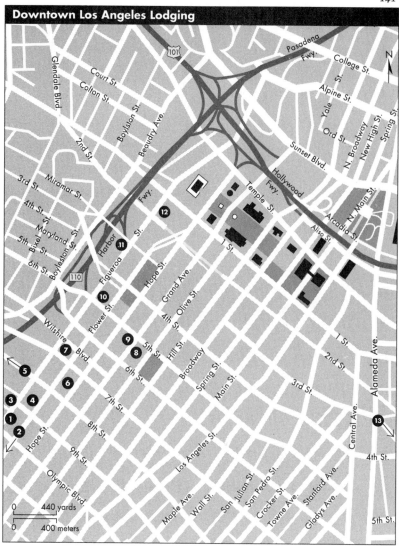

Downtown Los Angeles Lodging

Best Western Inn Towne, **1**

The Biltmore Hotel, **8**

Checkers Hotel, **9**

Comfort Inn, **13**

Figueroa Hotel, **3**

Holiday Inn L.A. Downtown, **5**

Hyatt Regency Los Angeles, **6**

Los Angeles Hilton Hotel, **7**

The New Otani and Garden, **12**

Orchid Hotel, **4**

Sheraton Grande Hotel, **11**

University Hilton Los Angeles, **2**

The Westin Bonaventure, **10**

Beverly Hills and Hollywood Lodging

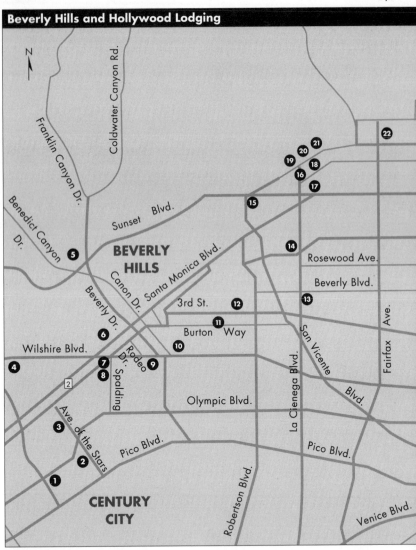

N

Coldwater Canyon Rd.

Franklin Canyon Dr.

Benedict Canyon Dr.

Sunset Blvd.

BEVERLY HILLS

Santa Monica Blvd.

Canon Dr.

Beverly Dr.

3rd St.

Rosewood Ave.

Beverly Blvd.

Burton Way

Rodeo Dr.

Spalding

Wilshire Blvd.

San Vicente Blvd.

Fairfax Ave.

La Cienega Blvd.

Olympic Blvd.

Ave. of the Stars

Pico Blvd.

Robertson Blvd.

Pico Blvd.

CENTURY CITY

Venice Blvd.

Beverly Hills Comstock, **4**
Beverly Hills Hotel, **5**
The Beverly Hilton, **7**
Beverly House Hotel, **8**
Beverly Pavilion Hotel, **10**
Beverly Rodeo, **6**

Century City Inn, **1**
Century Plaza Hotel, **3**
Chateau Marmont Hotel, **21**
Four Seasons Los Angeles, **12**
Hollywood Holiday Inn, **23**
Hollywood Roosevelt, **22**
Hyatt on Sunset, **20**

Hyatt Wilshire, **25**
JW Marriott Hotel at Century City, **2**
Le Bel Age Hotel, **15**
Le Dufy Hotel, **17**
L'Ermitage Hotel, **11**
Le Mondrian Hotel, **16**
Le Parc Hotel, **14**
Ma Maison Sofitel Hotel, **13**

Regent Beverly Wilshire Hotel, **9**
The Saint James's Club/Los Angeles, **18**
Sheraton Towne House, **26**
Sunset Dunes Motel, **24**
Sunset Marquis Hotel, **19**

Los Feliz Blvd.

Franklin Ave.

Hollywood **23** Blvd.

Sunset Blvd.

Vine Ave.

Gower Ave.

Fountain Ave.

Santa Monica Blvd.

24

H O L L Y W O O D 101

Van Ness Ave.

Wilton Pl.

Western Ave.

Virgil Ave.

Melrose Ave.

Beverly Blvd.

Highland Ave.

Rossmore Ave.

3rd St.

Normandie Ave.

Vermont Ave.

La Brea Ave.

Wilshire Blvd.

Arlington Ave.

25

26

Crenshaw Blvd.

Olympic Blvd.

Hoover St.

Pico Blvd.

Washington Blvd.

0   1 mile

0   1km

Airport Park Hotel, **21**
Amfac Hotel Los Angeles, **20**
Barnaby's Hotel, **14**
Bel Air Hotel, **28**
Best Western Royal Palace Hotel, **24**
Carmel Hotel, **1**
Century Wilshire, **26**
The Chesterfield Hotel Deluxe, **25**
Holiday Inn-LAX, **17**
Holiday Inn Santa Monica Pier, **6**
Hyatt Hotel-LAX, **15**
Loews Santa Monica Beach Hotel, **3**
The Los Angeles Airport Marriott, **18**
Marina Beach Hotel, **11**
Marina del Rey Hotel, **10**
Marina del Rey Marriott Inn, **12**
Marina International Hotel, **8**
Marina Pacific Hotel & Suites, **7**
Miramar Sheraton, **2**
Pacific Shore, **4**
Pacifica Hotel, **22**
Palm Motel, **5**
Radisson Bel Air Summit, **29**
The Ritz-Carlton, Marina del Rey, **9**
Sheraton Plaza, **23**
Sheraton Plaza La Reina, **16**
Sheraton at Redondo Beach, **13**
Stouffer Concourse Hotel, **19**
Westwood Marquis, **27**

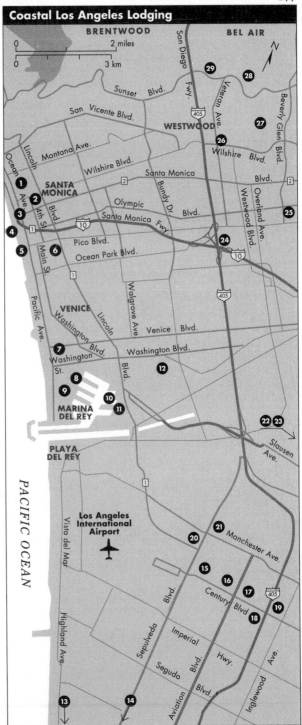

Coastal Los Angeles Lodging

St., 90071, tel. 213/617–1133 or 800/325–3535. 469 rooms. Facilities: restaurants, nightclub, outdoor pool, 23 meeting rooms, 4 movie theaters. AE, DC, MC, V.

The Westin Bonaventure. This is John Portman's striking masterpiece: a 35-story, circular-towered, mirrored-glass high rise in the center of downtown. Rooms have a wall of glass, streamlined pale furnishings, and comfortable appointments. The outside elevators provide stunning city views; there are also 5 acres of ponds and waterfalls in the lobby, several restaurants, including Beaudry's Gourmet, and the Bona Vista revolving lounge at the top of the hotel. The grand ballroom seats 3,000. A popular Sunday brunch is served in the atrium lobby. Parking is expensive. *404 S. Figueroa St., 90071, tel. 213/624–1000 or 800/228–3000. 1,474 rooms. Facilities: restaurant, lounge, entertainment, pool, and 5-level shopping arcade. AE, DC, MC, V.*

Expensive–Very Expensive ★

The New Otani and Garden. East meets west in L.A., and the exotic epicenter downtown is this 21-story, ultramodern hotel surrounded by Japanese gardens and waterfalls. The decor combines a serene blend of Westernized luxury and Japanese simplicity. Each room has a refrigerator, an alarm clock, color TV, and phone in the bathroom, and most provide a kimono. For the ultimate Little Tokyo experience, book a Japanese suite. These suites are so authentic that guests sleep on futons on mats on the floor. Concrete walls give great noise control. A Thousand Cranes offers classic Japanese cuisine; Commodore Perry's, steak and lobster. The Genji Bar features noted jazz artists. There is also a large conference center. *120 S. Los Angeles St., 90012, tel. 213/622–0980, 800/252–0197 in CA, or 800/421–8795 nationwide. 448 rooms. Facilities: restaurants, nightclubs, sauna and massage (fee), parking (fee). AE, DC, MC, V.*

University Hilton Los Angeles. If you're doing business at USC, the Coliseum, or the Sports Arena, this is the best hotel in the area. All the modern-style rooms have a view of the pool area, the lush gardens, or the nearby USC campus. It's well-equipped to handle banquets and conventions. *3530 S. Figueroa St., 90007, tel. 213/748–4141, 800/445–8667 nationwide, or 800/872–1104 in CA. 241 rooms. Facilities: restaurant, coffee shop, lounge, pool, parking (fee). AE, DC, MC, V.*

Moderate

Best Western Inn Towne. This three-story hotel has large beige and white rooms. It's 1½ blocks from the Convention Center and just down the street from the famous 24-hour Pantry restaurant. The swimming pool is surrounded by palm trees and small garden. *925 S. Figueroa St., 90015, tel. 213/628–2222 or 800/528–1234. 176 rooms. Facilities: restaurants, lounge, pool, room service, free parking. AE, DC, MC, V.*

Figueroa Hotel. This hotel has managed to keep its charming Spanish style intact as it enters its second half-century. There's a poolside bar. The hotel is on the Gray Line sightseeing tour route and there is airport service every hour to LAX. *939 S. Figueroa St., 90015, tel. 213/627–8971, 800/421–9092 nationwide, or 800/331–5151 in CA. 280 rooms. Facilities: restaurants, coffee shop, lounge, pool, free parking. AE, DC, MC, V.*

Holiday Inn L.A. Downtown. This offers Holiday Inn's usual professional staff and services, and standard room decor. Pets are allowed, and there is plenty of free parking. It's close to the Museum of Contemporary Art and Dodger Stadium. *750 Garland Ave., 90017, tel. 213/628–5242 or 800/465–4329. 204* *rooms. Facilities: restaurant, lounge, pool, parking. AE, DC, MC, V.*

Inexpensive **Comfort Inn.** With its central location between downtown and Hollywood, near the Wilshire commercial district, this is very convenient for businesspeople. The modern-style rooms offer color TVs and VCRs. *3400 Third St., 92020, tel. 213/385–0061. 120 rooms. Facilities: coffee shop, pool. AE, DC, MC, V.*

Orchid Hotel. One of the smaller downtown hotels, this is very reasonably priced. There are no frills, but the standard rooms are clean. Note that there is no parking at the hotel, but public lots are close by. *819 S. Flower St., 90017, tel. 213/624–5855. 66 rooms. Facilities: color TV, coin-operated laundry. AE, DC, MC, V.*

Mid-Wilshire

Expensive– Very Expensive **Hyatt Wilshire.** One of Wilshire Boulevard's largest hotels, this 12-story building's interior was renovated in 1987. There's a grand piano and concert pianist in the lobby. The rooms have views of either Hollywood or downtown. The Hyatt's corporate clients often use the large banquet and meeting rooms for up to 400 people. Extras include the Hyatt Regency Club, a full-security floor, and an excellent Sunday champagne brunch. *3515 Wilshire Blvd., 90010, tel. 213/381–7411 or 800/233–1234. 397 rooms. Facilities: restaurant, cafeteria, lounge, disco, room service, laundry service, parking (fee). AE, DC, MC, V.*

Sheraton Towne House. Howard Hughes slept (and lived) here. A great example of L.A.'s best Art Deco architecture, this hotel, built in the 1920s, retains its original charm and elegance. Marble fireplaces, antiques, and cedar-lined closets enhance the country-estate tone. It's convenient to Bullocks Wilshire shopping. *2961 Wilshire Blvd., 90010, tel. 213/382–7171 or 800/ 325–3535. 300 rooms. Facilities: restaurants, coffee shop, pool, tennis, parking (fee). AE, DC, MC, V.*

Hollywood/West Hollywood

Very Expensive **Le Bel Age Hotel.** This is a wonderful location for an all-suite,
★ European-style hotel with a distinctive restaurant, which features fine Russian meals with an elegant French flair. There are many extravagant touches, like three telephones with five lines in each suite, original art, private terraces, and courtesy limousine service. Ask for a suite that faces south for terrific views looking out as far as the Pacific over the L.A. skyline. The decor is French country style. *1020 N. San Vicente Blvd., West Hollywood 90069, tel. 213/854–1111 or 800/424–4443. 190 suites. Facilities: 2 restaurants, lounge, pool. AE, DC, MC, V.*

Le Dufy Hotel. Opened in 1984, this luxury hotel features all suites that are decorated in a modern style and shades of blue, pink, and salmon. All have private balconies. It's great for business travelers, near "Restaurant Row," and not as expensive as other hotels in this price category. *1000 Westmont Dr., West Hollywood 90069, tel. 213/657–7400. 103 suites. Facilities: restaurant, bar, pool, whirlpool, spa, sauna, sun deck. AE, DC, MC, V.*

Le Mondrian Hotel. This giant structure is a monument to the Dutch artist after whom the hotel takes its name. The outside of the 12-story hotel is actually a giant surrealistic mural; inside there's fine artwork. Accommodations are spacious, with pale wood furniture and curved sofas in the seating area. Ask for south-corner suites; they tend to be quieter than the rest. A chauffeured limo is placed at each guest's disposal. Nouvelle cuisine is served at Cafe Piet. The hotel is convenient to major recording, film, and TV studios. *8440 Sunset Blvd., West Hollywood 90069, tel. 213/650–8999 or 800/424–4443. 243 suites. Facilities: restaurant, pool, health club, parking. AE, DC, MC, V.*

★ **The Saint James's Club/Los Angeles.** Located on the Sunset Strip, this is the latest in the prestigious group of St. James's Clubs, and the first in the United States. The building has been around since the 1930s; today all the furnishings are exact replicas of Art Deco masterpieces, the originals of which are in New York's Metropolitan Museum of Art. Ask for a city or mountain view. Both are great but the cityside accommodations are more expensive. The hotel also features a 1930s-style supper club (California cuisine) with piano entertainment, a club bar, and a lounge. *8358 Sunset Blvd., West Hollywood 90069, tel. 213/654–7100 or 800/225–2637. 63 rooms. Facilities: restaurant, health center, sauna, pool, secretarial services, small meeting facilities. AE, DC, MC, V.*

Sunset Marquis Hotel. A garden area with lovely landscaping highlights this three-story property near La Cienega and Sunset Boulevard. The hotel also features nightly entertainment and a Jacuzzi. The Californian room decor adds to the hotel's relaxed atmosphere. *1200 N. Alta Loma Rd., West Hollywood 90069, tel. 213/657–1333 or 800/858–9758 in CA. 118 rooms. Facilities: dining room, pool, sauna, whirlpool, exercise room, in-room refrigerators, free parking. AE, DC, MC, V.*

Expensive **Chateau Marmont Hotel.** Although planted on the Sunset Strip amid giant billboards and much Hollywood glitz, this castle of Old World charm and French Normandy design still promises its guests a secluded hideaway close to Hollywood's hot spots. A haunt for many show-biz personalities and discriminating world travelers since it opened in 1927, this is the ultimate in privacy. All kinds of accommodations are available, including fully equipped cottages, bungalows, and a penthouse. *8221 Sunset Blvd., Hollywood 90046, tel. 213/656–1010 or 800/CHATEAU. 62 rooms. Facilities: dining room, gardens, pool, patios. AE, MC, V.*

Hollywood Roosevelt. This hotel across from Mann's Chinese Theater was once considered state-of-the-art Hollywood glamour and luxury before it gradually fell into disrepair. But in true Hollywood fashion, this site of the first Academy Awards ceremony made a comeback in 1985, thoroughly restored right down to the ornate Art Deco lobby and elegant courtyard. Highlights are the Olympic-size pool decorated by artist David Hockney and the Tropicana Bar in the courtyard. *7000 Hollywood Blvd., Hollywood 90028, tel. 213/466–7000, or 800/950–7667. 320 rooms plus 90 poolside cabanas. Facilities: restaurants, lounge, rental cars, airport transportation, valet parking. AE, DC, MC, V.*

Hyatt on Sunset. In the heart of the Sunset Strip, this Hyatt is a favorite of music-biz execs and rock stars. There are penthouse suites, some rooms with private patios, and a rooftop pool. The rooms are decorated in peach colors and modern furniture; some rooms even have aquariums. *8401 W. Sunset Blvd., West Hollywood 90069, tel. 213/656–4101 or 800/233–1234. 262* *rooms. Facilities: restaurant, lounge, entertainment, pool, parking (fee). AE, DC, MC, V.*

Moderate **Hollywood Holiday Inn.** You can't miss this hotel, one of the tallest buildings in Hollywood. It's 23 stories tall, topped by Windows, a revolving restaurant-lounge. The rooms are decorated in light gray and rose in standard Holiday Inn fashion. There is a safekeeping box in each room. The hotel is only minutes from the Hollywood Bowl, Universal Studios, and Mann's Chinese Theater, and it's a Gray Line Tour Stop. *1755 N. Highland Ave., Hollywood 90028, tel. 213/462–7181 or 800/465–4329. 468 rooms. Facilities: restaurant, coffee shop, pool, coin laundry, parking. AE, CB, DC, MC, V.*

Inexpensive **Sunset Dunes Motel.** Across the street from two TV stations, this hotel with Spanish-style rooms is a popular stop for studio folk. Its Dunes restaurant is open until 10 PM and the family-oriented Spaghetti Factory is nearby. *5625 Sunset Blvd., Hollywood 90028, tel. 213/467–5171. 56 rooms. Facilities: restaurant, lounge, free parking. AE, DC, MC, V.*

Beverly Hills

Very Expensive **Beverly Hills Hotel.** This is a California landmark: 12 acres of
★ beautiful grounds in a quiet location with tropical plants. The lovely rooms are all different, decorated with traditional furniture and overstuffed chairs and sofas. For the full flavor of this Beverly Hills legend, book a bungalow by the pool. Movie stars often take the bungalows and congregate in the famous Polo Lounge. Breakfast and lunch are served in the Coterie Restaurant overlooking the heated pool. *9641 Sunset Blvd., Beverly Hills 90210, tel. 213/276–2251 or 800/283–8885. 268 units. Facilities: restaurants, pool, wading pool, exercise room, parking. AE, DC, MC, V.*

The Beverly Hilton. This large hotel complex has a wide selection of restaurants and shops. Most rooms have balconies overlooking Beverly Hills or downtown. Trader Vic's and L'Escoffier are two of the city's better restaurants. There are a theater ticket desk, limo service, and free coffee in the lobby for hotel guests. *9876 Wilshire Blvd., Beverly Hills 90210, tel. 213/274–7777 or 800/445–8667. 592 rooms. Facilities: restaurants, pool, wading pool, exercise room, refrigerators, parking. AE, DC, MC, V.*

★ **L'Ermitage Hotel.** L'Ermitage features Old World charm with modern conveniences. Opened in 1976, it's one of the only hotels on the West Coast to garner both the Mobil Five Star Award and the AAA Five Diamond Award. The property is near Beverly Hills' elegant shopping, and Twentieth Century Fox. The suites have balconies and sunken living rooms with fireplaces. The best is the split-level town-house suite. The fine Cafe Russe is reserved exclusively for hotel guests. Complimentary Continental breakfast; chauffeured limo within Beverly Hills. *9291 Burton Way, Beverly Hills 90210, tel. 213/278–3344 or 800/424–4443. 114 rooms. Facilities: restaurant, pool, whirlpool, spa, private solarium, parking. AE, DC, MC, V.*

★ **Four Seasons Los Angeles.** This new hotel combines the best in East and West Coast luxury. Formal European decorative details are complemented by outpourings of flora from the porte cochere to the rooftop pool deck. There is an outstanding restaurant and a great shopping location within five minutes of Rodeo Drive and trendy Melrose Avenue. Many of the suites come with French glass doors and a walk-out balcony. *300 S. Doheny Dr., Los Angeles 90048, tel. 213/273–2222 or 800/332–3442. 285 rooms. Facilities: restaurant, 1-hr pressing service, pool, exercise equipment. AE, DC, MC, V.*

Ma Maison Sofitel Hotel. This two-year-old hotel offers first-class service and an intimacy usually reserved for small European-style hotels. The country French guest rooms are done in terra-cotta and blues, with small prints. The hotel is next to some of L.A.'s best shopping, restaurants, and boutiques. It also faces a large brick wall; insist on a northern view. *855 Beverly Blvd., Los Angeles 90048 (on the fringe of Beverly Hills), tel. 213/278–5444 or 800/221–4542. 311 rooms. Facilities: 2 restaurants, 24-hr room service, pool, sauna, fitness center, parking. AE, DC, MC, V.*

Le Parc Hotel. An intimate European-style hotel housed in a modern low-rise building in a lovely residential area. Suites are decorated in earth tones and shades of wine and rust with balconies, fireplaces, VCRs, and kitchenettes. Near Farmers' Market, CBS Television City, and the County Museum of Art. Cafe Le Parc, a private dining room, is reserved for guests only. *733 North West Knoll, West Hollywood 90069, tel. 213/855–8888, 800/424–4442 nationwide, or 800/424–4443 in CA. 152 rooms. Facilities: lighted tennis, heated pool, whirlpool, spa, sauna, exercise room, free parking, chauffeured limo to Hollywood and Beverly Hills. AE, DC, MC, V.*

Regent Beverly Wilshire. This famous hotel facing Rodeo Drive and the Hollywood Hills re-opened in 1989 after a major renovation (and under new management). It remains stylish, with personal service and extras to match. There are great restaurants, limo service to the airport, and a multilingual staff. *9500 Wilshire Blvd., Beverly Hills 90212, tel. 213/275–4282 or 800/421–4354. 401 rooms. Facilities: restaurants, pool, health spas, parking (fee). AE, DC, MC, V.*

Expensive **Beverly Hills Comstock.** Because this is a low-rise hotel (only three floors), guests need not walk through long corridors to reach their rooms. All the suites are situated off the pool. Furnishings are smart, some in Early American style and some contemporary; all feature kitchen/living room, one bedroom, and bath. *10300 Wilshire Blvd., Beverly Hills 90024, tel. 213/275–5575 or 800/343–2184. 150 rooms. Facilities: restaurant, pool, Jacuzzi, garage. AE, DC, MC, V.*

Beverly Pavilion Hotel. Located near fashionable shopping and movie theaters, this hotel is popular with commercial travelers and features the well-known restaurant Colette, with French cuisine and cocktail lounge. The rooms and executive suites have balconies and are decorated in contemporary styles, mostly in beige, yellow, and browns. *9360 Wilshire Blvd., Beverly Hills, 90212, tel. 213/273–1400, 800/421–0545 nationwide, or 800/441–5050 in CA. 109 rooms. Facilities: pool, laundry, restaurant, lounge. AE, DC, MC, V.*

Beverly Rodeo. Modern elegance characterizes the rooms of this small European-style hotel. Cafe Rodeo, an outdoor eatery popular with locals, is an added feature. Renovated in 1985, the understated rooms are decorated in floral prints, which enhance the homey atmosphere. Convenient to shopping. *360 Rodeo Dr., Beverly Hills 90210, tel. 213/273–0300. 100 rooms. Facilities: sun deck, restaurant, garage, bar, lounge. AE, DC, MC, V.*

Moderate
★
Beverly House Hotel. This is a small, elegantly furnished, European-style bed-and-breakfast hotel. Even though it's near busy areas of L.A. (Century City and Beverly Hills shopping), this hotel is quiet and actually quaint. *140 S. Lasky Dr., Beverly Hills 90212, tel. 213/271–2145 or 800/432–5444. 50 rooms. Facilities: laundry, free parking. AE, DC, MC, V.*

West Los Angeles

Very Expensive
★
Century Plaza Hotel. This 20-story hotel (on 14 acres of tropical plants and reflecting pools) features a new 30-story tower, which is lavishly decorated with signature art and antiques; it's furnished like a mansion, with a mix of classic and contemporary appointments. Each room has a refrigerator and balcony with ocean or city view. Complimentary car service is provided to Beverly Hills. There are four excellent restaurants: award-winning La Chaumiere for California/French cuisine, the Terrace for American/Continental, the Garden Pavilion for spa cuisine, and the Cafe Plaza, a French-style cafe. *2025 Ave. of the Stars, Century City 90067, tel. 213/277–2000 or 800/228–3000. 1,072 rooms. Facilities: restaurants, 2 pools, whirlpools, parking. AE, DC, MC, V.*

★
J W Marriott Hotel at Century City. This hotel, which opened in 1988, is the West Coast flagship for the multifaceted Marriott chain. Its elegant, modern rooms are decorated in soft pastels and equipped with minibars, lavish marble baths, and facilities for the handicapped. Ask for accommodations that overlook Twentieth Century Fox's back lot. The hotel offers complimentary limo service to Beverly Hills and boasts the 2,000 sq. ft. Presidential Suite and excellent service. *2151 Ave. of the Stars, Century City 90067, tel. 213/201–0440 or 800/228–9090. 375 rooms. Facilities: restaurant, indoor and outdoor pools, whirlpools, fitness center. AE, DC, MC, V.*

Expensive
The Chesterfield Hotel Deluxe. This new, more-than-comfortable hotel near the Century City business complex mixes California architecture with English fabrics and furnishings, epitomized in the red welcome carpet and the London phone booth at the entrance. *10320 W. Olympic Blvd., 90067, tel. 213/556–2777 or 800/243–7871. 126 rooms. Facilities: exercise salon, sun deck, garden whirlpool, retaurant, London taxi courtesy service to surrounding areas. AE, DC, MC, V.*

Moderate
Century City Inn. This hotel is small but well designed for comfort. Rooms have refrigerators, microwave oven, remote control TV, and VCR, as well as a 10-cup coffee unit with fresh gourmet-blend coffee and tea. Baths have whirlpool tubs and a phone. Complimentary breakfast is served as an added plus. *10330 W. Olympic Blvd., Los Angeles 90064, tel. 213/553–1000 or 800/553–1005. 46 rooms. Facilities: rental cars, parking. AE, DC, MC, V.*

Coastal Los Angeles

Very Expensive
Bel Air Hotel. This is a charming, secluded hotel (and celebrity mecca) with lovely gardens and a creek complete with swans. The rooms and suites are decorated individually in peach and earth tones. All are villa bungalow style with Mediterranean decor. For their quietest accommodation, ask for a room near the former stable area. *701 Stone Canyon Road, Bel Air 90077, tel. 213/472–1211 or 800/648–4097 outside CA. 60 rooms, 32*

suites. Facilities: pool, restaurant, lounge, parking. AE, DC, MC, V.

Westwood Marquis. This hotel near UCLA is a favorite of corporate and entertainment types. Each individualized suite in its 15 stories has a view of Bel Air, the Pacific Ocean, and downtown L.A. Ask for a suite that overlooks the pool and garden. Breakfast and lunch are served in the Garden Terrace, which is also famous for its Sunday brunch. The award-winning Dynasty Room features Continental cuisine plus special Minceur spa diet menu. European teas are served in the afternoon in the Westwood Lounge. *930 Hilgard Ave., Los Angeles 90024, tel. 213/208–8765 or 800/692–2140. 258 suites. Facilities: 2 pools, sauna, phones in bathrooms, banquet and meeting rooms, pay parking. AE, DC, MC, V.*

Expensive **Radisson Bel Air Summit.** This "bit of the Bahamas in Bel Air" (near Brentwood) has been recently renovated. The fixtures in the rooms are Art Deco–style; the furniture is Italian style, with sleek, modern shapes. *11461 Sunset Blvd., Los Angeles 90049, tel. 213/476–6571, 800/421–6649 nationwide, or 800/333–3333 in CA. 162 rooms. Facilities: restaurant, lounge, pool, tennis courts, free parking. AE, DC, MC, V.*

Moderate–Expensive **Century Wilshire.** Most units in this European-style hotel are suites featuring kitchenettes. There are tiled baths and homey English-style pastel decor. Within walking distance of UCLA and Westwood Village, this simple hotel has views of Wilshire and the courtyard. The clientele here is mostly European. *10776 Wilshire Blvd., West Los Angeles 90024, tel. 213/474–4506. 100 rooms. Facilities: heated swimming pool, complimentary Continental breakfast, free parking. AE, DC, MC, V.*

Inexpensive **Best Western Royal Palace Hotel.** This small hotel located just off I–405 has all suites, decorated with conservative, homey prints. In-room morning coffee and tea are complimentary, as is parking to hotel guests. Suites have kitchenettes. *2528 S. Sepulveda Blvd., West Los Angeles 90064, tel. 213/477–9066 or 800/528–1234. 58 rooms. Facilities: pool, Jacuzzi, exercise room and billiard room, laundry facilities. AE, DC, MC, V.*

Santa Monica

Very Expensive **Loews Santa Monica Beach Hotel.** Set on the most precious of L.A. real estate—beachfront—the Loews opened mid-1989 just south of the Santa Monica Pier. Most of the contemporary rooms have ocean views and private balconies, and all guests have private access to the beach. Its restaurant, Riva, serves Northern Italian cuisine with an emphasis on seafood. *1700 Ocean Ave., 90401, tel. 213/458–6700 or 800/223–0888. 350 rooms, including 35 suites. Facilities: restaurant, cafe, fitness center, indoor/outdoor pool, valet parking.*

Miramar Sheraton. This hotel, "where Wilshire meets the sea," is close to all area beaches, across the street from Pacific Palisades Park, and near deluxe shopping areas and many quaint eateries. The landscaping incorporates the area's second-largest rubber tree. Many rooms have balconies overlooking the ocean. The decor in some rooms is very contemporary, with bleached wood, marble, granite, glass, and brick. A new wing has traditional furnishings. *101 Wilshire Blvd., 90403, tel. 213/394–3731 or 800/325–3535. 305 rooms. Facilities: 3 restaurants, lounge, entertainment, pool. AE, DC, MC, V.*

Moderate **Holiday Inn Santa Monica Pier.** Close to many restaurants, major shopping centers, the beach, and Santa Monica Pier, this inn features standard Holiday Inn rooms and amenities. *120 Colorado Ave., 90401, tel. 213/451-0676. 132 rooms. Facilities: restaurant, lounge, pool, laundry facilities, meeting and banquet rooms, room service, free parking. AE, CB, DC, MC, V.*

Pacific Shore. Formerly the Royal Inn of Santa Monica, this modern building is a half block from the beach and many restaurants. The attractive rooms are decorated with contemporary fabrics and modern furniture; some have ocean views. *1819 Ocean Ave., 90401, tel. 213/451-8711, or 800/622-8711. 169 rooms. Facilities: restaurant, lounge, pool, sauna, therapy pool, Jacuzzi, laundry facilities, Avis Rent-a-Car, gift shop, free parking. AE, MC, V.*

Inexpensive **Carmel Hotel.** This charming hotel from the 1920s is one block from the beach and the new Santa Monica Shopping Plaza, as well as from movie theaters and many fine restaurants. Electric ceiling fans add to the room decor. There is a Mexican-American restaurant on the premises. *201 Broadway, 90401, tel. 213/451-2469. 110 rooms. Facilities: restaurant, parking (overnight fee). AE, DC, MC, V.*

Palm Motel. This quiet, unceremonious motel has old-fashioned rooms. The decorative highlight is the color TVs, but the motel does offer complimentary coffee, tea, and cookies at breakfast. It's only a short drive away from several good restaurants. *2020 14th St., 90405, tel. 213/452-3822. 26 rooms. Facilities: self-service laundry, free parking. MC, V.*

Marina del Rey

Very Expensive
★ **Marina Beach Hotel.** Opened in 1986, this luxurious nine-story high-rise hotel has high-tech design softened by a pastel decor accented in brass and marble. Ask for upper-floor rooms that face the marina. There are lovely touches, like a gazebo in the patio and rooms with water views. The restaurant Stones is known for its fresh seafood. The hotel offers 24-hour free transportation to and from LAX. All of the rooms are decorated in pastels and have a safe for valuables. *4100 Admiralty Way, 90292, tel. 213/301-3000, 800/528-0444 nationwide, or 800/862-7462 in CA. 386 rooms. Facilities: restaurant, lounges, pool, pay parking. AE, DC, MC, V.*

Marina del Rey Hotel. Completely surrounded by water, this deluxe waterfront hotel is on the marina's main channel, making cruises and charters accessible. Guest rooms (contemporary with a nautical touch) offer balconies, patios, and harbor views. For splendid views, book a room that faces the water. The hotel is within walking distance of shopping and only a bike ride away from Fisherman's Village. There are meeting rooms and a beautiful gazebo area for parties. *13534 Bali Way, 90292, tel. 213/301-1000, 800/822-1010, or 800/421-8145. 160 rooms. Facilities: 2 restaurants, lounge, pool, putting green, airport transportation, free parking. AE, DC, MC, V.*

Expensive–
Very Expensive **Marina del Rey Marriott Inn.** Located in a lively area—a shopping center near Fox Hills Mall and across the street from a movie theater—the building is only 10 years old. The Old World–style rooms are decorated in light blue, rust, or light green. Tropical trees and foliage enhance the pool area; a goldfish pond makes Sunday brunch by the water a delight. *13480 Maxella Ave., 90292, tel. 213/822-8555 or 800/228-9290. 287*

rooms. Facilities: meeting and banquet rooms, pool, restaurant, lounge, Jacuzzi. AE, DC, MC, V.

Marina International Hotel. Directly across from an inland beach, this hotel is unique for its village-style decor. The rooms are done in earth tones with California-style furniture. Each of the very private rooms offers a balcony or patio that faces the garden or the courtyard. Ask for a bungalow—they're huge. The Crystal Fountain restaurant has Continental cuisine. Boat charters are available for up to 200 people. *4200 Admiralty Way, 90292, tel. 213/301–2000, 800/528–0444 nationwide, or 800/862–7462 in CA. 110 rooms, 25 bungalows. Facilities: restaurant, lounge, pool, airport transportation, free parking. AE, DC, MC, V.*

The Ritz-Carlton, Marina del Rey. Opened in 1990, this sumptuous property sits on some prime real estate at the northern end of a basin, offering a resplendent panoramic view of the Pacific. The extremely attractive rooms have marble baths, honor bars, and plenty of amenities—from maid service twice a day to plush terry robes. *4640 Admiralty Way, Marina del Rey 90292, tel. 213/823–3656. 306 rooms. Facilities: pool, sun deck, fitness center, tennis courts, boutiques, complimentary transportation to LAX. AE, CB, DC, MC, V.*

Moderate   **Marina Pacific Hotel & Suites.** This hotel faces the Pacific and one of the world's most vibrant boardwalks; it's nestled among art galleries, shops, and elegant, offbeat restaurants. The marina is just a stroll away. The Spanish-style rooms are all decorated in pink. Comfortable accommodations include suites, conference facilities, full-service amenities, and a delightful sidewalk cafe. For the active traveler, there are ocean swimming, roller skating along the strand, racquetball, and tennis nearby. *1697 Pacific Ave., Venice 90291, tel. 213/399–7770, 800/421–8151 nationwide, or 800/826–2474 in CA. 125 rooms. 1-bedroom apartments available. Facilities: restaurant, laundry. AE, DC, MC, V.*

South Bay Beach Cities

Expensive–   **Sheraton at Redondo Beach.** Opened in 1987, this swank five-
Very Expensive   story hotel, located across the street from the Redondo Beach Pier, overlooks the Pacific. There are plenty of amenities, including indoor and outdoor dining and a nightclub. The rooms are decorated in a seaside theme of light woods and bright colors. *300 N. Harbor Dr., Redondo Beach 90277, tel. 213/318–8888 or 800/325–3535. 339 rooms. Facilities: restaurant, lounge, entertainment, pool, exercise room, game room, sauna, whirlpool, tennis, pay parking. AE, DC, MC, V.*

Moderate   **Barnaby's Hotel.** Modeled after a 19th-century English inn,
★   with four-poster beds, lace curtains, and antique decorations, Barnaby's also has an enclosed greenhouse pool. Rosie's Bar resembles a cozy pub, with live entertainment; Barnaby's Restaurant features Continental cuisine and curtained private booths. Afternoon tea is a highlight. An adjacent health club charges $10 per day. Weekend packages are available. *3501 Sepulveda Blvd., at Rosecrans, Manhattan Beach, tel. 213/545–8466 or 800/552–5285. 128 rooms. Facilities: restaurants, lounge, pool. AE, DC, MC, V.*

Airport

**Expensive–
Very Expensive**

Sheraton Plaza La Reina. A luxurious 15-story hotel befitting its name of "Plaza of the Queen," this is in a perfect setting for business and leisure travelers alike. The contemporary rooms are decorated in muted shades of mauve, brown, green, and purple. Ninety-six meeting rooms, with in-house audiovisual equipment, can accommodate groups up to 1,000. There are two restaurants: Plaza Brasserie, a coffee shop open from 6 AM to midnight, and Landry's, for steak and lobster, with an excellent sushi bar, open till 10 PM. 48 of the rooms are especially designed for the disabled. *6101 W. Century Blvd., Los Angeles 90045, tel. 213/642–1111. 852 rooms. Facilities: restaurants, lounges, live entertainment, multilingual concierge, room service, currency exchange, direct international dialing from guest-room telephones. AE, DC, MC, V.*

Expensive

Hyatt Hotel-LAX. Earth tones and brass decorate this elegant 12-story building, the hotel closest to LAX, Hollywood Park, the Forum, and Marina del Rey. The Hyatt keeps business travelers in mind, and it offers large meeting rooms with ample banquet space. The hotel's staff is bilingual and a concierge is on duty 24 hours a day. *6225 W. Century Blvd., 90045, tel. 213/670–9000 or 800/233–1234. 596 rooms. Facilities: restaurant, coffee shop, lounge, entertainment, pool, sauna, exercise room, pay parking. AE, DC, MC, V.*

The Los Angeles Airport Marriott. One of the first luxury hotels to be built in the airport area (it opened in 1973), this Marriott is a fully equipped convention center and convenient to the beach, Marina del Rey, Fisherman's Village, the Forum, and the Coliseum. Complimentary airport bus service gets you to LAX in just four minutes. Seven restaurants and lounges offer gourmet elegance, family-style dining, and lavish California-style buffets. All guest rooms are designed for maximum space and comfort in relaxing earth tones, some with sitting areas and balcony. *5855 W. Century Blvd., 90045, tel. 213/641–5700 or 800/228–9290. 1,012 rooms. Facilities: restaurants, lounges, entertainment, pool, health club, laundry facilities, pay parking. AE, DC, MC, V.*

★ **Stouffer Concourse Hotel.** This is a good place to stay if you're looking for pampering near the airport. Rooms and suites are decorated in soft pastels and some deeper colors to complement the contemporary decor; many suites have private outdoor spas. The expansive, luxurious lobby is decorated in earth tones and brass. The Trattoria Grande restaurant features pasta and seafood specialties. *5400 W. Century Blvd., Los Angeles 90045, tel. 213/216–5858 or 800/468–3571. 750 rooms. Facilities: 2 restaurants, lounge, entertainment, pool, sauna, fitness center, pay parking. AE, DC, MC, V.*

Moderate

Airport Marina Hotel. Located in a quiet, residential area, perfect for jogging, tennis, and golf, the hotel consists of four separate wings: The main building and the tower have contemporary rooms that recently have been redecorated in blue and orange; the Fountain and West wings have more traditional rooms in floral prints. Full services are provided, and there is excellent dining in the American Celebration Restaurant. The hotel also has a shuttle service to Fisherman's Village. *8601 Lincoln Blvd., Los Angeles 90045, tel. 213/670–8111* *or 800/227–1117 nationwide. 750 rooms. Facilities: restaurant, airport transportation. AE, DC, MC, V.*

Airport Park Hotel. Located on the grounds of the Hollywood Park racetrack, this hotel is next door to the Forum and close to major freeways. There are all types of rooms here: traditional to modern, in colors like blue, pink, brown, or gold. The hotel also features the Shanghai Gardens restaurant and convenient coffee shop, Champs. *600 S. Prairie, Inglewood 90301, tel. 213/673–5151. 350 rooms. Facilities: 2 restaurants, pool, free 24-hr shuttle to LAX. AE, DC, MC, V.*

Holiday Inn-LAX. This recently decorated, international-style hotel is ideal for families and business types. The hotel features standard Holiday Inn rooms in colors like beige, burgundy, pink, orange, or green. Other amenities include the well-known restaurant and cocktail lounge, Wings; multilingual telephone operators; and tour information. *9901 La Cienega Blvd., Los Angeles 90045, tel. 213/649–5151 or 800/238–8000. 403 rooms. Facilities: restaurant, pool, free parking. AE, DC, MC, V.*

Pacifica Hotel. Just three miles north of LAX and a few minutes from Marina del Rey, this deluxe Spanish American–style hotel is convenient for business types. There is both elegant and casual dining. The Culver's Club Lounge has lively entertainment and dancing. Extra special is the Shalamar Suite, with beautiful decorations and its own indoor pool. Package rates are available. *6161 Centinela Ave., Culver City 90230, tel. 213/649–1776 or 800/542–6082. 368 rooms. Facilities: restaurant, lounge, entertainment, pool, sauna, health club, free parking. AE, DC, MC, V.*

San Fernando Valley

Very Expensive **Sheraton Universal.** You're apt to see movie and TV stars in this large, 23-story hotel. The hotel is on the grounds of Universal City, where you'll see the renovated Universal Amphitheater and can tour the largest movie studio in the world. (Any guesses?—Universal.) The hotel overlooks Hollywood. The rooms have been decorated in muted shades of blue, beige, and gray. *333 Universal Terrace Pkwy., Universal City 91608, tel. 818/980–1212. 500 rooms. Facilities: 2 restaurants, rooftop pool, sauna, whirlpool spa, exercise room. AE, DC, MC, V.*

Sierra Hotel. This 24-story glass tower (opened in 1984) blends contemporary luxury with the charm of an Old World European hotel. The bright rooms are decorated in dark beige, brick, blue, and peach, and the bathrooms have wall-to-wall marble. Breathtaking views of the San Fernando Valley and hills can be enjoyed through floor-to-ceiling windows. Inside the 40-foot-high pavilions next to the guest tower are two restaurants and two lounges. There is a nearby tennis center and equestrian center, and golf courses are a short drive away. A popular place for TV location filming, this is close to the Universal Amphitheater, Universal Studios Tour, and the Hollywood Bowl. *555 Universal Terrace Pkwy., Universal City 91608, tel. 818/506–2500. 450 rooms. Facilities: 9 meeting rooms, an executive boardroom, grand ballroom, palm-studded gardens, oversize heated pool, health spa. AE, DC, MC, V.*

Expensive **Burbank Airport Hilton.** This Hilton is located across the street from the Hollywood-Burbank Airport and close to Universal Studios. There are rooms here for anyone's taste, though all are

Beverly Garland's
Howard Johnson
Resort Lodge, **4**

Burbank Airport
Hilton, **7**

St. George Motor
Inn, **2**

Safari Inn, **8**

Sheraton Universal, **6**

Sierra Hotel, **5**

Sportsman's Lodge
Hotel, **1**

The Valley Hilton, **3**

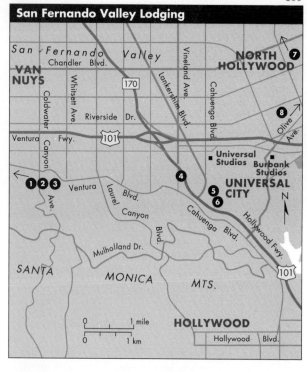

San Fernando Valley Lodging

done in standard hotel decor; the colors—browns to mauves
and reds—give each room a unique atmosphere. *2500 Hollywood Way, Burbank 91505, tel. 818/843–6000. 277 rooms. Facilities: pool, whirlpool spa, color TV and VCR in room, gift
shop, small meeting and banquet facilities, free parking. AE,
DC, MC, V.*

Moderate   **Beverly Garland's Howard Johnson Resort Lodge.** There's a
country-club atmosphere to this seven-story site, which is popular with business and entertainment folk, that offers private
balconies and patios. The lodge is on the historic El Camino
Real. *4222 Vineland Ave., North Hollywood 91602, tel. 818/
980–8000. 258 rooms. Facilities: swimming and wading pool,
cocktail lounge, tennis courts, free parking. AE, DC, MC, V.*

Sportsman's Lodge Hotel. An English country–style building
with a resort atmosphere, this hotel features beautiful grounds
with waterfalls. Guest rooms are large, with country decor in
colors like mauve and blue. Studio suites with private patios
are available, and there's an Olympic-size swimming pool and a
restaurant with American and Continental cuisine. The hotel is
close to the Universal Studios Tour and Universal Amphitheater. *12825 Ventura Blvd., Studio City 91654, tel. 818/769–4700.
196 rooms. Facilities: restaurant, coffee shop, room service,
pool, free parking. AE, DC, MC, V.*

The Valley Hilton. In addition to excellent service and comfort,
this Hilton boasts a convenient location (at the intersection of
I–405 and Hwy. 101). Aside from being not far from Universal
Studios and other Southland attractions, it's well equipped for
conventioneers: Its banquet and meeting rooms accommodate

up to 500 people. There are plush executive suites. *15433 Ventura Blvd., Sherman Oaks 91403, tel. 818/981–5400. 217 rooms. Facilities: Restaurant, lounge, pay parking. AE, DC, MC, V.*

Inexpensive **Safari Inn.** Often used for location filming, this hotel offers high-standard services. The rooms recently have been redone, with a modern flair. Some feature blond wood, some rattan furniture. Suites with bars are available. There's a fine French restaurant, LeSerene, on the premises. *1911 W. Olive, Burbank 91506, tel. 818/845–8586. 110 rooms. Facilities: restaurant, pool, Jacuzzi, cocktail lounge, free parking. AE, DC, MC, V.*

St. George Motor Inn. This English Tudor–style hotel, near the southwest end of the San Fernando Valley and close to the Warner Studios ranch, features stark, simple room decor. It's convenient for its proximity to such restaurants as Victoria Station and Charlie Brown's. *19454 Ventura Blvd., Tarzana 91356, tel. 818/345–6911. 57 rooms. Facilities: heated pool, Jacuzzi, kitchenettes, free parking. AE, DC, MC, V.*

8 The Arts and Nightlife

For the most complete listing of weekly events, get the current issue of *Los Angeles* or *California* magazine. The Calendar section of the Los Angeles *Times* also offers a wide survey of Los Angeles arts events, as do the more irreverent free publications the *L.A. Weekly* and the *L.A. Reader*.

Most tickets can be purchased by phone (with a credit card) from **Teletron** (tel. 213/410–1062), **Ticketmaster** (tel. 213/480–3232), **Ticketron** (tel. 213/642–4242), **Good Time Tickets** (tel. 213/464–7383), or **Murray's Tickets** (tel. 213/234–0123).

The Arts

The following credit card abbreviations are used: AE, American Express; CB, Carte Blanche; DC, Diners Club; MC, MasterCard; V, Visa.

Theater

If Los Angeles isn't quite the "Broadway of the West" as some have claimed—the scope of theater here really doesn't compare to that of the Great White Way—there are unique offerings worth any visitor's time in this entertainment-oriented city.

The growth is astounding. In 1978 only about 370 professional productions were brought to stages in Los Angeles; in 1982 more than 600 were scheduled. Small theaters are blossoming all over town, and the larger houses, despite price hikes to $35 for a single ticket, are full as often as not.

Even small productions might boast big names from "the Business" (the Los Angeles entertainment empire). Many film and television actors love to work on the stage between "big" projects as a way to refresh their talents or regenerate their creativity in this demanding medium. Doing theater is also an excellent way to be seen by those who matter in the more glitzy end of show business. Hence there is a need for both large houses—which usually mount productions that are road-company imports of Broadway hits or, on occasion, are the place where Broadway-bound material begins its tryout phase—and a host of small, intimate theaters for the talent that abounds in this city.

The following sampling includes some of the major houses in the area. All are located in Los Angeles unless otherwise noted.

Ahmanson Theater. With 2,071 seats, this is the largest of the three-theater Music Center complex (with the Dorothy Chandler Pavilion and the Mark Taper Forum), and productions include both classics and new plays. The list of artists who have worked at this theater reads like a Who's Who of stage and screen. *135 N. Grand Ave., tel. 213/972–7654. Tickets: $37–$50. AE, DC, MC, V.*
Dorothy Chandler Pavilion. Also part of the Music Center, this 3,200-seat house offers a smattering of plays in between performances of the L.A. Philharmonic. *135 N. Grand Ave., tel. 213/972–7211. Tickets: $7–$35. AE, DC, MC, V.*
James A. Doolittle. Located in the heart of Hollywood, this house offers an intimate feeling despite its 1,038-seat capacity. New plays, dramas, comedies, and musicals are presented here

year-round. *1615 N. Vine St., Hollywood, tel. 213/462–6666; charge line, 213/851–9750. Tickets: $26–$36. AE, DC, MC, V.*

John Anson Ford Theater. This 1,300-seat house in the Hollywood hills is best known for its Shakespeare and free summer jazz, dance, and cabaret concerts. *2580 Cahuenga Blvd., Hollywood, tel. 213/972–7211. Tickets: $10–$35. AE, MC, V.*

Mark Taper Forum. Also part of the Music Center, this house boasts 742 seats, excellent acoustics, and an intimate setting. The theater, under the direction of Gordon Davidson, is committed to new works and to the development of a community of artists. Many of its plays, including *Children of a Lesser God,* have gone on to Broadway. *135 N. Grand Ave., tel. 213/972–7353; charge line, 213/972–7654. Tickets: $17.50–$23.50. AE, DC, MC, V.*

Pantages. Once the home of the Oscar telecast and Hollywood premieres, this house is massive (2,300 seats) and (except for the acoustics) splendid. Musicals from Broadway are usually presented here. *6233 Hollywood Blvd., Hollywood, tel. 213/410–1062. Tickets: $15–$35. MC, V.*

Second City Theater. Built in 1911, this charming 282-seat theater (a former opera house) is decorated in an Old World style and now houses the infamous Second City comedy troupe. *214 Santa Monica Blvd., Santa Monica, tel. 213/451–0621. Tickets: $7–$15. AE, DC, MC, V.*

Westwood Playhouse. An acoustically superior theater with great sightlines, the 498-seat playhouse showcases new plays, primarily musicals and comedies in the summer. Many productions come in from Broadway; two—*Perfectly Frank* and *Passionate Ladies*—went on to Broadway. Jason Robards and Nick Nolte got their starts here. *10886 Le Conte Ave., Westwood, tel. 213/208–6500 or 213/208–5454. Tickets: $17.50–$30. AE, DC, MC, V.*

Wilshire Theater. The interior of this newly renovated, 1,900-seat house is Art Deco–style; musicals from Broadway are the usual fare. *8440 Wilshire Blvd., Beverly Hills, tel. 213/642–4242. Tickets: $14.50–$27.50. MC, V.*

Smaller houses are more specialized in their offerings. Here are a few of the best:

Cast Theater. Musicals, revivals, and avant-garde improv pieces are done here. The production of *Working* was picked up for PBS from here, and *The Hasty Heart* went on to the Ahmanson. *804 N. El Centro, tel. 213/462–0265. Tickets: around $15, previews around $10. AE, MC, V.*

The Coast Playhouse. This 99-seat house specializes in excellent original musicals and new dramas. *8325 Santa Monica Blvd., West Hollywood, tel. 213/650–8507. Tickets: $16–$20. AE, MC, V.*

Fountain Theater. Seating 80, this theater presents contemporary drama and comedies. Marian Mercer and Rob Reiner got their starts here. *5060 Fountain Ave., tel. 213/663–1525. Tickets: $7–$8. No credit cards.*

Japan America Theater. This community-oriented 880-seat theater at the Japan Cultural Arts Center is home to Kabuki troupes, local Japanese koto recitals, the East West Players, and numerous children's theater groups. *244 S. San Pedro, tel. 213/680–3700. Ticket prices vary. MC, V.*

Santa Monica Playhouse. This 99-seat house is worth visiting for its cozy, librarylike atmosphere; good comedies and dramas should add further incentive. *1211 4th St., Santa Monica, tel. 213/394–9779. Tickets: $10–$20. No credit cards.*

Skylight Theater. With 99 seats, this theater has hosted many highly inventive productions. *1816½ N. Vermont Ave., Los Feliz, tel. 213/466–1767. Tickets: $6–$15. AE, MC, V.*

Theatre/Theater. This 99-seater houses new, often terrific comedies and drama. *1713 Cahuenga Blvd., Hollywood, tel. 213/ 871–0210. Tickets: $7–$15. No credit cards.*

Concerts

Los Angeles is not only the focus of America's pop/rock music recording scene, after years of being regarded as a cultural invalid, but now also a center for classical music and opera.

The following is a list of Los Angeles's major concert halls:

The Ambassador Auditorium (300 W. Green St., Pasadena, tel. 818/304–6161). World-renowned soloists and ensembles perform in this elegant and acoustically impressive hall from September to May. *AE, MC, V.*

Dorothy Chandler Pavilion (135 N. Grand Ave., tel. 213/972–7211). Part of the Los Angeles Music Center and—with the Hollywood Bowl—the center of L.A.'s classical music scene, the 3,200-seat Pavilion is the home of the Los Angeles Philharmonic from November to April and the showcase for the Los Angeles Master Chorale Group, the Los Angeles Civic Light Opera, and, in the fall, the Joffrey Ballet. *AE, MC, V.*

The Greek Theater (2700 N. Vermont Ave., tel. 213/410–1062). This open-air auditorium near Griffith Park offers some classical performances in its mainly pop/rock/jazz schedule from June to October. Its Doric columns evoke the amphitheaters of ancient Greece. *AE, MC, V.*

The Hollywood Bowl (2301 Highland Ave., tel. 213/850–2000). Open since 1920, the Bowl is one of the world's largest outdoor amphitheaters, located in a park surrounded by mountains, trees, and gardens. The L.A. Philharmonic spends its summer season here. Concert-goers usually arrive early, bringing or buying picnic suppers. There are plenty of picnic tables, and box-seat subscribers can reserve a table right in their own box. Restaurant dining is available on the grounds (reservations recommended, tel. 213/851–3588). The seats are wood, so you might bring or rent a cushion—and bring a sweater. A convenient way to enjoy the Hollywood Bowl experience without the hassle of parking is to take one of the Park-and-Ride buses, which leave from various locations around town; call the Bowl for information. *MC, V.*

Royce Hall (405 N. Hilgard, tel. 213/825–9261). Internationally acclaimed performers are featured in this 1,800-seat auditorium at UCLA. The university's **Schoenberg Hall,** smaller but with wonderful acoustics, also hosts a variety of concerts. *MC, V.*

The Shrine Auditorium (665 W. Jefferson Blvd., tel. 213/749–5123). Built in 1926 by the Al Malaikah Temple, the auditorium's decor could be termed Basic Baghdad and Beyond. Touring companies from all over the world, along with assorted gospel and choral groups, appear in this one-of-a-kind, 6,200-seat theater. *AE, MC, V.*

The Wilshire Ebell Theater (4401 W. Eighth St., tel. 213/939–1128). The Los Angeles Opera Theatre comes to this Renaissance-style building (Spanish in architecture and design, built in 1924), as do a broad spectrum of other musical performers. *No credit cards.*

Wiltern Theater (Wilshire Blvd. and Western Ave., tel. 213/ 380–5005). Reopened in 1985 as a venue for the Los Angeles Opera Theater, the building was constructed in 1930, is listed in the National Register of Historic Places, and is a striking example of Art Deco in its green terra-cotta glory. *MC, V.*

Dance

Los Angeles offers not only its own Bella Lewitsky and the Los Angeles Chamber Ballet, but also yearly visiting dance companies including the Joffrey, American Ballet Theatre, Martha Graham, and Paul Taylor, to name a few. Most dance events in Los Angeles will be listed each Sunday in the Los Angeles *Times* Calendar section. The **Dance Resource Center of Greater Los Angeles** (tel. 213/281–1918) also offers current dance information.

The Music Center (135 N. Grand, tel. 213/972–7211). At the western home of the late Robert Joffrey's bicoastal ballet company, you'll find (in spring and fall) the company dancing a range of works from the elegant *pas de trois Monotones* to the full production of *Romeo and Juliet.* The yearly Folk Dance Festival is held in March. *AE, MC, V.*

The Shrine Auditorium (665 W. Jefferson, tel. 213/749–5123). This is host of the American Ballet Theatre (ABT) in March. ABT's repertoire includes Baryshnikov's *Cinderella* and Saint Leon's classic *Coppelia. AE, MC, V.*

UCLA Center for the Arts (405 N. Hilgard, tel. 213/825–9261) attracts masters of modern dance, jazz, and ballet, including Martha Graham, Bella Lewitsky, Paul Taylor, Hubbard Street Dance Company, and Bejart, along with its own UCLA Dance Company. Rush tickets priced at $7 are available on the night of the performance for full-time students and senior citizens. *MC, V.*

Film

Spending two hours at a movie while visiting Los Angeles needn't be taking time out from sightseeing. Some of the country's most historic and beautiful theaters are found here, hosting both first-run and revival films.

Movie listings are advertised daily in the Calendar section of the papers. The price of admission to first-run movies is, as of this writing, $6–$7. Bargain prices as low as $3.50 are common for the first showing of the day.

First, a sampling of L.A.'s palaces:

Egyptian Theater (6712 Hollywood Blvd., tel. 213/467–6167) Built in 1922, this theater also was owned by Sid Grauman, and it was the site of many premieres. Now run by United Artists, it's been converted into a triple-screen facility for first-run movies, but the lobby maintains the ornate Egyptian decor that made it famous.

Pacific Cinerama Dome (6360 Sunset Blvd., tel. 213/466–3401). This futuristic, geodesic structure was the first theater designed specifically for Cinerama in the United States. The gigantic screen and multitrack sound system create an unparalleled cinematic experience.

Mann's Chinese Theater (6925 Hollywood Blvd., tel. 213/464–8111). Formerly owned by Sid Grauman, this Chinese pagoda structure is perhaps the world's best-known movie theater. It still carries on one of the oldest of Hollywood traditions: its famous hand- and footprinting ceremony, which was inspired by the mason who supervised the construction of the theater's forecourt. Grauman came upon Jean W. Klossner, a French immigrant, as he put his handprint in wet cement near the marquee after he finished laying the entrance to the theater. A descendant of generations of French masons, Klossner explained that his father, grandfather, and great-grandfather had placed their handprints and signatures at the curbstone of Notre Dame in Paris to mark their contributions to civilization. Grauman offered the Frenchman a 34-year contract to place the imprints of Hollywood's greatest stars in the secret cement mixture that Klossner had devised to stand the test of time. Mary Pickford and Douglas Fairbanks, Sr., were the first to place their hand- and footprints at the entrance to the theater during the opening ceremony on May 18, 1927. Today the Chinese houses three movies, and it still hosts many gala premieres.

The less prestigious movie houses often offer double bills for a good price. Here are some of the best:

Aero (Montana and 14th St., Santa Monica, tel. 213/395–4990). A movie theater with a cozy, hometown atmosphere; the glowing neon clock near the screen is an unusual touch.

AMC Century Fourteen Theaters (10250 Santa Monica Blvd., Century City, tel. 213/553–8900). This complex is located amid the restaurants and shops of the Century City Shopping Center.

Clinton (526 N. Western, tel. 213/461–3064). The Clinton features $1.25 seats all week.

Rialto Theater (1023 S. Fair Oaks Blvd., South Pasadena, tel. 818/799–9567). A richly decorated, spacious house that hasn't been converted—yet—into a multiscreen theater, as have most large, older theaters in town.

Vista Theater (4473 Sunset Dr., Hollywood, tel. 213/660–6639). Good double bills and special late shows of cult films (*The Rocky Horror Picture Show, Eraserhead,* and others) on weekends.

Los Angeles art houses (a vanishing breed, due to home video) bill revivals, foreign films, and animation festivals on neon-decorated marquees preserved to convey the original feeling of neighborhood movie theaters.

American Film Institute Festival L.A. (tel. 213/520–2000). An annual event, usually in March, screening innovative and controversial films.

The **Laemmle Theater** chain hosts the best of the latest foreign releases. See their L.A. *Times* Calendar ad for listings. In addition, the 14-theater **Cineplex** (8522 Beverly Blvd., in the Beverly Center, tel. 213/652–7760) offers foreign films and first-run features.

Melnitz Hall (405 Hilgard Ave., tel. 213/825–2581). UCLA's main film theater runs a mixture of the old, the avant-garde, and the neglected.

New Beverly Cinema (7165 Beverly Blvd., tel. 213/938–4038). Film festivals, Hollywood classics, documentaries, and notable foreign films are the fare at this theater. There is always a double bill.

Nuart (11272 Santa Monica, tel. 213/478–6379). The best-kept of L.A.'s revival houses, with an excellent screen, good double bills, and Dolby stereo.

Vagabond Theater (2509 Wilshire Blvd., tel. 213/387–2171). The Vagabond specializes in double bills of musicals, vintage drama, and comedy films.

Nightlife

Nightlife in Los Angeles has come to mean anything from catching a stand-up routine at the Comedy Store to frenetic disco dancing at Chippendale's. This city offers a potpourri of specialized entertainment, not only in the hub of the city but also in the outlying suburbs.

Despite the high energy level of the nightlife crowd, Los Angeles nightclubs aren't known for keeping their doors open until the wee hours. This is an early-to-bed city, and it's safe to say that by 2 AM, most jazz, rock, and disco clubs are closed for the night. Perhaps it's the temperate climate and the sports orientation of the city: Most Angelenos want to be on the tennis court or out jogging by 9 AM, so a late-night social life is out of the question.

The accent in this city is on trendy rock clubs, smooth country-and-western establishments, intimate jazz spots, and comedy clubs. City residents generally don't gravitate toward hotels for nighttime entertainment, but you can discover there a quiet evening of soft piano music, often accompanied by sentimental vocalists, for a refreshing change of pace.

The Sunset Strip, which runs from West Hollywood to Beverly Hills, offers a wide assortment of nighttime diversions. Comedy stores, restaurants with piano bars, cocktail lounges, and hard-rock clubs proliferate.

Westwood, home of UCLA, is a college town, and this section of Los Angeles comes alive at night with rock and new-wave clubs playing canned and live music. It's one of the few areas in the city with a true neighborhood spirit. For years, downtown Los Angeles hasn't offered much in the way of nighttime entertainment (with the exception of the Music Center for concerts and theater), but that has gradually changed over the last year, with the openings of more theaters and trendy clubs.

Don't think that the city suburbs have no nightlife. Some of Los Angeles's best jazz clubs, discos, and comedy clubs are scattered throughout the San Fernando and San Gabriel valleys. For example, the Palomino Club in North Hollywood boasts nationally recognized country-and-western performers as well as top rock acts.

Dress codes vary depending on the place you visit. Jackets are expected at cabarets and hotels. Discos are generally casual, although some will turn away the denim-clad. The rule of thumb is to phone ahead and check the dress code, but on the whole, Los Angeles is oriented toward casualwear.

The following night spots are divided according to their orientation: jazz, folk/pop/rock, cabaret, disco/dancing, country, hotel rooms and piano bars, and comedy and magic. Consult *Los Angeles* and *California* magazines for current listings. The Sunday Los Angeles *Times* Calendar section, the *Herald Examiner*

Style section, and the free *L.A. Weekly* and *L.A. Reader* also provide listings.

The following credit card abbreviations are used: AE, American Express; CB, Carte Blanche; DC, Diners Club; MC, MasterCard; V, Visa.

Jazz

The Baked Potato. A tiny club where they pack you in like sardines to hear a powerhouse of jazz. The featured item on the menu is, of course, baked potatoes; they're jumbo and stuffed with everything from steak to vegetables. *3787 Cahuenga Blvd. W, North Hollywood, tel. 818/980-1615. AE, MC, V.*

Birdland West. This is the place to come for contemporary jazz, Art Deco decor, and great happy hours. *105 W. Broadway, Long Beach, tel. 213/436-9341. Closed Mon.-Tues. AE, DC, MC, V.*

Bon Appetit. This cozy room spotlights different talent every night. A young, lively crowd turns up as much for the Continental cuisine as for the entertainment. *1061 Broxton Ave., Westwood, tel. 213/208-3030. AE, DC, MC, V.*

Catalina Bar and Grill. Big name acts and innovators like Latin-influenced saxophonist Paquito D. Rivera light up this top Hollywood jazz spot. Continental cuisine is served. *1640 N. Cahuenga Blvd., Hollywood, tel. 213/466-2210. AE, MC, V. Cover varies.*

Jax. An intimate club serving a wide variety of food, from sandwiches to steak and seafood. Live music is an added draw. *339 N. Brand Blvd., Glendale, tel. 818/500-1604. AE, MC, V. No cover.*

Le Cafe. The Room Upstairs is of high-tech design, and it features mellow jazz. Downstairs is a dynamic restaurant-cafe offering everything from onion soup to the best fresh duck in town. Le Cafe is open seven nights. *14633 Ventura Blvd., Sherman Oaks, tel. 818/986-2662. AE, MC, V.*

The Lighthouse. One of Los Angeles's finest offers a broad spectrum of music, from reggae to big band. Jam sessions are often held on weekends. Freddie Hubbard, Woody Herman, and Jimmy Witherspoon all have played here. The decor is wood, brass, and brick, with a lot of plants. Dine on fettuccine, appetizers, or steaks while listening to the sounds. *30 Pier Ave., Hermosa Beach, tel. 213/372-6911 or 213/376-9833. MC, V with a $5 minimum. No cover.*

Marla's Memory Lane. This club is now owned by comedy star Marla Gibbs of "The Jeffersons" and "227." Newly remodeled, the room pops with blues, jazz, and easy listening. Kenny Burrell and Ernie Andrews play here from time to time. A new menu includes prime rib of beef and Alaskan king crab legs. *2323 W. Martin Luther King, Jr. Blvd., Los Angeles, tel. 213/294-8430. AE, DC, MC, V.*

Nucleus Nuance. This Art Deco restaurant features vintage jazz on Friday and Saturday nights. *7267 Melrose Ave., West Hollywood, tel. 213/939-8666. AE, DC, MC, V.*

Vine Street Bar and Grill. This elegant club in the heart of Hollywood (across the street from the James Doolittle Theater) features two shows nightly. Past performers have included Eartha Kitt, Cab Calloway, and Carmen McRae. Italian food is served. *1610 N. Vine St., Hollywood, tel. 213/463–4375. AE, MC, V.*

Folk/Pop/Rock

At My Place. This enterprise features a provocative blend of jazz/fusion, pop, and rhythm-and-blues music acts. Comedy performers open the weekend shows. Culinary specialties include quiche and potato skins. *1026 Wilshire Blvd., Santa Monica, tel. 213/451–8596. MC, V.*

The Central. A musician's hangout. Road crews, pop-act managers, and famous guitarists alike come to hear live music in the pop, soul, and jazz/fusion genres. Many celebrity musicians attend the Tuesday night jam sessions. *8852 Sunset Blvd., West Hollywood, tel. 213/855–9183. No credit cards.*

Club 88. Rock and roll nightly. *11784 Pico Blvd., West Los Angeles, tel. 213/479–6923. No credit cards.*

Club Lingerie. One local describes it as "clean enough for the timid, yet seasoned quite nicely for the tenured scenester." Best of all is its mix of really hot bands. *6507 Sunset Blvd., Hollywood, tel. 213/466–8557.*

Gazzarri's. A Sunset Strip landmark offering pure rock and roll with a 19–early 20s age group. Dress is casual. *9039 Sunset Blvd., West Hollywood, tel. 213/273–6606. No credit cards.*

Madame Wong's West. In a nutshell: a young crowd, local bands, dancing, and video games. Over 21 only. *2900 Wilshire Blvd., Santa Monica, tel. 213/829–7361.*

McCabe's Guitar Shop. Folk, acoustic rock, bluegrass, and soul in an intimate concert-hall setting. Coffee, herb tea, apple juice, and homemade sweets are served during intermission. The club is open Friday–Sunday only. *3101 Pico Blvd., Santa Monica, tel. 213/828–4497. AE, DC, MC, V.*

The Palace. The "in" spot for the upwardly mobile. It's plush Art Deco—truly a palace—and boasts live entertainment, a fabulous sound system, full bar, and dining upstairs. Patrons dress to kill. *1735 N. Vine St., Hollywood, tel. 213/462–3000 or 213/462–6031. AE, MC, V.*

The Palladium. This club is known for its events, the live bands that appear on Saturdays, and the funky, hip, younger crowd. *6215 W. Sunset Blvd., Hollywood, tel. 213/962–7600.*

Pier 52. From Tuesday through Sunday there are live dance bands playing pure rock and roll and Top 40s. Monday night is saved for top bands, including new wave and heavy metal. *52 Pier Ave., Hermosa Beach, tel. 213/376–1629. No credit cards.*

The Roxy. The premier Los Angeles rock club, classy and comfortable, offers performance art as well as theatrical productions. Many famous Los Angeles groups got their start here as opening acts. *9009 Sunset Blvd., West Hollywood, tel. 213/276–2222. No credit cards.*

Sasch. A live band plays Top 40s for the 21–35 age group. *11345 Ventura Blvd., Studio City, tel. 818/769–5555. AE, MC, V.*

The Strand. This major concert venue covers a lot of ground, hosting hot new acts like Asleep at the Wheel, bluesman Albert King, rock vet Robin Trower, and Billy Vera, all in the same week. Who says you can't have it all? *1700 S. Pacific Coast Hwy., Redondo Beach, tel. 213/316–1700. AE, MC, V.*

Sunset Saloon. This club draws a beach crowd with mostly rock-and-roll entertainment. *1 Washington St., Venice, tel. 213/821–2874. MC, V.*

The Troubador. In the early '70s this was one of the hottest clubs in town for major talent. Then business entered a shaky phase for a few years as the music industry changed its focus, but now it's rolling again, this time with up-and-coming talent. The adjoining bar is a great place to see and be seen. *9081 Santa Monica Blvd., West Hollywood, tel. 213/276–6168. No credit cards.*

Cabaret

Gio's Cabaret Theatre. This place is highly eclectic in its programs: One night will feature comedians, another night it's big-band time or jazz quartets or aspiring singers doing Broadway vignettes. The adjoining restaurant specializes in Brazilian cuisine. *7574 Sunset Blvd., Hollywood, tel. 213/876–1120. AE, DC, MC, V.*

L.A. Cabaret. The club features a variety of comedy acts nightly. Famous entertainers often make surprise appearances. *17271 Ventura Blvd., Encino, tel. 818/501–3737. AE.*

La Cage Aux Folles. A cabaret supper club featuring female impersonators who do impressions of such stars as Liza Minelli and Barbra Streisand. The ambience—with a shocking pink and stark blue color scheme—resembles a European bistro of 40 years ago. An unusual and fun place to go. There's an extensive French/Continental menu. There's a cover charge for diners. *643 N. La Cienega Blvd., West Hollywood, tel. 213/657–1091. Closed Mon. AE, DC, MC, V.*

Studio One Backlot. An elegant, classy night spot featuring excellent musical acts, singers, comedians, and dancers. *657 N. Robertson Blvd., West Hollywood, tel. 213/659–0472. AE, MC, V.*

Disco/Dancing

Bar One. Celebrities such as Warren Beatty and Charlie Sheen enjoy this restaurant and bar. A hot, hip place to dance, this is L.A.'s club of the moment. There's also a pool table and comfortable lounging areas. *9229 Sunset Blvd., Beverly Hills, tel. 213/271–8355.*

Carnavale. The motto here is: "where adults can be kids, too." The bar is set as a party in Rio with neon palms surrounding two long bars. Musicians, jugglers, and mimes entertain during happy hour. *223 N. Glendale Ave., Glendale, tel. 818/500–1665. AE, MC, V.*

China Club. This is the new West Coast branch of the notoriously hip New York danceteria. A serious attitude and the latest in performance art-wear will help you get in the door. *1600 N. Argyle, Hollywood, tel. 213/469–1600.*

Chippendale's. A popular Los Angeles disco, known for its male exotic dancers/waiters who strip down to G-strings for women only at the 8:30 PM shows. Men are welcome after 10 PM. There is dancing (too-loud funk, punk, and new wave) every night. Chippendale's is not for the timid or prudish. The cover varies; there are occasional free nights for ladies. *1024 S. Grand Ave., Los Angeles, tel. 213/396–4045. AE, MC, V.*

Circus Disco. A gay-owned and -operated club, featuring funk, rock, and exclusively new wave on Thursday nights. Open nightly. *6655 Santa Monica Blvd., Hollywood, tel. 213/462–1291. No credit cards.*

Coconut Teaszer. Disco dancing, a great barbecue menu, and killer drinks make for lively fun. *8177 Sunset Blvd., Los Angeles, tel. 213/654–4773. AE, MC, V.*

DC3. Hip and uptown, this club/restaurant in the Santa Monica Airport plays pop music until 2 AM. Look for an older, upscale crowd and sophisticated lighting effects. *2800 Donald Douglas Loop North, Santa Monica, tel. 213/399–2323.*

Florentine Gardens. One of Los Angeles's largest dance areas, with spectacular lighting to match. *5951 Hollywood Blvd., Hollywood, tel. 213/464–0706. Closed Mon.–Thurs. No credit cards.*

Nucleus Nuance. Casual, cool, and swinging, with dancing until 1:30 AM. *7262 Melrose Ave., Los Angeles, tel. 213/939–8666. AE, DC, MC, V.*

Samba E Saudade. The serious dance action in L.A. these days moves to a Latin beat. This Brazilian club dishes it up hot, with a sexy, infectious flair. At press time, the club was only open Thursday and Sunday. *9300 W. Jefferson Blvd., Culver City, tel. 213/962–1953.*

The Stock Exchange. Along with Vertigo, this is the hottest place to be downtown. This multilevel Art Deco palace was once the Pacific Stock Exchange; now it's a star-filled dance spot open Wednesday–Saturday. *618 S. Spring St., Los Angeles, tel. 213/627–4400. AE, MC.*

20/20. Once the Playboy Club, this night spot is where the beautiful people party, with plenty of mirrors for checking themselves out. Music runs from oldies to top 40. *2020 Ave. of the Stars, Century City, tel. 213/933–2020.*

Vertigo. A New York–style club with restricted entrance policy, large dance floor, balcony bar, and restaurant. Open Friday and Saturday until 4 AM, which is unusual for this city. *1024 S. Grand Ave., Los Angeles, tel. 213/747–4849. MC, V.*

Country

The Palomino. There's occasionally a wild crowd at this premier country showcase in Los Angeles. Good old boys and hip cowboys meet here, and everybody has a good time. *6907 Lankershim Blvd., North Hollywood, tel. 818/764–4010. AE, DC, MC, V.*

Hotel Lounges and Piano Bars

Alberto's Ristorante. This piano bar draws a neighborhood crowd, mostly over 40 and well-to-do. Alberto's serves excellent Italian food. *8826 Melrose Ave., Los Angeles, tel. 213/278–2770. AE, DC, MC, V.*

Bel-Air Sands Hotel. The Bimini Bar features a singer/pianist who performs music from the '40s as well as more contemporary tunes. *11461 Sunset Blvd., Bel Air, tel. 213/476–6571. AE, DC, MC, V.*

Beverly Hills Hotel. There's late supper and after-theater piano entertainment in the Polo Lounge nightly. This stately old hotel is a celebrity mecca. *9641 Sunset Blvd., Beverly Hills, tel. 213/276–2251. AE, DC, MC, V.*

Century Plaza Hotel. The Lobby Lounge features piano music nightly. *2025 Ave. of the Stars, Century City, tel. 213/277–2000. AE, DC, MC, V.*

Hotel Bel Air. There's entertainment Tuesday–Sunday, alternating between a pianist and a vocalist, in one of Los Angeles's most famous hotels. *701 Stone Canyon Rd., Bel Air, tel. 213/472–1211. AE, DC, MC, V.*

Hyatt Regency. There's a good piano lounge in this spectacularly designed hotel. *711 S. Hope St., Los Angeles, tel. 213/683–1234. AE, DC, MC, V.*

Hyatt Wilshire. Entertainment is featured in the Cafe Carnival Lounge. *3515 Wilshire Blvd., Los Angeles, tel. 213/381–7411. AE, DC, MC, V.*

Los Angeles Marriott. The Hangar Room on the top floor of the hotel offers a panoramic view of the city and especially of arrivals and departures from the Los Angeles International Airport. It's a romantic place to go for a drink and soft piano music accompanied by a soothing vocalist. Both standard and contemporary songs are featured. *5855 W. Century Blvd., Los Angeles, tel. 213/641–5700. AE, DC, MC, V.*

The New Otani Hotel and Garden. The Genji Bar of this Japanese-style hotel offers a sentimental vocalist. *120 S. Los Angeles St., Los Angeles, tel. 213/629–1200. AE, DC, MC, V.*

Regent Beverly Wilshire. Sofas and high tables set the atmosphere for this elegant piano bar, in one of L.A.'s premier and most historical hotels. *9500 Wilshire Blvd., Beverly Hills, tel. 213/275–5200. AE, DC, MC, V.*

Smoke House. There's a lounge room with assorted entertainment separate from the restaurant. Many musical acts of the 1950s are featured. *4420 Lakeside Dr., Burbank, tel. 818/845–3731. AE, DC, MC, V.*

Sportsmen's Lodge Restaurant. The lounge connected to the main hotel features a pianist; the setting, with brooks and swan-filled ponds, is very attractive. *12833 Ventura Blvd., Studio City, tel. 818/984–0202. AE, DC, MC, V.*

SS Princess Louise Restaurant. This ship sails to nowhere but stays afloat with a piano bar and a good restaurant. Enjoy a romantic view of the ocean and incoming ships. If you get carried away, you can get married at the ship's chapel. *Berth 95, Port of Los Angeles, San Pedro, tel. 213/831–2351. AE, DC, MC, V.*

Westin Bonaventure Hotel. In the Lobby Court there is music nightly. Another room, Top of Five, features two pianists in a revolving lounge, which offers breathtaking sights of the whole city. *5th and Figueroa St., L.A., tel. 213/624–1000. AE, DC, MC, V.*

Westwood Marquis. The Westwood Lounge of this chic hotel offers cozy settees, soft lights, and a piano or harp player. Vocalists are featured occasionally. *930 Hilgard Ave., Westwood, tel. 213/208–8765. AE, DC, MC, V.*

Comedy and Magic

Comedy and Magic Club. This beachfront club features many magicians and comedians seen on TV and in Las Vegas. The Unknown Comic, Elayne Boosler, and Pat Paulsen have all played here. Reservations are suggested. The menu features light American fare and many appetizers. *1018 Hermosa Ave., Hermosa Beach, tel. 213/372–2626. Closed Mon. AE, MC, V.*

Comedy Store. Los Angeles's premier comedy showcase for over a decade. Many famous comedians, including Robin Williams and Steve Martin, make unannounced appearances here. The cover varies. *8433 Sunset Blvd., Hollywood, tel. 213/656–6225. AE, MC, V.*

Groundlings Theater. Original skits, music, and improv, with each player contributing his/her own flavor to the usually hilarious performance. Junior Groundlings performs on Sundays. *7307 Melrose Ave., Hollywood, tel. 213/934–9700. MC, V.*

The Ice House Comedy Showroom. Three-act shows here feature comedians and magicians from Las Vegas as well as from television shows. Special bargain prices include show and dinner. *24 N. Mentor Ave., Pasadena, tel. 818/577–1894. MC, V.*

Igby's Comedy Cabaret. You'll see familiar television faces as well as up-and-coming comedians Tuesday through Saturday. Cabaret fare includes cocktails and dining in a friendly ambience. Reservations are necessary. *11637 Tennessee Place, Los Angeles, tel. 213/477–3553. AE, DC, MC, V.*

The Improvisation. The Improv is a transplanted New York establishment: 18 years in the Big Apple, seven in the Big Orange. Comedy is showcased, with some vocalists. The Improv was the proving ground for Liza Minelli and Richard Pryor, among others. Reservations are recommended. *8162 Melrose Ave., West Hollywood, tel. 213/651–2583 and 321 Santa Monica Blvd., Santa Monica, tel. 213/394–8664. MC, V for food and drinks only.*

The Laugh Factory. A variety of comedy acts and improvisation, seven days a week. No age limit. *8001 Sunset Blvd., Hollywood, tel. 213/656–8860. No credit cards.*

Merlin McFly Magical Bar and Grill. If you're seeing double here, it might not be the drinks: Magical illusions are featured nightly until midnight. Ladies, watch out for the powder room; lights will dim there, and you'll see a Houdini-like figure with a crystal ball in the mirror. *2702 Main St., Santa Monica, tel. 213/392–8468. AE, DC, MC, V.*

Second City. The Chicago comedy institution behind SCTV and innumerable top performers has finally come to L.A. Improv is the specialty of the house, and it's almost always well done. *214 Santa Monica Blvd., Santa Monica, tel. 213/451–0621. Closed Mon.*

Casinos

In the late 1930s the famed gambling ship *Rex*, anchored just outside the three-mile limit, catered to Los Angelenos looking for the occasional fling with Lady Luck. Each night tuxedoed men and gowned ladies took a motor launch out to the ship for an evening of gaming—blackjack, roulette, craps, or poker. Readers of Raymond Chandler's *Farewell My Lovely* will recognize the scene.

Today the *Rex* is only a memory perpetuated mainly through a restaurant in downtown Los Angeles that bears its name and Art Deco motif. Anyone who lusts for the thrill of "bones" dancing across green felt has to hop a jet to Las Vegas; it's just an hour away.

Poker players, though, don't have to make that trek. Just 15 miles south of the Los Angeles Civic Center is the community of Gardena, home of six combination card rooms, restaurants, and cocktail lounges. These are not full gaming casinos, and there are no attached hotels. Although California law prohibits gambling, Gardena enacted an ordinance years ago allowing operators to run draw-poker, low-ball, and pan card games.

The six card rooms are fairly standardized, even though the decor varies and limits on maximum bets differ. A card room, for example, can have no more than 35 tables. Typically a poker table has eight seats and a designated limit on bets. The minimum bet is $1 before the draw and $2 after the draw, with no limits on the number of raises. Some tables have a "house" dealer; the card room collects a fee, ranging from $1 up to $24 an hour in the $100–$200 games, from the players every half hour.

Gardena card rooms are open 24 hours a day, and you can play as long as your cash and stamina hold out. Card rooms also have surprisingly good food in their restaurants at reasonable prices. Law requires that the bar be separate and outside the building. Usually these bars are unimaginative and rarely offer entertainment, but they are a welcome oasis for someone who thirsts for a gin and tonic after a few hours at the table. You can't have a drink brought to your table.

There's no entertainment other than the excitement of winning a fat pot, and craps, "21," roulette, baccarat, and slot machines are banned. Yet Gardena is a great break for the $2 or $2,000 bettor.

The Eldorado Club (15411 S. Vermont Ave., Gardena, tel. 213/323–2800). This is the high rollers' club, and the only card room with a $100–$200-limit game going nonstop. That means that your first bet can be up to $100, and after the draw (cards from the dealer), the maximum bet is $200. With eight players and no limits on the number of times players can raise, pots easily can double or triple. The food, at bargain prices, is superb. One-third of the tables have house dealers. Establish credit and you can cash checks easily, but no credit cards are accepted for chips.

Normandie Club (1045 W. Rosecrans, Gardena, tel. 213/515–1466). Most of the table games at this European-style card room are $40–$80 stakes, but some are lower. Free instruction is offered by staffers. The Candlelight Room offers good Italian dinners for less than $10.

Bars

Despite its well-publicized penchant for hedonism, Los Angeles, unlike New York City, Chicago, and San Francisco, is not a saloon town. The practiced art of pub-crawling has never flourished here, mainly because the city has few real neighborhoods and plenty of freeways. Your favorite Mexican cantina may be in Marina del Rey, or the premier Irish pub may be in Pasadena, more than 25 miles away.

Although the sheer sprawl has stunted the growth of a true saloon society, there are hundreds of great cozy bars, lively pubs, and festive watering holes to quench your thirst for conversation and fine spirits. Traditionally, unlike New Yorkers, Los Angelenos rarely pledge loyalty to any libational hangout; they're too nomadic.

Before you begin your expedition, keep these guidelines in mind: **South Bay** bars and any place near the water have younger, hipper, more hedonistic crowds. Rugby shirts and cutoffs are commonplace, and the talk is largely about volleyball, beach parties, real estate syndications, and sports cars. **Westside** is typically more trendy; casual chic is the watchword. In **West Hollywood** and **Hollywood** environs, the attire is even more relaxed: young directors in jogging suits, out-of-work actors in jeans. Here bars buzz with the intoxicating talk of "deals," as in "three-picture deals," "development deals," "album deals." Deals are the lifeblood of the entertainment industry. Autograph hounding of celebrities is discouraged by owner-managers who are thrilled whenever stars frequent their places. **Pasadena** pubs, once fiercely conservative, have loosened and livened up. But the attire is still traditional: button-down shirts, rep ties, blue blazer—decidedly preppy. **Downtown** bars are generally a bastion for bankers, brokers, and other business folk. Two- and three-piece suits are de rigueur.

The best specific advice we can offer is to monitor your intake of spirits if you're driving. California has enacted some very tough laws to rid its roads of intoxicated motorists. A first-time offender who has more than a 0.1% blood-alcohol reading gets 20 hours in jail and a stiff fine. So beware.

Otherwise, welcome to Los Angeles—and bottoms up.

Airport and South Bay
Orville and Wilbur's (401 W. Rosecrans, tel. 213/545–6639). The clientele is an eclectic mix of surfers, business folks, and rugby-shirted beach rats. With its spectacular view of the Pacific this is a real sundown place.
Sausalito South (3280 Sepulveda Blvd., Manhattan Beach, tel. 213/546–4507). This lively spot showcases a variety of live jazz, encouraging a crowded, colorful dance scene.

Beverly Hills
Ten years ago you'd never have found a corner saloon in Beverly Hills—too déclassé. But as the world citizenry flocked to this enclave of wealth, they brought with them the customs of the leisurely rich. This small city is now riddled with libational refuges from the rat race.

Chrystie's Bar (8442 Wilshire Blvd., tel. 213/655–8113). The bar of Chrystie's Restaurant caters to the after-work bunch and soothes the eye with its Art Deco style.
The Ginger Man (369 N. Bedford Dr., tel. 213/273–7585). Decorated with tile floors and green-shaded tables, this is the stand-up-and-rap haunt of young execs and lovely women.
La Scala (410 N. Canon, tel. 213/275–0579). A quaint bar with an immense wine cellar; honeycombed with celebrities nightly.
Polo Lounge (9641 Sunset Blvd., tel. 213/276–2251). This bar in the Beverly Hills Hotel still attracts the trendy Hollywood crowd.
Rangoon Racquet Club (9474 Little Santa Monica Blvd., tel. 213/274–8926). One of Beverly Hills' busiest. The house special is a Pimm's Cup served by snappy regimental bartenders.
R.J.'s (252 N. Beverly Dr., tel. 213/274–3474 or 213/274–7427). Behind the oak bar and brass rail are 800 bottles stacked to the ceiling. You can either listen to the piano player pound out his favorite ditty, or elbow-bend at the bar with a brace of new buddies.

Century City
Once the backlot of Twentieth Century Fox, this sprawling complex of towering office buildings and luxury condominiums is not without fine bars and saloons. Two of the best:

Avenue Saloon (2040 Ave. of the Stars, tel. 213/553–1855). A central place to meet friends for cocktails before or after the show at the Shubert Theater; warm decor and generous drinks.
Harry's Bar and American Grill (ABC Entertainment Center, 2020 Ave. of the Stars, tel. 213/277–2333). A reasonably authentic version of the famed Venice bar and grill that Heming-

way and other rogues of the pen frequented, Harry's is unrivaled for its potent cappuccino.

Downtown   Downtown Los Angeles, once a ghost town after dusk, is enjoying a renaissance as a dining, drinking, and socializing center for nighttime Angelenos. But go with someone who knows the territory; downtown isn't the safest place for a novice to go exploring.

Al's Bar (305 S. Hewitt, tel. 213/687–3558). Downtown's greatest dive, a dimly lit, SoHo-like haven for artist-types and the adventurous.
Casey's Bar (613 S. Grand, tel. 213/629–2353). Probably the area's most popular pub.
Cocola (410 Boyd St., tel. 213/680–0756). One of downtown's hot new restaurants has a popular, neon-lit bar.
Engine Co. #28. (644 S. Figueroa, downtown, tel. 213/624–6996). This cozy bar (and restaurant), with dark mahogany accents and high-backed booths, attracts a lot of stockbrokers and lawyers.
Grand Avenue Bar (515 S. Olive, tel. 213/612–1595). This sleek bar in the Biltmore Hotel serves until 2. There's also excellent jazz. Bring money.
Little Joe's (900 N. Broadway, tel. 213/489–4900). A must for sports buffs. Prices are cheap and the big-screen TV is always tuned to the hottest game. W.C. Fields frequented the bar in the '30s.
O'Shaughnessy's (515 S. Flower, tel. 213/629–2565). Not the most authentic Irish pub, but one of the most popular. Sample a Bailey's Irish Cream and milk on the rocks to soothe your ulcer.
Pacific Dining Car (1310 W. 6th St., tel. 213/483–6000). This Los Angeles landmark has a large bar open 24 hours that serves gourmet hors d'oeuvres nightly at no charge.
Redwood Second Street Saloon (316 W. Second St., tel. 213/617–2867). A gaudy, gabby hangout for the L.A. press corps. Reporters from the Los Angeles *Times* and United Press International pack this place after 5 PM to postmortem the day's stories or to drink their lunch if they're working nightside.
Rex (617 S. Olive, tel. 213/627–2300). This bar on the ground floor of the historic Oviatt Building radiates the Art Deco ambience of a 1930s cruise liner. Sip slowly and enjoy.
Top of the Five (404 S. Figueroa, tel. 213/624–1000). Share a cognac with a friend while this rotating bar atop the Westin Bonaventure takes you on a leisurely 360-degree trip.

Hollywood   The bar and saloon scene in the film capital of the world is no longer the raucous, gin-soaked setting that Zelda and Scott Fitzgerald, Errol Flynn, Robert Benchley, or even Sinatra and Burton adored. The great Sunset Strip nightclubs—the Mocambo, Ciro's, Trocadero, Interlude—are gone. The bar-hopping ritual of the 1940s, crawling down Sunset in a top-down '47 convertible in quest of the next Cuba Libre, has been replaced by cruisers who clog that boulevard and others the moment the sun sets. But for the patron of the libational arts who'd like to briefly relive yesteryear, there are some oases that should be visited.

The Columbia Bar & Grill (1448 N. Gower, tel. 213/461–8800). Its proximity to several television studios helps this casually elegant spot draw quite a show-business crowd.
Fellini's (6810 Melrose Ave., tel. 213/936–3100). The bar next

door to this Italian restaurant is a cozy cantina packed with a young, hip crowd.

L.A. Nicola Martini Lounge (4326 Sunset Blvd., tel. 213/660–7217). Decorated with a modern touch almost reaching new wave status. The clientele of this friendly place is usually a mix of business and "biz" folk who take full advantage of its proximity to ABC Studios.

Magic Castle (7001 Franklin Ave., tel. 213/851–3313). As the guest of a member, you'll still pay the $7.50 admission at the door, but once you utter the magic words "open sesame" to a blinking owl, a bookcase slides back to reveal a secret panel and a three-level celebration of the magical arts. Watch out for the first bar stool on the left—perch on it and you get this sinking feeling.

Martoni's (1523 Cahuenga Blvd., tel. 213/466–3441). A venerable Italian restaurant launched decades ago by Frank Sinatra's former valet. The cozy bar is packed nightly with agents, studio musicians, and stars on the ascent.

Musso and Franks (6667 Hollywood Blvd., tel. 213/467–5123). Once the host of film-studio moguls and $2-a-day extras alike. Now the Rob Roys are just as smooth and the clientele just as eclectic. No-nonsense bartenders will give you an oral history of the boulevard; just ask.

Nucleus Nuance (7267 Melrose Ave., tel. 213/939–8666). Offering a variety of mixed imbibements and earfuls of music of the '30s and '40s performed live at night in an adjacent room.

Nickodell (5507 Melrose Ave., tel. 213/469–2181). Located next to Paramount Studios. You're apt to see some familiar TV faces.

Yamashiro's (1999 N. Sycamore Ave., tel. 213/466–5125). A lovely tradition is to meet at this Japanese restaurant/bar at sunset for cocktails on the terrace.

Vine St. Bar & Grill (1610 N. Vine St., tel. 213/463–4375). The Art Deco–style bar re-creates the glamour of Duke Ellington's swingtime 1940s.

Marina del Rey/ Venice

Brennan's (4089 Lincon Blvd., tel. 213/821–6622). This Irish pub's big open bar is a pleasant backdrop for easy conversation. Turtle racing, a parking-lot grand prix, is a fixture here.

Black Whale (3016 Washington Blvd., tel. 213/823–9898). For swashbuckling saloon-goers; plenty of mates ready to swig rum with you.

Casablanca (220 Lincoln, tel. 213/392–5751). A Mexican bar and grill where you can watch a woman pounding and cooking tortillas.

Crystal Fountain Lounge (Marina International Hotel, 4200 Admiralty Way, tel. 213/301–2000). Even locals often overlook this dark and cozy spot. The pianist at the bar alternates with a guitarist.

The Warehouse (4499 Admiralty Way, tel. 213/823–5451). Ex-cinematographer Burt Hixon collected tropical drink recipes on his South Seas forays and whips up one of the most sinfully rich piña coladas this side of Samoa. The bar is popular, so get there early.

West Beach Cafe (60 N. Venice Blvd., tel. 213/823–5396). A popular night spot. The bar is often crowded with Westside Yuppies, and it has a changing contemporary art show.

Mid-Wilshire Wilshire Boulevard links downtown to Beverly Hills, Santa Monica, and the Pacific Ocean. It's lined with good—and some great—bars.

HMS Bounty (3357 Wilshire Blvd., tel. 213/385–7275). An après-work businessperson's watering hole; very clubby, very gabby.

Molly Malone's (575 S. Fairfax, tel. 213/935–1577). A real Irish pub. Gaelic music on weekends, Harp beer all the time, and a hamburger that is a feast in itself. Small and cozy.

Red Onion (3580 Wilshire Blvd., tel. 213/386–7295). A classic cantina, though a chain operation. Packed during happy hour, a throbbing disco later in the evening.

Tom Bergin's (840 S. Fairfax, tel. 213/936–7151). One of L.A.'s best Irish pubs, plastered with Day-Glo shamrocks perpetuating the names of the thousands of patrons who have passed through the door.

Pasadena Famed for the Rose Bowl game and the New Year's Day Rose Parade, Pasadena also boasts some of the friendliest bars and pubs in Southern California.

Beckham Place (77 W. Walnut, tel. 818/796–3399). A rather fancy "Olde English" pub known for its huge drinks, free roast beef sandwiches, and wingback chairs placed near a roaring fire. Packed with engineers and science buffs; the conversation is heady, the serving wenches friendly.

Chronicle (897 Granite Dr., tel. 818/792–1179). This restaurant/bar with the feel of a turn-of-the-century mansion features friendly bartenders and generous drinks.

The Crossbow (1400 Huntington Dr., S. Pasadena, tel. 818/799–0758). A dark, clubby atmosphere pervades this piano bar, attracting an older, Pasadena-esque group of people.

Crown City Brewery (300 S. Raymond Ave., tel. 818/577–5548). Beer brewed on the premises is the main attraction, and for good reason.

John Bull (958 S. Fair Oaks, tel. 818/441–4353). A British pub that looks as if it's straight out of London.

Lobby Bar (150 S. Los Robles, tel. 818/577–1000). A turn-of-the-century Victorian bar, on the lower level of the Pasadena Hilton. There are no little old ladies from Pasadena here; this is action central.

Maldonado's (1202 E. Green, tel. 818/796–1126). A tiny European-style bar attached to one of Pasadena's finest restaurants. Perch on a bar stool, order a glass of French wine, and enjoy live opera and Broadway show tunes.

Monahan's Pub (110 S. Lake Ave., tel. 818/449–4151). Single women can comfortably perch on a bar stool in this warm, woodsy setting and not be hassled—many of the patrons are off-duty police who favor it because author and ex-cop Joseph Wambaugh elbow-bends here regularly.

Tap Room (1401 S. Oak Knoll, tel. 818/792–0266). Pasadena's best hideaway bar is tucked away in the Huntington Sheraton Hotel. Debs and dowagers alike, plus business folks, nibble on thick roast beef sandwiches and drink cold beers. Other draws are the comfortable captain's chairs and tables and munchies in the afternoon.

Restaurant Row Most of the bars on La Cienega Boulevard in West Hollywood are part of the boulevard's restaurants and are usually small alcoves off dining rooms, more European than Californian.

La Cage Aux Folles (643 N. La Cienega, tel. 213/657–1091). A saucy saloon and cabaret featuring female impersonators romping through an ever-changing revue. The bar is Paris circa

1920, the drinks are a bit steep, and the barkeeps talk your ear off.

L'Ermitage (730 N. La Cienega, tel. 213/652–5840). This restaurant—generally considered one of the five best in L.A.—has an intimate, personable bar.

San Fernando Valley The San Fernando Valley, once known for acres of tract houses supplanting fields of orange trees, is rapidly becoming a sophisticated suburban bedroom community, especially the southern (closer to Ventura Boulevard) slice of this 1.2 million–person mini-megalopolis. Commuters traverse the Ventura Freeway east to west and often stop to dine and drink at a potpourri of French, Italian, Asian, and trendy American bistros.

Houlihans (17150 Ventura Blvd., Encino, tel. 818/986–2100). One of the better antique-crammed, fern-filled "meet market" bar-restaurants proffering just-over-a-dollar beer, wine, and single mixed drinks in the late afternoon and early evening. Stick around at night and boogie in the disco.

Sagebrush Cantina (23527 Calabassas Rd., tel. 818/888–6062). An indoor-outdoor saloon, sort of the Valley version of the Via Veneto cafe scene. Motorcycle hippies mix comfortably with computer moguls and showbiz folk including a platoon of stunt people. Country-pop entertainment nightly.

Santa Monica and the Beaches Santa Monica may be the most cosmopolitan city in Southern California. The British, for example, love its cool weather and its proximity to the ocean. Not surprisingly, there are some authentic British pubs here as well as good bars.

Chez Jay (1657 Ocean, tel. 213/395–1741). A shack of a saloon that has endured for 30 years and seen the likes of Warren Beatty, Julie Christie, and former California governor Jerry Brown.

Galley Steak House (2442 Main, tel. 213/452–1934). A tiny restaurant/bar recommended for nostalgics who want to recapture Santa Monica circa 1940. Thick with nautical mementos and people who appreciate the sea.

The Oar House (2941 Main, tel. 213/396–4725). Something old has been glued or nailed to every square inch of the place, from motorcycles to carriages. Drinks are downright cheap.

Ye Olde King's Head (116 Santa Monica Blvd., tel. 213/451–1402). Reeking of brew, it's stocked with Brits eager to hear or dispense news from home.

West Hollywood **Carlos and Charlie's** (8240 W. Sunset, tel. 213/656–8830). A slick L.A. version of the funky cantinas found throughout Mexico, this bar is a beautiful-people hangout and big with the record industry crowd.

Dan Tana's (9071 Santa Monica Blvd., tel. 213/275–9444). Mainly a restaurant but blessed with a busy bar that's a favorite late-night haunt.

Le Dome (8720 W. Sunset, tel. 213/659–6919). A circular bar that draws the likes of Rod Stewart and Richard Gere. The best time to visit is after 11 PM, when it really starts to jump.

Dominick's (8715 Beverly Blvd., tel. 213/659–5171). A virtually unknown, secluded bar and grill frequented by Hollywood heavies. Dominick's draws include wood paneling and traditional pictures and a staff that's courteous, never obsequious.

MaBe (8722 West 3rd St., tel. 213/276–6223). Rich oak, Art Nouveau mirrors, brass tables, and a plush sofa along the wall make this place as inviting as one of the enormous martinis served here.

Morton's (8800 Melrose Ave., tel. 213/276–1253). A small bar with a big-name clientele.

Spago (8795 W. Sunset, tel. 213/652–4025). Celebrity watching is a polished art here. The tiny bar tucked away inside this ultrachic bistro is immensely popular; consider yourself fortunate if you can stake out a bar stool.

Trumps (8764 Melrose Ave., tel. 213/855–1480). Sink into soft sofas and sip a tall gin and tonic. The European ambience— clean, contemporary design—makes you feel like a jet-setter.

Westwood/Westside Westwood is the front door to UCLA and a popular hangout for kids of all ages. Both it and the area around it have some outstanding bars.

Acapulco (1109 Glendon, tel. 213/208–3884). Once an Irish pub, this Mexican restaurant/bar still has an air of conviviality. It also stocks a good assortment of Mexican beers.

Alice's (1043 Westwood Blvd., Westwood, tel. 213/208–3171). In the heart of Westwood Village, this restaurant bar has plenty of tables as well as a long, marble bar. Two television monitors are bound to be tuned to the latest sporting event.

Hamburger Hamlet (11648 San Vicente, tel. 213/826–3558). One of the Westside's hottest singles bars, so don't walk in looking for solitude.

Radisson Bel Air Summit (11461 Sunset, tel. 213/476–6571). A bar for anyone who wants to avoid the madding crowds. Sit on the patio out by the pool as the sun sets or inside at night when the piano music starts.

San Francisco Saloon (11501 W. Pico Blvd., tel. 213/478–0152). Thrift-store ambience, but the crowd is adventurous and there are always rabid chess and backgammon players at their boards.

Stratton's (10886 Le Conte, tel. 213/208–8880). A restaurant/bar that looks like the inside of an 11th-century castle. Drinks are imaginative but prices are semisteep.

Westwood Marquis Hotel (930 Hilgard, tel. 213/208–8765). A one-time UCLA dorm, this European-style hostelry has turned its bar into a giant living room with pillow-soft sofas, coffee tables, a harpist and a pianist nightly, and silk-gowned waitresses serving canapes on sterling silver trays.

Yesterday's (1056 Westwood Blvd., tel. 213/208–8000). Sit amid $750,000 worth of antiques. There's a small bar downstairs, and upstairs is a veranda bar, where you can listen to a guitarist and other musicians.

9 Excursions from Los Angeles

by Aaron Sugarman

Even if Los Angeles is the center of your vacation plans, you are probably planning trips out of the city. Disneyland (*see* Chapter 10) is less than an hour's drive away; Santa Barbara (*see* Chapter 12) and Palm Springs (*see* Chapter 11) can be reached in a couple of hours. This chapter explores some excursions more off the beaten track.

Big Bear/Lake Arrowhead

Local legend has it that in 1845, Don Benito Wilson—General George Patton's grandfather—and his men charged up along the San Bernardino River in pursuit of a troublesome band of Indians. As Wilson entered a clearing, he discovered a meadow teeming with bear. The rest, of course, is history: Wilson later became mayor of Los Angeles, and Big Bear was developed into a delightful mountain playground.

Today, Angelenos seeking escape from urban life and other vacationers are more plentiful in these mountain resort areas than bears ever were. They come for downhill and cross-country skiing in the winter, a wide variety of water sports when the weather is warmer, and breathtaking vistas and romantic retreats at rustic cottages and inns year-round.

Running along the edge of the San Bernardino Mountains, connecting Lake Arrowhead and Big Bear Lake, is a truly great scenic drive. The alpine equivalent of the Pacific Coast Highway, the aptly named Rim of the World Drive reaches elevations of 8,000 feet, offering views of sprawling San Bernardino, the San Gabriel range, and the Mojave Desert to the north.

Arriving and Departing

By Car Take Interstate 10 east from Los Angeles to Highway 330, which connects with Highway 18—the Rim of the World Drive. The trip should take about 90 minutes to Lake Arrowhead, two hours to Big Bear. Highway 38, the back way into Big Bear, is a longer route, but it can be faster when there is heavy traffic on the more direct route.

Exploring

Numbers in the margin correspond with points of interest on the Big Bear Lake map.

As you wind your way along Rim of the World Drive, there are several places to park, sip cool water from spring-fed fountains, and enjoy the view. At the village of Crestline, a brief ❶ diversion off of Highway 18 leads you to **Lake Gregory.** The newest of the high mountain lakes, Lake Gregory was formed by a dam constructed in 1938. Because the water temperature in summer is seldom extremely cold, this is the best swimming lake in the mountains. Rowboats can be rented at Lake Gregory Village.

❷ Continuing east on Highway 18, you will pass the **Baylis Park Picnic Ground,** where you can have a barbecue in a wooded setting. A little farther along, just past the town of Rim Forest, is ❸ the **Strawberry Peak** fire lookout tower. Visitors braving the steep stairway to the tower are treated to a magnificent view and a lesson on fire-spotting by the lookout staff.

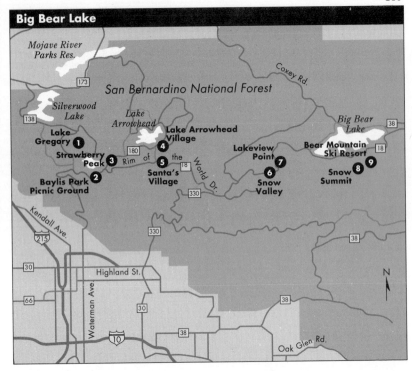

Big Bear Lake

❹ Heading north on Highway 173 will lead you to **Lake Arrowhead Village** and the lake itself. Arrowhead Village draws mixed reviews: For some it is a quaint alpine village with shops and eateries; others feel it has all the ambience of a shopping mall. The lake, on the other hand, is decidedly a gem, although it can get crowded with speedboats and water-skiers in the summer. The *Arrowhead Queen* provides 45-minute cruises around the lake, leaving from the waterfront marina. Boat rentals are available on nearby public docks. Arrowhead Sports cruise boats leave at noon from the south shore for a one-hour cruise. Call the Arrowhead Chamber of Commerce (tel. 714/337–3715) for information on events, camping, and lodging.

❺ If you are traveling with children, you may want to consider a stop at nearby **Santa's Village.** A petting zoo, rides, riding stables, and a bakery full of goodies make this a natural for kids. *Located on Hwy. 18, Box 638, Skyforest 92385, tel. 714/337–2484. Admission: $6.50 adults, $3 senior citizens, $7.50 for children 3–16. Hours change from season to season, so call ahead for information.*

❻ Farther along the Rim Drive is **Snow Valley** (tel. 714/867–5151 or 714/867–2751), one of the major ski areas in the San Bernardinos with a dozen lifts and snowmaking capabilities to fill in those dry spells. The facilities are closed during the summer.

❼ Beyond Snow Valley, the road climbs to **Lakeview Point,** where a spectacular view unfolds of the deep Bear Creek Canyon, with Big Bear Lake usually visible in the distance. A 15.5-mile drive will take you completely around the lake. **Big Bear Lake Village** is located on the lake's south shore. The town is charming. Equipment for whatever sport you fancy—from fishing to skiing to sailboarding—is available, and there are even some surprisingly good restaurants. For general information, contact the Big Bear Tourist and Visitor Bureau (Box 3050G, Big Bear Lake 92315, tel. 714/866–5878).

❽ ❾ **Snow Summit** and **Bear Mountain Ski Resort** are both just to the southeast of the Village. Snow Summit is probably the best of the area ski resorts, with challenging runs and carefully controlled lift-ticket sales to keep lift lines from getting out of hand. On busy winter weekends and holidays, your best bet is to reserve your tickets before you head for the mountain. *Snow Summit: snow report, tel. 213/613–0362, 818/888–2233, or 714/972–0601; lift ticket reservations, tel. 714/866–5841; general information, tel. 714/866–5766. Bear Mountain: information and snow report, tel. 714/585–2519.*

Dining

Big Bear **The Iron Squirrel.** Hearty French cooking is presented in a country French setting. The veal Normande comes highly recommended, and other traditional dishes like rack of lamb with garlic are nicely prepared. *646 Pineknot Ave., Big Bear Lake, tel. 714/866–9121. MC, V. Expensive (over $20).*

George and Sigi's Knusperhauschen. Don't let the campy gingerbread-house look fool you; this restaurant offers wonderful Eastern European fare in a warm, charming atmosphere. The schnitzels and sauerbraten are a delight. *829 W. Big Bear Blvd., Big Bear City, tel. 714/585–8640. Reservations are a good idea. MC, V. Open Thurs.–Sun. and holidays. Moderate ($15–$20).*

Blue Ox Bar and Grill. Another rustic restaurant, this one has peanut shells on the floor. Oversize steaks, ribs, burgers, and chicken are done simply, but well. *441 W. Big Bear Blvd., Big Bear City, tel. 714/585–7886. AE, MC, V. Inexpensive (under $15).*

Lake Arrowhead **Cliffhanger.** Go with traditional dishes—moussaka and lamb—and don't worry about the cliffside locale, it's part of the charm. *25187 Hwy. 118, Lake Arrowhead, tel. 714/338–3806. MC, V. Moderate ($15–$20).*

Lodging

Big Bear Central Reservations (tel. 714/866–5877) can answer any questions you have and make arrangements for you.

Arrowhead **Arrowhead Hilton Lodge.** The design and Old World graciousness of the lodge are reminiscent of the Alps. In addition to the lakeside luxury, guests receive membership privileges at the Village Bay Club and Spa. *Box 1699, Lake Arrowhead 92352, tel. 714/336–1511. 257 rooms. Facilities: restaurant, coffee shop, lounge, beach, pool, whirlpools, health club, tennis (fee). AE, MC, V. Expensive (over $100).*

Storybook Inn. The inn offers nine antique-furnished rooms and suites in an elegant estate, with a view over the valley. Breakfast is included, and can be served in your room or in the main dining area. *Box 362, Sky Forest 92385, tel. 714/336–1483.*

10 rooms. Facilities: whirlpool. MC, V. Moderate–Expensive ($95–$175).

Big Bear **Big Bear Inn.** This is a gem of a mountain chateau in the European tradition. The rooms are furnished with brass beds and antiques. Developer Paul Rizos's family has three luxury hotels on the Greek island of Corfu and the inn shows its classy, classic lineage. *Box 1814, Big Bear Lake 92315, tel. 714/866–3471 or 800/BEAR–INN. 80 rooms. Facilities: restaurants, lounge, pool, sauna, whirlpool. AE, MC, V. Moderate–Expensive ($65 –$450).*

Gold Mountain Manor. A restored shingled mansion dating from the Roaring '20s now serves as a historic bed-and-breakfast inn. It earned its fame when Clark Gable and Carole Lombard honeymooned in what is now the Clark Gable Room. The rooms are furnished with quilts and antiques. Rates include country breakfast. *Box 2027, Big Bear City 92314, tel. 714/585–6997. 8 rooms. No credit cards. No smoking on the premises. Moderate ($70–$100).*

Knickerbocker Mansion. This is another historic bed-and-breakfast (built of logs), complete with brass kerosene lanterns, breakfast served on the veranda, and afternoon tea. The rooms have a country decor. *Box 3661, Big Bear Lake 92315, tel. 714/866–8221. 9 rooms, 7 with bath. MC, V. Smoking limited. Moderate ($85–$150).*

Club View Chalets. Adjacent to the Goldmine Ski area, some of the chalets include sitting room, fireplace, and complete kitchen. The decor is contemporary eclectic. *Box 2817, Big Bear Lake 92315, tel. 714/866–5753. 7 rooms. AE, MC, V. Inexpensive–Moderate ($50–$225).*

Robinhood Inn and Lodge. Well located, reasonably priced rooms (with or without kitchen) and condos near Snow Summit. Each room (some with fireplaces) is individually decorated with modern furniture and bright colors. *Box 3706, Big Bear Lake 92315, tel. 714/866–4643. 20 rooms. Facilities: restaurant, spa. AE, MC, V. Inexpensive (under $80).*

Catalina Island

When you approach Catalina Island through the typical early morning ocean fog, it's easy to wonder if perhaps there has been some mistake. What is a Mediterranean island doing 22 miles off the coast of California? Don't worry, you haven't left the Pacific—you've arrived at one of the Los Angeles area's most popular resorts.

Though lacking some of the sophistication of a European pleasure island, Catalina offers virtually unspoiled mountains and canyons, coves and beaches. It is Southern California without the freeways, a place to relax and play golf or tennis, go boating, hiking, diving, or fishing, or just lay on the beach. Avalon is the island's only "city," a charming old-fashioned beach community. Yachts are tied up in neat rows in the crescent-shape bay, palm trees rim the main street, and there are plenty of restaurants and shops to attract the attention of day-trippers out strolling in the sunshine.

Of course, life was not always this leisurely on Catalina. Discovered by Juan Rodriguez Cabrillo in 1542, the island has sheltered many dubious characters, from sun-worshiping

Indians, Russian fur trappers (seeking sea-otter skins), slave traders, pirates, and gold miners, to filmmakers and movie stars. Avalon was named in 1888 after the island of Avalon in Tennyson's *Idylls of the King*. In 1919, William Wrigley, Jr., chewing-gum magnate, purchased controlling interest in the company developing the island. Wrigley had the island's most famous landmark, the Casino, built in 1929, and he made Catalina the site of spring training for his Chicago Cubs baseball team. The Santa Catalina Island Conservancy, a nonprofit foundation, acquired about 86% of the island in 1974 to help preserve Catalina's natural resources.

A wide variety of tours offer samples of those resources, either by boat along the island's coast or by bus or van into Catalina's rugged interior country. Depending on which route you take, you can expect to see roving bands of buffalo, deer, goats, and boar or unusual species of sea life, including such oddities as electric perch, saltwater goldfish, and flying fish. The buffalo originally came to the island in 1924 for the filming of *The Vanishing American;* apparently, they liked it well enough to stay.

Although Catalina can certainly be done in a day, there are several inviting romantic hotels that promise to make it worth extending your stay for one or more nights. Between Memorial Day and Labor Day we strongly suggest you make reservations *before* heading out to the island. After Labor Day, rates drop dramatically and rooms are much easier to find.

Arriving and Departing

By Boat   Boats to Catalina run from San Pedro and Long Beach. **Catalina Express** (tel. 213/519–1212) makes the run in 90 minutes; round-trip fare is $25 for adults. **Catalina Cruises** (tel. 800/888–5939) is a bit slower, taking two hours, and cheaper, charging about $20. Service is also available from Newport Beach through **Catalina Passenger Service** (tel. 714/673–5245), leaving from Balboa Pavilion. Catalina Express launches regularly scheduled service from San Pedro ($27.70 round-trip) and Long Beach ($32 round-trip). Advance reservations for all lines are recommended.

By Plane   **Helitrans** (tel. 213/548–1314 or 800/262–1472) offers helicopter service from San Pedro's Catalina Island Terminal to Pebbly Beach, five minutes by van from Avalon. **Island Express** (tel. 213/491–5550) flies from San Pedro and Long Beach. The trip takes about 14 minutes and costs between $40 and $53 one-way. Commuter air service is available from Long Beach Airport and John Wayne Orange County Airport to Catalina's Airport in the Sky. Call **Allied Air Charter** (tel. 213/510–1163) for schedules and fares.

Guided Tours

The major tour operators on the island are the **Santa Catalina Island Co.** (tel. 213/510–2000 or 800/428–2566) and **Ultimate Destinations** (tel. 213/510–0575). Tours include: inland motor tour, Skyline Drive, coastal cruise to Seal Rocks (summer only), the Flying Fish boat trip (evenings, summer only), casino tour, Avalon scenic tour, and the glass-bottom boat tour. Advance reservations are highly recommended for the first four tours; the other three are offered several times daily. Costs range from $4.50 for the casino tour (adults) to $17 for the four-hour inland motor tour; discounts are available for children under 12 years and senior citizens over 55. Catalina Adventure Tours also offers para-sailing, fishing, and diving options.

The Catalina Conservancy (tel. 213/510–1421) offers walks led by knowledgeable docents.

Exploring

Catalina Island is one of the very few places in the L.A. environs where walking is considered quite acceptable. In fact, you cannot bring a car onto the island nor can you rent one once you get there. If you are determined to have a set of wheels, rent a bicycle or golf cart along Crescent Avenue as you walk in from the docks. To hike into the interior of the island you will need a permit, available for free from the L.A. County Department of Parks and Recreation (Island Plaza, Avalon, tel. 213/510–0688).

The **Visitors Center** and the **Chamber of Commerce Visitors Bureau** are good places to get your bearings, check into special events, and plan your itinerary. The Visitors Center (tel. 213/510–2000) is located on the corner of Crescent Avenue and Catalina Avenue, across from the Green Pier; the Chamber's Visitors Bureau is on the pier.

Housed on the northwest point of Crescent Bay is the **Casino.** The round structure is an odd mixture of Spanish, Moorish, and Art Deco modern style, with Art Deco murals on the porch as you enter. In the Casino are an art gallery, museum, movie theater (tel. 213/510–0179), and ballroom. Guided tours are available.

The Wrigley Memorial and Botanical Garden is 2 miles south of Avalon via Avalon Canyon Road. Wrigley's family commissioned this monument to Wrigley, replete with grand staircase and Spanish mausoleum with Art Deco touches. Despite the fact that the mausoleum was never used by the Wrigleys, who are buried in Los Angeles, the structure is worth a look, and the view from the mausoleum is worth even more. The garden is small but exceptionally well planted. Tram service between the memorial and Avalon is available daily between 8 AM and 5 PM. There is a nominal entry fee of 50¢.

If modern architecture interests you, make sure to stop by the **Wolfe House** (124 Chimes Rd.). Built in 1928 by noted architect Rudolph Schindler, its terraced frame is carefully set into a steep site, affording extraordinary views. The house is a private residence, rarely open for public tours, but you can get a good view of it from the path below it and from the street.

El Rancho Escondido is a ranch in Catalina's interior, home to some of the country's finest Arabian horses. The ranch can be visited on the Inland motor tour *(see* Guided Tours, above).

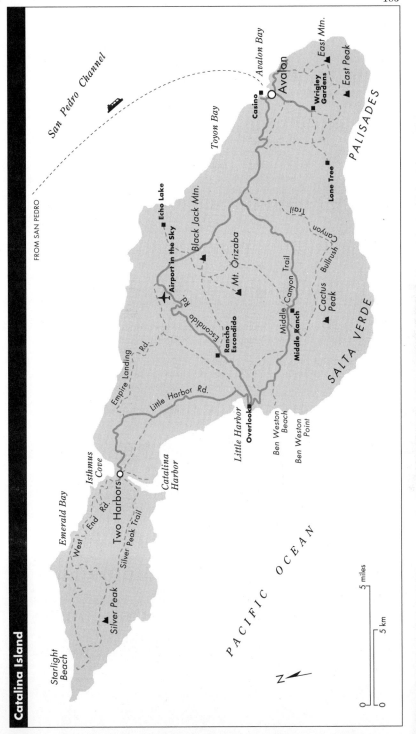

Catalina Island

San Pedro Channel

FROM SAN PEDRO

Avalon Bay

Avalon

East Mtn.

East Peak

Casino

Wrigley Gardens

Toyon Bay

PALISADES

Echo Lake

Lone Tree

Black Jack Mtn.

Airport in the Sky

Mt. Orizaba

Bullrush Canyon

Canyon Trail

Rancho Escondido

Cactus Peak

Escondido Rd.

Middle Canyon Trail

Middle Ranch

SALTA VERDE

Empire Landing Rd.

Little Harbor Rd.

Little Harbor Overlook

Ben Weston Beach

Ben Weston Point

Isthmus Cove

Emerald Bay

West End Rd.

Two Harbors

Catalina Harbor

Silver Peak Trail

Silver Peak

Starlight Beach

PACIFIC OCEAN

N

5 miles

5 km

0

Dining

American **The Sand Trap.** Omelets are the specialty at this local favorite located on the way to Wrigley Botanical Garden. *Bird Park Rd., tel. 213/510–1349. No credit cards. Inexpensive (under $10).*

Italian **Cafe Prego.** This restaurant features an intimate setting on the waterfront, several good pasta dishes, and a hearty minestrone. *603 Crescent Ave., tel. 213/510–1218. AE, MC, V. Dinner only. Moderate ($10–$20).*
Antonio's Pizzeria. You'll find spirited atmosphere, decent pizza, and appropriately messy Italian sandwiches. *2 locations: 230 Crescent Ave., tel. 213/510–0008, and 114 Sumner, tel. 213/510–0060. MC, V. Inexpensive (under $10).*

Seafood **Pirrone's.** This brand-new restaurant with bird's-eye view of the bay serves fresh seafood. *417 Crescent Ave., tel. 213/510–0333. MC, V. Open Mon.–Sat. for dinner and for Sun. brunch in winter, daily for lunch and dinner in summer. Moderate ($10– $20).*

Lodging

Inn on Mt. Ada. The former Wrigley Mansion is now the island's most exclusive hotel. There are only six rooms, the views spectacular, the grounds superbly planted. *Box 2560, Avalon 90704, tel. 213/510–2030. 6 rooms. AE, MC, V. Very Expensive ($170–$440).*
Glenmore Plaza Hotel. This striking Victorian hotel dating from 1891 has hosted the likes of Clark Gable, Teddy Roosevelt, and Amelia Earhart. Located near the beach, the hotel offers complimentary breakfast and suites with whirlpool or Jacuzzi. *120 Sumner Ave., Avalon 90704, tel. 213/510–0017. 50 rooms. AE, MC, V. Moderate–Expensive ($80–$180).*
Hotel Villa Portofino. This is a Mediterranean-style waterfront hotel with a sun deck, an art gallery, and ambitious Italian restaurant. *111 Crescent Ave., Avalon 90704, tel. 213/510–0555. 34 rooms. AE, MC, V. Moderate–Expensive ($70–$150).*
Hotel Catalina. A renovated Victorian, half a block from the beach, the Catalina offers a choice of rooms and cottages. Extra touches include an attractive sun deck with Jacuzzi and free movies every afternoon. *129 Whittley Ave., Avalon 90704, tel. 213/510–0027. 32 rooms, 4 cottages. AE, MC, V. Moderate ($70–$100).*
Zane Grey Pueblo Hotel. The former home of the famous American novelist, this hotel offers a stunning harbor view from its hilltop perch. Built in 1926 in Hopi Indian pueblo style, the Zane Grey offers such amenities as eccentric decor, a swimming pool, and a courtesy bus. No phones or TVs in rooms; no children allowed. *199 Chimes Tower Rd., Avalon 90704, tel. 213/510–0966. 18 rooms. AE, MC, V. Moderate ($75–$125).*
Atwater Hotel. This family-oriented hotel is a half-block from the beach. *Box 737, Avalon 90704, tel. 213/510–1788. 84 rooms. AE, CB, DC, MC, V. Inexpensive (under $70).*

Antelope Valley

The most memorable parts of a trip are often its surprises—the places and people you stumble onto when you least expect to. Antelope Valley, which makes up the western corner of the Mojave Desert, holds several unexpected pleasures. A sudden turn along a desert road reveals a riot of flaming orange poppies on acres of rolling hills nestled between barren rises and desolate flatlands. In the late summer and fall, after the flowers have faded, you can pick your own cherries, peaches, and pears at nearby orchards incongruously set in the desert. Head east and you can hike to the top of Saddleback Butte for a spectacular view of where the desert ends and the San Gabriel Mountains begin, their snow-capped peaks a beautiful contrast to the arid valley.

Another surprise is the valley's wildlife. No, don't look for the hoary antlers of the antelope that lent their name to the area. Once practically overrunning the region, the antelope went into decline with the arrival of the railroad in 1876. They apparently refused to cross the tracks that blocked the route to their traditional grazing grounds and many starved to death. A severe winter in the 1880s and the growth of ranching and farming in the early 1900s spelled the end for the few that had survived.

What you can see on an Antelope Valley safari are the eminently amusing and increasingly rare desert tortoises. Thanks to preservationists, a safe haven has been created for California's official state reptile. Visiting the tortoise in its natural habitat is a great opportunity for budding photographers—not noted for their speed, the tortoises make willing subjects. If birds are more your fancy, there is also a 40-acre wildlife sanctuary in the valley noted for its winged inhabitants.

Man, of course, has also made his mark in Antelope Valley. You'll find gold mines and historic railroad towns that still evoke the spirit of the Old West. Some $40 million in gold and silver has been taken out of the hills between Rosemond and Mojave since a Mr. Hamilton hit pay dirt on what is now called Tropico Hill in the 1890s. The Burton Mining Company believes there is still some gold to be found in Tropico and is today still excavating the same hill Hamilton made his fortune on.

Arriving and Departing

By Car Heading north from Los Angeles, I–5 will lead you to Highway 14, which runs north through Palmdale, Lancaster, Rosamond, and Mojave. It should take about 90 minutes to reach Palmdale and another hour between Palmdale and Mojave. To reach the Antelope Valley California Poppy Reserve, take the Avenue I exit in Lancaster off Highway 14 and head west about 10 miles. Rosemond and the Tropico Mine are just north of Lancaster on Highway 14. Take the Rosamond Boulevard exit and go west for 3 miles to Mojave-Tropico Road; turn north here and you will see the mine shortly. For the Desert Tortoise Natural Area, take Highway 14 about 4 miles past Mojave and then turn east on California City Boulevard through California City; turn left on Randsburg-Mojave Road and follow signs about 5 miles to the preserve. Take Avenue J (Rte. N5) east from Lancaster for about 19 miles to get to Saddleback Butte State Park. To reach the Devil's Punchbowl Natural Area Park and nearby Hamilton Preserve, take Highway 138 southwest from Palmdale; just past Pearblossom turn south on Route N6 (Longview Rd.) and go about 8 miles. On Highway 138, you can continue southeast along the San Gabriel Mountains, pick up I–15 south through Cajon Pass, and return to Los Angeles via I–10 heading west.

Exploring

You can't miss the **Antelope Valley California Poppy Reserve**— its orange glow with dots of purple lupine and yellow goldfields and fiddleneck can be seen long before you reach the reserve itself. The best time to visit is between March and May, peak flower time. There are four short (between a mile and 2 miles) walking trails leading through the fields, some reaching wonderful viewpoints. While there is a perfectly serviceable picnic area by the parking lot, a snack on the bench atop Kitanemuk Vista (an easy five-minute stroll up a well-marked trail) offers much finer scenery. Do take a few minutes to walk through the visitor center. The uniquely designed building is burrowed into a hill to keep the building cooler during the summer and warmer during the winter. You can pick up trail maps and other useful information. *Visitor Center open Mar.–May, daily 9–3. State Park day-use fee: $3 per car. For more information and schedules of guided tours, call the California Dept. of Parks and Recreation, tel. 805/942–0662.*

You will find the area's orchards along State Highway 138 in the communities of **Littlerock** and **Pearblossom,** and in **Leonia,** just to the southwest of Lancaster. Harvesting season starts in June. Contact the Lancaster Chamber of Commerce and Visitors Center (44335 Lowtree, Lancaster 93534, tel. 805/948–4518) for more information.

A short drive north of Lancaster to **Rosamond** will take you back a long way in years. Gold was first discovered in Tropico Hill in 1894 and Burton's Tropico Mine and Mill, hanging awkwardly against the hill, looks just as it did during the height of the gold rush. Unfortunately, the high cost of liability insurance put an end to mine tours and led to the closing of an informative museum, but you can still get a close look at the old buildings and let your imagination fill in the sights and sounds of a turn-of-the-century mining town.

The **Desert Tortoise Natural Area** is a good place to commune with nature. Cars must be left behind as you stroll through the preserve's peaceful and picturesque landscape. Be sure to do two things: look around and consider the fact that there isn't a sign of civilization to be seen; and breathe deeply, because you won't find air this fresh too often in and around Los Angeles or any urban center. The best time of the year for viewing the tortoises is generally March through June, but avoid the midafternoon. The tortoises sensibly stay cool during the heat of the day by retiring to their shallow burrows. Two warnings about the natural area: The road into the area is wide and flat, but not paved, so your car is bound to get a bit dusty; also, there is no water available at the preserve. The preserve is open land, there is no admission, and you may feel free to roam about whenever you like. For more information and to arrange guided tours call the California City Recreation Department (tel. 619/373–4278).

East of Lancaster is **Saddleback Butte State Park,** a favorite among hikers and campers. A 2½-mile trail leads to the 3,651-foot summit of the butte the park is named for, which offers some grand views. Throughout the park there is a great deal of typical high-desert plant and animal life—stands of Joshua trees, desert tortoises, golden eagles, and many other species of reptiles, mammals, and birds. Near park headquarters is a picnic area with tables, stoves, and rest rooms. The Los Angeles County Department of Parks and Recreation (tel. 805/259–7721) offers a fact sheet on the various wildlife sanctuaries near the park. Information on camping at Saddleback Butte is available from the State Department of Parks (tel. 805/942–0662).

Farther south is another popular spot for hikers—**Devils Punchbowl Natural Area Park**. Once at the bottom of an ocean, and currently nestled between the active San Andreas and San Jacinto faults, the park offers a network of well-planned trails. The nearby **Hamilton Preserve** consists of 40 acres of pinyon-juniper woodland sheltering numerous bird species.

Antelope Valley is also home to **Edwards Air Force Base** and the **NASA Ames-Dryden Flight Research Facility** (off State Hwy. 14, northeast of Lancaster). Tours of the facility are available, with a film describing the history of flight test programs, a walk through a hangar, and a look at experimental aircraft. Now that the space shuttle is flying again, this is the place to see it land. *Free tours weekdays 10:15 AM and 1:15 PM. Call ahead (tel. 805/258–3446) as the base is occasionally closed for security reasons.*

Dining

Antelope Valley is not known for its fine dining. There are several fast food and very average roadside restaurants in Lancaster, Palmdale, and Mojave. You might be better off to pack a gourmet picnic basket before you leave Los Angeles and dine alfresco at one of the many scenic spots you will come across throughout the valley.

Riverside

Where Los Angeles tends to focus on the newest and latest—a place where '50s furniture is considered antique—Riverside wears its history on its sleeve. A delightful array of historic buildings rises up on almost every street corner in downtown Riverside. The range of styles is striking and eclectic, from Mission Revival and Beaux Arts to Renaissance Revival and Victorian. The centerpiece is the 100-year-old Mission Inn. A national historic landmark, the Mission Inn is a romantic affair, with jutting turrets and towers, arches, balconies, fountains, sculptures, and unusual rooms.

Riverside is a good place to wander leisurely for a morning or afternoon. Options include several worthwhile museums, a pleasant pedestrian mall lined with ornamental citrus trees and intriguing small shops, and even a chance to see the tree that launched the billion-dollar citrus industry in the western United States.

Arriving and Departing

By Car Take I–10 east out of Los Angeles to I–15E heading south. The trip should take about 90 minutes.

By Bus **Greyhound-Trailways** (213/620–1200 or 800/531–5332) offers over a dozen daily departures to Riverside. The ride costs $8.75 one-way, $14.95 round-trip and takes about 1½ hours. The station is downtown and within walking distance from all downtown attractions.

Exploring

To get the proper historical perspective, make a quick stop at the **Parent Tree** (intersection of Market St. and Arlington Ave.). Planted in 1875 and still bearing fruit, this navel orange tree is the sole survivor of two trees brought to Riverside from Brazil. Cuttings from this tree have grown into today's citrus groves. Much of the money behind Riverside's architectural wealth did in fact grow on trees, so don't be surprised when you discover downtown streets named Orange, Lemon, and Lime.

In 1990, after four years of loving restoration work, the remarkable **Mission Inn** reopened and was once again Riverside's prime attraction. You can either tour the collection of Spanish paintings and antiques, Tiffany stained-glass windows, and priceless international objets d'art, or just dine in the colorful courtyard cafe. The St. Francis Chapel and its gold-leaf altar from Mexico are worth seeing. There are 240 guest rooms as well. *3649 Seventh St., tel. 714/784–0300. Room rates start at $120; call for a tour schedule.*

Across the street from the Mission Inn is the **Municipal Museum.** A Renaissance Revival building constructed in 1912, the museum contains exhibits on local history, Indian culture, and natural history. *3720 Orange St., tel. 714/782–5273. Small donations accepted. Closed Mon.*

Continuing down Seventh Street, you'll pass the **First Congregational Church,** a good example of the Mission Revival style, built in 1914. Note the differences between it and the **Municipal Auditorium** across the street. Built in 1929 in Hispanic Revival style, the auditorium has distinctive blue, yellow, and white tile domes and is topped by an all-American eagle.

At Seventh and Lime is the **Riverside Art Museum,** designed in 1929 by Julia Morgan, the chief architect of Hearst Castle. Several galleries display the work of Southern California artists. *3425 Seventh St., tel. 714/684–7111. Donation: $1. Closed Sun.*

Time Out **Jeanines,** in the courtyard of the art museum, is a charming eatery in a delightful location. There are only a dozen small tables and the moderately priced menu changes regularly. *Tel. 714/684–4476. Open 7–10 AM for breakfast, 11 AM–2 PM for lunch. Dinner Fri. and Sat. is by reservation only; the fixed-price dinner menu weighs in at just under $20 for seven courses. Closed Sun.*

Riverside's other main strip is **Main Street,** a pedestrian mall running from Fifth Street to Eleventh Street, where there are several shops and cafes to look into. The **California Museum of Photography** (3824 Main St., tel. 714/787–4787) is located in the historic Kress Variety Store building. The museum is open Tues.–Sat. 10–5, Sun. noon–5. When you reach the **Riverside County Courthouse,** built in 1903, be prepared for a bit of a shock. Not even remotely Hispanic, this Beaux Arts beauty was modeled after the Grand Palace of Fine Arts in Paris.

A short distance south of downtown Riverside is the **Heritage House,** a Victorian building dating from 1891. The house, built for the family of a successful citrus grower, features period furniture, tile fireplaces in every room, and gas lamps. *8193 Magnolia Ave., between Adams and Jefferson, tel. 714/689–1333. Open Tues. and Thurs. noon–2:30, Sun. noon–3:30.*

Castle Park is a family-oriented amusement park spread over 27 pleasantly landscaped acres. A state-of-the-art video arcade, miniature golf course, and collection of rides—including a restored carousel dating from 1909—are sure to keep the kids entertained. *3500 Polk St., tel. 714/785–4140. Admission: $4 adults, $3 age 11 and under for golf; 35¢ per ride in the ride park (discount books available). Golf and arcade open Sun.–Thurs. 10–10, Fri.–Sat. 10–midnight; ride park open Fri. 6–11, Sat. noon–11, Sun. noon–8.*

The **Riverside Botanic Gardens,** on the campus of the University of California, covers 37 acres of hilly terrain. Spring, when many of the 2,000 plant species bloom, is the best time to visit. *Univ. of California–Riverside, tel. 714/787–4650. Admission free. Open daily 8–5.*

10 Orange County

Orange County is a proverbial land of contrasts: It is beach and city, Republican and liberal, old society and high technology.

Sometime during the recessions of the 1970s, Middle America packed up its bags and moved west, settling comfortably in Orange County. Stretching between two major cities—Los Angeles and San Diego—Orange County is essentially one vast suburb. It is perhaps America's foremost suburb, a place where Mickey Mouse rules, the average home costs $200,000, and finding the right wave and beach volleyball action are daily concerns among the younger set. The county's affluence continues to attract an ever-growing number of exclusive shopping malls, new performing arts arenas, and luxurious oceanfront resorts—along with traffic jams, slow-growth initiatives, and an occasional metallic haze to the sky. It is a region some travelers love and others love to hate, but when it comes to theme parks, shopping, and beach life, few places do it better than Orange County.

Served by convenient airports and only an hour's drive from Los Angeles, Orange County is both a destination on its own and a very popular excursion from Los Angeles.

Getting Around

By Plane Several airports are accessible to Orange County. **John Wayne Orange County Airport** (tel. 714/755–6500) is the county's main facility; it is 14 minutes from Anaheim and centrally located within the county. It is serviced by Alaska Airlines (tel. 800/426–0333); America West Airlines (tel. 800/AWA–WEST); American (tel. 800/433–7300); Delta (tel. 800/221–1212); TWA (tel. 800/221–2000); United (800/241–6522).

Los Angeles International Airport is only 35 miles from Anaheim and from **Ontario Airport,** 30 miles. LAX is still the destination of some nonstop transcontinental flights.

Long Beach Airport (tel. 213/421–8295) is another good choice for Orange County visits. It is about 20 minutes by coach from Anaheim. Airlines flying into Long Beach include America West, American Airlines, Delta, TWA, and United.

Airport Coach (tel. 800/772–5299 in CA or 800/491–3500 nationwide) services LAX to Anaheim, Long Beach, and Pasadena. Fare from the airport to Anaheim is $12 one-way, $22 round-trip; to Long Beach, $9 one-way, $16 round-trip.

Prime Time Airport Shuttle (tel. 213/558–1606 or 818/901–9901) offers door-to-door service to LAX, Burbank Airport, and San Pedro Harbor. The company's motto is "We're on time or you don't pay." The fare is $10 from Anaheim hotels to LAX. Children under 2 ride free.

SuperShuttle (tel. 213/417–8427) provides 24-hour door-to-door service from all the airports to all points in Orange County. Fare to the Disneyland district is $10 a person from any airport. Phone for other fares and reservations.

By Car Two major freeways, I–405 and I–5, run north and south through Orange County. Past Laguna they merge into I–5. Try to stay away from these during rush hours (7–9 AM and 4–6 PM) when they can slow for miles. Coming off I–405 is I–605, another major Orange County route. Highways 22, 55, and 91 go west to the ocean and east to the mountains: Take Highway 91 or Highway 22 to inland points (Buena Park, Anaheim) and take Highway 55 to Newport Beach.

Pacific Coast Highway (Highway 1) allows easy access to beach communities, and it is the most scenic route. It follows the entire Orange County coast, from Huntington Beach to San Clemente.

By Train **Amtrak** (800/USA–RAIL) has several stops in Orange County: Santa Ana, San Juan Capistrano, San Clemente, Anaheim, and Fullerton. There are six departures daily. A special motor-coach also takes people to Disneyland from the Fullerton station.

By Bus In Southern California, relying on public transportation is usually a mistake, unless you have plenty of time and patience. The **Los Angeles RTD** has limited service to Orange County. At the downtown Los Angeles terminal, on 6th Street, you can get the No. 460 to Anaheim; it goes to Knott's Berry Farm and Disneyland.

The **Orange County Transit Department** (tel. 714/636–7433) will take you virtually anywhere in the county, but, again, it will take time; OCTD buses go from Knott's Berry Farm and Disneyland to Huntington and Newport beaches. The No. 1 bus travels south along the coast.

Greyhound/Trailways (tel. 213/394–5433) as well has scheduled bus service to Orange County. For **Gray Line's** schedule and fare information, call 213/856–5900.

Pacific Coast (tel. 714/978–8855) provides transportation from Orange County hotels to the San Diego Zoo, Tijuana, the *Queen Mary/Spruce Goose*, and Knott's Berry Farm.

Scenic Drives Winding along the seaside edge of Orange County on the **Pacific Coast Highway**, is an eye-opening experience. Here, surely, are the contradictions of Southern California revealed—the powerful, healing ocean vistas and the scars of commercial exploitation; the appealingly laid-back, simple beach life and the tacky bric-a-brac of the tourist trail. Oil rigs line the road from Long Beach south to Huntington Beach, suddenly giving way to pristine stretches of water and dramatic hillsides. Prototypical beach towns like Laguna Beach, Dana Point, and Corona del Mar serve as casual stopping points irregularly arrayed along the route. This is a classic coastline drive.

For a scenic mountain drive, try **Santiago Canyon Road,** which winds through the Cleveland National Forest in the Santa Ana Mountains. Tucked away in the mountains are Modjeska Canyon, Irvine Lake, and Silverado Canyon, of silver mining lore. The terrain is rugged and you hardly feel as if you are anywhere near urban civilization.

Guided Tours

General-Interest Tours **Gray Line** (tel. 213/856–5900) has all-day tours to Disneyland and Knott's Berry Farm, as well as a combination tour of Knott's and Movieland Wax Museum.

For those who want specialized sightseeing services for small-group or personal tours, **The Orange County Experience** (tel. 714/680–3550) has been showing groups around the county for many years. Owner Louis Reichman is the author of *The Orange County Experience*. Stories behind Disneyland, Knott's

Berry Farm, and some of Orange County's most interesting cities make up these insiders' tours. The Crystal Cathedral, Mission San Juan Capistrano, and many local beaches can be part of the tour. A special tour, "From Orange to Wine," visits the Callaway Winery in scenic Rainbow Gap via the old Butterfield Stage Route.

Boat Tours At the **Cannery** in Newport Beach, you can hop a boat and go for a brunch cruise around the harbor on Sundays. Cruises last two hours and depart at 10 AM and 1:30 PM. Champagne brunches cost $25 per person. For more information call 714/675–5777.

Catalina Passenger Service (tel. 714/673–5245) at the Balboa Pavilion offers a full selection of sightseeing tours and fishing excursions to Catalina and around Newport Harbor. The 45-minute narrated tour of Newport Harbor, at $5, is the least expensive. Whale-watching cruises (Dec.–Mar.) are especially enjoyable. Narrated by a speaker from the American Cetacean Society, the tours follow the migration pattern of the giant gray whales.

Hornblower Yachts (tel. 714/548–8700) offers a number of special sightseeing brunch cruises. Whale-watching brunches (Jan.–Apr.) are scheduled each Saturday and Sunday; special cruises take place on such holidays as Valentine's Day, Easter, Halloween, Thanksgiving, and Christmas.

Walking Tours If you want to walk in Orange County, you're going to have to drive somewhere first. For a respite from suburban sprawl and urban smog, the **Tucker Wildlife Preserve** in Modjeska Canyon (tel. 714/649–2760), 17 miles southeast of the city of Orange, is worth the effort. The preserve is a haven for more than 140 bird species, including seven varieties of hummingbird—bizarre creatures that are surprisingly amusing to watch.

Free walking tours of **Mission San Juan Capistrano** are offered every Sunday at 1 PM, whether the swallows are in town or not. The tours take in the ruins of the Great Stone Church, destroyed by an earthquake in 1812, the Serra Chapel, the Mission's courtyards and fountains, and other historical sights.

Shopping Tours Several shopping shuttles help visitors make their own shopping tours. Six days a week, **South Coast Plaza's Shuttle Service** (tel. 714/241–1700) furnishes free round-trip transportation from many coastal-area hotels to this ritzy shopping area. Santa Ana's **Main Place** (tel. 714/547–7800), a newly improved shopping center, offers several shuttles a day from Anaheim hotels. One-way fare is $2 adults and $1 children under 13. **The City Shopper** offers transportation to the Crystal Cathedral, the City Shopping Center in Orange, and local hotels for $1 one-way. Information is available at hotels.

Important Addresses and Numbers

Tourist The main source of tourist information is the **Anaheim Area**
Information **Convention and Visitors Bureau,** located at the Anaheim Convention Center (800 West Katella Ave., 92802, tel. 714/999–8999). The **Guest Information Hot Line** (tel. 714/635–8900) offers information on entertainment, special events, and sightseeing tours in Orange County. This recording also describes amusement park hours and major attractions.

Other area chambers of commerce and visitors bureaus are generally open Monday–Friday 9–5 and will help with information. These include the following:

Buena Park Visitors Bureau (7711 Beach Blvd., 90261, tel. 714/994–1511).

Newport Harbor Chamber of Commerce (1470 Jamboree Rd., 92660, tel. 714/644–8211).

Huntington Beach Chamber of Commerce (Seacliff Village, 2213 Main St., 92648, tel. 714/536–8888).

Laguna Beach Chamber of Commerce (357 Glenneyre, 92651, tel. 714/494–1018).

Dana Point Chamber of Commerce (Box 12, 92629, tel. 714/496–1555).

San Juan Capistrano Visitors Center (inside the mission, 31882 Camino Capistrano, tel. 714/493–1424), **San Juan Capistrano Visitors Bureau** (31682 El Camino Real, 92675, tel. 714/493–4700).

San Clemente Tourism Bureau (31199 N. El Camino Real, 92672, tel. 714/492–1131).

Emergencies Dial 911 for **police** and **ambulance** in an emergency.

Doctor Orange County is so spread out and comprises so many different communities that it is best to ask at your hotel for the closest emergency room. Here are a few: **Anaheim Memorial Hospital** (1111 W. La Palma, tel. 714/774–1450), **Western Medical Center** (1025 S. Anaheim Blvd., Anaheim, tel. 714/533–6220), **Hoag Memorial Hospital** (301 Newport Blvd., Newport Beach, tel. 714/645–8600), **South Coast Medical Center** (31872 Coast Hwy., South Laguna, tel. 714/499–1311).

Exploring Orange County

Residents have long battled the popular belief that Orange County's borders start and end at Disneyland. We take the more enlightened view that there are two sides to the county—the theme parks that dominate the inland area (of which Disneyland is certainly first and foremost), and the coastline. Our Exploring section is therefore divided in two.

As the county lacks any definitive center, day trips will typically be destination-oriented rather than open explorations. If you're traveling with children, you can easily devote several full days to the theme parks: a day or two for Disneyland, a day for Knott's Berry Farm, perhaps a day driving between some of the area's lesser-known attractions. To rent a sailboard or other water sport paraphenalia, you'll have to head to the beach towns. For cultural fare, you'll need to drive to the Orange County Performing Arts Center. Only on the coastline is there any real wandering to be done. Beach days can be a mix of sunning, studying surf culture, and browsing the small shops native to the beach communities.

Inland Orange County

Numbers in the margin correspond with points of interest on the Orange County map.

Anaheim is indisputably the West's capital of family entertainment. With Disneyland, Knott's Berry Farm, and Movieland Wax Museum, there are as many rides and attractions, color and merriment, as anyone could want. The Anaheim Convention Center attracts almost as many conventions as Disneyland attracts children. For many visitors to Anaheim, a family trip to Disneyland may be an added attraction of an Anaheim meeting.

❶ Perhaps more than any other attraction in the world, **Disneyland,** the lasting physical evidence of Walt Disney's dream, is a symbol of the enduring child in all of us, a place of wonder and enchantment—also an exceptionally clean, well-managed, and imaginatively developed wonder. Decades ago, when the Yippies staged a small demonstration there, the papers reported that a woman stepped from behind a stroller to remind them that there were children present. There always are—plus many jaded adults who find they can't help enjoying themselves.

Disney built the park in 1955, and new attractions are added every year. The newest, open just a year, is Splash Mountain in the Bear County area of the park. The highlight here is an eight-passenger flume ride inspired by the Disney film *Song of the South*. The combination thrill-and-show ride features more than 100 of Disney's signature robotic characters, including Brer Fox, Brer Rabbit, and Brer Bear. At one point the flume drops 52 feet at 40 miles an hour, the longest, fastest flume ride anywhere, according to Disney.

Star Tours is based on the popular movie *Star Wars*, and is guided by those charming robots C3PO and R2D2. The story goes like this: The robots are now working for an intergalactic travel agency and you go on a trip with them in a star speeder; as you head for space, you find yourself in the middle of a battle between the rebel and imperial forces. The very realistic ride uses flight simulator technology.

All of the old standbys in Disneyland are still going strong. Disney's ideal turn-of-the-century Main Street is what first greets visitors; through it are Tomorrowland, Frontierland, Fantasyland, and Adventureland. Tomorrowland is the site of Star Tours, and also of the popular *Captain EO*, the Michael Jackson 3-D movie directed by Francis Ford Coppola. Space Mountain is a thrilling ride through space.

Fantasyland is the favorite domain of kids: The Pinocchio's Daring Journey ride takes you through this favorite puppet's escapade; a fly-through waterfall is only one element of the Peter Pan Flight; and logs turn into crocodiles in Snow White's Scary Adventure.

Frontierland takes visitors back to the Wild West. Big Thunder Mountain, one of the newer rides, is a runaway mine-car roller coaster. For a much more relaxing ride, the *Mark Twain* and *Columbia* river vessels take passengers on an exploration of the river, complete with Tom Sawyer's Island.

Time Out **Blue Bayou,** featuring Creole food, is a great place to eat. It is located in the entrance to the Pirates of the Caribbean, so you can hear the antics in the background.

Adventureland's Jungle Cruise is another popular water-based ride, with jungle sounds and realistic snapping crocodiles. The Pirates of the Caribbean is a swashbuckling adventure with cannonballs flying overhead to the accompaniment of a catchy

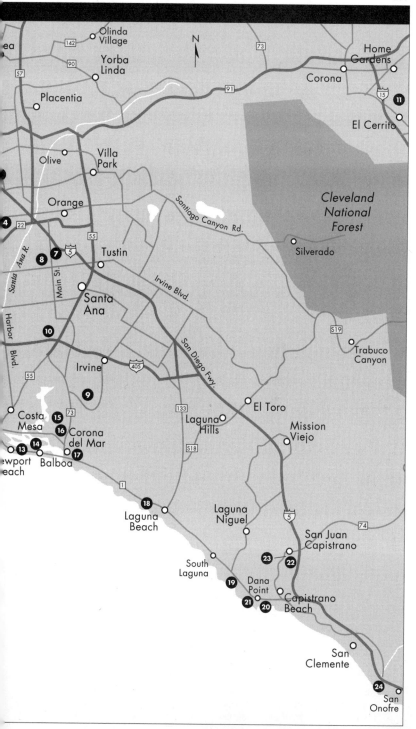

pirate tune. *1313 Harbor Blvd., Anaheim, tel. 714/999–4565. Admission: $25.50 adults, $20.50 children 3–12; this allows entrance to all the rides and attractions. In summer, open Sun.–Fri. 9 AM–midnight, Sat. 9 AM–1 AM; in fall, winter, and spring, open Mon.–Fri. 10–6, weekends 9–midnight.*

❷ Knott's Berry Farm, another family tradition, is located in nearby Buena Park. Several decades ago, people used to come to a 10-acre fruit patch here for Mrs. Knott's home cooking and the re-created ghost town. Now Knott's is a 150-acre complex with more than 60 eating places, 60 shops, and 100 rides and attractions. The recently opened Boomerang is a thrill ride with six loops—it moves slow to fast, giving you the sensation that you're falling out. Recent addition Wild Water Wilderness, set in a California river wilderness park of the early 1900s, has a raging white-water river, cascading waterfall, and geysers, landscaped with indigenous California trees. Bigfoot Rapids, a white-water rafting ride, incorporates the legend of Bigfoot; the ride itself is more than a third of a mile long. Floating rafts pass towering cliffs, race under waterfalls, and shoot the rapids. Bigfoot memorabilia—photos, footprints, etc.— are on hand in the "ranger's station."

Time Out   Don't forget what made Knott's famous, Mrs. Knott's fried chicken dinners and boysenberry pies at **Mrs. Knott's Chicken Dinner Restaurant,** just outside the park in Knott's Marketplace.

The other themed areas at Knott's include Camp Snoopy, a children's wonderland set in California's High Sierras; Ghost Town, an authentic 1880s Old West town; and Fiesta Village, a salute to California's Spanish heritage. Knott's is known for its daring thrill rides. "Montezooma's" Revenge accelerates from 0 to 55 mph in less than five seconds. The Corkscrew is the world's first upside-down roller coaster, featuring two 360-degree loops. And the Parachute Sky Jump falls 20 stories. *8039 Buena Park Blvd., Buena Park, tel. 714/220–5200. Admission: $21 adults, $16 children 3–11, $15 senior citizens over 60, expectant mothers, and disabled visitors. Open in summer, Sun.–Fri. 10 AM–midnight, Sat. 10 AM–1 AM; in winter, Mon.–Fri. 10–6, Sat. 10–10, Sun. 10–7.*

Visitors will find 70 years of movie magic immortalized at **❸ Movieland Wax Museum** in 240 wax sculptures of Hollywood's greatest stars. Realistic movie sets are the backdrop for such celebs as George Burns, Clint Eastwood, Mel Gibson, and Roger Moore. The Black Box is the newest attraction here; it takes visitors through scary scenes from *Alien, Halloween,* and *Altered States. 7711 Buena Park Blvd., one block north of Knott's, tel. 714/522–1155. Admission: $9.95 adults, $5.95 children. Open daily in summer 9 AM–10PM; daily in winter 10–9.*

Garden Grove, a community adjacent to Anaheim and Buena Park, is the site of one of the most impressive churches in the **❹** country, the **Crystal Cathedral.** The domain of television evangelist Robert Schuller, the glass edifice resembles a four-pointed star. More than 10,000 panes of glass cover the weblike steel truss to form translucent walls. The feeling as you enter is nothing less than mystical. A *Newsweek* writer called the building, designed by the renowned architect Philip Johnson, "the most spectacular religious edifice in the world." In addition to tours of the cathedral, two pageants are offered yearly —"The Glory of Christmas" and "The Glory of Easter." These dramas, which include live animals in the cast, flying angels, and other special effects, are seen by more than 200,000 people each year. *12141 Lewis St., Garden Grove, tel. 714/971–4013. Admission free. Usually open for self-guided tours Mon.–Sat. 9–3:30, Sun. 1:30–3:30. For reservations for the Easter and Christmas productions, call 714/54–GLORY.*

⑤ Several unique museums fill the inland area. The **Anaheim Museum,** which recently moved to the Carnegie Library Building, circa 1908, explores the prehistory and geology of the area as well as Anaheim's wine-producing story. *133 S. Anaheim Blvd., tel. 714/778–3301. Suggested admission: $1.50 adults, $1 senior citizens. Open Wed.–Fri. 10–4, Sat. noon–4. Closed Sun.*

⑥ The **Museum of World Wars and Military History** will fascinate history buffs. Included in the $2-million collection are military field equipment, armor, uniforms, posters, and armored vehicles. *7884 E. La Palma Ave. (at Beach Blvd.), Buena Park, tel. 714/952–1776. Admission: $1 adults. Open Mon.–Sat. 11–6, Sun. noon–6.*

⑦ The **Bowers Museum** presents cultural arts of the Americas, the Pacific Rim, and Africa. Each year it does exhibitions of international, national, and regional scope. *2002 N. Main St., Santa Ana, tel. 714/972–1900. Admission free. Open Tues.–Sat. 10–5, Sun. noon–5.*

Santa Ana, the county seat, is undergoing a dramatic restoration in its downtown area. Gleaming new government buildings meld with turn-of-the-century structures to give a sense of **⑧** where the county came from and where it is going. The **Fiesta Marketplace** is a new downtown development that has been recognized as a grass-roots effort involving businessmen and government. The Spanish-style, four-block project brings life to one of the traditionally most successful Hispanic marketplaces in Southern California.

Known for its forward-looking concept of community planning, **⑨** Irvine is also a center for higher education. The **University of California at Irvine** was established on land donated by the Irvine Company in the mid-1950s. The Bren Events Center, Fine Art Gallery on campus sponsors exhibitions of 20th-century art (free, Tues.–Sat. 10–5). Tree lovers will be enthralled by the campus; it's an arboretum with more than 11,000 trees from all over the world. *Take the San Diego Frwy. (I-405) to Jamboree Rd. Go west to Campus Dr. S.*

It is no small irony that the Costa Mesa/South Coast Metro area is known first for its posh shopping mall and then for its per- **⑩** forming arts center. **South Coast Plaza** (3333 South Bristol St., Costa Mesa) attracts more than 20 million visitors a year, making it the busiest mall in southern California. This is Adventureland for the credit card set, built around attractions with names like Polo/Ralph Lauren, Charles Jourdan, Godiva Chocolates, and Courreges. The adjacent **Orange County Performing Arts Center,** (600 Town Center Dr., tel. 714/556–2787), is a world-class complex, hosting such notables as the Los Angeles Philharmonic, the Pacific Symphony and the New York Opera. *California Scenario,* a 1.6 acre sculpture garden designed by artist Isamu Noguchi, connects the arts center and the mall, completing this unusual union of art and upscale consumerism. Noguchi uses sandstone, running water, concrete, and native plants to evoke different aspects of the California environment.

Time Out For a quick, healthful meal during a South Coast Plaza visit, try **Forty Carats** on the lower level between Saks and Bullocks. This spin-off of a restaurant in Bloomingdale's has a selection of tasty natural muffins, carrot and pumpkin among them.

After you have sightseen yourself to exhaustion, you might want to try the ultimate in the California spa experience at **①** **Glen Ivy Hot Springs.** Thirty-five miles east of Anaheim, the spa is a day-use-only resort. It features an Olympic-size mineral water pool, seven outdoor whirlpool baths, and a pool designed for tanning. The highlight is California's only European-style clay bath. Certified massage therapists are on duty. *Take Hwy. 91 east to I–15 south. Continue 8 mi to Temescal Canyon Rd. and exit. Make 2 immediate rights and take Glen Ivy Rd. to its end. Tel. 714/277–3529. Admission: $14.75 Sat., Sun., and holidays; $12.50 weekdays. Open daily 10–6.*

The Coast

To explore Orange County's coast you need four things: a car, the Pacific Coast Highway, comfortable walking shoes, and a fair supply of sun block. The highway serves as the main thoroughfare for all the beach towns along the coast. Small in scale, these communities are eminently walkable, so park the car to have a look about. We'll start our tour in the north and head south.

A popular surfer hangout, **Huntington Beach** is practically a living museum of southern California beach life. Each September, surfers from around the world converge on the city for its annual surfing competition. Unfortunately, Huntington pier, the best place to observe the sporting and social scene is closed this year for a major renovation. The facelift also includes a new theater, restaurant, and shopping complex scheduled to open this summer across the street from the pier.

② You won't find surfers at the **Bolsa Chica Ecological Reserve**, but you may well encounter a great blue heron, light-footed clapper rail, or harlequin duck. Close to 200 different species of birds have been sighted at the 300-acre salt marsh located off the Pacific Coast Highway, between Warner Avenue and Golden West Street. On the first Saturday of each month, October through March, the Amigos de Bolsa Chica offer guided tours of the reserve. *Tel. 714/897–7003. Call for a schedule.*

Newport Beach is the county's bastion of high society. Yacht clubs and country clubs thrive and host one gala party after the next. The community got its start as a commercial shipping center, but now it has become one of the county's most popular recreation and shopping areas.

In this Beverly-Hills-by-the-sea community, boats are as vital as BMWs; nearly 10,000 of them bob gently on the swells in **③** **Newport Harbor.** During the Christmas season the boats are decorated with more lights than most homes, making for a lively, definitely showy, boat parade. In June, the annual Flight of the Snowbirds is held in the harbor. An exceptionally popular race featuring small, Snowbird-class boats, this regatta was first run in 1926.

The U-shaped harbor, with the mainland along one leg and Balboa Peninsula along the other, shelters eight small islands. The ⑭ eost visited is **Balboa Island,** connected to the peninsula by a three-car ferry. You can drive directly to the island (via Jamboree, off the Pacific Coast Highway), but the ferry—one of the few remaining in the state—offers significantly more character. The **Victorian Balboa Pavilion** is the architectural jewel of the peninsula. Built in 1902 as a bath and boat house, the pavilion was a haven for the big band sound in the 1940s. Today it hosts boating facilities for harbor cruises, a sport-fishing fleet, whale watching boats (December through February), and a restaurant. The Newport Pier is older still, dating to 1888.

Time Out   **Irvine Ranch Farmer's Market** in Fashion Island Shopping Center sells a vast array of fresh produce, deli fare, and any other exotic food that you can imagine. It is best to visit off-hours; the place is mobbed at lunchtime.

Near the pier is a section called the Fun Zone. It has a carnival feel with an old-fashioned Ferris wheel, arcades, and novelty concessions. And you can get a notorious Balboa Bar (chocolate-covered frozen banana) here without going to Balboa Island.

To get to the Balboa Peninsula, take Hwy. 55 (Newport Frwy.) southwest until it becomes Newport Blvd. At the end, bear left onto Balboa Blvd.

⑮ The **Newport Harbor Art Museum** is internationally known for its impressive collection of works by California artists. The emphasis is on contemporary art, and there are many changing exhibits. Snacks are available in the Sculpture Garden Cafe. *850 San Clemente Dr., tel. 714/759-1122. A donation is requested. Open Tues.-Sun. 10-5.*

⑯ **Fashion Island** is another Newport Beach signature venue. Atrium Court, a Mediterranean-style plaza, is especially popular with upscale shoppers. Splash and Flash, with trendy swimwear; Amen Wardy, with the most haughty of women's fashions; and Posh, a unique men's store, are just some of the entries. In the first-floor court, you can relax to the sounds of a a grand piano. A recent expansion and renovation has added several new stores. *On Newport Center Dr. between Jamboree and MacArthur Blvds., just off Pacific Coast Hwy.*

Just south of Newport Beach, **Corona del Mar** is a small jewel of a town with an exceptional beach. You can walk clear out onto the bay on a rough-and-tumble rock jetty. The town itself stretches only a few blocks along the Pacific Coast Highway, but some of the fanciest stores and ritziest restaurants in the ⑰ county are located here. **Sherman Library and Gardens,** a lush botanical garden and library specializing in Southwest flora and fauna, offers diversion from sun and sand. Colorful seasonal flowers adorn the grounds, and you can have pastries and coffee in the tea garden. *2647 E. Coast Hwy., Corona del Mar, tel. 714/673-2261. Admission: $2. Open daily 10:30-4.*

If Newport is a seaside Beverly Hills, Laguna Beach is the SoHo of the surf. Some 60 art galleries peacefully coexist with the endless volleyball games and parades of people on Main Beach. Local shops offer crafts and current fashion in addition to canvases and sculptures. In the true spirit of the 60s, when Timothy Leary and his hippy cronies used to hang out in Laguna's fast-food joints along Pacific Coast Highway, the artistic style here can best be described as anything goes. Expect to see placid dune and ocean watercolors as well as shocking neon colored works and out of the ordinary assemblages of found objects.

⑱ The **Laguna Beach Museum of Art** has two locations. In Laguna Beach (307 Cliff Dr., tel. 714/494–6531), right near Heisler Park, the museum offers exhibits of historical and contemporary American art. The smaller gallery near the Carousel Court at South Coast Plaza (tel. 714/662–3366), offers smaller scale exhibits in the same vein.

In front of the Pottery Barn on the Coast Highway is a bit of local nostalgia—a life-size statue of Eiler Larson, the town greeter. For years he stood at the edge of town saying hello and goodbye to visitors.

Laguna's many festivals are what give it a worldwide reputation in the arts community. During July and August, the Sawdust Festival and Art-a-Fair, the Festival of the Arts, and the **Pageant of the Masters** take place. The Pageant of the Masters (tel. 714/494–1147) is Laguna's most impressive event, a blending of life and art. Live models and carefully orchestrated backgrounds are arranged in striking mimicry of famous paintings. Participants must hold a perfectly still pose for the length of their stay on stage. It is an impressive effort, requiring hours of training and rehearsal by the 400 or so residents who volunteer each year.

Going to Laguna without exploring its beaches would be a shame. To get away from the hubbub of Main Beach, go north to Woods Cove, off the Coast Highway at Diamond Street; it's especially quiet during the week. Big rock formations hide lurking crabs. As you climb the steps to leave, you'll see a stunning English-style mansion. It was once the home of Bette Davis. At the end of almost every street in Laguna, there is another little cove with its own beach.

⑲ **The Ritz Carlton** in Laguna Niguel is the classiest hotel for miles and has become a watering hole for the movers and shakers of Orange County. Gleaming marble and stunning antiques fill this posh hotel, and traditional English tea is served each afternoon to the strains of live piano music. *33533 Ritz Carlton Dr., Laguna Niguel, tel. 714/240–2000.*

⑳ Although it's been a popular port town for some 150 years, it's only recently that **Dana Point** has started to boom. New shops, restaurants, and hotels appear regularly. The town's main attraction is its harbor, set on a secluded cove surrounded by steep, jagged cliffs. Boats can be rented at Dana Wharf Sportsfishing (tel. 714/496–5794) for fishing or recreation. The beach here is quite good. In the summer, it's not unusual to see the adventurous parasailing above the sun worshipers; come winter, attention typically turns to whale watching (for information, call 714/496–4794). Mariners Village is the harbor's shopping area, a nautically themed, not terribly original, affair.

㉑ The **Orange County Marine Institute** is a unique educational facility that helps adults and children explore the ocean environment. A 65-foot diesel sportfishing boat is a floating laboratory; hands-on opportunities allow you to study marine life. Anchored near the institute is *The Pilgrim*, a full-size replica of the square-rigged vessel on which sailed Richard Henry Dana, the author of *Two Years Before the Mast*, for whom the town is named. Tours of *The Pilgrim* are offered one Sunday each month. *Dana Point Harbor Dr. and Del Obispo, tel. 714/496–2274. Open daily 9–3.*

San Juan Capistrano is best known for its Mission, and, of course, for the swallows that migrate here each year from their winter haven in Argentina. The arrival of the birds on St. Joseph's Day, March 19, launches a week of celebration. After summering in the arches of the old stone church, the swallows head home on St. John's Day, October 23.

㉒ Founded in 1776 by Father Serra, **Mission San Juan Capistrano** was the major Roman Catholic outpost between Los Angeles and San Diego. Although the original Great Stone Church lies in ruins, the victim of an 1812 earthquake, many of the mission's adobe buildings have been restored, and the grounds are well kept. The impressive Serra Chapel is believed to be the oldest building still in use in California. The knowledgeable staff in the mission's visitors center can help you with a self-guided tour. *Camino Capistrano and Ortega Hwy., tel. 714/493–1111. Admission: $2 adults, $1 children 11 and under. Open daily 7:30 AM–5 PM.*

㉓ Near the mission is the postmodern **San Juan Capistrano Library,** built in 1983. Architect Michael Graves mixed classical design with the style of the mission for a striking effect. It has a courtyard with private places for reading as well as a running water fountain. *31495 El Camino Real. Open Mon.–Thurs. 10–9, Fri.–Sat. 10–5.*

Time Out   The **Capistrano Depot** (26701 Verdugo St., tel. 714/496–8181) is not only a train station for Amtrak but also a restaurant and jazz spot. White tablecloths, linen napkins, and flowers grace the restaurant, which specializes in rack of lamb, prime rib, and combinations of filet mignon and scampi for dinner. It's a perfect way to see San Juan if you are based in Los Angeles—a train ride, a meal, and then a little sightseeing.

The southernmost city in Orange County, San Clemente, is probably best remembered as the site of the Western White House during the Nixon years. Casa Pacifica made the news often in those years. The house, on a massive 25.4-acre estate, is visible from the beach; just look up to the cliffs.

㉔ Perhaps even more infamous than Nixon's house is the **San Onofre Nuclear Power Plant,** a controversial installation lending an eerie feeling to the nearby beach, where surfers surf nonetheless. Off the Coast Highway, the San Onofre Nuclear Information Center is a must for those who want to know more about the mechanics of nuclear energy.

San Clemente also offers a wide selection of activities that make Southern California the playground that it is: swimming, surfing, sailing, fishing, and picnicking. San Clemente State Beach is one of the least crowded and most beautiful of the state beaches.

In the summer, San Clemente is awhirl for nine days during La Christianita Pageant. The three-act play commemorates the first baptism of an Indian in California. (This may or may not be an event you feel needs honoring. Christianized Indians throughout the state died in very large numbers.) The pageant is presented in La Christianita Bowl, three miles from a wilderness clearing where it was first presented. Soldiers, priests, Indian rites, and singing make up the colorful production.

For avid bicycle riders, the next 20 miles south of San Clemente is prime terrain. Camp Pendleton welcomes cyclists to use its roads. But don't be surprised if you see a troop helicopter taking off right beside you. This is the country's largest Marine Corps base. Training involves off-shore landings; overland treks are also conducted on the installation's three mountain ranges, five lakes, and 250 miles of roads.

What to See and Do with Children

Disneyland and Knott's Berry Farm are the prime attractions (*see* Inland Orange County, above), but there are many other amusements designed for children and families.

Raging Waters is a water theme park sure to please the whole family. It's actually in southeast Los Angeles County, but not far from Anaheim. Clean beaches and river rapids (man-made), water slides, and safe water fun for the smallest of children are found here. *111 Via Verde, San Dimas, where I–10 and I–210 meet (take the Raging Waters Blvd. exit), tel. 714/592–6453. Admission: $14.95 adults, $8.50 children 42–48 inches, children under 42 inches free, reduced rates for senior citizens and nonsliders. Open May and June daily 10–6, the rest of the summer Mon.–Thurs. 10–9, weekends 9–10.*

Wild Rivers is Orange County's newest water theme park. It has more than 40 rides and attractions. Among them: a wave pool, several daring slides, a river inner-tube ride, and several places to eat and shop. *8800 Irvine Center Dr., Laguna Hills (just off I–405 at Irvine Center Dr.), tel. 714/768–WILD. Admission: $14.95 adults, $10.95 children 3–9; discounts after 4 PM. Open mid-May–Sept. Call for hours.*

Golf-n-Stuff offers unusual family golfing fun. This miniature golf and arcade center is near Disneyland. Colored lights sparkle on geyser fountains amid windmills, castles, and waterfalls. *Admission: $4.75 adults, $3.75 children. Special family rates. Open Mon.–Fri. 9–10, weekends 9–midnight.*

Hobby City Doll and Toy Museum houses antique dolls and toys from around the world in a replica of the White House. It is one of the world's largest hobby, craft, and collector centers. *1238 S. Beach Blvd., Anaheim, tel. 714/527–2323.*

La Habra Children's Museum features all kinds of diversions for children. The restored 1923 railroad depot has a beehive, railroad cars, and several touchable displays. *301 S. Euclid St., tel. 714/905–9793.*

Laguna Moulton Playhouse has a special children's theater with changing fare. *606 Laguna Canyon Rd., tel. 714/494–0743.*

Off the Beaten Track

If you find time to visit any of these spots during your trip to Orange County, you can term yourself local. These are some of the "in" spots that natives know well.

Lido Island. This beautiful island in Newport Harbor is the location of some of the most elegant homes in Orange County. It's an inviting spot for a walk and a great view of the boats. *Take Hwy. 55 to Pacific Coast Hwy. in Newport Beach. Turn left at the signal onto Via Lido and follow this street onto the island.*

Orange County Swapmeet. This is no ordinary flea market. With a huge collection of items at big discounts, it's truly a Southern Californian way to spend the day, enjoying some beer and hot dogs in the sun. There are more than 1,000 vendors every Saturday and Sunday. Good bargains to look for include stereo equipment, plants, and artwork. *Orange County Fairgrounds, 88 Fair Dr., Costa Mesa (off Hwy. 55), tel. 714/751–3247.*

C'est Si Bon. This little cafe resembles quaint sidewalk cafes in Paris. It offers the best selection of coffee and croissants anywhere around; there is also a great selection of cheeses and pâtés. *Riverside Ave., off Pacific Coast Hwy. in Newport Beach, tel. 714/645–0447. Open Mon.–Fri. 6:30–6, Sat. 8–5, Sun. 8:30 AM–1:30 PM.*

Shopping

Shopping is Orange County's favorite indoor sport, and the region has the facilities to prove it. Some of the most exclusive shopping areas in the world fill the Newport Beach area, and South Coast Plaza in Costa Mesa is the second-largest mall in the country. Following is just a small selection of the shopping available in the county.

South Coast Plazas (Bristol and Sunflower Sts.) 270 stores offer everything from tires to ball gowns. Saks Fifth Avenue, Nordstrom, Neiman Marcus, Bullocks, I. Magnin, May Company, Sears, the Broadway, and Robinson's are the department stores anchoring the mall. For literary buffs, there is a branch of the famous Rizzoli's International Bookstore.

Fashion Island on Newport Center Drive in Newport Beach sits on the top of a hill, so shoppers enjoy a distinct ocean breeze. It is an open-air, single-level mall of more than 120 stores. Don't miss the Irvine Ranch Farmers Market, on the first level of the Atrium Court. This awesome market is a high-quality specialty gourmet store, surrounded by international eateries—a salsa bar, Italian bakery, and gourmet chocolate stand to name a few.

The **City Shopping Center,** in Orange, is an enclosed mall enhanced with attractive landscaping. May Company and J.C. Penney are the department stores. **Buena Park Mall,** near Disneyland and Knott's, has more than 160 stores.

If you can look past the inflatable palm trees, unimaginative T-shirts and other tourist novelties, there is some good browsing to be done in Laguna Beach. This is Main Street USA shopping, with the sort of antiques dealers and craftsmen you won't find in a generic shopping mall. Dozens of art and custom jewelry shops dot the streets. There are more jewelers per capita in Laguna than in any other town in the country. Some of the more unusual Laguna stores include: **Chicken Little Emporium,** Coast Highway, with whimsical gifts and clothing; **From Laguna,** 241 Forest Avenue, for unique fashions; **Khyber Pass,** 384 Forest Avenue, with gifts from the Middle East and Afghanistan; and **Toni's Kids Closet,** Coast Highway, with designer children's clothing and handcrafted wooden toys.

Beaches

Huntington Beach State Beach runs for miles along Coast Highway (take Beach Blvd. if you are coming from inland). There are changing rooms, concessions, and lifeguard vigilance on the premises. **Bolsa Chica State Beach,** down the road and across from the Bolsa Chica Ecological Reserve, has facilities for barbecues and picnics.

Lower Newport Bay provides an enclave sheltered from the ocean. This area, off Coast Highway on Jamboree, is a 740-acre preserve for ducks and geese. **Newport Dunes Aquatic Park,** nearby, offers picnic facilities, changing rooms, and a place to launch boats.

Just south of Newport Beach, **Corona del Mar State Beach** has a tide pool and caves waiting to be explored. It also sports one of the best walks in the county—a beautiful rock pier jutting into the ocean.

The county's best place for scuba diving is in the **Marine Life Refuge,** which runs from Seal Rock to Diver's Cove in Laguna. Farther south, in South Laguna, **Aliso County Park** is a recreation area with a pier for fishing.

Doheny State Park, near the Dana Point Harbor, has food stands and shops nearby. Camping is permitted here; there are also picnic facilities and a pier for fishing. **San Clemente State Beach** is one of the least crowded. It has ample camping facilities and food stands. Boogie boards and small boats can be rented nearby as well.

Participant Sports

Orange County is a sportsperson's playground; from surfing to walking, from sailing to biking, there is something for everyone who wants to be active.

Bicycling   Bicycles and roller skates are some of the most popular means of transportation along the beaches. Again, most beaches have rental stands. A bike path spans the whole distance from Marina del Rey all the way to San Diego, with some minor breaks. In Laguna, try the **Laguna Cyclery** (tel. 714/552–1798); in Huntington Beach, **Two Wheel Transit Authority** (tel. 714/951–4896).

Golf   Golf is one of the most popular sports in Orange County, and owing to the climate, almost 365 days out of the year are perfect golf days. Here is a selection of golf courses:

Anaheim Hills Public Country Club (tel. 714/637–7311); **Costa Mesa Public Golf and Country Club** (tel. 714/540–7500); **Mile Square Golf Course,** Fountain Valley (tel. 714/545–3726); **Meadowlark Golf Course,** Huntington Beach (tel. 714/846–1364); **Rancho San Joaquin Golf Course,** Irvine (tel. 714/786–5522); **Costa del Sol Golf Course,** Mission Viejo (tel. 714/581–9040); **Newport Beach Golf Course** (tel. 714/852–8681); **San Clemente Municipal Golf Course** (tel. 714/361–8278); **San Juan Hills Country Club,** San Juan Capistrano (tel. 714/837–0361); **Aliso Creek Golf Course,** South Laguna (tel. 714/499–1919).

Snorkeling Corona del Mar is off-limits to boats; this fact—along with its two colorful reefs—makes it a great place for snorkeling. Laguna Beach is also a good spot for snorkeling and diving; the whole beach area of this city is a marine preserve.

Surfing Orange County's signature sport may be too rough-and-tumble for some; you can get the same feel with a boogie board. Rental stands are found at all beaches. Body surfing is also a good way to start. Huntington Beach is popular for surfers and spectators. "The Wedge" at Newport Beach is one of the most famous surfing spots in the world. Don't miss the spectacle of surfers, who look tiny in the middle of the waves, flying through this treacherous place. San Clemente surfers are usually positioned right across from the San Onofre Nuclear Reactor.

Swimming All of the state, county, and city beaches in Orange County allow swimming. Make sure there is a manned lifeguard stand nearby and you are safe. Also keep on the lookout for posted signs about undertow as it can be mighty nasty in certain places.

Tennis Most of the larger hotels have tennis courts. Here are some other choices; try the local Yellow Pages for further listings.

Huntington Beach **Edison Community Center** (21377 Magnolia St., tel. 714/960–8870) has four courts available on a first-come, first-served basis, or reservations can be made. The **Murdy Community Center** (70000 Norma Dr., tel. 714/960–8895) requires reservations.

Laguna Beach Eight metered courts can be found at **Laguna Beach High School,** on Park Avenue. On Monday, Wednesday, and Friday, courts are also available at the **Irvine Bowl,** Laguna Canyon Road.

Newport Beach Call the recreation department at 714/644–3151 for information about court use at **Corona del Mar High School,** 2102 East Bluff Street. There are eight courts for public use.

San Clemente There are four courts at **San Luis Rey Park,** on Avenue San Luis Rey. They are offered on a first-come, first-served basis. Call the recreation department at 714/361–8200 for further information.

Water Sports Rental stands for surfboards, windsurfers, small power boats, and sailboats can almost always be found near most of the piers. Here are some of the more well-known rental places: **Hobie Sports** has three locations for surfboard and boogie board rentals—two in Dana Point (tel. 714/496–2366 or 714/496–1251) and one in Laguna (tel. 714/497–3304).

In the biggest boating town of all, Newport Beach, you can rent sailboats and small motorboats at **Balboa Boat Rentals** in the harbor (tel. 714/673–1320; open Fri.–Sun. 9 AM–sundown).

Sailboats rent for $20 an hour, and motorboats for $26 an hour. You must have a driver's license, and some knowledge of boating is helpful; rented boats are not allowed out of the bay.

In Dana Point, power and sailboats can be rented at **Embarcadero Marina** (tel. 714/496–6177), near the launching ramp at Dana Point Harbor. Boat sizes vary—sailboats range from $12 to $50 for two hours, motorboats are $17 an hour.

Spectator Sports

Orange County has some of the best, unplanned, casual spectator sports; besides the surfers, you are bound to catch a volleyball or basketball game at any beach on a weekend. Professional sports in Orange County include the following:

Baseball The **California Angels** (tel. 714/634–2000) play at the Anaheim Stadium from April through October.

Football The **Los Angeles Rams** (tel. 714/937–6767) have called Anaheim Stadium their home since 1980. The season runs from August through December.

Horse Racing The **Los Alamitos Race Course** (tel. 714/995–1234) has quarter horse racing and harness racing on a ⅝-mile track. Thoroughbred racing is part of the fare here as well.

Horse Shows Twice monthly at the **Orange County Fair Equestrian Center** (714/641–1328) show jumping is featured. Admission is free.

Dining

by Bruce David Colen Orange County seems to prove that nothing improves the quality of restaurants quite so much as being in a high-rent district. Since the region became one of the most costly places to buy a home, the dining scene is vastly improved. Restaurant prices, however, are not as high as in the upscale communities of Los Angeles and San Francisco; perhaps high mortgage payments have made the natives dining-dollar wary. The growing number of luxury hotels, with dining rooms to match, has also broadened gastronomic choices. The French cuisine at Le Meridien, for example, in Newport, is the best of any California hotel. At each of these restaurants, it is safest to call ahead for reservations.

The most highly recommended restaurants are indicated by a star ★.

Category	Cost*
Very Expensive	over $40
Expensive	$30–$40
Moderate	$15–$30
Inexpensive	under $15

per person, without tax (7%), service, or drinks

Anaheim **JW's.** You would never guess you were in a hotel—the dining
Expensive room looks like a French country inn, complete with a fireplace. The food is well prepared classic French, featuring roasted saddle of lamb, venison, and wild boar. *Marriott Hotel, 700 W. Convention Way, tel. 714/750–8000. Reservations re-*

quired. *Jacket required. AE, DC, MC, V. Valet parking. Dinner only. Closed Sun.*

Moderate **Bessie Wall's.** Citrus rancher John Wall built this house for his bride-to-be in 1927. It has been restored, and the rooms have been converted into dining areas decorated with Wall memorabilia. Bessie's favorite chicken-and-dumplings recipe is on the menu, which features Southern California–Mexican dishes. The place is nostalgic fun. *1074 N. Tustin Blvd., tel. 714/630–2812. Reservations advised. Jacket advised. AE, DC, MC, V. Closed Sat. lunch.*

Overland Stage. A dining Disneyland of sorts. The theme here is California in its Wild West days. There's a stagecoach over the entrance, and all sorts of Western bric-a-brac within. The daily specials are intriguing: wild boar, buffalo, rattlesnake, bear, and elk. *1855 S. Harbor Blvd., tel. 714/750–1811. Reservations advised. Jacket advised. AE, DC, MC, V. Closed for lunch weekends.*

Corona del Mar **Trees.** The contemporary look, atmosphere, and menu of this
Expensive upscale restaurant are among the most appealing in Orange County. The three dining rooms, with walls and table appointments done in shades of pink, surround a glassed-in atrium planted with towering ficus trees. Each room has its own fireplace. Satisfying cooking matches the setting: Maryland crab cakes, roast turkey dinners on Sunday; Chinese chicken salad, potstickers and spring rolls; veal sweetbreads in puff pastry. Don't pass up the apricot mousse dessert. There's also a piano bar. *440 Heliotrope Ave., tel. 714/673–0910. Reservations required. Jacket required. AE, DC, MC, V. Closed for lunch.*

Moderate **The Five Crowns.** A surprisingly faithful replica of Ye Old Bell,
★ England's oldest inn. The barmaids and waitresses are costumed in Elizabethan dress; there's a wide array of British ales and, of course, Guinness stout. The roast beef with Yorkshire pudding and the rack of lamb are very good, as are the fish dishes, all at reasonable prices. *3801 E. Pacific Coast Hwy. tel. 714/760–0331. Reservations required. Jacket advised. AE, DC, MC, V. Closed lunch; open for Sun. brunch.*

Costa Mesa **Gemmel's.** This sophisticated, charming restaurant is in a
Expensive not-very-attractive commercial neighborhood. But once you're through the front door, you'll think you're in New York or London. Chef Gemmel's cooking is cosmopolitan: He smokes his own salmon and makes a hearty duck pâté; there's smoked quail with dill and noodles, sautéed Maine lobster, and poached whitefish in a mustard sauce. All in all, worth dressing for. *3000 Bristol St., tel. 714/751–1074. Reservations required. Jacket and tie required. AE, DC, MC, V. Closed Sat. lunch and Sun.*

Moderate–Expensive **Alfredo's.** Northern Italian dishes served in an attractive, multi-level dining room, beneath a huge skylight. There's lots of cheerful greenery with service to match. Menu suggestions include mozzarella marinara, scampi sautéed with garlic and white wine, chicken and spinach cannelloni, and a fine seafood salad. Brunch is served on Sunday. *666 Anton Blvd., tel. 714/540–1550. Reservations advised. Jacket required. AE, DC, MC, V. Closed Sat. lunch and Sun. dinner.*

Dana Point **Watercolors.** This light, cheerful dining room gives a clifftop
Expensive view of the harbor and an equally enjoyable Continental/California menu, along with low-calorie choices. Try the baked breast of pheasant, roast rabbit, grilled swordfish, and either

the Caesar or poached spinach salad. *Dana Point Resort, tel. 714/661–5000. Reservations suggested. Dress: resort casual. AE, DC, MC, V. Valet parking.*

Moderate **Chart House.** This is one of the most popular of the small chain of steak-and-seafood houses in Southern California. Mud pie is the dessert everyone asks for. This particular location has a sensational view of the harbor from most of the tables and booths. *34442 Green Lantern, tel. 714/493–1183. Reservations advised. Jacket advised. AE, DC, MC, V. Closed lunch; open for Sun. brunch.*

Delaney's Restaurant. Seafood from nearby San Diego's fishing fleet is what this place is all about. Your choice is prepared as simply as possible. If you have to wait for a table, pass the time at the clam and oyster bar. *25001 Dana Dr., tel. 714/496–6196. Reservations advised. Dress: casual. AE, DC, MC, V.*

Fullerton **The Cellar.** And it is just that, a subterranean dining room,
Expensive with beamed ceiling and stone walls, wine casks and racks. The
★ list of wines from Europe and California is among the best in the nation. The classic French cuisine is lightened for the California palate. *305 N. Harbor Blvd., tel. 714/525–5682. Reservations required. Jacket and tie advised. AE, DC, MC, V. Closed lunch and Sun. and Mon.*

Huntington Beach **MacArthur Park.** Modeled after the popular San Francisco res-
Moderate taurant, this casual eatery has a view of Huntington Harbor. Contemporary art hangs on brick walls. Standouts on the California menu are smoked filet mignon appetizers and sweet potatoes with tequila-and-lime sauce. *16390 Pacific Coast Hwy., tel. 714/846–5553. Weekend reservations advised. Jacket advised. AE, MC, V.*

Inexpensive **Texas Loosey's Chili Parlor & Saloon.** This place serves up Tex-Mex cooking with hot fixings, plus steaks, ribs, and burgers. Country-and-western music is played at night. *14160 Beach Blvd., tel. 714/898–9797. Dress: informal. MC, V.*

Irvine **Chanteclair.** This Franco-Italian country house is a lovely,
Moderate–Expensive tasteful retreat in an island of modern high-rise office buildings. French Riviera–type cuisine is served; Chateaubriand for two and rack of lamb are recommended. *18912 MacArthur Blvd., tel. 714/752–8001. Reservations advised. Jacket required. AE, DC, MC, V. Closed Sat. lunch; open for Sun. brunch.*

Moderate **Gulliver's.** Jolly old England is the theme of this groaning board. Waitresses are addressed as "wenches" and busboys as "squires." Prime rib is the specialty. *18482 MacArthur Blvd., tel. 714/833–8411. Reservations advised. Jacket advised. MC, V.*

Pavilion. Excellent Chinese food is offered in what resembles a formal eating hall in Chef Hu's native Taiwan. Specialties include steamed whole fish, ginger duck, and Hunan lamb. *14110 Culver Drive, 714/551–1688. Reservations advised. Dress: casual. AE, MC, V.*

Prego. A much larger version of the Beverly Hills Prego, this one is located in an attractive approximation of a Tuscan villa, with an outdoor patio. A favorite of Orange County's Yuppies, who rave about the watch-the-cooks-at-play open kitchen and the oak-burning pizza oven. Try the spit-roasted meats and chicken, or the charcoal-grilled fresh fish. Also try the California or Italian wines. *18420 Von Karman Ave., tel. 714/553–1333. Dress: casual. AE, MC, V. Valet parking. Closed for lunch weekends.*

Laguna Beach
Expensive

The Ritz-Carlton. The Dining Room in this ocean-side resort hotel serves rather pretentious pseudo-nouvelle cuisine, but the lavish Sunday brunch, served in The Cafe, is considered the best in Southern California. Be sure to make reservations several days in advance and ask for a table on the terrace, overlooking the swimming pool. *33533 Ritz-Carlton Dr., Niguel, tel. 714/240–2000. Reservations required. Dress: casual but neat. AE, DC, MC, V.*

Moderate

Las Brisas. A long-time coastal favorite with a spectacular view of the rugged coastline from the clifftop terrace, wonderful margaritas, addictive guacamole, and nouvelle Mexican dishes. The first three compensate for the last. *361 Cliff Dr., tel. 714/497–5434. Reservations advised. Dress: casual. AE, DC, MC, V.*

Partners Bistro. Beveled glass, antiques, and lace curtains adorn this neighborhood hangout. Fresh fish and tournedos of beef are featured on the Continental menu. *448 S. Coast Hwy., tel. 714/497–4441. Reservations advised. Dress: casual. MC, V.*

The White House. Bing Crosby and Cecil B. DeMille dined at this local hangout. The broad American menu has everything from bagels and lox to Mexican favorites. There's also a salad bar, for while you're making up your mind. *340 S. Coast Hwy., tel. 714/494–8088. No reservations. Dress: casual. AE, DC, MC, V.*

Inexpensive

The Beach House. A Laguna tradition, the Beach House has a white-water view from every table. Fresh fish, lobster, and steamed clams are the drawing cards. *619 Sleepy Hollow La., tel. 714/494–9707. Reservations advised. Jacket advised. AE, MC, V.*

The Cottage. The menu is heavy on vegetarian dishes, and the price is right. Specialties include fresh fish, Victoria Beach scallops, and chicken Alfredo. *308 N. Pacific Coast Hwy., tel. 714/494–3023. Weekend reservations advised. Dress: casual. AE, MC, V.*

Tortilla Flats. This hacienda-style restaurant specializes in first-rate chile relleno, carne Tampiquena, soft-shell tacos, and beef or chicken fajitas. There's a wide selection of Mexican beers and tequilas. *1740 S. Coast Hwy., tel. 714/494–6588. Dinner reservations advised. Dress: casual. AE, MC, V. Brunch only on Sun.*

Newport Beach
Expensive

Antoine's. This lovely, candle-lit dining room is made for romance and quiet conversation. It serves the best French cuisine of any hotel in Southern California; the fare is nouvelle, but neither skimpy nor tricky. *4500 MacArthur Blvd., tel. 714/476–2001. Reservations advised. Jacket and tie required. Closed lunch; open for brunch Sun.*

★ **The Ritz.** One of the most comfortable Southern California restaurants—the bar area has red leather booths, etched glass mirrors, and polished brass trim. Don't pass up the smorgasbord appetizer, the roast Bavarian duck, or the rack of lamb from the spit. This is one of those rare restaurants that pleases everyone. *880 Newport Center Dr., tel. 714/720–1800. Reservations advised. Jacket required. AE, DC, MC, V. Lunch Sat., closed Sun.*

Moderate **Le Biarritz.** Newport Beach natives have a deep affection for this restaurant, with its country French decor, hanging greenery, and skylit garden room. There's food to match the mood: a veal-and-pheasant pâté, seafood crepes, boned duckling and wild rice, sautéed pheasant with raspberries, and warm apple tart for dessert. *414 N. Newport Blvd., tel. 714/645–6700. Reservations advised. Dress: casual. AE, DC, MC, V. Closed weekend lunches.*

Bubbles Balboa Club. This whimsical take-off on a 1930s nightclub has cigarette girls and canned music from the Big Band Era. While you're taking in the scene, order a steak or the grilled lamb chops. *111 Palm St., tel. 714/675–9093. Reservations advised. Dress: casual. AE, DC, MC, V.*

Cannery. The building was a cannery, and it has wonderful wharf-side views. The seafood entrées are good, and the sandwiches at lunch are satisfying, but the location and lazy atmosphere are the real draw. *3010 Lafayette Ave., tel. 714/675–5777. Reservations advised. Dress: casual. AE, DC, MC, V. Open for Sun. brunch.*

Marrakesh. In a casbah setting straight out of a Bob Hope road movie, diners become part of the scene—you eat with your fingers while sitting on the floor or lolling on a hassock. Chicken *b'stilla*, rabbit couscous, and skewered pieces of marinated lamb are the best of the Moroccan dishes. It's what-the-heck fun. *1100 Pacific Coast Hwy., tel. 714/645–8384. Reservations advised. Dress: casual. AE, DC, MC, V. Closed lunch.*

Inexpensive **Crab Cooker.** If you don't mind waiting in line, this shanty of a place serves fresh fish grilled over mesquite at low-low prices. The clam chowder and cole slaw are good, too. *2200 Newport Blvd., tel. 714/673–0100. No reservations. Dress: casual. No credit cards.*

★ **El Torito Grill.** Southwestern cooking incorporating below-the-border specialties is the attraction here. The just-baked tortillas with a green pepper salsa, the turkey mole enchilada, and the blue-corn duck tamalitos are good choices. The bar serves 20 different tequila brands and hand-shaken margaritas. *951 Newport Center Dr., tel. 714/640–2875. Reservations advised. Dress: casual. AE, DC, MC, V.*

Orange **Chez Cary.** Orange County residents have been celebrating
Very Expensive special events here for over 25 years. It will be a costly evening, indeed, but you'll get excellent Continental cuisine with impeccable service, in an opulent, red-plush dining room—and gold matchbooks imprinted with your name. *571 S. Main St., tel. 714/542–3595. Reservations required. Jacket and tie required. AE, DC, MC, V.*

Expensive **The Hobbit.** This is the place to feast, if you can make reservations two to three months in advance. The six- to eight-course French-Continental meal starts in the wine cellar at 7:30 and ends about three hours later. *2932 E. Chapman Ave., tel. 714/997–1972. Reservations required far in advance. Jacket and tie required. DC, MC, V. One seating only.*

Moderate **La Brasserie.** It doesn't look like a typical brasserie but the varied French cuisine fits the name over the door. One dining room in the multi-floor house is done as an attractive, cozy library. There's also an inviting bar-lounge. *202 S. Main St., tel. 714/978–6161. Reservations advised. Dress: casual. AE, DC, MC, V. Closed Sat. lunch and Sun.*

San Clemente **Andreino's.** Pasta is the key word at this Italian restaurant dec-
Moderate orated with antiques, flowers, and lace curtains. *1925 S. El
Camino Real, tel. 714/492–9955. Reservations advised. Jacket
advised. AE, MC, V.*

Etienne's. Smack-dab in the center of town, this restaurant is
housed in a white stucco historical landmark. There is outdoor
seating in a terra-cotta patio with fountains. Indoors, the decor
is French château. Only fresh fish is served; chateaubriand,
frog legs, and other French favorites are on the menu, along
with flaming desserts. *215 S. El Camino Real, tel. 714/492–
7263. Reservations advised. Jacket advised. AE, DC, MC, V.
Closed for lunch Fri.; closed Sun.*

The Fish Tale. Twenty-five different kinds of beer are part of
the fare at this seafood restaurant with turn-of-the-century decor. *111 W. Palizada, tel. 714/498–6072. Reservations advised.
Jacket advised. AE, MC, V.*

Swallow's Cove. This elegant restaurant has peach linen cloths,
high-backed upholstered chairs, and rosebuds on every table.
The menu offers seafood, steak, and chicken. Chicken Judy—
Mediterranean baked chicken—is a house special. *In the San
Clemente Inn, 2600 Ave. del Presidente, tel. 714/492–6103.
Weekend reservations advised. Jacket advised. AE, DC,
MC, V.*

San Juan **El Adobe.** President Nixon memorabilia fills the walls in this
Capistrano Early American–style eatery serving Mexican-American food.
Moderate Mariachi bands play Wednesday–Sunday. *31891 Camino Capi-
strano, tel. 714/830–8620. AE, MC, V.*

L'Hirondelle. There are only 12 tables at this charming French
inn. Duckling is the specialty, prepared three different ways.
*31631 Camino Capistrano, tel. 714/661–0425. Reservations
necessary. MC, V. Closed Mon. and Tues.*

Inexpensive **Swallow Inn.** The food is Mexican, but the atmosphere is American West, complete with sawdust on the floor. Live entertainment Tuesday–Sunday. *31786 Camino Capistrano, tel. 714/
493–3188. No credit cards.*

Santa Ana **Saddleback Inn.** The decor here takes Orange County back in
Inexpensive time to hacienda days, blending Old Spain and Mission California. Slow-cooked barbecued roast beef is the house specialty;
filet of sole amandine, barbecued baked chicken, and filet mignon with bordelaise sauce are other possibilities. *1660 E.
First St., tel. 714/835–3311. AE, V. Closed Sun.*

Lodging

Like cuisine, hotels have also come a long way in Orange County. Sophistication seems to grow with each new hotel opening. The beaches are the most expensive for lodging; family areas, like Anaheim, are full of more inexpensive, simpler motels,
which are too numerous to list. Categories here are based on
prices for summer; winter rates tend to be lower. Be sure to ask
about discounted promotional and weekend rates, which can be
as much as 50% below standard "rack" rates.

The most highly recommended lodgings in each price category
are indicated by a star ★.

Category	Cost*
Very Expensive	over $110
Expensive	$80–$110
Moderate	$60–$80
Inexpensive	under $60

for a double room

Anaheim
Very Expensive
★

Anaheim Hilton and Towers. This hotel is one of the largest on the West Coast. It is truly a city unto itself complete with its own post office. The lobby is dominated by a bright, airy atrium, and rooms are decorated in pinks and greens with light-wood furniture. *777 Convention Way, 92702, tel. 714/750–4321 or 800/445–8667. 1,600 rooms. Facilities: 4 restaurants, several lounges and shops, outdoor pool, fitness center, sun deck, concierge. AE, DC, MC, V.*

Anaheim Marriott. With outstanding meeting facilities, this hotel caters to convention attendees. Its lobby is filled with windows and colorful Spanish tile. Rooms, decorated with pastels, have balconies. *700 W. Convention Way, 92802, tel. 714/750–8000. 1,042 rooms. Facilities: gift shops, beauty salon, 2 heated swimming pools, Jacuzzi, weight rooms, video games, 3 restaurants, lounge, and entertainment. AE, CB, DC, MC, V.*

Disneyland Hotel. Always bustling with activity, this hotel is connected to Disneyland by monorail. It encompasses a 60-acre resort that carries on the fun atmosphere of its neighbor. New towers and tropical village make for unique accommodations; rooms, decorated in contemporary colors, all have balconies with views of Disneyland or the hotel marina. *1150 W. Cerritos Ave., 92802, tel. 714/778–6600 or 800/MICKEY–1. 1,132 rooms. Facilities: waterfront bazaar with wares from all over the world, tennis courts, pool, marina with playland and pedalboats. AE, CB, DC, MC, V.*

Pan Pacific Anaheim. This hotel is geared toward the business traveler. Its distinctive atrium lobby has glass-enclosed elevators. Contemporary graphics fill the rooms. Nonsmoking rooms are available. *1717 S. West St., 92802, tel. 714/999–0990 or 800/821–8976. 507 rooms. Facilities: 3 restaurants, pool, sun deck, and Jacuzzi. AE, CB, DC, MC, V.*

Expensive

Anaheim Holiday Inn. Large glass chandeliers greet the visitor to this establishment one block south of Disneyland. *1850 S. Harbor Blvd., 92802, tel. 714/750–2801. 312 rooms. Facilities: heated pool, sauna, suites, dining room, lounge, and coffee shop. AE, CB, DC, MC, V.*

Anaheim Plaza Resort. Soft pastels and plants fill the lobby of this hotel near Disneyland. Wheelchair units and suites are available. *1700 S. Harbor Blvd., 92602, tel. 714/772–5900 or 800/228–9000. 300 rooms. Facilities: heated pool, restaurant. AE, CB, DC, MC, V.*

Grand Hotel. Lobby and rooms are decorated in a pleasant plum–teal green combination. This property is adjacent to Disneyland and offers a free shuttle. Each room in the nine-story high rise has a balcony. *7 Freedman Way, 92802, tel. 714/772–7777. 242 rooms. Facilities: pool, gift shop, dining room, coffee shop, the Grand Dinner Theater. AE, CB, DC, MC, V.*

Inn at the Park. Mountains of all kinds can be seen from private balconies—the man-made Matterhorn at Disneyland and the

Santa Ana Mountains. *1855 S. Harbor Blvd., 92802, tel. 714/ 750–1811. 500 rooms. Facilities: heated pool, exercise room, suites, restaurant, coffee shop, lounge with entertainment. AE, CB, DC, MC, V.*

Sheraton-Anaheim Motor Hotel. This Tudor-style hotel offers a free shuttle to Disneyland. *1015 W. Ball Rd., 92802, tel. 714/ 778–1700 or 800/325–3535. 500 rooms. Facilities: dining room, coffee shop, deli, heated pool, suites, game room, and bar. Wheelchair units. AE, CB, DC, MC, V.*

Moderate **Quality Hotel and Conference Center.** A large, open, red-tile lobby is filled with mirrors, plants, and flowers; rooms are decorated in greens and yellows. The hotel is close to Disneyland. *616 Convention Way, 92802, tel. 714/750–3131. 284 rooms. Facilities: suites, heated pool, gift shop, bar restaurant. AE, CB, DC, MC, V.*

Ramada Hotel Maingate. A clean, reliable, two-year-old member of the worldwide chain. Located across the street from Disneyland, with free shuttle service to the park. *1460 S. Harbor Blvd., 92802, tel. 714/772–6777. 467 rooms. Facilities: pool, restaurant. AE, MC, V.*

Inexpensive **Hampton Inn.** Basic lodging at a basic price. *300 E. Katella Way, 92802, tel. 714/772–8713. 136 rooms. Facilities: pool, cable TV. AE, MC, V.*

Buena Park **Buena Park Hotel and Convention Center.** A spiral staircase
Moderate leading to the mezzanine centers a lobby of marble, brass, and glass. Sleeping rooms are done in blues, greens, and peaches. *7675 Crescent Ave., 90620, tel. 714/995–1111. 328 rooms. Facilities: heated pool, dining rooms, lounge, coffee shop. AE, CB, DC, MC, V.*

Costa Mesa **Westin South Coast Plaza.** The lobby lounge dominates a sunk-
Very Expensive en lobby here; rooms are all decorated in a different style. This is the perfect hotel for die-hard shoppers, who only have to cross the street to get to South Coast Plaza, one of the poshest shopping centers in the country. A special weekend package is available at 50% off regular price. *666 Anton Blvd., 92626, tel. 714/540–2500. 400 rooms. Facilities: volleyball, shuffleboard, tennis courts, 2 restaurants, 3 bars, live entertainment, gift shop. AE, CB, DC, MC, V.*

Dana Point **Dana Point Resort.** This two-year-old resort brings Cape Cod
Very Expensive to Southern California in pleasant shades of sea-foam green
★ and peach. The lobby is filled with large palm trees and original artwork. It is casual yet elegant; every room has an ocean view. A special parasailing package deal is offered. *25135 Park Lantern Ave., 92629, tel. 714/661–5000. 350 rooms. Facilities: 2 pools, 3 spas, health club, restaurant, and lounge. AE, CB, DC, MC, V.*

Moderate **Marina Best Western.** Set right in the marina, this hotel is accessible to many restaurants and shops. All rooms have balconies and vary in size from a basic room to a family suite with kitchen and fireplace. *24800 Dana Point Dr., 92629, tel. 714/ 496–1203. 135 rooms. Facilities: pool. AE, CB, DC, MC, V.*

Huntington Beach **Best Western Huntington Beach Inn.** This inn, decorated in
Expensive light green and mauve, is right across from the ocean. *21112 Pacific Coast Hwy., 92648, tel. 714/536–1421. 94 rooms. Facilities: restaurant, pool, coffee shop, lounge, gift shop, 3-par golf course. AE, CB, DC, MC, V.*

Moderate
★

Huntington Shore Motor Hotel. Also across from the ocean, some rooms at this small hotel have ocean views. The cozy lobby is set off with a fireplace. The extra-large rooms are decorated in earth tones. Complimentary Continental breakfast is offered. *21002 Pacific Coast Hwy., 92648, tel. 714/536–8861. 50 rooms. Facilities: heated pool. AE, MC, V.*

Irvine
Very Expensive

Irvine Hilton and Towers. This beautiful hotel has all the amenities of a first-class resort. It is elegantly decorated in pale earth tones; the marble lobby is flanked by glass-enclosed elevators. Weekend rates are a great deal. *17900 Jamboree Rd., 92714, tel. 714/863–3111. 550 rooms. Facilities: pool, Jacuzzi, tennis, workout room, entertainment, 2 restaurants, 2 cocktail lounges, concierge. AE, CB, DC, MC, V.*

Irvine Marriott. Mauve and sea-foam green fill this contemporary hotel, and flower arrangements beautify the lobby. *1800 Von Karman, 92715, tel. 714/553–0100. 502 rooms. Facilities: restaurant, indoor-outdoor pool, tennis courts, sports-oriented bar, massage room, concierge floors, American Airlines and Hertz Rent-a-Car desks. AE, CB, DC, MC, V.*

Moderate

Airporter Inn Hotel. To cater to businesspeople, all rooms here have a work area and are decorated in earth tones. One deluxe suite even has its own private pool. *18700 MacArthur Blvd., 92715, tel. 714/833–2770. 213 rooms. Facilities: Heated pool, dining room, coffee shop, cocktail lounge, suites. AE, DC, MC, V.*

Laguna Beach
Very Expensive
★

Inn at Laguna. This Southwest-style inn has just been renovated and enlarged. It's got one of the best locations in town— close to Main Beach and Las Brisas restaurant and bar, one of Laguna's most popular watering holes, yet far enough away to be secluded. The inn is decorated in peacock blue and peach and overlooks the ocean from a high bluff. *211 No. Coast Hwy., 92651, tel. 714/497–9722. 70 rooms, Facilities: VCRs in the rooms, heated pool, Jacuzzi, complimentary Continental breakfast in the rooms. AE, CB, DC, MC, V.*

Surf and Sand Hotel. The largest hotel in Laguna, the Surf and Sand has a shopping area with antique, clothing, and gift stores. Newly done rooms sport soft sand colors and wooden shutters; they feature private balconies and honor bars. *15555 S. Coast Hwy., 92651, tel. 714/497–4477. 157 rooms. Facilities: private beach, pool, lounge, concierge, 2 restaurants, entertainment, art gallery. AE, CB, DC, MC, V.*

Expensive–
Very Expensive

The Carriage House. This New Orleans–style bed-and-breakfast is surrounded by a lush garden. Complimentary family-style breakfast is offered daily. Fresh fruit and wine gifts welcome guests. *1322 Catalina St., 92651, tel. 714/494–8945. 6 suites. No credit cards. 2-night minimum on weekends.*

Expensive

Eiler's Inn. A light-filled atrium centers this newly remodeled B&B. All rooms are unique and decorated with antiques. Outdoor breakfast is served; in the afternoon there's wine and cheese, often to the accompaniment of live music. With only 12 rooms, you'll need to book well in advance. *741 S. Coast Hwy., 92651, tel. 714/494–3004. 12 rooms. AE, MC, V.*

Hotel Laguna. This downtown landmark, the oldest hotel in Laguna, was totally redone three years ago. Lobby windows look out on manicured gardens, and a patio restaurant overlooks the ocean. *425 S. Coast Hwy., 92651, tel. 714/494–1151. 68 rooms.*

Facilities: 2 restaurants, private beach, lounge, entertainment. AE, CB, DC, MC, V.

Laguna Niguel
Very Expensive
★

The Ritz Carlton. The only Mobil five-star and AAA five-diamond resort in California, this hotel has become *the* place for the county's haute society. The Mediterranean architecture and extensive landscaping make it feel like an Italian country villa. *33533 Ritz Carlton Dr., 92677, tel. 714/240–2000. 393 rooms. Facilities: beach access, health club, 2 pools, 3 restaurants, 3 lounges and a club with entertainment, concierge. Adjacent to an ocean-view 18-hole golf course. AE, CB, DC, MC, V.*

Newport Beach
Very Expensive
★

Four Seasons Hotel. This four-year-old hotel lives up to the quality of its fellow chain members. Marble and antiques fill the airy lobby; all rooms—decorated with beiges, peaches, and other southwestern tones—have spectacular views. *690 Newport Dr., 92660, tel. 714/759–0808. 285 rooms. Facilities: pool, whirlpool, lighted tennis courts, health club, 2 restaurants, lounge, concierge. AE, CB, DC, MC, V.*

Hotel Meridien Newport Beach. An eye-catching cantilevered design is the trademark of this ultramodern hotel in Koll Center. Decor is Southern Californian with striking pastels. Weekend rates dip almost 50 %. *4500 MacArthur Blvd., 92660, tel. 714/476–2001. 435 rooms. Facilities: restaurant, cafe, lounge, health club with Jacuzzi, pool, tennis courts, complimentary bicycles, concierge. AE, CB, DC, MC, V.*

Expensive

Marriott Hotel and Tennis Club. A distinctive atrium surrounded by a fountain greets guests. Location is directly across the street from Fashion Island shopping center. *900 Newport Center Dr., 92660, tel. 714/640–4000 or 800/228–9290. 600 rooms. Facilities: pools, adjacent golf course, tennis courts, Jacuzzi, 2 restaurants, lounge, entertainment. AE, CB, DC, MC, V.*

The Newporter Resort. Terra-cotta reigns supreme at this recently redecorated and expanded resort. Upper Newport Bay is an added attraction for soothing walks or invigorating runs. Guests have access to the John Wayne Tennis Club right next door. *1107 Jamboree Rd., 92660, tel. 714/644–1700. 410 rooms. Facilities: par-3, 9-hole golf course, jogging paths, exercise room, 3 pools, 2 restaurants, lounge, entertainment, concierge. AE, CB, DC, MC, V.*

Sheraton Newport Beach. Bamboos and palms decorate the lobby in this Southern California beach–style hotel. Vibrant teals, mauves, and peaches make up the color scheme. Complimentary morning paper, buffet breakfast, and cocktail parties are offered daily. *4545 MacArthur Blvd., 92660, tel. 714/833–0570. 358 rooms. Facilities: pool, Jacuzzi, tennis courts, restaurant, lounge, entertainment. AE, CB, DC, MC, V.*

Orange
Expensive

Doubletree Inn. This hotel has a dramatic lobby of marble and granite with silent waterfalls cascading down the walls. The oversize guest rooms come equipped with a small conference table. Location is near the popular shopping center called The City. *100 The City Dr., 92668, tel. 714/634–4500. 450 rooms. Facilities: 2 concierge floors, 2 restaurants, bar, heated pool, 2 tennis courts, spa. AE, CB, DC, MC, V.*

Inexpensive

Best Western El Camino. This motel is close to Knott's Berry Farm and Disneyland. The large lobby is comfortably decorated with overstuffed sofas. Complimentary Continental breakfast is offered. *3191 N. Tustin Ave., 92665, tel. 714/998–0360. 56 rooms. Facilities: heated pool. AE, CB, DC, MC, V.*

San Clemente
Expensive

San Clemente Inn. Located in the secluded southern part of San Clemente, this inn is adjacent to the state beach. Refurbished each year in soft earth tones, all the condo units are equipped with bars and kitchens. *2600 Avenida del Presidente, 92672, tel. 714/492–6103. 96 units. Facilities: large pool, tennis, exercise equipment, restaurant. MC, V.*

Moderate

Ramada San Clemente. This four-year-old Mission-style hotel is beautifully set on a lush hillside. The lobby has a dramatic vaulted ceiling. A private patio or balcony is part of each room. *35 Calle de Industrias, 92672, tel. 714/498–8800. 110 rooms. Facilities: pool, restaurant with American cuisine, lounge, cable TV, HBO in rooms. AE, CB, DC, MC, V.*

San Juan Capistrano
Moderate
★

Country Bay Inn. Built in the 1930s, all the rooms here are decorated with antiques of brass, wood, and rattan. The rooms in this cozy inn also all have a wood-burning fireplace. It is right across from the beach, and some rooms have balconies or patios. Continental breakfast is complimentary; champagne is served on arrival. *34862 Pacific Coast Hwy., 92624, tel. 714/ 496–6656. 28 rooms. Facilities: Jacuzzi. AE, MC, V.*

The Arts

The biggest draw on the arts scene is the **Orange County Performing Arts Center** (600 Town Center Dr., tel. 714/556–ARTS) in Costa Mesa. Among the groups that perform here are the American Ballet Theatre and the New York City Ballet, the Opera Pacific, and symphony orchestras from around the country.

Concerts
The **Irvine Meadows Amphitheater** (8800 Irvine Center Dr., tel. 714/855–4515) is an open-air structure offering musical events from May through October.

Anaheim Stadium (2000 State College Blvd., tel. 714/937–6750) hosts a variety of musical events throughout the year.

The **Pacific Amphitheater** (Orange County Fairgrounds, Costa Mesa, tel. 714/634–1300) offers musical entertainment and stages plays from April through October.

Theater
South Coast Repertory Theater (655 Town Center Dr., tel. 714/ 957–4033), near the Orange County Performing Arts Center in Costa Mesa, has been a tradition in the county for the last 24 years. Twelve productions are offered each year on two different stages. A resident group of actors forms the nucleus for this facility's innovative productions.

La Mirada Theater for the Performing Arts (14900 La Mirada Blvd., tel. 714/994–6150) presents a wide selection of Broadway shows, concerts, and film series.

Muckenthaler Cultural Center (1201 W. Malvern Ave., tel. 714/ 738–6595) often presents cabaret theater. Located in a beautiful Spanish house, the center was a gift to the city of Fullerton by the Muckenthaler family.

Nightlife

Bars
The **Cannery** (3010 Layfayette Ave., tel. 714/675–5777) and the **Warehouse** (3450 Via Osporo, tel. 714/673–4700) are two more crowded Newport Beach bars. The **Studio Cafe** (100 Main St.,

on the Balboa Peninsula, tel. 714/675–7760) presents jazz musicians every night.

In Laguna Beach, the **Sandpiper** (1183 Coast Hwy., tel. 714/494–4694) is a tiny dancing joint that attracts an eclectic crowd. And **Laguna's White House** (340 Coast Hwy., tel. 714/494–8088) has nightly entertainment that runs the gamut from rock to motown, reggae to pop.

Comedy **The Improvisation** (4255 Campus Dr., Irvine, tel. 714/854–5455) is probably the funniest place in the county. From well known to lesser known, comedians try out their acts nightly.

Country **Bandstand** (1721 S. Manchester, Anaheim, tel. 714/956–1410) offers live country music Sunday, Tuesday, Thursday, and Friday. Other nights, there is Top 40s music. Six dance floors and four bars are part of the complex.

Dinner Theater Several night spots in Orange County serve up entertainment with dinner. **Tibbie's Music Hall** (16360 Coast Hwy., Huntington Beach, tel. 714/840–5661) offers rowdy musical revues along with prime rib, fish, or chicken.

Medieval Times Dinner and Tournament (7662 Beach Blvd., tel. 714/521–4740) is a new Buena Park attraction that takes guests back to the days of knights and ladies. Knights on horseback compete in medieval games, sword fighting, and jousting. Dinner, all of which is eaten with your hands, includes vegetables, roast chicken, potatoes, pastry, and cocktails.

Other area dinner theaters include **The Grand Dinner Theater** (Grand Hotel, Anaheim, tel. 714/772–7777), **Curtain Call** (690 El Camino Real, Tustin, tel. 714/838–1540), and **Hampton's** (3503 S. Harbor Blvd., Santa Ana, tel. 714/979–7550).

Nightclubs **Crackers** (710 Katella Ave., Anaheim, tel. 714/978–1828) is a zany restaurant and nightclub where waiters and waitresses double as on-stage performers. The live entertainment seven days a week varies, with music from the '40s to the '90s.

The Hop (18774 Brookhurst St., Fountain Valley, tel. 714/963–2366) is a 1950s–'60s-style diner/nightclub owned by the Righteous Brothers. Nostalgia fills this fun place, which has a basketball court-dance floor and a '56 Chevy attached to the front of the DJ booth. Only music circa 1950–60 is played.

11 Palm Springs

by Aaron
Sugarman

What do you get when you start with dramatic scenery, add endless sunshine, mix in deluxe resorts, and spice things up with a liberal dash of celebrities? Palm Springs, a mecca for socialites, sun worshipers, and star gazers.

This fashionable desert resort community, nestled beneath 10,831-foot Mt. San Jacinto, sports more than 70 golf courses in a 20-mile radius, more than 300 tennis courts, 35 miles of bicycle trails, horseback riding, 7,000 or so swimming pools, and even cross-country skiing. Those inclined to less strenuous activities are attracted by such names as Gucci, I. Magnin, and Saks Fifth Avenue. The "in crowd" gathers at exclusive country clubs and openings at the city's numerous art galleries. It's often said that socializing is the top industry in Palm Springs; after a few days here, you're sure to agree.

Year-round, Palm Springs is both a vacation retreat and a residence for celebrities and famous politicians. Bob Hope is the city's honorary mayor, and Gene Autry, Frank Sinatra, Gerald Ford, and other luminaries can be spotted at charity events and restaurants and on the golf course. Carrie Fisher and Bette Midler have done stints at the Palms spa, while Donna Mills, Goldie Hawn, and Kurt Russell have been poolside stars at the Ingleside Inn. Palm Springs resorts are not new territory to celebrity visitors: Esther Williams once practiced her strokes at the El Mirador pool, Spencer Tracy played chess at the Racquet Club, and Joan Bennett pedaled her bicycle down Palm Canyon Drive.

Palm Springs became a haven for the stars in 1930, after the arrival of noted silent-film pros Charlie Farrell and Ralph Bellamy. For $30 an acre, the two actors bought 200 acres. This was the beginning of the Palm Springs Racquet Club, which soon listed Ginger Rogers, Humphrey Bogart, and Clark Gable among its members. Today you can take a tour that points out the homes of the celebrities of yesterday and today. Some of the most impressive include the Frank Sinatra, Elvis Presley, and Liberace estates.

The desert's stunning natural beauty is a major contributor to its magnetism. Nature dominates the area: City buildings are restricted to a height of 30 feet; flashing, moving, and neon signs are prohibited, preserving an intimate village feeling; and 50% of the land consists of open spaces with palm trees and desert vegetation.

This beauty is particularly evident in the canyons surrounding Palm Springs. Lush Tahquitz Canyon, one of the five canyons that line the San Jacinto Mountains, was the setting for Shangri-La in the original version of *Lost Horizon*. The original inhabitants of these rock canyons were the Cahuilla Indians. Their descendants came to be known as Agua Caliente— "hot water"—Indians, named after the hot mineral springs that flowed through their reservation. The Agua Caliente still own about 30,000 acres of Palm Springs desert, making them one of the richest tribes in the country.

Despite the building restrictions, Palm Springs has a suitable array of sophisticated spots, from the outstanding Desert Museum and Annenberg Theatre to the chic shops and galleries along the palm tree–lined Palm Canyon Drive. The trendy El Paseo Drive, 10 miles south of Palm Springs in neighboring

Palm Desert, is often compared to Rodeo Drive in Beverly Hills.

One brief comment on the weather: While daytime temperatures average a pleasantly warm 88° Fahrenheit, you are still in the desert. And that means during the middle of the day in the summer it is going to be very hot—sometimes uncomfortably hot. You're bound to be told that "it is a dry heat." It is. But it is still desert hot: Plan activities in the morning and late afternoon, and wear a hat and plenty of sunscreen if you're out for a midday stroll.

Arriving and Departing

By Plane Major airlines serving Palm Springs Municipal Airport include Alaska Airlines, American Airlines, American Eagle, America West, Continental Airlines, Skywest/Delta Connection, Trans World Airlines, United Airlines, and United Express. The airport is about 2 miles east of the city's main downtown intersection; most hotels provide service to and from the airport.

By Train **Amtrak** passenger trains service the Indio area, 20 miles east of Palm Springs. For information and reservations call 800/USA–RAIL. From Indio, **Greyhound/Trailways** bus service is available to Palm Springs.

By Bus **Greyhound/Trailways** Bus Lines (311 N. Indian Ave., tel. 619/325–2053).

By Car Palm Springs is about a two-hour drive east of Los Angeles and a three-hour drive northeast of San Diego. Highway 111 brings you right onto Palm Canyon Drive, the main thoroughfare in Palm Springs. From Los Angeles take the San Bernardino Freeway (I–10E) to Highway 111. From San Diego, I–15N connects with the Pomona Freeway (I–60E), leading to the San Bernardino Freeway (I–10E). If you're coming from the Riverside area, you might want to try the scenic Palms-to-Pines Highway (Hwy. 74). This 130-mile route begins in Hemet and connects directly with Highway 111; the trek from snowcapped peaks to open desert valley is breathtaking.

Getting Around

Downtown Palm Springs is distinctly walkable. Beyond that, you will find that having a car is the easiest way to get around and take in nearby attractions like the Aerial Tramway and El Paseo Drive.

By Bus **SunBus** serves the entire Coachella Valley from Desert Hot Springs to Coachella with regular routes. Call 619/323–4010 or 619/323–4058 for route and schedule information. The company also operates the **Sun Trolley,** which runs up and down Palm Canyon Drive from December through mid-May; the Trolley runs from 9 AM to 7:30 PM. The fare is 50¢.

By Taxi **Desert Cab** (tel. 619/325–2868) and **Caravan Yellow Cab** (tel. 619/346–2981).

By Car The easiest way to get around Palm Springs is by automobile. If you're not driving to Palm Springs, you might do well to check with one of the many rental agencies, all of which offer fairly competitive rates. Agencies include Avis (tel. 619/325–1331), Aztec (tel. 619/325–2294), Budget (tel. 619/327–1404),

Dollar (tel. 619/325–7334), Enterprise (tel. 619/328–9393), Hertz (tel. 619/778–5120), and National (tel. 619/327–4100).

Important Addresses and Numbers

Tourist Information **The City of Palm Springs Tourism Division** (Welwood Murray Memorial Library, 100 S. Palm Canyon Dr., tel. 800/347–7746) provides tourist information and maintains an information desk in the airport's main terminal.
Greater Palm Springs Convention and Visitors Bureau (tel. 619/327–8411) is located 300 yards north of the airport at Airport Park Plaza (255 N. Cielo, Suite 315).

Emergencies Dial 911 for **police** and **ambulance** in an emergency.

Doctor **Desert Hospital** (tel. 619/323–6511).

Dentist Dental emergency service is available from R. Turnage D.D.S. (tel. 619/327–8448) 24 hours a day.

Guided Tours

Orientation Tours **Gray Line Tours** (tel. 619/325–0974) offers several good general bus tours, from the hour-long Palm Springs Special highlight tour to the Palm Springs and Living Desert tour through Palm Springs, Cathedral City, Rancho Mirage, and Palm Desert, with stops at a date shop and the Living Desert. Prices are $14.25 for adults, $8.25 for children. Most departures are in the morning; call for reservations. Pick-up and drop-off service is available to most hotels. For a different perspective of the desert, try floating over the valley in a balloon. Trip lengths and prices vary; call **Fantasy Balloon Flights** (tel. 619/568–0997), **Sunrise Balloons** (tel. 619/346–7591), and the **American Balloon Society** (tel. 619/568–6700) for information.

Special-Interest Tours In Palm Springs, special-interest tours mean one thing: celebrity homes. **Gray Line** and **Palm Springs Celebrity Tours** (tel. 619/325–2682) both cover this turf well. Prices range from $10 to $14 for adults. **Desert Off Road Adventures** (tel. 619/773–3187) takes to the wilds with jeep tours of Indian canyons, unexpected waterfalls, and other off-the-beaten-track desert highlights. Customized helicopter tours are available from **Sunrise Balloons:** 40-minute trips start at $270 for two people.

Exploring

Numbers in the margin correspond with points of interest on the Palm Springs map.

Palm Springs proper is pretty easy to understand. Palm Canyon Drive runs north–south through the heart of downtown; the intersection with Tahquitz-McCallum is pretty much the center of the main drag. Heading south, Palm Canyon Drive splits: South Palm Canyon Drive leads you to the Indian Canyons and East Palm Canyon takes you through the growing satellite resort areas of Cathedral City, Rancho Mirage, and Palm Desert. The Aerial Tramway is at the northern limits of Palm Springs. Joshua Trees National Monument is about an hour's drive north.

Most Palm Springs attractions can be seen in anywhere from an hour or two to an entire day. Do you want to take the tram up Mt. San Jacinto, see the view, and come right back down, or spend the day hiking? Would you rather linger for a picnic lunch in one of the Indian Canyons, or double back for a snack and people-watching at Hyatt's sidewalk cafe? Your best bet is to look at the list of sights and activities as if it were an à la carte menu and pick and choose according to your appetite. To help you organize your outings, we will start in the north and work our way south and southeast. A separate tour of Joshua Trees follows.

Palm Springs and Environs

❶ The **Palm Springs Aerial Tramway** is the place for a real over-view of the desert. The 2½-mile ascent brings you to an elevation of 8,516 feet in under 20 minutes. On clear days, which are common, the view stretches some 75 miles from the peak of Mt. San Gorgonio to the north to the Salton Sea in the southeast. Mt. San Jacinto State Park offers 54 miles of hiking trails and camping and picnic areas; the Nordic Ski Center is open for cross-country skiing November 15 to April 15, snow permitting. *Tram cars depart at least every 30 min from 10 AM weekdays and 8 AM weekends. Last car up is at 8 PM, last car down 9:45 PM; May–Labor Day, last car up is at 9 PM, last car down at 10:45 PM. Cost: $13.95 adults, $8.95 children 3–12. Closed for 2–4 wks after Labor Day for maintenance. Call 619/325–1391 for information; 619/325–4227 for ski and weather conditions.*

Strolling down **Palm Canyon Drive,** Palm Springs' version of Main Street, should satisfy even the most avid shopper. With a good pair of comfortable walking shoes you should be able to walk from one end of the drive to the other in a couple of hours. Some exceptional art galleries, such as the **Elaine Horwitch collection** of studios, have taken root along the route and are well worth the browsing time. *Elaine Horwitch Galleries, 1090 N. Palm Canyon Dr., tel. 619/325–3490. Open Mon.–Sat. 9:30–5:30, Sun. noon–5.*

Downtown **horse-drawn carriages** promenade the city streets to the narrative of their guide/drivers. *Carriage Trade LTD, tel. 619/327–3214. $20 for 1 to 4 people. Rides start at the Hyatt Regency, 285 N. Palm Canyon Dr.*

Downtown Palm Springs is not without its historical treasures. **❷** The **Village Green Heritage Center** comprises two 19th-century pioneer homes. The adobe house built by "Judge" John McCallum in 1885 is now a museum housing the major portion of the collection of the Palm Springs Historical Society. McCallum, a San Francisco attorney, brought his family to the area hoping to restore the health of his son, who had taken ill during a typhoid epidemic. Next door is the Cornelia White House, built in 1894 from railroad ties. Inside are such historical tidbits as the first telephone in Palm Springs. *221 and 223 S. Palm Canyon Dr. Nominal admission. Both open Wed.–Sun. noon–3, Thurs.–Sat. 10–4. Closed June–mid-Oct.*

❸ If further evidence is needed to prove that the desert is no barren wasteland, there is the **Desert Museum.** Art exhibits here tend to favor a Western flavor, from California Contemporary to shows like "Art and Treasures of the Old West" from the Buffalo Bill Historical Center. But it is not unusual to catch the likes of a Matisse exhibition or works from the impressive Armand Hammer Collection that toured the region last year. Natural-history and science exhibits illuminate aspects of the surrounding desert. The museum's Annenberg Theatre has

Palm Springs

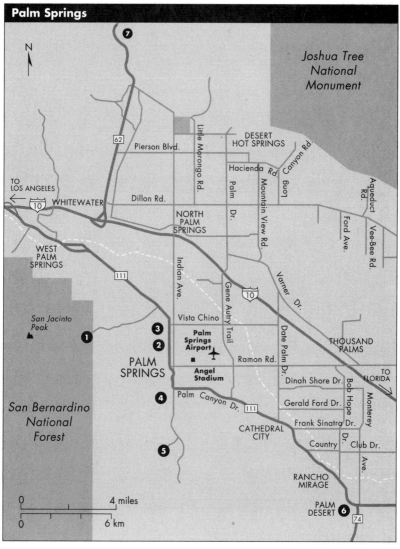

featured Liza Minnelli and Frank Sinatra in concert. *Museum Dr., just north of Tahquitz Way (on the south side of the Desert Fashion Plaza), tel. 619/325–7186. Admission: $4 adults, $2 children under 17. Open Tues.–Fri. 10–4, weekends until 5. Closed Mon. and June 5–Sept. 22.*

4 A short drive or distinctly long walk farther south on Palm Canyon is the **Moorten Botanical Garden.** More than 2,000 plant varieties cover the 4-acre site in settings that simulate the plants' original environments. Indian artifacts and rock, crystal, and wood forms are exhibited. *1701 S. Palm Canyon Dr., tel. 619/327–6555. Nominal admission fee. Open daily 9–4:30.*

5 The **Indian Canyons** begin 5 miles south of downtown Palm Springs. Inside this Indian-owned sanctuary, visitors can gaze at pictographs, bedrock mortar holes for grinding grain, and stone houses and shelters built atop high cliff walls—all relics of ancient Indian history. Streams of icy mountain water wind through the dense growth of willows, sycamores, and mesquite and groves of stately Washingtonia palms. Bands of wild ponies roam through Murray Canyon, and Andreas Canyon has towering rock faces and mysterious crevices and caves. Desert wildlife scampers around the more than 3,000 palm trees in Palm Canyon. Experiencing the canyons leaves visitors with the sensation of slipping through a time warp into a prehistoric era. *End of S. Palm Canyon Dr., tel. 619/327–2714. Admission: $3 adults, children 75¢. Open Sept.–June daily 8–5.*

6 Bighorn sheep, coyotes, eagles, and other desert wildlife roam in naturalistic settings at the **Living Desert Reserve,** in Palm Desert. There is a 6-mile nature walk, a walk through an aviary, a coyote grotto, a desert reptile exhibit, and regularly scheduled animal shows. This is a particularly enjoyable learning experience for children. *47-900 Portola Ave., less than 2 mi south of Hwy. 111. Admission: $5 adults, $2 children 6–15. Open daily 9–5, closed mid-June–Aug.*

Time Out Tired from all your hiking around? Then sample the healing waters that have made Palm Springs famous for centuries. The Cahuilla Indians have leased 8 acres of land to form the site of the **Palm Springs Spa Hotel.** Visit the inhalation room with its soothing menthol vapors and, of course, the mineral baths. Facials and massage are also available. *100 N. Indian Ave., tel. 619/325–1461. Prices begin at $25. Open daily, 10–5.*

Joshua Trees National Monument

7 **Joshua Trees National Monument** is about a one-hour drive from Palm Springs, whether you take I–10 north to Highway 62 to the Oasis Visitor Center or I–10 south to the Cottonwood Visitor Center. The northern part of the park is in the Mohave (or high) Desert and has the joshua trees. The southern part is Colorado (or low) Desert; you'll see fine displays of wildflowers here in the spring. It is possible to drive through the monument and come back to Palm Springs from the other direction. This would be a good long day's exploring, but you would travel through the two major California deserts.

On the northern route to the national monument, you may want to consider stopping at the **Big Morongo Wildlife Reserve.** Once an Indian village, then a cattle ranch, and now a regional park, the reserve is a serene natural oasis supporting a wide variety of plants, birds, and animals. There is a shaded meadow for picnics and choice hiking trails. *From I–10 or Indian Ave., take Hwy. 62 east to East Dr. Admission free. Open 8–sunset.*

The monument itself is immense, complex, and ruggedly beautiful. It marks the meeting place of the Mojave and Colorado deserts with mountains of twisted rock and exposed granite monoliths, lush oases shaded by tall, elegant fan palms, and natural cactus gardens. Extensive stands of Joshua trees, which look like something the late Muppet-maker Jim Henson designed to amuse kids, give the monument its name. The trees were named by early white settlers who felt their unusual forms resembled Joshua raising his arms toward heaven. With so much to see—the monument covers more than half a million acres—the **Oasis Visitor Center** is probably the best place to start. The center has an excellent selection of free and low-cost brochures, books, posters, and maps as well as several educational exhibits. Knowledgeable and helpful rangers are on hand to answer questions and offer advice. *Hwy. 62 to the town of 29 Palms, follow the signs a short distance south to the Visitor Center. There is a $5-per-vehicle entry fee to the monument.*

Right at the Visitor Center is the **Oasis of Mara.** Inhabited first by Indians and later by prospectors and homesteaders, the oasis now provides a good home for birds, small mammals, and other wildlife. Once inside the monument, you will find nine campgrounds with tables, fireplaces, and rest rooms and several picnic areas for day use. Beyond those basics, sights range from the Hidden Valley, a legendary cattle rustlers' hideout reached by a trail winding through massive boulders; and the Lost Horse Mine, a remnant of the gold-mining days; to Keys View, an outstanding scenic point commanding a superb sweep of valley, mountain, and desert. Sunrise and sunset are magic times to be at the monument, when the light throws rocks and trees into high relief before (or after) bathing the hills in brilliant shades of red, orange, and gold. The National Parks Service map available at the Visitor Center tells you where to find these and other impressive sights within the monument.

Palm Springs for Free

The North Palm Canyon Gallery Association (tel. 619/322–0966) regularly offers a free "art stroll" touring the area galleries.

There are two dozen or so municipal and school **tennis courts** scattered throughout Palm Springs that are absolutely free. Check the "Courts and Courses" listing in *Desert Guide*, available at most hotels, at the Convention and Visitors Bureau, and at the Palm Springs Tourism Division.

What to See and Do with Children

The Dinosaur Gardens are a must-see. Claude Bell designed and built the 150-foot-long brontosaurus and matching Tyrannosaurus rex right off the main highway. The dinosaurs starred in the movie *Pee-wee's Big Adventure. 5800 Seminole Dr., Cabazon, just off I–10, just before Hwy. 111, 18 mi northwest of Palm Springs, no phone. Open Wed.–Mon. 9–5.*

At the **Palm Springs Swim Center,** an Olympic-size swimming pool has a separate swimming section for children only. Swimming instruction is available for all ages. *411 South Pavilion,* *adjacent to the corner of Sunrise Way and Ramon Rd., tel. 619/323–8278. Hours and admission vary by season.*

Kids can also make a splash at the **Oasis Water Resort.** Tubing, water slides, "Squirt City," and other watery delights will entertain a wide range of age groups. *1500 Gene Autry Trail, between Hwy. 111 and Ramon Rd., tel. 619/325–7873. Hours and admission prices vary by season.*

California Angels spring-training baseball games, with a requisite autograph hunt, makes for a fun afternoon *(see* Spectator Sports, below, for more information).

Aerial Tramway *(see* Exploring, above).

The Living Desert *(see* Exploring, above).

Indian Canyons. Hiking and picnic areas, Indian cultural remains *(see* Exploring, above).

Off the Beaten Track

Dog sled races in Palm Springs? Why not . . . ? The **Moosehead Championship Sled Dog Races** are held in January, atop Mt. San Jacinto. Take the Aerial Tramway up. Call 619/325–1391 for more information.

The Eldorado Polo Club (50-950 Madison Blvd., Indio, tel. 619/342–2223) is known as the "Winter Polo Capital of the West." Pack a picnic hamper and hobnob with the elite from November to April. Admission is free except for a $5 charge on Sundays.

Shopping

The Palm Springs area is full of custom boutiques and lively art galleries. The resort community also has several large air-conditioned indoor malls with major department stores and chic boutiques. El Paseo in nearby Palm Desert is the desert's other shopping mecca, with its own collection of upscale and elegant galleries and shops. Most stores are open 10–5 or 6, Monday–Saturday. A fair number are open on Sunday, typically noon–5. The sales tax in Palm Springs is 6½%.

Shopping Districts **Palm Canyon Drive** is Palm Springs' main shopping destination. It began as a dusty two-way dirt road and is now a one-way, three-lane thoroughfare with parking on both sides. Its shopping core extends from Alejo Road on the north to Ramon Road on the south. Expect to find everything your heart desires—though your wallet may have a tough time keeping up. Furs, jewelry, sportswear, home furnishings, books, shoes, and crafts will tempt you on this busy street. Anchoring the center of the drive is the Desert Fashion Plaza, sporting big names like Saks Fifth Avenue, I. Magnin, Gucci, The Hyatt Regency Suites, and many smaller surprises.

The Courtyard at the Bank of Palm Springs Center brings Paris to Palm Springs. Expect to be dazzled by the high fashion of Rodier and Yves St. Laurent. There's also a six-screen movie theater.

El Paseo Village is touted as a true shopping experience rather than a shopping center. Unique stores, architecturally designed with a Spanish motif, are clustered among flower-lined paths and fountained courtyards. Don't miss Polo/Ralph

Lauren (73-111 El Paseo, tel. 619/340–1414), featuring Lauren's classic fashions and accessories for men and women, and Cabale Cachet (73-111 El Paseo, tel. 619/346–5805) for a collection of European haute couture.

The Palm Desert Town Center is the desert's latest major addition to convenient and stylish shopping. Five major department stores anchor the center including Bullocks and The May Co. There are also seven movie theaters and a skating rink.

Rancho las Palmas at Highway 111 and Bob Hope Drive, Rancho Mirage, offers gourmet kitchenware, antiques, imported chocolate and confections, and fine restaurants.

Department Stores The exclusive **I. Magnin** (151 S. Palm Canyon Dr., tel. 619/325–1571) is a department store with class, so do expect the latest fashions, but don't expect flea market prices. Another I. Magnin (tel. 619/325–1531) is located at Desert Fashion Plaza. Other major department stores can be found in the various malls listed above.

Specialty Shops **Jacqueline's** (Desert Fashion Plaza, tel. 619/322–4114) features *Jewelry* beautiful original designs; rings are a specialty.
Robanns (125 S. Palm Canyon Dr., tel. 619/325–9603) offers an elegant collection.

Discount Although Palm Springs is known for glamour and high prices, the city does offer bargains if you know where to look. Several outlets can be found in the **Loehmann's Shopping Center** (2500 North Palm Canyon Dr.), including **Fieldcrest-Cannon** (tel. 619/322–3229), **Dansk** (tel. 619/320–3304), and **Loehmann's** (tel. 619/322–0388).

Participant Sports

The *Desert Guide* from Palm Springs Life, available at most hotels and the Convention and Visitors Bureau, lists "Courts and Courses," with a map showing all of the city's golf courses and tennis courts and information on whether the facilities are public or private.

Bicycling There are more than 35 miles of bike trails, with six mapped-out city tours. Trail maps are available at the **Palm Springs Recreation Department** (401 S. Pavilion, tel. 619/323–8276) and bike-rental shops. You can rent a bike at **Mac's Bike Rental** (70–155 Highway 111, tel. 619/327–5721) and **Burnett's Bicycle Barn** (429 S. Sunrise Way, tel. 619/325–7844).

Golf Palm Springs is known as the "Winter Golf Capital of the World." The area has more than 70 golf courses within its limits, a number of which are open to the public. Among these are the **Palm Springs Municipal Golf Course** (1885 Golf Club Dr., tel. 619/328–1005) and **Fairchilds Bel Aire Greens** (1001 El Cielo Rd., tel. 619/327–0332). Don't be surprised to spy well-known politicians and Hollywood stars on the greens.

Hiking Nature trails abound in the Indian Canyons, Mt. San Jacinto State Park and Wilderness, and Living Desert Reserve (*see* Exploring above).

Physical Fitness The **Clark Hatch Physical Fitness Center** (Hyatt Regency Suites Hotel, 285 N. Palm Canyon Dr., tel. 619/322–2778) is the latest in a worldwide chain of Hatch health clubs. The facilities are high quality and low key. Fees are $10 daily, $60 monthly.

Tennis Of the 350 or so tennis courts in the area, you'll find these open to the public: the **Palm Springs Tennis Center** (1300 Baristo Rd., tel. 619/320–0020), nine lighted courts; **Ruth Hardy Park** (Tamarisk and Caballeros, no phone), eight lighted courts, with no court fee; and **Demuth Park** (4375 Mesquite Ave., tel. 619/323–8279), four lighted courts.

Spectator Sports

Baseball The **California Angels** hold their annual spring training and play a number of exhibition games in Palm Springs during March and early April. Games typically begin at 1 PM at Palm Springs Angels Stadium, east of Sunrise Way near Ramon Road. Reserved and general admission seats are available. Call 619/323–8272 for more information.

Golf More than 100 golf tournaments are presented in Palm Springs; the two most popular are the **Bob Hope Desert Classic** (Jan.) and the **Dinah Shore Championship** (Mar. or Apr.). Call the Convention and Visitors Bureau or Palm Springs Tourism for exact dates and places.

Tennis The **Newsweek Champions Cup** tournament (Feb. or Mar.), held at Hyatt Grand Champions Resort in Indian Wells, attracts the likes of Boris Becker and Yannick Noah.

Dining

So many L.A. natives have second homes or condos "down in the Springs" that local restaurateurs are outdoing themselves to match the Big City's standards—and more and more are succeeding. Most of the restaurants listed below can be found on or near Highway 111 running from Palm Springs to Palm Desert.

Category	Cost*
Expensive	over $35
Moderate	$15–$30
Inexpensive	under $15

* *per person, without tax (6%), service, or drinks*

Palm Springs **Melvyn's Restaurant.** "Lifestyles of the Rich and Famous" calls
Expensive this Old World–style spot "one of the 10 best." Snugly nestled in the gardens of the Ingleside Inn, weekend brunch here is a Palm Springs tradition. Nightly piano bar. *200 W. Ramon Rd., tel. 619/325–2323. Reservations advised. Jacket required. AE, MC, V.*
Le Vallauris. Formerly a private club, this stylish, rather romantic setting is now open to the public. The cuisine ranges from classic French to nouvelle dessert. *385 W. Tahquitz-McCallum Way, tel. 619/325–5059. Reservations advised. Jacket and tie required. Valet parking. AE, DC, MC, V.*

Moderate–Expensive **Banducci's Bit of Italy.** Homemade dishes in a friendly, family atmosphere are served: Try the cannelloni or lasagna. There is a piano bar. *1260 S. Palm Canyon Dr., tel. 619/325–2537. Reservations suggested. Dress: casual. AE, MC, V. Closed for lunch.*

Lyon's English Grille. When was the last time you had real honest-to-goodness roast beef and Yorkshire pudding the way only the Brits can make it? Lyon's has it and other old-country favorites. Good value and good food make this a popular stop for the locals. *233 E. Palm Canyon Dr., tel. 619/327–1551. Reservations suggested. Dress: casual. AE, CB, DC, MC, V. Closed summer. Closed for lunch. Closed for dinner Mon.*

Moderate **Bono.** Palm Springs' mayor, Sonny Bono, of Sonny and Cher fame, serves the southern Italian dishes his mother used to make. It's a favorite feeding station for show-biz folk and the curious, and a good place for pasta, chicken, veal, and scampi dishes. Outdoor dining is available. *1700 N. Indian Ave., tel. 619/322–6200. Reservations advised. Dress: casual. Valet parking. AE, MC, V. Closed lunch.*

Brussels Cafe. The best spot in town for people-watching is this sidewalk cafe in the heart of Palm Canyon Drive. Try the Belgian waffles or homemade pâté. Beers from around the world are featured, and there's nightly entertainment. *109 S. Palm Canyon Dr., tel. 619/320–4177. Reservations required. Dress: casual. AE, CB, DC, MC, V.*

Cafe St. James. Dine while seated on a plant-filled balcony, and watch the passing parade below. The lunch menu features excellent salads and thick, imaginative sandwiches. *254 N. Palm Canyon Dr., tel. 619/320–8041. Reservations advised. Dress: casual. AE, CB, DC, MC, V. Closed Mon.*

Las Casuelas Original. A long-time favorite among natives and visitors alike, this restaurant offers great (in size and taste) margaritas and average Mexican dishes: crab enchilada, carne asada, lobster Ensenada. It gets very, very crowded during winter months. *368 N. Palm Canyon Dr., tel. 619/325–3213. Reservations advised. Dress: casual. AE, DC, MC, V.*

Flower Drum. Related to highly popular New York Flower Drum, this health-conscious Chinese restaurant features Hunan, Peking, Shanghai, Canton, and Szechuan cuisines in a Chinese village setting. *424 S. Indian Ave., tel. 619/323–3020. Reservations advised. Dress: casual. AE, MC, V.*

Rennick's. This local landmark recently celebrated its silver anniversary. The health-conscious chef watches calorie and cholesterol counts. Fresh fish and grilled items are recommended. *100 N. Indian Ave., tel. 619/325–1461. Reservations suggested. Jacket required. AE, DC, MC, V.*

Riccio's. Tony Riccio, formerly of the Marquis and Martoni's, in Hollywood, knows the old-fashioned Italian food that comforts his steady patrons: fettucini Alfredo, veal piccata, chicken Vesuvio, and a luscious Italian cheesecake. *2155 N. Palm Canyon Dr., tel. 619/325–2369. Reservations advised. Jacket required.*

Inexpensive **Di Amico's Steak House.** Hearty eaters will enjoy this early-California–style restaurant. Prime Eastern corn-fed beef, liver steak vaquero, and son-of-a-gun stew are featured. *1180 S. Palm Canyon Dr., tel. 619/325–9191. Reservations advised. Dress: casual. MC, V. Closed Sun. lunch.*

Elmer's Pancake and Steak House. Forget about Aunt Jemima. Elmer's offers 25 varieties of pancakes and waffles. There are steaks, chicken, and seafood on the dinner menu. A children's menu is available too. *1030 E. Palm Canyon Dr., tel. 619/327–8419. Dress: casual. MC, V.*

Louise's Pantry. Another local landmark, in the center of downtown Palm Springs for almost 40 years, its down-home cooking

1940s-style features chicken and dumplings and short ribs of beef. You can get soup, salad, entree, beverage, and dessert for under $15. There's usually a line to get in. *124 S. Palm Canyon Dr., tel. 619/325–5124. Dress: casual. No credit cards.*

Cathedral City, Rancho Mirage, Palm Desert
Expensive

Dominick's. An old favorite of Frank Sinatra's and what's left of his "rat pack." Steaks, pasta, and veal dishes are the order of the day. *70-030 Hwy. 111, tel. 619/324–1711. Reservations advised. Dress: casual. AE, DC, MC, V. Closed lunch.*

Mama Gina's. Generally considered the best Italian food in the Palm Springs area, this attractive, simply furnished trattoria was opened by the son of the original Mama Gina in Florence, Italy. There is an open kitchen where you can watch the chef from Tuscany prepare specialties including deep fried artichokes, fettucine with porcini mushrooms, and prawns with artichoke and zucchini. The soups are excellently robust. *73-705 El Paseo, tel. 619/568–9898. Reservations required. Dress: casual. AE, DC, MC, V. Closed lunch.*

Wally's Desert Turtle. If price is no object and you like plush, gilded decor, then this is where you'll be surrounded by the golden names of Palm Springs and Hollywood society. Old-fashioned French cooking is served: rack of lamb, imported Dover sole, braised sea bass, veal Oscar, chicken Normande, and dessert souffles. *71-775 Hwy. 111, tel. 619/568–9321. Valet parking. Reservations required. Jacket required. MC, V. Closed lunch except Friday.*

Moderate

The Rusty Pelican. Fresh seafood is flown in from both coasts and served in a nautical atmosphere. The Oyster Bar shucks to order. There's live entertainment and dancing. *72-191 Hwy. 111, Palm Desert, tel. 619/346–8065. Dress: casual. Reservations suggested. AE, CB, DC, MC, V.*

The Wilde Goose. The award-winning restaurant is popular with celebrities for its beef and lamb Wellington and five varieties of duck. A specialty of the house is duck with apricot and triple sec sauce. Dependable food and service. *67-938 Hwy. 111, Cathedral City, tel. 619/328–5775. Dress: casual. Reservations recommended. AE, MC, V. Closed for lunch.*

Inexpensive

Stuft Pizza. What would any listing be without at least one pizza parlor? This one is popular for its thick, Chicago-style crusts and generous heaps of fresh toppings. *67-555 Hwy. 111, Cathedral City, tel. 619/321–2583. No credit cards.*

La Quinta
Expensive
★

Cunard's. Robert Cunard converted his French-style villa to a restaurant three years ago and hired chef Jay Trubee to devise a Franco-Italian menu. Today, the warm atmosphere and inventive cuisine have made it the area's biggest hit. *73-045 Calle Cadiz, tel. 619/564–4443. Reservations advised. (MC, V. Closed for lunch.) Jacket and tie requested. Closed July and Aug.*

Lodging

One of the reasons Palm Springs attracts so many celebrities, entertainment-industry honchos, and other notables is its stock of luxurious hotels. There is a full array of resorts, inns, clubs, spas, lodges, and condos, from small and private to big and bustling. Room rates cover an enormous range—from $20 to $1,600 a night—and also vary widely from summer to winter season. It is not unusual for a hotel to drop its rates from 50% to 60% during the summer (June through early Sept.). For a growing number of off-season travelers, the chance to stay in a $180 room for $60 is an offer they just can't refuse.

Don't even think of visiting here during winter and spring holiday seasons without advance reservations. The Palm Springs Chamber of Commerce (tel. 619/325–1577), the Convention and Visitors Bureau (tel. 619/327–8411), and Palm Springs Tourism (tel. 800/347–7746) can help you with hotel reservations and information. For a more complete hotel guide complete with prices, pick up a copy of the *Convention and Visitors Bureau Accommodations Guide (tel. 800/347–7746)*.

The most highly recommended lodgings are indicated by a star ★.

Category	Cost*
Very Expensive	over $150
Expensive	$100–$150
Moderate	$70–$100
Inexpensive	under $70

double occupancy

Rentals. Condos, apartments, and even individual houses may be rented by the day, week, month, or longer period. Rates start at about $400 a week for a one-bedroom condo, $500–$600 a week for two bedrooms, and $3,200 for a three-bedroom house for a month. Contact **The Rental Connection** (170 E. Palm Canyon Dr., Palm Springs 92264, tel. 619/320–7336, 800/468–3776, or 800/232–3776 in CA). For small, exclusive hotels, contact **Palm Spring's Best-Kept Secrets** (tel. 800/344–5646).

Palm Springs
Very Expensive

Doubletree Resort at Desert Princess. This two-year-old luxury resort hotel has a full slate of amenities: 18-hole championship golf course, tennis and racquetball courts, pools, spas, and health club. Three restaurants, including gourmet dining room. *Vista Chino at Desert Princess Dr., Box 1644, 92263, tel. 619/322–7000. 300 rooms and suites. AE, CB, DC, MC, V.*

Hyatt Regency Suites. Located stage center in the heart of downtown shopping at the Desert Fashion Plaza. Striking six-story asymmetrical lobby, three restaurants, including fine Continental cuisine at Le Jardin and a popular sidewalk cafe. Health club and pool. *285 N. Palm Canyon Dr., 92262, tel. 619/322–9000. 194 suites. AE, CB, DC, MC, V.*

La Mancha Private Pool Villas and Court Club. Only four blocks from downtown Palm Springs, this Hollywood-style retreat blocks out the rest of the world with plenty of panache. Villas are oversized and opulent; one is even equipped with a screening room and private pool. *444 N. Avenida Cabilleros, tel. 619/323–1773. Facilities: tennis courts, paddle tennis courts, pool, croquet lawns. AE, CB, DC, MC, V.*

Palm Springs Hilton Resort and Racquet Club. The cool, white marble elegance of this plant-filled resort hotel just off Palm Canyon Drive and its two superb restaurants make it a top choice for the city. Tennis, body spa, swimming pool, Jacuzzi. *400 E. Tahquitz Way, 92262, tel. 619/320–6868 or 800/522–6900. 257 units. AE, CB, DC, MC, V.*

The Palm Springs Marquis. Posh, desert-modern style marks this centrally located hotel, featuring gourmet restaurant and cafe, two pools, Jacuzzis, health spa, tennis courts, plus extensive meeting and convention facilities. *150 S. Indian Ave., 92262, tel. 619/322–2121. 262 units. AE, CB, DC, MC, V.*

★ **Spa Hotel and Mineral Springs.** Therapeutic mineral springs, outdoor pool, 35 swirlpool tubs, gym, and tennis are the big attractions here. A coffee shop, restaurant, and cocktail lounge with entertainment round out the features. *100 N. Indian Ave., 92262, tel. 619/325–1461. 230 units. AE, CB, DC, MC, V.*

Sundance Villas. Beautifully decorated, spacious villas include fireplace, wet bar, kitchen, and private patio for dining or sunning. Each villa has a private pool or Jacuzzi. The hotel also has tennis courts. Not for the weak of pocketbook. *303 Cabrillo Rd., 92262, tel. 619/325–3888. 19 villas. AE, MC, V.*

Expensive **Gene Autry Hotel.** Well decked out for activities with six tennis courts, three swimming pools, two therapy spas, horseback riding, hiking, and desert tours. Dining and entertainment are offered nightly. *4200 E. Palm Canyon Dr., 92262, tel. 619/328–1171. 187 units. AE, CB, DC, MC, V.*

★ **Ingleside Inn.** A hacienda-style inn furnished with antiques. Each room is equipped with a steam shower and whirlpool. Swimming pool, Jacuzzi, sauna. *200 W. Ramon Rd., 92262, tel. 619/325–0046. 29 units. AE, MC, V.*

Racquet Club of Palm Springs. Built by Charlie Farrell and Ralph Bellamy in 1933, the Racquet Club marked the beginning of Palm Spring's glamour era. Four swimming pools, therapy pool, sauna, tennis courts (where, it is said, Marilyn Monroe was "discovered"), cocktail lounge. *2743 N. Indian Ave., 92262, tel. 619/325–1281. 120 units. AE, CB, DC, MC, V.*

Moderate **Courtyard by Marriott.** This new property represents the Marriott chain's effort to expand into comfortable, smaller hotels offering a good value. The concept works nicely. Pool, weight room, restaurant. *1300 Tahqu Way, tel. 619/322–6100. 149 rooms. AE, MC, V.*

Mira Loma Hotel. Small, friendly family atmosphere with rooms and suites decorated in 1940s Hollywood Art Deco style. Marilyn Monroe slept here! Swimming pool. *1420 N. Indian Ave., 92262, tel. 619/320–1178. 12 units. AE, MC, V.*

Mt. View Inn. A friendly atmosphere and convenient location make this small inn a great favorite. The inn has a swimming pool. *200 S. Cahuilla Rd., 92262, tel. 619/325–5281. 11 units. No credit cards.*

Tuscany Manor Apartment-Hotel. Lovely apartments. Pool, therapeutic pool. Esther Williams shot her first movie here. *350 Chino Canyon Rd., 92262, tel. 619/325–2349. 24 units. MC, V.*

Villa Royale. Charming bed-and-breakfast, each unit individually decorated in an international theme. Some rooms with private Jacuzzis, fireplaces. *1620 Indian Trail, 92262, tel. 619/327–2314. 34 units. AE, MC, V.*

Inexpensive **Monte Vista Hotel.** Located in a prime Palm Canyon Drive location, this hotel is replete with swimming pool and comfortable accommodations. *414 N. Palm Canyon Dr., 92262, tel. 619/325–5641. 32 units. AE, MC, V.*

Westward Ho Seven Seas Hotel. A swimming pool, therapy pool, and cocktail lounge grace this modest property. *701 E. Palm Canyon Dr., 92262, tel. 619/320–2700. 209 units. AE, MC, V.*

Outside of Palm Springs
Very Expensive

Hyatt Grand Champions Resort. This elegant resort takes its fun seriously with two 18-hole golf courses, tennis courts featuring three court surfaces, the largest tennis stadium in the West, and a health club with a full complement of workout equipment and pampering treatments. Jasmine's nouvelle American menu is getting raves; the more casual Trattoria mixes Italian and Californian cuisines with delightful results. *44-600 Indian Wells Ln., Indian Wells, 92210, tel. 619/341–1000. 334 units. AE, CB, DC, MC, V.*

Marriott's Desert Springs Resort and Spa. The most luxurious spa facilities in the desert, two 18-hole golf courses, and a complex of waterways with boat transport around the resort let you know this is no run-of-the-mill resort. There are 16 tennis courts, five restaurants, and a European spa. *74855 Country Club Dr., Palm Desert, 92260, tel. 619/341–2211. 891 rooms. AE, CB, DC, MC, V.*

★ **The Ritz Carlton Rancho Mirage.** The newest, poshest gem in the desert collection is located on a 650-foot-high plateau in the foothills of the Santa Rosas, adjacent to a reserve for bighorn sheep. Needless to say, it has all the amenities you would expect from one of the world's classiest hotel chains: restaurants, entertainment, pools, bar, fitness center, and tennis. *68-900 Frank Sinatra Dr., Rancho Mirage, 92270, tel. 619/321–8282. 240 rooms including 19 suites. AE, CB, DC, MC, V.*

Expensive

Two Bunch Palms. Reputedly built by Al Capone to escape the pressures of gangsterdom in 1920s Chicago, this collection of white-walled villas is still something of a secret hideaway. Antiques recapture the flavor of the pre–World War II years. *67-425 Two Bunch Palms Trail, Desert Hot Springs, CA 92240, tel. 619/329–8791 or 800/472–4334. 44 villas. Facilities: tennis courts, thermal pools, restaurant. AE, MC, V.*

The Arts

For complete listings of upcoming events, pick up a copy of *Palm Springs Life* magazine or Palm Springs Life's *Desert Guide*, a free monthly publication found in any hotel.

The McCallum Theatre (73-000 Fred Waring Dr., Palm Desert, tel. 619/325–0698) in the Bob Hope Cultural Center is probably the desert's premier venue for the performing arts. Since opening in January 1988 with a tribute to Bob Hope, the theater has hosted such varied artists as Rudolf Nureyev and the Paris Ballet, the Los Angeles Philharmonic, pantomimist Marcel Marceau, and a rock-and-roll revival starring Fabian.

The Annenberg Theatre (Museum Dr., just north of Tahquitz Way, on the south side of the Desert Fashion Plaza, tel. 619/325–7186) of the Palm Springs Desert Museum is the area's other major arts center. Featured performers have ranged from the Second City improv troupe to Liza Minnelli, Frank Sinatra, and a slew of international musicians in its Sunday Afternoon Concerts series.

Concerts

The College of the Desert (43-500 Monterey Ave., Palm Desert, tel. 619/346–8041). This is home to the annual Joanna Hodges Piano Conference and Competition.

Theater

VPG Theatre (225 S. El Cielo Rd., tel. 619/320–9898). Home of the Valley Players Guild, the VPG offers a lively mix of theater fare.

Nightlife

Two good sources for finding current nightlife attractions are the *Desert Sun* (the local newspaper) and *Guide* magazine, a monthly publication distributed free at most downtown merchants' counters.

Live entertainment, ranging from soft dinner music to song-and-dance numbers, is frequently found in the city's hotels and restaurants. The piano bars at **Rennick's** and **Melvyn's Ingleside Inn** are popular. **Moody's Supper Club** (1480 S. Palm Canyon Dr., tel. 619/323–1806) has an inviting party atmosphere, and you can hear everything from Puccini to pops.

Jazz **The Great American Bar & Grill** (777 E. Tahquitz Way, tel. 619/322–1311) is a cool place for jazz on Monday and Tuesday nights. Brussels Cafe (tel. 619/320–4177) features jazz and blues Sunday nights.

Discos Between the flashing lights of its Top-40 disco and the retro-memorabilia in its new '50s–'60s room, **Cecil's** (1775 E. Palm Canyon Dr., tel. 619/320–4202) is bound to keep you dancing.
Dance to live country music at the **Cactus Corral** (67-501 E. Palm Canyon Dr., Cathedral City, tel. 619/321–8558).
Mary's (1700 N. Indian Ave., tel. 619/322–6200), below Bono's restaurant, is one of the newest discos, catering to an older, Hollywood crowd. Contemporary music is played here.
Zelda's (169 N. Indian Ave., tel. 619/325–2375) is another nightclub that regularly attracts a full house and a young crowd.

Comedy Clubs **The Comedy Haven.** Stand-up comics and improv groups dished up with American/Italian fare. *Desert Fashion Plaza (enter parking lot from Tahquitz Way), tel. 619/320–7855. Shows start at 9 PM.*
The Laff Stop. Stand-up comedy shows are the nightly attraction, interspersed with live and recorded music of the '50s, '60s, and '70s. *Corner of Tahquitz and Caballeros across from the Convention Center, tel. 619/327–8889.*

12 Santa Barbara

by Marie Felde

A staff writer specializing in environmental subjects for the Oakland *Tribune, Marie Felde also writes on travel.*

Santa Barbara sports the famed sandy beaches and sunny days of Southern California, but works hard to retain a more reserved atmosphere and a smaller, cozier scale than the Los Angeles area 90 miles to the south. Wedged as it is between the Pacific and the Santa Ynez Mountains, there never was much room for sprawl. The mountains to the north assure a sunny climate and a Riviera-like setting. There is an outdoor emphasis on everything here. The waterfront—with its beaches, pier, and harbor—and the Spanish-style downtown are the centers of business, and the number-one business here is tourism. Further up the hills are the exclusive residential areas of Montecito and Hope Ranch, home to movie stars and celebrities.

Getting Around

By Plane **American** and **American Eagle** (tel. 800/433–7300), **Sky West/ Delta** (tel. 800/453–9417), **United** and **United Express** (tel. 800/ 241–6522), and **Trans World Express** (tel. 800/221–2000) fly into **Santa Barbara Municipal Airport** (tel. 805/967–5608), 8 miles from the downtown on Marxmiller Road.

Airport Express (tel. 805/965–1161) runs service to and from the airport. **Santa Barbara Airbus** (tel. 805/964–7374) shuttles travelers between Santa Barbara and Los Angeles International Airport. **Metropolitan Transit District** (tel. 805/963– 3364) bus No. 11 runs from the airport to the downtown transit center.

By Bus Local service is provided by the **Santa Barbara Municipal Transit District** (tel. 805/963–3364).

By Train **Amtrak** (tel. 800/USA–RAIL or 805/687–6848) runs the *Coast Starlight* train along the coast from Santa Barbara to San Luis Obispo and inland for the rest of the route to the San Francisco Bay area.

By Car You can drive to Santa Barbara from Los Angeles in two hours (along U.S. 101 and Highway 1). Once in Santa Barbara, you may run into some horrendous traffic if work on the highway through town isn't finished. Try to route yourself around without depending on U.S. 101 during rush hours (it's not a freeway all the way through Santa Barbara anyway); just getting across it may take five minutes. Downtown parking may be difficult but there are several large multistory, inexpensive public parking lots, so you'll find something.

Guided Tours

Santa Barbara Trolley Co. (tel. 805/565–1122) has three daily, regularly scheduled runs in Santa Barbara. Motorized San Francisco–style cable cars deliver visitors to major hotels, shopping areas, and attractions. Stop or not as you wish and pick up another trolley when ready to move on. All depart and return to Stearns Wharf.

Walking Tours Through History (tel. 805/967–9869). A longtime Santa Barbara resident takes small groups on walking tours of gardens and historic buildings. Morning and afternoon tours begin at the courthouse lobby.

Important Addresses and Numbers

Tourist Information An excellent selection of free pamphlets on accommodations, dining, sports, and entertainment is available at the **Visitors Information Center.** *1 Santa Barbara St. at Cabrillo Blvd., tel. 805/965–3021. Open Mon.–Thurs. 9–4, Fri. 9–6.*

Before arriving contact the **Santa Barbara Conference and Visitors Bureau** (222 E. Anapamu St., 93101, tel. 805/966–9222).

Exploring

Numbers in the margin correspond with points of interest on the Santa Barbara map.

Santa Barbara's attractions begin with the ocean, with most everything else along Cabrillo Boulevard. In the few miles between the beaches and the hills, you pass the downtown and then reach the old mission and, a little higher up, the botanic gardens. A few miles up the coast is the exclusive residential district of Hope Ranch. To the east is the district called Montecito, where Charlie Chaplin built the Montecito Inn to house visiting guests during the days he was making movies in Santa Barbara before moving to Hollywood. Montecito is also where the exclusive San Ysidro Ranch is located.

Because the town is on a jog in the coastline, it faces south, making directions confusing. Up the coast is west, and down toward Los Angeles is east. The mountains are north.

Everything is so close, the 8-mile drive to the airport seems like a long trip. A car is handy, but not essential. The beaches and downtown are easily explored by bicycle or on foot. The Santa Barbara Trolley takes visitors to most of the major hotels and sights, which can also be reached on the local buses.

The Visitors Information Center publishes a free pamphlet to a scenic drive that circles the town with a detour into the downtown. It passes the harbor, beaches, Hope Ranch, and the old mission, offers fine views on the way to Montecito, and returns to the beaches. You can pick up the drive, marked with blue "Scenic Drive" signs, anywhere along the loop. A free guide to the downtown, the "Red Tile Walking Tour," is also available free from the tourist office. It hits historical spots in a 12-block area.

The town of Goleta, the home of the University of California at Santa Barbara, is located a few miles up the coast via U.S. 101.

❶ If you decide to start at the Pacific and move inland, then one of the first spots to visit is **Stearns Wharf** on Cabrillo Boulevard, at the foot of State Street. You can drive out and park on the pier, then wander through the shops or dine at the wharf's restaurants or snack bar. The **Sea Center,** a recent addition to the pier, is a branch of the Museum of Natural History that specializes in exhibits of marine life. First built in 1872, then rebuilt in 1981 after a fire, the wharf extends three blocks into the Pacific. It is a fine place to look back on the city for a sense of its size and general layout.

❷ The nearby **Santa Barbara Yacht Harbor** is sheltered by a manmade breakwater at the west end of Cabrillo Boulevard. You

Santa Barbara

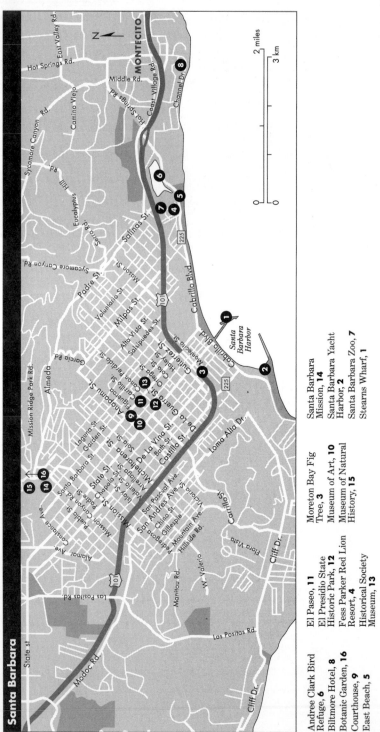

Andree Clark Bird
Refuge, **6**
Biltmore Hotel, **8**
Botanic Garden, **16**
Courthouse, **9**
East Beach, **5**

El Paseo, **11**
El Presidio State
Historic Park, **12**
Fess Parker Red Lion
Resort, **4**
Historical Society
Museum, **13**

Moreton Bay Fig
Tree, **3**
Museum of Art, **10**
Museum of Natural
History, **15**

Santa Barbara
Mission, **14**
Santa Barbara Yacht
Harbor, **2**
Santa Barbara Zoo, **7**
Stearns Wharf, **1**

can take a half-mile walk along the paved breakwater, check out the tackle and bait shops, or hire a boat from here.

3 Planted in 1877, the **Moreton Bay Fig Tree,** at Chapala Street and Highway 101, is so huge it reportedly can provide shade for 10,000 people. Unfortunately, in recent years the tree has become a gathering place for an increasing number of homeless people, and the area has become somewhat seedy.

Back along Cabrillo, sandy beaches stretch for miles. The sprawling reddish Spanish-style hotel across from the beach is **4** the **Fess Parker Red Lion Resort.** Parker, the actor who played Davy Crockett and Daniel Boone, owned the oceanfront acreage and spent years trying to convince city fathers to allow him to develop a hotel. He finally did, and the hotel opened in 1987 as the largest in Santa Barbara.

5 Just beyond the hotel is the area's most popular beach, **East 6 Beach,** at the east end of Cabrillo. Nearby is the **Andree Clark Bird Refuge,** a peaceful lagoon with gardens. *1400 Cabrillo Blvd. Admission free.*

7 Adjoining the lagoon is the **Santa Barbara Zoo,** a small, lushly landscaped home to big cats, elephants, and exotic birds. *500 Ninos Dr., tel. 805/962–6310. Admission: $4 adults, $2 senior citizens and children under 13. Open winter, daily 10–5; summer, 9–6.*

Where Cabrillo Boulevard ends at the lagoon, Channel Drive **8** picks up and a short distance east passes the **Biltmore Hotel,** now owned by the Four Seasons chain. For more than 60 years, the rich have come here to indulge in quiet elegance.

To get downtown, return to Cabrillo and head inland along **9** State Street. **The Courthouse,** in the center of the downtown area, has all the grandeur of a Moorish palace. In fact, as you wander the halls, admiring the brilliant hand-painted tiles and spiral staircase, you'll forget you are in a public courthouse unless a handcuffed group of offenders marches through. This magnificent building was completed in 1929 at the height of the city's cultural reawakening. An elevator to the tower takes visitors to a panoramic view of the city and a fine place to take photos. The second-floor supervisors' ceremonial chambers contain murals painted by the same artist who did backdrops for Cecil B. De Mille's silent films. *1100 block of Anacapa St. Admission free. Open weekdays 8–5, weekends 9–5. 1-hr guided tours Tues.–Sat. 2 PM.*

Continue one block down Anapamu Street past the Spanish-**10** style **Public Library** to the **Santa Barbara Museum of Art.** This fine small museum houses a permanent collection featuring ancient sculpture, Oriental art, a collection of German expressionist paintings, and a sampling of American artists. *1130 State St., tel. 805/963–4364. Donation requested. Open Tues.–Sat. 11–5 (9 PM Thurs. eve.), Sun noon–5. Free guided tours Tues.–Sun. at 2.*

11 Walking south you'll pass **El Paseo,** a shopping arcade built around an old adobe home. There are several such arcades in this area and many small art galleries. A few blocks north is the **12** **El Presidio State Historic Park.** Built in 1782, the Presidio was one of four military strongholds established by the Spanish along the coast of California. The guard house, El Cuartel, is one of two original adobe buildings that remain from the complex and is the oldest building owned by the state. *123 E. Canon Perdido St. Admission free. Open daily 10:30–4:30.*

⑬ A block away is the **Historical Society Museum,** with an array of items from the town's past including a silver-clad riding saddle and a collection of fancy ladies' fans. *136 E. De la Guerra St. Admission free. Open Tues.–Sat. 10–5, Sun. noon–5.*

⑭ A short distance from downtown (take State Street north and make a right on Los Olivos), at the base of the hills, is the **Santa Barbara Mission,** the gem of the chain of 21 missions established in California by Spanish missionaries in the late 1700s. One of the best preserved of the missions, it still functions as a Catholic church. *Laguna St. Admission: $1 adults, children under 16 free. Open daily 9–5.*

⑮
⑯ Continuing north a block you pass the **Museum of Natural History** (2559 Puesta del Sol) and then the **Botanic Garden,** 1½ miles north of the mission. The 60 acres of native plants are particularly beautiful in the spring. *1212 Mission Canyon Rd. Admission $3 adults. Open daily 8:30 AM–sunset. Guided tours Thurs., Sat., Sun. 10:30 AM and Sun. 2 PM.*

Ojai

A half-hour drive east of Santa Barbara, over the narrow and winding Highway 150, will put you in **Ojai,** a surprisingly rural town whose surroundings are reminiscent of earlier days in California. You'll see acres of ripening orange and avocado groves. Movie maker Frank Capra used the Ojai Valley as a backdrop for his 1937 classic *Lost Horizon.* Be aware that the valley can sizzle in the summer when temperatures reach 90 degrees.

The works of talented local artists can be seen in the Spanish-style shopping arcade along the main street. Each Sunday they display their paintings and crafts at the outdoor exhibition in the Security Bank parking lot (205 W. Ojai Ave.).

A stroll around town should include a stop at **Bart's Books** (302 W. Matilija, tel. 805/646–3755), an outdoor store sheltered by native oaks and overflowing with used books.

Nearby **Lake Casitas** on Highway 150 offers boating, fishing, and camping. It was the venue for the 1984 Olympic rowing events.

The spa at **Wheeler Hot Springs** emerges like an oasis 7 miles from town on Highway 33. Its tall palms and herb gardens are fed by an adjacent stream, and natural mineral waters fill the four redwood hot tubs and a large pool at the well-kept spa. Massage by the half-hour is also available. An on-site restaurant offers dinner and weekend brunch. *16825 Maricopa Hwy., tel. 805/646–8131. Open Mon., Wed.–Fri. 10 AM–9 PM, Sat. 9 AM–10 PM, Sun. 9 AM–9 PM. Reservations for the spa advised on weekends.*

What to See and Do with Children

Santa Barbara Zoo. Kids particularly enjoy the scenic railroad and barnyard petting zoo (*see* Exploring, above).

Beach Playground. For children who tire of the beach quickly, there is an elaborate jungle-gym play area at Santa Barbara's East Beach, next to the Cabrillo Bath House.

Whale Bones. Outside the Museum of Natural History in Santa Barbara is the skeleton of a blue whale, the world's largest creature. Kids are dwarfed by the bones and invited to touch them (they just can't climb on them). *See* Exploring.

Off the Beaten Track

Hearty travelers will be rewarded with a day visit or overnight camping trip to one of the five **Channel Islands** that often appear in a haze off the Santa Barbara horizon. The closest of the islands and the most often visited is Anacapa Island, 11 miles off the coast. The islands' remoteness and unpredictable seas have protected them, providing a naturalist's paradise—both underwater and on land. In 1980 the islands became the nation's 40th national park, and the water a mile around each is protected as a marine sanctuary.

On a good day, you'll view seals, sea lions, and an array of bird life. From late December through March, migrating whales can be seen close up. On land, tide pools alive with sea life are often accessible. Underwater, divers view fish, giant squid, and coral. Off Anacapa Island, scuba divers can view the remains of a steamship that sank in 1853. Frenchy's Cove, on the west end of the island, has a swimming beach and fine snorkeling.

A visit to the islands can be a rugged trip, often in rough waters. You can charter a boat and head out on your own, if you wish, but most visitors make the 40-minute drive south to the Ventura Harbor. There, a park-district concessionaire carries small groups to the islands for day hikes, barbecues, and primitive overnight camping.

Boat Trips **Island Packers** provides day trips to the islands and overnight camping to three of them. Boats link up with National Park naturalists for hikes and nature programs. A limited number of visitors are allowed on each island, and unpredictable weather can limit island landings. *1867 Spinnaker Dr., Ventura, CA 93001, tel. 805/642–1393. Reservations are essential in the summer.*

Shopping

Antiques A dozen antique and gift shops are clustered in restored Victorians on Brinkerhoff Avenue, two blocks west of State Street at W. Cota Street, in Santa Barbara.

Arcade Thirty-two shops, art galleries, and studios share the courtyard and gardens of El Paseo, a shopping arcade rich in history. Lunch at the outdoor patio is a nice break from a downtown tour. The arcade is located between State and Anacapa streets at Canon Perdido Street.

Beachwear If you want to go home with the absolute latest in California beachwear, stop by **Pacific Leisure.** They specialize in volleyball fashions, shorts, tops, and beach towels. *808 State St., Santa Barbara, tel. 805/962–8828. Open Mon.–Sat. 10–6, Sun. noon–5.*

Beaches

Santa Barbara's beaches don't have the big surf of beaches farther south, but neither do they have the crowds. A short walk from the parking lot and you can usually find a solitary spot. Be aware that fog often hugs the coast until about noon in May and June.

East Beach. At the east end of Cabrillo Boulevard, this is *the* beach in Santa Barbara. There are lifeguards, volleyball courts, a jogging and bike trail, and the Cabrillo Bath House with a gym, showers, and changing rooms open to the public.

Arroyo Burro Beach. A little west of the harbor on Cliff Drive at Las Positas Road, this state beach has a small grassy area with picnic tables and sandy beaches below the cliffs. The Brown Pelican Restaurant on the beach is nice for breakfast.

Goleta Beach Park. To the north in Goleta, this is a favorite with the college kids from the nearby University of California campus. The easy surf makes it perfect for beginning surfers and families with young children.

State Beaches. West of Santa Barbara on Highway 1 are **El Capitan, Refugio,** and **Gaviota** state beaches with campsites, picnic tables, and fire pits. East of the city is the state beach at **Carpenteria,** a sheltered, sunny, and often crowded beach.

Participant Sports

Bicycling Santa Barbara's waterfront boasts the level, two-lane Cabrillo Bike Lane. In just over 3 easy miles, you pass the city zoo, bird refuge, beaches, and harbor. There are restaurants along the way, or you can stop for a picnic along the palm-lined path looking out on the Pacific. Rent bikes from **Beach Rentals.** It also has rollerskates for hire. *8 W. Cabrillo Blvd., tel. 805/963-2524. Open 7:30AM–8 PM.*

Bikes can also be rented from the **Cycles 4 Rent** concession (Fess Parker's Red Lion Resort, 633 E. Cabrillo, tel. 805/564–4333, ext. 444) near the pool.

Boating Rent sailboats and powerboats by the hour or the day from **Santa Barbara Boat Rentals** (Breakwater near the harbor, tel. 805/962–2826).

Fishing Surf and deep-sea fishing are possible all year. Fully equipped boats leave the harbor area for full- and half-day trips, dinner cruises, island excursions, and whale watching. Contact **SEA Landing** (Cabrillo Blvd. at Bath, tel. 805/963–3564).

Golf Play nine or 18 holes at the **Santa Barbara Golf Club** (Las Positas Rd. and McCaw Ave., tel. 805/687–7087). **Sandpiper Golf Course** (7925 Hollister Ave., Goleta, tel. 805/968–1541), 15 miles west in Goleta, offers a challenging course that used to be a stop in the women's professional tour.

Horseback Riding The **San Ysidro Ranch** hotel offers trail rides for parties of no more than six into the foothills by the hour. *900 San Ysidro Lane, Montecito, tel. 805/969–5046. Reservations advised.*

Tennis Many hotels have their own courts, but there are also excellent public courts. Day permits for $3 are available at the courts. **Las Positas Municipal Courts** (1002 Las Positas Rd.) has six lighted courts. Large complexes are also at the **Municipal**

Courts (near Salinas St. and Hwy. 101) and **Pershing Park** (Castillo and Cabrillo).

Volleyball The east end of East Beach has more than a dozen sand lots for this truly Southern California sport. There are some casual, pickup games, but be prepared—these folks play serious volleyball.

Spectator Sports

Polo The public is invited to watch the elegant game at the **Santa Barbara Polo Club,** 7 miles east in Carpinteria. *Take the Santa Claus Lane exit from Hwy. 101, turn left under the freeway and then left again onto Via Real. The polo grounds are ½ mi further, surrounded by high hedges, tel. 805/684–6683. Modest admission. April–Oct., Sun.*

Dining

The variety of good food in Santa Barbara is astonishing for a town its size. Menu selections range from classic French to Cajun to fresh seafood, and the dining style from tie and jacket to shorts and T-shirt hip. A leisurely brunch or lunch will take the best advantage of the beach and harbor views afforded by many restaurants and cafes. At the Biltmore's acclaimed and expensive Sunday brunch, however, all attention is on the spread of fresh fruits, seafood, and pastries. Served in the hotel's airy glass-roofed courtyard, it is a perfect choice for special occasions.

But a tasty and satisfying meal certainly doesn't have to cost a fortune. If it is good, cheap food with an international flavor you are after, follow the locals to Milpas Avenue on the east edge of the downtown. This is as close as Santa Barbara comes to a working-class area. The eateries change often, but a recent count found three Thai restaurants, one Hawaiian, one Greek, and one New Mexican. Freshly made tortillas are easily found in the markets on Milpas, and a place called La Supericha Tacqueria is rumored to be one of Julia Child's favorites for a quick Mexican snack.

Casual dress is acceptable, unless otherwise noted.

Category	Cost*
Expensive	$40–$50
Moderate	$15–$40
Inexpensive	under $15

per person, without tax (6.5% in California), service, or drinks

Santa Barbara **The Harbor Restaurant.** This place tops annual surveys on
Moderate– where locals like to take out-of-town guests. The entire estab-
Expensive lishment has undergone a complete renovation and has reopened in 1989. The upstairs, now a bar and grill, offers an extensive menu of fresh seafood, sandwiches, large salads, and a huge variety of appetizers. The nautical decor boasts much more space and a complete new video system. Head downstairs for healthy portions of fresh seafood, prime rib, or steaks, and order one of the house's specialty drinks; every seat in the re-

modeled restaurant has a harbor view. *210 Stearns Wharf, tel. 805/963–3311. Reservations accepted on a limited basis. Dress: casual. AE, DC, MC, V.*

★ **The Stonehouse.** This farmhouse restaurant, part of the San Ysidro Ranch, features the best light French-California cuisine in Santa Barbara. For lunch order Chef Marc Ehrler's Mediterranean-style pizza while sitting on the deck. At night, the cooking gets more serious, with game, roasts, and fresh fish entrées. *900 San Ysidro Ln., 805/969–5046. Reservations required. Jacket required.. MC, V. Breakfast, lunch, and dinner daily. Full bar.*

Moderate **Don the Beachcomber.** Don offers lots of bamboo and tiki carvings, plus an expansive view of the ocean. Breakfast, lunch, and dinner are served; the dinners feature Polynesian and Oriental specials. This is a great place for exotic drinks with names like Cobra Fang. *E. Cabrillo Blvd. at Milpas (in the Santa Barbara Inn), tel. 805/966–2285. Reservations accepted. Dress: informal. AE, DC, MC, V.*

The Palace Cafe. This stylish and lively restaurant has won acclaim for its Cajun and Creole dishes such as blackened redfish and jambalaya with dirty rice. Caribbean fare features Bahamian Slipper Lobster Tails—tender lobster sautéed with garlic, mushrooms, and tomatoes, then flambéed in a Madeira sauce. If the dishes aren't spicy enough, each table has its own bottle of hot sauce. The Palace offers dinner only; be prepared for a wait. *8 E. Cota St., tel. 805/966–3133. Reservations accepted for 5:30 PM seating only on Fri. and Sat. Dress: informal. AE, MC, V.*

Inexpensive **Castagnola Bros. Fish Galley.** This is an unassuming spot a quick two blocks from the beach where wonderfully good, fresh fish is served on paper plates. Newly extended indoor space and an outdoor patio provide ample seating with plenty of tables and booths. *205 Santa Barbara St., tel. 805/962–8053. No credit cards. Closes Tues.–Thurs. and Sun. at 6 PM, Fri. and Sat. at 9 PM.*

East Beach Grill. Watch the waves break and the happenings at this busy beach from a surprisingly pleasant outdoor cafe right on the beach. It's a step above a fast food joint, with its friendly table service and pleasant shoreline view. You'll find basic breakfast fare served with real plates and cutlery, and hotdogs and burgers for lunch. *At the Cabrillo Bath House, East Beach, tel. 805/965–8805. No credit cards. Closes daily at 3 PM, at 5 PM during summer.*

Joe's Cafe. The vinyl checked tablecloths and simple round stools at the hefty wooden counter tell the story: nothing fancy, but solid cafe fare in generous portions. Joe's is a popular hangout and drinking spot, particularly for the younger crowd. *536 State St., tel. 805/966–4638. AE, MC, V. No lunch Sun.*

Ojai **Wheeler Hot Springs Restaurant.** The menu changes weekly but *Moderate* always features herbs and vegetables grown in the spa's garden. In Ojai, 6 miles north on Highway 33. The restaurant serves brunch on weekends. *16825 Maricopa Hwy., tel. 805/646–8131. AE, MC, V. No lunch weekdays. Closed Mon.–Wed.*

Lodging

Bargain lodging is hard to come by in Santa Barbara, where high-end resorts are more the style. Long a favorite getaway for congestion-crazed Los Angeles residents, the resorts promise, and usually deliver, pampering and solitude in romantic settings. The beach area is certainly the most popular locale for lodging. It is also where you will find the largest concentration of moderately priced motels. Many places offer discounts in the winter season. Come summer weekends, when 90% of the town's 46,000 motel and hotel rooms are filled, reservations well in advance are highly recommended.

The most highly recommended lodgings in each price category are indicated by a star ★.

Category	Cost*
Very Expensive	over $140
Expensive	$100–$140
Moderate	$60–$100
Inexpensive	under $60

for a double room

Santa Barbara
Very Expensive
★

Fess Parker's Red Lion Resort. This resort complex has a Spanish flair. Two- and three-story stucco buildings are located directly across the street from the beach. This is Santa Barbara's newest luxury hotel and, with its huge and lavishly appointed lobby, a showplace for the chain. Spacious rooms, all with private patios, many with ocean views, are furnished with pastels and light woods. *633 E. Cabrillo Blvd., 93103, tel. 805/564–4333. 360 rooms. Facilities: pool, sauna, tennis courts, exercise room, Jacuzzi, gift shop, lounge with dance floor, bar, cafe, restaurant. AE, DC, MC, V.*

Four Seasons Biltmore. Santa Barbara's grande dame has been given a $15-million facelift by its new owners. A decor featuring muted pastels and bleached woods gives the cabanas a light, airy touch without sacrificing the hotel's reputation for understated elegance. It's a bit more formal than elsewhere in Santa Barbara, with lush gardens and palm trees galore. *1260 Channel Dr., 93108, tel. 805/969–2261. 236 rooms. Facilities: Olympic-size pool, whirlpool, croquet, shuffleboard, raquet ball, health club, casino, putting green, tennis courts, restaurants, bar. AE, CB, DC, MC, V.*

San Ysidro Ranch. At this luxury "ranch" you can feel at home in jeans and cowboy boots, but be prepared to dress for dinner. A hideout for the Hollywood set, this romantic place hosted John and Jackie Kennedy on their honeymoon. Guest cottages, some with antique quilts and all with wood-burning stoves or fireplaces, are scattered about 14 acres of orange trees and flower beds. There are 500 acres more left in open space to roam at will on foot or horseback. The hotel welcomes children and pets. *900 San Ysidro Lane, Montecito 92108, tel. 805/969–5046. 43 rooms. Facilities: pool, tennis courts, horseback riding, croquet, badminton, restaurant. AE, DC, MC, V. Minimum stay: 2 days on weekends, 3 days on holidays.*

Moderate–Expensive

Ambassador by the Sea. Near the harbor and Stearns Wharf, this place has a real California beach feel. Sun decks look over the ocean and beach bike path. Complimentary breakfast is included. *202 W. Cabrillo Blvd., 93101, tel. 805/965–4577. 32 units. Facilities: pool, 2 units with kitchenettes. AE, DC, MC, V.*

Old Yacht Club Inn. Built as a private home near the beach in 1912, the inn was one of Santa Barbara's first bed-and-breakfasts. Rooms feature period antiques and Oriental rugs. Guests receive complimentary breakfast and evening wine, along with the use of bikes and beach chairs. *431 Corona del Mar Dr., 93103, tel. 805/962–1277. 9 rooms. Facilities: dining room, airport pickup service, non-smoking section. AE, MC, V.*

Pacific Crest Motel. A block from East Beach on a quiet residential street, this motel has clean and comfortable rooms, avoiding the austerity of some budget operations. Kitchens are available. *433 Corona Del Mar Dr., 93103, tel. 805/966–3103. 26 rooms. Facilities: pool, laundromat. AE, DC, MC, V. Minimum stay: 2 nights on weekends, 3 on holidays.*

Santa Barbara Inn. Wicker and floral prints give a Polynesian feel to this three-story motel, directly across the street from East Beach. Many rooms have ocean views, but the lower-price ones with mountain views look over the parking lot. *435 S. Milpas, 93103, tel. 805/966–2285. 74 rooms. Facilities: pool, whirlpool, restaurant. AE, DC, MC, V.*

Villa Rosa. The atmosphere is of a private club, housed in a 50-year-old Mediterranean house a block from the beach. The rooms and intimate lobby are decorated with a southwestern style. Rates include Continental breakfast and wine and cheese in the afternoon. *15 Chapala St., 93101, tel. 805/966–0851. 18 rooms. Facilities: pool, spa. AE, MC, V.*

Inexpensive **Motel 6.** Low price and great location near the beach are the pluses for this no-frills place. Reserve well in advance all year. *443 Corona Del Mar Dr., 93103, tel. 805/564–1392. 52 units. Facilities: pool. AE, MC, V.*

Ojai
Very Expensive **Ojai Valley Inn and Country Club.** Reopened by Hilton International in January 1988 after a $40-million renovation, the hotel is set in landscaped grounds lush with flowers. The peaceful setting comes with hillside views in nearly all directions. Some of the nicer rooms are in the original adobe building, where the best of the old—like huge bathrooms—is enhanced with contemporary touches. The suites in cabanas are more expensive. Interesting works by the famed local art community are featured throughout the resort. *Country Club Dr., 93023, tel. 805/646–5511. 233 units. Facilities: championship golf course, lighted tennis courts, 2 pools, men's and women's sauna and steam room, complimentary bicycles, 2 restaurants, bar. AE, DC, MC, V.*

Expensive **Oaks at Ojai.** Well-known, comfortable spa with a solid fitness program that includes lodging; three nutritionally balanced, low-calorie meals (surprisingly good); complete use of spa facilities; and 16 optional fitness classes. *122 E. Ojai Ave., 93023, tel. 805/646–5573. 50 rooms. Facilities: complete spa.*

Inexpensive **Los Padres Inn.** This is a modern hotel on the main street of town across from the Soule Park Golf Course. *1208 E. Ojai Ave., 93023, tel. 805/646–4365. 31 units. Facilities: pool, whirlpool. AE, MC, V.*

The Arts

Santa Barbara prides itself on being a top-notch cultural center. It supports its own professional symphony and chamber orchestra and an impressive art museum. The proximity to the

University of California at Santa Barbara assures an endless stream of visiting artists and performers.

The performing arts find a home in two theaters that are themselves works of art. The enormous Moorish-style **Arlington Theater** on State Street is home to the Santa Barbara Symphony. You can also catch a first-run movie there. The **Lobero,** a state landmark, at the corner of Anacapa and Canon Perdido streets, shares its stage with community theater groups and touring professionals.

For a more casual art experience, catch the beachfront display of wares from local artists and craftspeople each Sunday from 10 AM to dusk along Cabrillo Boulevard.

The **Santa Barbara Arts Council** (tel. 805/966–7022) provides information on performances and events.

Nightlife

Most of the major hotels offer nightly entertainment during summer season and live weekend entertainment all year. To see what's scheduled at the hotels and many small clubs and restaurants, pick up a copy of the free weekly Santa Barbara *Independent* newspaper for an extensive rundown.

Dancing   **Zelo.** This high-energy restaurant doubles as a progressive rock and punk dance club featuring off beat videos and innovative lighting. *630 State St., tel. 805/966–5792. Closed Mon.*
The Pacific Coast Dance Company (500 Anacapa St., tel. 805/966–6411). Popularly known as the PCDC to the college crowd it attracts, this is a lively place featuring bands and DJs.

Index

Personal Itinerary

Departure *Date*

Time

Transportation

Arrival *Date*   *Time*

Departure *Date*   *Time*

Transportation

Accommodations

Arrival *Date*   *Time*

Departure *Date*   *Time*

Transportation

Accommodations

Arrival *Date*   *Time*

Departure *Date*   *Time*

Transportation

Accommodations

Personal Itinerary

Arrival *Date* *Time*

Departure *Date* *Time*

Transportation

Accommodations

Arrival *Date* *Time*

Departure *Date* *Time*

Transportation

Accommodations

Arrival *Date* *Time*

Departure *Date* *Time*

Transportation

Accommodations

Arrival *Date* *Time*

Departure *Date* *Time*

Transportation

Accommodations

Personal Itinerary

Arrival *Date* *Time*

Departure *Date* *Time*

Transportation

Accommodations

Arrival *Date* *Time*

Departure *Date* *Time*

Transportation

Accommodations

Arrival *Date* *Time*

Departure *Date* *Time*

Transportation

Accommodations

Arrival *Date* *Time*

Departure *Date* *Time*

Transportation

Accommodations

Addresses

Name	*Name*
Address	*Address*
Telephone	*Telephone*
Name	*Name*
Address	*Address*
Telephone	*Telephone*
Name	*Name*
Address	*Address*
Telephone	*Telephone*
Name	*Name*
Address	*Address*
Telephone	*Telephone*
Name	*Name*
Address	*Address*
Telephone	*Telephone*
Name	*Name*
Address	*Address*
Telephone	*Telephone*
Name	*Name*
Address	*Address*
Telephone	*Telephone*
Name	*Name*
Address	*Address*
Telephone	*Telephone*

Addresses

Name	*Name*
Address	*Address*
Telephone	*Telephone*
Name	*Name*
Address	*Address*
Telephone	*Telephone*
Name	*Name*
Address	*Address*
Telephone	*Telephone*
Name	*Name*
Address	*Address*
Telephone	*Telephone*
Name	*Name*
Address	*Address*
Telephone	*Telephone*
Name	*Name*
Address	*Address*
Telephone	*Telephone*
Name	*Name*
Address	*Address*
Telephone	*Telephone*
Name	*Name*
Address	*Address*
Telephone	*Telephone*

Fodor's Travel Guides

U.S. Guides

Alaska	Florida	New York State	The Upper Great
Arizona	Hawaii	Pacific North Coast	Lakes Region
Boston	Las Vegas	Philadelphia	Vacations on the
California	Los Angeles	Puerto Rico	Jersey Shore
Cape Cod	Maui	(Pocket Guide)	Virgin Islands
The Carolinas & the	Miami & the	The Rockies	Virginia & Maryland
Georgia Coast	Keys	San Diego	Waikiki
The Chesapeake	New England	San Francisco	Washington, D.C.
Region	New Mexico	San Francisco	
Chicago	New Orleans	(Pocket Guide)	
Colorado	New York City	The South	
Disney World & the	New York City	Texas	
Orlando Area	(Pocket Guide)	USA	

Foreign Guides

Acapulco	Egypt	London	Spain
Amsterdam	Europe	(Pocket Guide)	Sweden
Australia	Europe's Great	Madrid & Barcelona	Switzerland
Austria	Cities	Mexico	Thailand
The Bahamas	France	Montreal &	Tokyo
The Bahamas	Germany	Quebec City	Toronto
(Pocket Guide)	Great Britain	Morocco	Turkey
Baja & the Pacific	Greece	Munich	Vienna
Coast Resorts	The Himalayan	New Zealand	Yugoslavia
Barbados	Countries	Paris	
Belgium &	Holland	Paris (Pocket Guide)	
Luxembourg	Hong Kong	Portugal	
Bermuda	India	Rio de Janeiro	
Brazil	Ireland	Rome	
Budget Europe	Israel	Saint Martin/	
Canada	Italy	Sint Maarten	
Canada's Atlantic	Italy's Great Cities	Scandinavia	
Provinces	Jamaica	Scandinavian Cities	
Cancun, Cozumel,	Japan	Scotland	
Yucatan Peninsula	Kenya, Tanzania,	Singapore	
Caribbean	Seychelles	South America	
Central America	Korea	South Pacific	
China	London	Southeast Asia	
Eastern Europe	London Companion	Soviet Union	

Special-Interest Guides

Cruises and Ports	Smart Shopper's	Shopping in Europe
of Call	Guide to London	Skiing in North
	Healthy Escapes	America